W9-BAW-273

THE
CURIOUS
COOK

HAROLD McGEE

THE CURIOUS COOK

MORE KITCHEN SCIENCE AND LORE

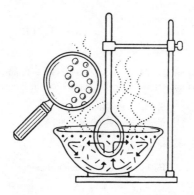

COLLIER BOOKS · MACMILLAN PUBLISHING COMPANY · NEW YORK

Maxwell Macmillan Canada
Toronto

Maxwell Macmillan International
New York   Oxford   Singapore   Sydney

Copyright © 1990 by Harold McGee

Illustrations copyright © 1990 by Laurie Anderson

All rights reserved. No part of this book may be reproduced or transmitted in any
form or by any means, electronic or mechanical, including photocopying, recording,
or by any information storage and retrieval system, without permission in writing
from the Publisher.

Collier Books   Maxwell Macmillan Canada, Inc.
Macmillan Publishing Company   1200 Eglinton Avenue East
866 Third Avenue   Suite 200
New York, NY 10022   Don Mills, Ontario M3C 3N1

Macmillan Publishing Company is part of the Maxwell Communication
Group of Companies.

Library of Congress Cataloging-in-Publication Data

McGee, Harold.
    The curious cook : more kitchen science and lore / Harold McGee. —
1st Collier Books ed.
        p.   cm.
    Originally published: San Francisco : North Point Press, 1990.
    Includes bibliographical references and index.
    ISBN 0-02-009801-4
    1. Cookery.   2. Food.   I. Title.
TX651.M36   1992   91-34092   CIP
641.5—dc20

Macmillan books are available at special discounts for bulk purchases for sales
promotions, premiums, fund-raising, or educational use. For details, contact:

Special Sales Director
Macmillan Publishing Company
866 Third Avenue
New York, NY 10022

First Collier Books Edition 1992

10 9 8 7 6 5 4 3

Printed in the United States of America

To Sharon

Contents

Acknowledgments

My thanks to the generous people who answered questions, asked questions, cast a critical eye over the manuscript, bravely tasted experimental dishes, or otherwise helped me cook up this book.

A number of experts kindly responded to my requests for information. Millard Cohen passed along his dossier on the history of the toque. A bibliographical tip from Charles B. Heiser of Indiana University led to Nancy J. Turner of the Royal British Columbia Museum, who introduced me to the anthropological literature on inulin-containing foods. Adrian Fuchs of Wageningen Agricultural University shared his extensive knowledge of the life and works of Petrus Hondius. Kay Engelhardt of the American Egg Board and Owen J. Cotterill of the University of Missouri unearthed some early history of the mayonnaise industry. Helen Stafford of Reed College sent a helpful reference on the chemistry of tannins and fruit ripening. Raymond Blanc of Le Manoir aux Quat' Saisons offered a professional perspective on the making of fruit ices. Historical and technical information on metal utensils was supplied by Robert Friedel of the University of Maryland, Ronald M. Kasperzak of the Commercial Aluminum Cookware Co., Elinore S. Thomas of Alcoa, Paul Uetzmann of the Cookware Manufacturers Association, and Janet Zapata of Tiffany's. Frederic L. Holmes of Yale University and Rhoda Rappaport of Vassar College clarified some obscure references in early French chemistry. And Ron G. Buttery of the U.S. Department of Agriculture, Hildegarde Heymann of the University of Missouri, and Miriam Rothschild expanded on their research into the chemistry and biology of odors.

I'm especially grateful to several scholars of biology and medicine for taking the time to read chapters that venture into their specialties: at the University of California's Berkeley campus, Bruce Ames; and at Stanford University, Paul Ehrlich, Philip Hanawalt, Richard Scheller, Robert Simoni, and Lawrence Steinman.

Acquaintances, friends, and family provided encouragement and all kinds of help. Arthur Grossman and Ann McGee looked over a number of draft chapters. Sharon Long improved every one, and lent equipment and expertise for several experiments. Harold Long pointed out the affinity of sawdust for eyeglasses. Edward Behr got me thinking about cooking times, Alan Davidson revealed his source for the "square rule," and Paul Green helped me understand it. Betsy Curtis called my attention to the Jerusalem artichoke, and Joyce Schink translated some lines of Petrus Hondius from the Dutch. Chuck McGee spotted the recipe for streamlined hollandaise sauce. Bob Togasaki told me about the persimmon in Japan, Ginny Walbot furnished experimental material from her Hachiya tree, and Marti Crouch encouraged some of her students to do parallel studies on the American persimmon. Annette Smith tracked down some information on L.-C. Maillard. Louise Hammersmith and Florence Long kept raising interesting questions. Shirley and Arch Corriher, Hank Greely and Laura Butcher, Jean Swanson and other members of the Long laboratory, and my wife and children were all good-humored, outspoken participants in a number of taste tests.

Finally, my thanks to Mildred Marmur for finding an orphaned manuscript a good home, and to Jack Shoemaker, Jennifer McDonald, Barbara Ras, and their colleagues at North Point for turning manuscript into book with care and enthusiasm.

THE
CURIOUS
COOK

Introduction

Modern times have dished up a strange stew to the food lover. Much of the developed world is now eating better and more variously than ever before. We're affluent enough to spend great efforts and sums on the pleasures of the table. Thanks to a demanding public and the technologies of transportation and storage, our markets stock ever more fresh, exotic, and well-made foods; and a crowd of cookbooks, food magazines, and instructional shows advises us what to do with this bounty. Yet despite all the possibilities for delectation, and despite a life expectancy unmatched in our history, we're more anxious than ever that eating will do us in. Some of the most feared diseases of the day have been blamed in one way or another on our diet, and usually on its most tempting features. So we enjoy and we worry. We seek out a velvety pâté or make our own double-rich ice cream, and then stand in line for penitential oat bran and fish oil.

In this peculiar atmosphere, the word "science" has taken on some pretty dyspeptic connotations. It suggests either the dissection of a food into two opposing rosters, the Nutrients and the Toxins, or else the industrial synthesis of bottled chemicals into a spuriously appetizing item, the culinary equivalent of a jigsaw creature with a bolt through its neck. True enough, science has given us some mass-produced monstrosities and dietetic anxieties. It's just as true, however, that for anyone cooking or eating nowadays, science can be an especially valuable ally. As a critical way of thinking, it helps us winnow traditional kitchen lore and glean the kernels of genuine craft. And as a far-reaching body of knowledge, it helps us distinguish between prudent attention to what we eat and an unrealistic preoccupation with it.

Food scientists have been delving into the chemical makeup and behavior of our foods for several productive decades. A few years ago, in a book called *On Food and Cooking*, I translated into plain English the food science that seemed relevant to everyday cooking. In the process, I came to realize that the professionals have overlooked much of what goes on in our kitchens. Their research generally centers on questions of commercial importance: such things as the properties of "restructured" fish protein, or methods for detecting adulteration, or the effects of various gases on fruit quality. Sometimes the answers turn out to apply to everyday cooking as well, but usually they don't. So when I finished *On Food and Cooking*, I decided to try a little research of my own, and see whether an amateur could shed some light on matters closer to home.

The result is the first part of *The Curious Cook*: eleven chapters that describe my experiments with various foods and ways of preparing them. I found that by thinking about how a traditional technique works and then tinkering with it, I was able to pare it down to its essential steps, and to come up with useful alternatives. The experience has made me a more effective cook, and I'm sure it can do the same for others. My interests may sometimes seem a bit eccentric, but I hope that won't stop you from trying the experimental approach on the dishes that intrigue you. I've narrated my experiments in detail to show how easily an interested amateur can test the received wisdom or a new idea.

Received wisdom of a different sort is my subject in the second part of *The Curious Cook*. These days we're on the receiving end of all kinds of nutritional advice and information, down to news of the very latest medical research. The question is what kind of wisdom it all adds up to. We hear, for example, that some foods are probably good for the heart and others bad; some may cause cancer and others may prevent it. We also hear that researchers disagree about the actual significance of such findings. So: maybe our traditional eating habits doom us to deadly disease, while a carefully chosen diet will spare us. On the other hand, maybe some scientists are just being officious, interfering experts, and their prescriptions for this oil, that bran, that relative of cabbage aren't necessarily any more trustworthy than some similarly eccentric fad diet.

One important reason for our confusion, I think, is that while the purveyors of news and advice dutifully pass along the latest scientific word on these matters, they don't take the time to tell us about all the words that preceded it. The latest word in scientific research is only one piece of evidence in a broad investigation, one brief episode in a long, continuing story. It gets its meaning from the way it fits into the research effort as a whole. Unfortunately, we seldom hear the rest of the story. No wonder, then, that new findings and recommendations can end up sounding authoritative to some of us, arbitrary to others, and puzzling to the rest.

A couple of years ago it dawned on me that although I was managing to keep up with the dietary debates, I knew next to nothing about their basic premises. I really had no idea how saturated fats could possibly affect the heart, or brussels sprouts the development of cancer, or why the rumor had even gotten started that aluminum pots can cause brain damage. So I tracked down some answers. These in turn suggested more questions. In the end, I tried to piece together coherent research stories for the role of diet in heart disease, in cancer, and in Alzheimer's disease. As you'll see in part two, these stories are mysteries in progress, full of surprising twists and tantalizing clues. Though they remain unresolved, they explain a great deal. They show what these diseases actually are, how certain foods and utensils have come to be scrutinized, and why unequivocal dietary recommendations are so elusive. Most important, these stories give us a realistic idea of what medical science can say about the healthfulness of particular foods, and what we can hope to do for ourselves by watching what we eat. If a balanced diet has become an important element in the good life, so too has a balanced outlook.

It's my hope that much of *The Curious Cook* will be useful: that it will help you cook and eat well. But science is more than merely handy. As the product of a basic human hunger, the hunger for understanding, it also has uncommon satisfactions to offer. Just as private memories and meanings give an emotional dimension to cooking and eating, so scientific understanding connects these activities with the larger world of physical and chemical transformation and supplies a resonance of its own. I devote the third and final part of *The Curious Cook* to reflections on this theme, and I'll give a brief preview in a few pages. But there are also the firsthand pleasures of experimentation and discovery: that is, the fun of playing with foods. And even the sobering study of disease has generated provocative insights into our relationship with the world that nourishes us. I hope that many of the following chapters will give you a taste of these less tangible rewards.

Even if science does happen to offer a valuable perspective on cooking, it may still seem that the two disciplines make an unlikely pair. In fact, cooking and science go way back together. It may even be that one begat the other. In a moment some history, but first an experiment. Consider the following piece of advice, which was composed by one Thomas Norton some five hundred years ago (I've modernized the language). What is Norton talking about?

A perfect master you may call him true
Who knows his heats, both high and low.
Nothing may so ruin your desires
As ignorance of the heats of your fires.
In many authors written you may see,
"Everything depends on the fire's degree":
Wherefore in all chapters you must so proceed
That heat work neither more nor less than it need;
Wherein many of Gebar's cooks
Deceived were, though they were wise in books.

One line seems to give it away: these are sentiments with which most cooks, Gebar's or not, would agree. One plausible description of the essence of cooking is the application of heat to foodstuffs. And firsthand experience with oven or flame cannot be substituted for by books, whether the *Joy of Cooking* or its fourteenth-century predecessor the *Forme of Cury*.

But Thomas Norton was not some medieval rhyming gastronome; he was an alchemist. "Gebar's cooks" is his disparaging phrase for the disciples of Jabir ibn Hayyan, renowned alchemist to the eighth-century caliph Harun al-Rashid. Norton and his associates were concerned with the secrets of transformation. They sought to prepare the *elixir*, which would make humans immortal, and to transmute common metals into gold. And for alchemist as for cook, the principal means of transformation was heat. So "everything depends on the fire's degree."

True, I rigged the experiment. But there's more here than a coincidental interest in heat on the part of cooks and antique pseudoscientists. Alchemical practice was the crucible in which modern chemistry was formed. And the crucible itself had been fired in the ovens of ancient crafts, preeminently cookery.

It's thought that our ancestors mastered fire in southern Africa around a million years ago. Almost surely the first things they managed to heat into something short of ashes were foods. In time, they found that animal musculature could be made into roasts, tough roots and stalks into edible vegetables, and certain otherwise toxic or spoiling materials into safe, digestible nutriment.

Cooking, then, is a strong candidate for the human animal's initial discovery that natural materials can be transformed by means of heat, and that the results are consistent, predictable, and often useful. The same principles were applied only much later in ceramics, which came to fire soft clays into pots about thirty thousand years ago, and in metallurgy, which first fired brittle ores into ductile metals some six thousand years ago. The crafts in turn contributed to cookery such essential implements as bowls, pots, measures, and ovens. Together with the older stone mortars and fiber sieves, these tools then became standard equipment for perhaps the first practical chemists—Sumerian perfumers of the second millennium B.C., who extracted aromatic substances in oil and water and by distillation—and eventually for the alchemists.

The heating of foodstuffs to make foods was more than a practical turning point. It also became an important conceptual model by which transformations in the natural world could be explained and related to each other. The great systematizer Aristotle saw cooking as the artificial version of a natural process. He thought that all material change is caused by the two active and contrary principles of heat and cold. Perhaps influenced by the fact that cooking so evidently improves the flavor and texture of foods, Aristotle claimed that heat's mode of influence on matter is to "perfect" things: to bring them to their proper end, to mature them. The word he used for this process, *pepsis*, meant "softening," "ripening," "digestion," or "cooking," all of which were presumed to require heat. Aristotle's synoptic view of heat survived for better than a thousand years, and exerted an important influence on the alchemists. They thought that precious metals were "concocted," or incubated in the earth's womb by the sun's heat; and the alchemical degrees of fire, whose details were based on craft lore, were meant to mimic this natural transformation.

So it is that practical chemistry can be traced back to our ancestral cooks. Before human beings could develop an experimental science of matter, we had to discover that matter could be manipulated; and the first molecules to be transformed by human hands were probably food molecules. Though the current cultural prestige of science, its pervasive influence on everyday life, might suggest the reverse, cooking is the parent discipline. Each time we enter the kitchen to make a meal, we engage in the primal alchemy; we rehearse the domestic origins of laboratory chemistry. To bring modern science to bear on cooking, then, is not a matter of forcing together two alien entities like oil and water. In the beginning, cooking supplied experience and ideas to science. Today, science stands ready to return the favor.

Parentage and practicalities aside, it might still seem that science is inherently a reductive affair: that its demystifying tendencies will "unweave the rainbow,"

as the poet John Keats said with reference to Isaac Newton, will kill pleasure by
dissecting it and enumerating its costs. It's true that, for the purposes of analysis,
science is reductive. But when we undertake the effort of fitting the pieces back
together into a coherent picture, the result is usually a gain in richness of pattern
and detail.

One brief example. Aristotle wrote that cooking and the ripening of fruit
are analogous processes because both involve the maturation or "perfection" of
the material by means of heat. That idea has a certain appeal even today; it con-
fers a kind of natural dignity on cooking. But to modern eyes, the grounds for
comparison look weak. Fruit need not be heated directly by the sun to ripen,
and cooking generally involves the *dis*organization of organized materials,
rather than any further development. However, thanks to the sciences, we can
now say with some confidence that ripening is indeed analogous to cooking,
and in a much more interesting way than Aristotle imagined.

The sciences tell us that, together with mother's milk, fruits are the only
foods we eat that are meant to be our foods. Ripening is the purposeful preparation of food by plants for other creatures, a preparation in which, just as in
good cooking, both palatability and nutritiousness matter. Plants, being rooted
to their particular spots, must enlist the aid of the mobile agents in nature to disperse their offspring, the seeds. Fruit is one especially elaborate enticement that
is aimed at animals. The more appealing and nutritious the fruit, the more
likely it is that some creature will carry it off and deposit the seeds in a freshly
manured bed. Ripening, that sudden transformation of a fruit's color, flavor,
and texture, takes place only when the seeds are mature and ready to be dispersed. It is both the final confection of the meal, and the formal invitation to
dine.

One last thing. Experience teaches that it's a short step from ripe to rotten,
and ripening does indeed turn out to be the first stage in the fruit's demise. Softness and high flavor result from a carefully orchestrated crescendo of disinte-
gration. For the parent plant, then, the death of its fruit is purposeful. By generating pleasure and sustenance for another creature, it holds the promise of
new life for the plant's own kind. What better exemplum with which to reflect
on the ambiguous art of the cook? Cooking robs living flesh, both plant and animal, of its vital complexity in order to delight and nourish human life; and the
cook's creation fulfills its purpose only in the very process of being destroyed.

Far from reducing its subject to a dry, dusty specimen, this botanico-biochemico-ecological portrait of fruit gives it a fresh vitality. It dispels for a moment the haze of familiarity that envelops everyday objects. It even recalls and lends new force to great poetry: to Edgar's words in *King Lear*, "Ripeness is all," as his father lies under a tree and wishes for death; to the "soft-dying day" of Keats's ode on ripeness, "To Autumn"; to the "Sunday Morning" of Wallace Stevens, who asks

> Is there no change of death in paradise?
> Does ripe fruit never fall?

These days we easily forget that the natural world invented us and feeds us. It is our home, and it is an astonishing place. Our best efforts to understand it, the sciences, are a form of homage to its fascination. They can do much to enrich the experiences of cooking and eating, and living.

PART ONE

PLAYING WITH FOOD: EXPERIMENTS

The scientific study of foods can be both entertaining and immediately useful. Science offers the cook practical advice based on objective experiments and proven principles, rather than on anonymous kitchen lore. We still have much to learn about the culinary possibilities offered by the physical and chemical nature of our foodstuffs, and such research need not be left to professionals in industrial laboratories. The curious cook can make interesting discoveries (or rediscoveries) simply by taking some time to play with ingredients and observe their behavior. The first eleven chapters are devoted to experiments I've done in a modestly equipped kitchen. I hope that their simplicity and often surprising results will encourage other cooks to test the established lore and try out fresh approaches.

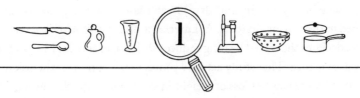

The Searing Truth

It's in the best of cookbooks and the worst of cookbooks, the simple and the sophisticated. "Sear the meat to seal in the juices," they say. This catchy phrase is probably the best-known explanation of a cooking method. It originated with an eminent scientist. And it's pure fiction.

A nineteenth-century German chemist, Justus von Liebig, conceived the idea that high temperatures quickly coagulate proteins at the surface of a piece of meat, and that this coagulum forms a juice-trapping shell that keeps the interior moist. The cooking technique that Liebig accordingly recommended—start the meat at a high temperature to seal it, then reduce the heat to cook it through—ran counter to the traditional ways of roasting and boiling. Despite this, or perhaps exactly because it offered a modern, "scientific" alternative to tradition, the technique caught on immediately in England and America, and eventually in France. Unfortunately, Liebig never bothered to test his theory by experiment. When home economists did so in the 1930s, they found that seared beef roasts lose somewhat more moisture than roasts cooked throughout at a moderate temperature. But Liebig's brainchild continues to turn up in many recipes for roasting, frying, and grilling. It refuses to die.

I think that the searing myth lives on because it offers a vivid and commonsensical picture of what happens to meat during cooking. Some of its persuasiveness may come from searing's resemblance to cautery, the time-honored surgical technique of using boiling liquid, a red-hot piece of metal, a burning lens, or—these days—an electrical current, to seal wounds and stop the bleeding. Centuries before Fannie Farmer applied the term to meat cookery (hers is the first such usage I've come across), *sear* was a synonym for *cauterize*. (Originally, and tellingly, *sear* meant "dry.") In any case, even some experts have succumbed to the searing myth. R. A. Lawrie's authoritative *Meat Science*, for example, declares that rapid heating reduces shrinkage, and cites a 1949 English study as evidence. That study actually comes to the opposite conclusion: it reports that "there was less loss of weight in slow than in quick roasting." If scientists are capable of such a lapse, it's hardly surprising that cookbooks perpetuate the same error.

Of course, in a way it doesn't really matter that the rationale for searing is false. A technique that produces tasty meat is a good technique. But a false rationale can lead people to misapply the technique. And why should cooks settle for a fairy tale instead of hard facts? If we don't really know what's going on when we cook meat, we may not be doing it as well as we might.

I think I've finally found a fatal weapon, a steak knife that all cooks can drive into the heart of the searing myth and thereby liberate themselves forever. The careful work of home economists and meat scientists hasn't made much of an impression because it's too far removed from the kitchen. Much more persuasive is the testimony of a cook's own eyes. All we have to do is watch the meat we cook, and think about what we see. It soon becomes apparent that the searing myth just doesn't hold water.

Imagine the scene. You're about to pan-fry a steak. You dry the raw steak with a paper towel to help it sear faster. You drop the raw steak on a very hot pan. Immediately it begins to sizzle and steam. The sound slowly subsides, but neither it nor the steam stops. After a couple of minutes, you turn the steak. The sizzling suddenly intensifies again. It seems to be caused by a bubbling in the fat around the edges of the steak.

Exhibit One: the steak's sizzle.

Once the second side has been seared, you turn the heat down, and turn the steak again. And after a few more minutes, once again. Soon you begin to notice red fluid appearing on the top of the steak. An important sign. Many cookbooks tell us that searing seals in juices, and then, a few sentences later, that the steak has reached a rare doneness when juices show up on the top surface—which, having been seared, is supposedly sealed. Since you prefer your meat medium rare, you turn the steak over for another minute or two of cooking. As you do so, the red liquid pours onto the hot pan and sizzles away.

Exhibit Two: the sign of the red juices.

You now remove your medium-rare steak from the pan to a serving platter, where it continues to steam. Left behind in the pan is a sticky brown mass, some of which, you noticed, formed rapidly as the red fluid sizzled away, and which accumulated throughout the cooking. You pour in some red wine to deglaze the pan. As the wine hits the hot pan, it bubbles violently, sizzles, and steams, until the pan has cooled down. You scrape and stir the brown material into the wine, then swirl in a piece of butter to thicken and enrich the sauce.

Exhibit Three: the brown pan.

Having deglazed the pan, you pour the sauce onto the still-steaming steak, which has yet to feel the knife. As you do so, you notice a pool of red fluid surrounding the steak. You are slightly annoyed at having forgotten these juices, since they will thin the sauce.

Exhibit Four: the juices on the platter.

Exhibit Five: the omnipresent steam.

Now consider the evidence. First, the sizzle. The steak makes this familiar noise throughout the entire cooking period. Why does the steak sizzle? The best clues are the bubbling along the side of the steak, and the burst of noise that results when wine and juices hit the pan. The crackling hiss is produced when a droplet of water comes in contact with a metal surface far hotter than the boiling point. Almost instantaneously, the liquid vaporizes and expands tremendously in volume. When the water vapor is surrounded by oil or by still-liquid juices, it forms a bubble that immediately bursts. And when the water makes its sudden transition from liquid to gas, its molecules collide energetically with the pan and with each other. All this violence generates noise. The fact that the steak continues to sizzle as long as it's cooked can mean only one thing: water is leaking continuously through the steak's bottom surface to the pan below.

Second, the juices that appear at the top of the steak after several minutes of cooking. There's not much to say about this piece of evidence, except the obvious: even after searing, meat juices leak through the upper surface of the meat as it continues to cook. Searing seals neither the side being cooked nor the side off the heat.

Third, the brown pan. The deeply colored, marvelously flavorful residue is formed from proteins, amino acids, and sugars, which react with each other at high temperatures to generate hundreds of new compounds. (Chapter 17 explores the browning reactions in more detail.) Those proteins, amino acids, and sugars clearly come from the meat. But how do they get to the pan? In the meat, they are dispersed in cells that are 75% water. So if they end up in the pan, they must have been carried there by a substantial volume of liquid. We never see this liquid because the water in the meat's juices is vaporized the instant it hits the pan. But the ever-accumulating residue of brown material is an indication that liquid has been leaving the meat.

Fourth, the juices on the serving platter. Again the conclusion is obvious. Even after the steak has been taken from the heat, and before it has been cut, it exudes considerable quantities of juice. If you keep an eye on it, you'll see the juice seep through both sides.

Finally, the omnipresent steam. Steam is water vapor. So from the first moment of cooking until it has cooled off, the steak exudes water and exhales it into the air.

Five observations, one conclusion. Cooking meat at a high temperature does not render its surfaces impervious to liquid. Searing does not seal in juices.

I can't imagine that any cook would argue with this evidence or with the conclusion. However, I can imagine that some cooks would try to salvage a modified version of the myth. Granted that searing doesn't create a juice-tight seal, they might say, but it does create a juice-resistant seal. Searing may not prevent the loss of juices, but it reduces the loss. Now that's conceivable, and the possibility isn't ruled out by simple visual observation. To test this weak version of the searing myth, we have to compare a seared piece of meat with an unseared one, and determine which one loses more juice. Tasting is one way to do this, but judging moistness is a subjective and difficult exercise. A more objective measure is to weigh the pieces of meat before and after cooking, and see which one has lost a greater proportion of its original weight.

I did just that, with a digital scale designed for letters and small packages. Instead of steaks, I used slices of the cheaper beef eye of round. Because this cut is very lean, irrelevant weight losses due to the rendering of fat are minimal. In each case, I cut a 1-inch slice of meat, weighed it, and inserted the small temperature probe from a digital thermometer so that I could cook each slice to the same internal temperature—the same doneness. (I arbitrarily chose 140°F, or 60°C, medium rare.) I cooked each slice in an electric skillet, using 350°F (177°C) on the thermostat for searing, and 250°F (121°C) for cooking through.

When the meat was done, I removed it from the pan, dried it quickly with a paper towel, and weighed it again. Finally, I figured what percentage of the meat's weight had been left behind in the pan and the air.

The results varied somewhat from slice to slice, so I did five slices each way and calculated the averages. Slices cooked without an initial searing took about 11 minutes to reach medium rare, and lost 14% of their weight in the process. Slices seared for 90 seconds to 2 minutes per side took 12 minutes to reach medium rare, and lost 18% of their weight. By the time the meat had cooled down on a plate, the unseared slices had lost about 22%, and the seared slices 25% of their original weight.

It was impossible to cut slices exactly and uniformly 1 inch thick, or to place the temperature probe precisely in the center of each slice. So the differences in these figures can't be taken too seriously. In fact, the striking thing is how similar the cooking losses are. They were about the same when I upped the searing temperature from 350°F to 425°F (219°C) and even higher when I broiled or charcoal-grilled the beef slices: between 25% and 30% fresh off the fire. So whether you sear or not, whether you fry or grill, the meat will lose a substantial amount of juice. For a medium-rare steak weighing half a pound, that loss turns out to be at least 2 tablespoons during the cooking, and another tablespoon as the steak sits on the plate.

Not only does searing fail to seal in the meat's juice, then: it allows just as much juice to escape as does cooking continuously at a moderate temperature. And sometimes more.

The searing myth claims to give us a closeup picture of the meat surface as it cooks. When meat is suddenly exposed to a very high temperature, the story goes, proteins at the surface quickly coagulate and form a solid, impenetrable layer that holds the meat's fluids inside. Obviously, this can't be correct. Juices seep and evaporate from the meat throughout the cooking, and even for some time afterwards. So what's really happening in the meat? If the surgeon can cauterize a wound, why can't the cook cauterize a steak?

The "juice" that the surgeon worries about is blood, which is carried in vessels composed of many cells. High heat can fuse artery or capillary walls together and coagulate blood, and clots eventually form in damaged tissue. Now it's true that meat was once animal muscle. But it's no longer alive, and there's very little blood left in it. A steak's juices come not from blood vessels, but from the individual muscle cells themselves. Pervasive damage on such a small scale isn't easy to control. And meat juices don't thicken as readily as blood does.

Muscle is made up of long cells, or fibers, which are packed with the protein machinery that does the work of contracting and relaxing. Each fiber is surrounded by a thin layer of connective tissue. Groups of fibers are bundled together into larger working units by thicker layers of connective tissue. The connective tissue is somewhat elastic, and it appears to exert some pressure on the muscle cells. (If you "skin" a single fiber by removing the sheath around it, the fiber expands.)

Nearly all the fluid in meat is contained within the muscle fibers, which are about 75% water. Raw meat doesn't leak much fluid because most of the water in each fiber is trapped in the semisolid matrix of proteins that does the mechanical work. When meat is heated, though, the violent motions of the molecules disrupt the intricate pattern of protein bonds, and the proteins begin to attach themselves to each other indiscriminately: that is, they coagulate. The matrix of proteins that once filled a fiber from edge to edge collapses to form a denser mass at the center of the cell. And as the protein matrix shrinks, some of the water that it originally contained is squeezed out. When meat scientists look at a cross section of cooked meat through the microscope, they see sheaths of connective tissue surrounding shrunken protein cores, and a space in between. That space is almost certainly filled with water.

Leaving aside the moistness contributed by fat, it is this free water—free, that is, from the protein machinery in which it had been immobilized—that gives the sensation of juiciness when we bite into a rare steak. The more of it that stays in the meat, the juicier the meat will seem. Yet we've seen that cooking inevitably removes a substantial amount of this liquid. So how does it get out?

British scientists at the Meat Research Institute in Bristol have proposed the following scenario. Remember that the connective tissue sheath exerts some pressure on the cell inside it. As long as the semisolid protein matrix is intact, it resists that pressure, and the water stays inside the matrix. When the matrix coagulates and shrinks, beginning around 100°F (38°C), a tube of liquid collects around it. The pressure from the connective tissue is now exerted on this liquid, which, like any liquid under pressure, responds by trying to flow. The only place it can flow is out an opening in the sheath. And since nearly all cuts of meat

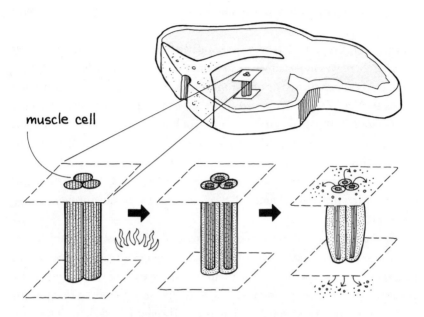

muscle cell

How cooking forces moisture from meat. Water molecules (dots) are bound up in the matrix of proteins (lines) that fills each muscle cell (left). As the meat is heated, the proteins coagulate and squeeze out much of the water they had contained (center). The elastic sheath of connective tissue around each muscle cell then squeezes this unbound water out the cut ends of the cell (right).

are sliced across the grain of the muscle fibers, each side of a steak or chop is nothing but a sheet of open fiber ends, all of them ready exits for the juice within. Searing does coagulate the protein at the exposed end of the muscle fiber, but coagulation entails general disorganization and shrinkage. Rather than sealing up the thousands of little liquid-filled tubes, cooking of any kind probably further damages their ends and makes them more prone to leakage, not less.

It turns out that this scientific picture of meat cookery bears some resemblance to prescientific explanations of cautery. A number of cultures have believed that cautery heals wounds or infected areas by making them too hot for the demons that inhabit them. Well, now we know that cooking too chases an elemental presence from animal flesh. Unfortunately, that presence is moisture.

Having seen the searing theory evaporate before my own eyes, I wondered whether there was in fact any way to reduce the loss of juices during frying or grilling. My search turned up one promising lead: Some time ago, two meat scientists in New Zealand reported that the farther apart they made two cuts across a muscle, the smaller the proportion of liquid the meat lost during cooking. In other words, thick steaks should lose less moisture than thin ones. Intuitively, this makes a certain amount of sense. If the freed juice at the center of a steak has to travel a long way to reach the open fiber ends, then maybe it can't escape during the cooking and will be reabsorbed by the fiber proteins as they cool down.

The meat scientists determined that most of the juice lost from a thick piece of meat comes from the 2 centimeters (or ¾ inch) closest to each side. So any significant savings would only show up in very thick cuts. However, when I experimented with 1½-inch and 2-inch slices of the eye of round, I didn't find any great improvement over the 1-inch slices I had been using all along. Three 1½-inch slices cooked to 140°F (60°C) lost an average of 18% fresh out of the pan, and 24% on standing. The figures for the one 2-inch slice I tried were 17% out of the pan and 22% after it had cooled down. Any advantage in moisture retention may well have been counterbalanced by the longer cooking times required: 25 minutes for a 1½-inch slice, and 35 minutes or so for the 2-inch slab. (The New Zealanders immersed all their samples, no matter the size, for 40 minutes in water at 180°F, or 82°C.)

The similarity of the cooking losses for all three thicknesses suggested to me that the most important influence on juiciness is simply the final internal temperature, or doneness, to which the meat is cooked. As a last experiment, I fried 1-inch and 1½-inch slices of beef up to an internal temperature of 170°F (77°C), or more than well done. At intervals, I quickly weighed them, then put them back in the pan to continue cooking. The thin piece lost weight much more rapidly than the thick one. But at a given doneness, the cooking losses were almost identical: at 130°F, 10% for the 1-inch piece and 11% for the 1½-inch piece; at 140°F, 12% and 13%; at 150°F, 15% and 16%; at 160°F, 18% and 20%.

Evidently what minimizes cooking loss is minimal cooking. Rare meat is juicy, well-done meat much less so. Searing doesn't alter this basic rule; in fact, high cooking temperatures may force out even more liquid. If meat is to be cooked well-done, all we can do to compensate for the inevitable loss of juice is to start with a well-marbled piece; the melting fat will permeate the meat with a less evanescent moistness.

The searing myth offered a comforting sense of control: begin with a dose of high heat and you're guaranteed a succulent piece of meat. That control turns out to be illusory. On the other hand, if searing caused any great harm, cooks would have seen through the myth long ago. Searing does have its uses. It assures that the pan won't cool down too far when you first put the meat on, and it enriches flavor by accelerating the browning reactions. So sear on. Just don't fall for the myth.

Happily, the death of this particular illusion actually simplifies life. Because juiciness is determined almost entirely by the meat's doneness, there's no point in worrying about it. Just cook meat to your taste. The juices will take care of themselves.

SUMMARY: SEARING MEAT

Searing meat does not seal in juices. Nor does searing reduce the loss of juices. The juiciness of meat is determined by the doneness to which the meat is cooked: the rarer the juicier. Meat marbled with fat will seem moister than a lean cut when cooked well-done; the fat melts and permeates the meat during cooking.

Even though searing doesn't seal in juices, it is a useful technique. A very hot pan will begin cooking the meat right away and will intensify the meat's flavor by browning the juices that flow from it.

Oil Drops Keep
Falling on My Toque

If anyone can be said to have founded kitchen science—the study of everyday cooking—it would have to be Benjamin Thompson, Count Rumford, who contributed to the modern designs of our stoves, coffee pots, and fireplaces. This remarkable man was born in Massachusetts, declared a traitor by the American revolutionaries, welcomed and knighted by George III, and given his title by a ruler of Bavaria for his service as chief military aide. His initial foray into the kitchen was less than promising: British soldiers under his command on Long Island used tombstones from a churchyard to build the camp oven, and sent the local citizens loaves of bread with the inscriptions for their deceased relatives baked backwards into the crusts. Rumford married the widow of the great chemist Lavoisier, who had been guillotined in the aftermath of the French Revolution, and founded the Royal Institution of Great Britain, a scientific society that is still active. Soldier of fortune, engineer, and experimentalist, Rumford also valued the pleasures of reflection. He wrote memorably of his desire "to inspire cooks with a just idea of the importance of their art, and of the intimate connection there is between the various processes in which they are daily concerned, and many of the most beautiful discoveries that have been made by experimental philosophers in the present age."

An inspiring idea indeed, that our everyday, routine activities and our most penetrating sciences both illuminate the world, and that each can illuminate the

Benjamin Thompson, Count Rumford. From a portrait done in 1797, when he was 44 years old.

other. Not long ago, I thought that I'd hit on a fine illustration of this idea. I soon proved myself wrong: the inspiration was fleeting and unfounded. But I now see the frying pan more clearly than ever before.

I am one of the millions of people in the world whose vision requires correction, and I noticed long ago that the activity of frying leaves an oily deposit on the cook's eyeglasses. Over the course of years of cleaning my glasses after cooking, I gradually registered the fact that most of the oil is deposited in small specks on the *inside* surface of the glasses. Even more gradually, I came to realize that this is a very strange phenomenon. After all, the outside surface is the one that directly faces the frying pan, and it presumably also shields the inside surface—and our eyes—from the spatter emanating from the pan. These vague thoughts eventually crystallized into two questions. How does the oil manage to get to the inside surface of our glasses? And how might we prevent it from getting there, so as to leave us with one item less to clean up?

Two other observations suggested a plausible hypothesis. As I paid more attention to the vicissitudes of my glasses, I noticed that at the end of the day most of the dust had ended up on the inside surface as well. And my wife's father, no habitué of the kitchen but a veteran of the wood shop, pointed out to me that sawdust too coats the inside surface. He knew something else about sawdust: it often carries a charge of static electricity.

Aha! Static electricity can manifest itself in repulsion as well as attraction. And I remembered from grade school that a glass rod can be given a charge by rubbing it with silk. Furthermore, because glass is an insulator, you can presumably build up local areas of charge, and perhaps generate a difference between the two surfaces of a lens. Maybe oil droplets are charged, like sawdust, and maybe the lens is electrified when wiped with a tissue or held with one surface close to the skin. That might explain the preference of spatter and sawdust for the protected surface.

Another aha! Charged oil droplets! Certainly one of the most beautiful discoveries of the present age was the precise determination of the electrical charge carried by a single electron, and the demonstration that electrical charge exists only in discrete amounts, or quanta. Robert Millikan received the Nobel Prize in physics for his "oil-drop" experiments, which he began in 1909 and which are simple enough that they're often repeated today in high school courses. Improving on earlier unsuccessful attempts that involved water droplets, which have an inconvenient tendency to evaporate, Millikan created a cloud of small oil droplets by forcing a clock lubricant through an atomizer into his apparatus, where individual droplets could be observed by means of a short-focus telescope. The droplets were electrically charged by friction as they were formed in the small nozzle of the atomizer. That the droplets had been charged was evident from the fact that their free fall in gravity could be disturbed by the application of a voltage across two metal plates, one at the top and one at the bottom of the apparatus. Millikan measured the changes in velocity induced by the electrical field for hundreds of individual droplets, and then deduced the total charge on each droplet. Because the droplets were minute, on the order of a ten-thousandth of an inch across, he was also able to notice small, sudden changes in velocity that were the result of a droplet "catching" another charged particle from the air. Millikan found that all the charges he computed were multiples, between 1 and 150, of a particular, apparently irreducible charge. That basic charge is the charge of a single electron.

Drawing a connection between kitchen spatter and Millikan's classic experiment was thrilling. Now my spatter hypothesis seemed even more credible.

Since culinary oil drops are also formed in a violent sort of expulsion, they too might be electrically charged. And for a moment I had the vertiginous sense that I might be seeing through my oily glasses darkly into the heart of matter itself. Perhaps Millikan could have determined the charge on the electron at his kitchen stove.

As I discovered when I went to investigate the nature of static electrification, much is known but little is understood. One modern student of the subject has written that this oldest branch of electricity is also the most backward. The word *electricity* derives from the Greek *elektron*, meaning "amber"; the Greek Thales is credited by the ancient writers with having discovered that amber could attract pieces of straw and grass. Lightning and "St. Elmo's fire," a glowing corona over the masts of sailing ships, are two of the most spectacular natural manifestations of static electricity; in the nineteenth century it was discovered that the spray from a waterfall is negatively charged.

Today we're probably most aware of the mildly annoying aspects of *triboelectricity*—the generation of electricity by friction—from the shock of osculation after we've walked across a carpet, to the clinginess of clothes fresh from the dryer, to the dust that sticks to phonograph records and compact discs, and the crackling that emanates from our speakers. In industrial settings, static electricity can be downright lethal. Both liquids and powders are easily charged as they pass through pipes, and small sparks can ignite large masses of material. This is what causes explosions in grain silos; one well-studied incident involved the ignition of chocolate particles in a British biscuit factory. But static electricity also does us some good. It's exploited in a variety of applications, from the spraying of paint and insecticides to photocopying (the ink particles are attracted to the paper by static) and the "scrubbing" of emissions from industrial smokestacks—the soot particles are charged and then trapped on large electrified plates.

The physical basis for such effects as these is not well understood, partly because scientific attention has been diverted to the much more versatile phenomenon of continuous electrical current, and partly because it's very difficult to study the atomic effects of, say, rubbing a glass surface with silk, or atomizing some oil. Like the chemistry of cooking, static electricity looks to be an aspect of everyday life that may be ripe for contributions by interested amateurs. In fact, I came across one paper in the *Journal of Electrostatics* that, judging by the author's residential address, appeared to be just such a contribution: a study of the charging of small salt crystals that are formed and ejected during the evaporation of small drops of water on a very hot surface. We create similar conditions when we test the temperature of our frying pan or griddle by flicking a few drops of water onto it; the more agitated the droplets' demise, the hotter the surface.

But back to oil drops. My working hypothesis was that frying causes small charged oil droplets to be ejected from the pan into the air. For reasons having to do with the cook's wiping the lenses with a tissue or the proximity of one surface to the body, which itself can easily become charged, the inner and outer surfaces of the glasses are electrically asymmetrical. The charged droplets are therefore repelled from the outer surface and attracted to the inner. And so grease ends up on the surface farthest away from the frying pan.

Should this explanation turn out to be true, I could already envision possible remedies. There might be some way to eliminate the charge on our glasses just before we begin to cook, or eliminate the influence of body on glasses. One practical measure for the bespectacled frequent fryer might be to interpose a metal shield between lens and face, a sort of mask of Agamemnon fashioned from heavy-duty aluminum foil. Now that had possibilities for personalizing the *batterie de cuisine*.

First, though, I needed to test my hypothesis. I began by trying to determine whether the lenses' proximity to the face was indeed a factor. To do this, I propped several extra pairs of glasses atop breakfast cereal boxes a foot or so from the frying pan. I heated a tablespoon of oil, then repeatedly flicked water onto the pan. The resulting spatter generated plenty of airborne droplets; in fact, most of the tablespoon was ejected. The pan ended up looking as though it had been gently rubbed with an oily cloth.

I turned off the gas and checked my detectors. The glasses I was wearing were speckled with droplets on the inside, as usual. The others, though, showed a variety of results. Two pairs had collected plenty of oil on the outer surface and none on the inside, just as would be predicted if facial proximity were the important factor. But one pair had very little on either surface. All three pairs had been cleaned at the same time and in the same way. So something else was at work here.

After staring at the setup for a while, I figured it out. Due to the wobbly condition of some sidepieces, one pair had been propped up so that the lenses were essentially vertical, while the others were slumping backward so that the outer

Spatter detectors.

surface was facing upward and protecting the inner surface. Of course the first pair would be clean and the other two coated on the outside. I just had to be more careful with such details so as not to complicate the story.

On the other hand, maybe this *was* the story. I had assumed that the spatter that dirties our glasses comes on a beeline from the frying pan. After all, that's clearly how our skin sometimes gets burned or our shirt soiled, and that's why it seemed so strange that the droplets could duck around the outer surface to land on the inside of my glasses. But my old glasses were telling me that their angle relative to the vertical was important. This indicated that much of the oil was hitting the lenses from above. Furthermore, it was obvious on a moment's consideration that the cook always looks *down* at the stovetop. And when the cook looks down, the inner surface of the eyeglass lens faces *upward*.

An alternative hypothesis formulated itself: Most of the oil that reaches our glasses falls from above; and because the inner surface is uppermost as we look down at the stove, the oil settles on the inner surface, not the outer. I immediately tested this idea by repeating the artificial spatter experiment, but this time

I held my head rigidly erect, my newly cleaned glasses directly facing the wall above the stove. I moved only my eyes when aiming the water at the pan. The result: pristine lenses.

So much for the Millikan oil-drop parallel and the window onto the heart of the physical world. The true explanation was a disappointingly surburban, trivial, even obvious one. Although the few oil droplets that get our immediate attention do come straight at us, most of them are carried straight up in the currents of hot air rising from the pan. It's from high in the room that they fall onto any and all exposed surfaces, including the inner surface of our down-tilted glasses. The same goes for dust and sawdust. We look down at our work or play all day long, and all day long debris floats past our brows to the near side of the lens.

There was only one thing to salvage from my eager research into Millikan's experiments: an estimate of how long the fallout from frying lasts. His droplets were on the order of a ten-thousandth of an inch across, and took on average 23 seconds to fall a centimeter, or something less than 12 minutes to fall a foot. The atmosphere in a kitchen is very turbulent by comparison to Millikan's small enclosed chamber, but it's clear that the oily rain continues for some time after the cook turns the burner off.

So much, too, for culinary masks of Agamemnon. If indeed the droplets are raining down from above, then the obvious remedy for the bespectacled cook is a hat with a visor that shields the face—a baseball cap. My old Cubs cap has proven to be altogether satisfactory for this purpose. Unfortunately, given its popularity and widespread use as a prefrontal billboard, the baseball cap is unlikely to catch on as a distinctive item of kitchenwear.

Of course, the matter of kitchen headgear immediately brings to mind the outlandish tower of cloth that is the true chef's hat, or *toque* (French for a soft, brimless, usually small hat). Could it be that this edifice had evolved or been invented for venerable chefs with career-weakened eyes? It is something like a vertical visor, and as such might cast a tremendous droplet shadow.

The origins of the chef's toque are somewhat obscure. The distinguished gastronomical authority André Simon said that it is a copy of the hat worn by Greek Orthodox priests and dates from a time of upheaval (some say the sixth century A.D.) when "many famous cooks to escape persecution sought refuge in

The geometry that results in back-spattered eyeglasses.

monasteries." Other investigations into the subject, however, make it clear that regardless of what may have happened in early Greek monasteries, today's toque was reinvented around 1900. In both France and England in the seventeenth and eighteenth centuries, those cooks who bothered with headgear at all wore a soft cotton hat, or *bonnet*, that looked very much like a nightcap. The great transition from shapeless to shaped can be attributed with some certainty to Marie-Antoine Carême, the renowned chef of the early nineteenth century, who at the time was in the service of the English ambassador to Vienna, Lord Stewart. As Carême wrote in his *Maître d'Hôtel français* (1822):

> Meditating ceaselessly on the elegance of our work, I had dreamed for a long time of ways to change the manner in which we wear our cotton cap; for it appeared to me absolutely necessary not to change the cap itself, whose whiteness allies it so well to the rest of our uniform, and

whose extreme cleanliness is the handsomest endowment of the cook. Professionals distinguish themselves by it, and by the order that they bring to their work, I mean by kitchens that are redolent of cleanliness.

At the time that I had the idea of wearing my cap thus trimmed with a circle of cardboard (one could make it an octagon), which lends it more grace, I found myself in Vienna during my last stay in 1821.

Every day around eleven in the morning, I presented the dinner menu to his Excellency Lord S————. The Ambassador looked at me, smiled, and said: "This new style better suits a cook." I pointed out to his Excellency that a cook should be the image of good health, while our ordinary cap is more reminiscent of the state of convalescence. My Lord agreed, and I never gave up my new headgear. My young men took it up, and several cooks of Vienna admired their newly fashionable selves, never doubting that they would find devotees in Paris.

Carême's modest effort at bestowing a little "grace" on the chef's cap ushered in a new era of experimentation. The following decades tossed up a number of new styles, from pillbox-shaped porkpie hats (in France likened to charlotte molds) to tam o'shanters (the French thought of these as resembling a *galette*, a round, flat cake), from black berets to great cotton puffs swept backwards. Out of this welter of invention arose the modern toque, which Phillis Cunnington and Catherine Lucas, two historians of English costume, call "one of the tallest hats ever to dignify man." Dignity, they suggest, is the true meaning of the toque; high hats have quite frequently adorned the leaders of social groups and lent them a commensurately imposing physical stature. So head chefs wear the toque to signify their status as *gros bonnets*, or bigwigs. Oil drops have nothing to do with it.

And so an experiment confirmed. When put to the test, a disposable 9-inch paper toque performed poorly at intercepting oily rain. Despite the toque's impressive overhang, there's apparently enough of a gap between hat and glasses for droplets to fall on slight tangents to the back of the lenses. The baseball cap remains unsurpassed for maintaining the cook's clarity of vision, if not the cleanliness of his or her hair, which the modern cap's coarse mesh does less to protect. Knowing now how easily large quantities of oil can be projected high above the stove, I wonder whether the time has come for another step in the evolution of the toque. Say, a tall, closed cylinder with a broad bill, which would confer dignity while it protected head and spectacles. Southwesterners might consider modifications of the ten-gallon hat. Then there's the apron, which is clearly designed for head-on, not overhead assaults. The home *brigade de cuisine* might profit from washable epaulets, or perhaps from a version of the lab coat.

Of course there is such a thing as a spatter guard, a dense meshwork of metal strips that rests over the frying pan and intercepts oil drops while allowing water vapor to escape. But it's hard to clean and, like a lid left partly ajar, blocks the cook's view of the food. Nor are all of us lucky enough to have a hood and exhaust fan over the stove. Now if the oil droplets are indeed charged by their expulsion from the pan, it might be possible to design the stovetop equivalent of a smokestack scrubber. One could erect a veil of window screening, so that the food remains visible, and charge it with a transformer or electrostatic generator with enough kilovolts to snatch the droplets as they whiz by.

It may be some time before a modern Rumford arises to address this problem. Meanwhile, we'll be able to make do with a Cubs cap or the equivalent, which is the more elegant solution anyhow.

SUMMARY: FRYING AND EYEGLASSES

When a bespectacled cook fries food, more oil droplets collect on the inner surface of the lens than on the outer surface. This happens because most of the spatter rises high in the air and falls from above. Since cooks always look down at the stovetop, the inner surface of the lens is exposed to this oily rain, which continues for some time after the cooking is over. A baseball cap does a good job of protecting glasses from the fallout of frying.

Simmering Down

"It could hardly be possible that precisely the temperature of 212 degrees of Fahrenheit thermometer should be that which is best adapted for cooking *all sorts of foods*."

Count Rumford expressed this suspicion of culinary providence two centuries ago, when apparently much cooking was done at a full boil. Thanks in part to Rumford, we're enlightened enough today to bring our cooking liquids down to a simmer, especially for fish and tender cuts of meat. But the simmer is usually defined as a point just short of the boil, so even then we stay in the neighborhood of 200°F (93°C). I think that we're drawn there irresistibly for a simple reason. The three basic elements of cooking are the raw ingredients, heat, and time. We're quite used to measuring the first with cups and spoons, the last with clocks and timers. When it comes to stovetop temperatures, we could certainly call on a thermometer for assistance. But the boiling point is so unmistakable and constant a benchmark, and has been for so many generations of cooks, that we really don't feel the need for any other measure—or any other temperature range. The appearance of bubbles, or the roiling that indicates their imminent arrival, is sufficiently reassuring: when we see them, we know that the liquid is hot enough to do its job. At least as far back as the time of Brillat-Savarin, the French have had a saying that a barely bubbling stewpot "smiles." It's a smile that says things are cooking along just fine.

As it happens, there's a smile lurking in the background of the English word *simmer* as well. But it's not an especially encouraging one. The original form of the word was *simper*, which then as now meant an affected, conceited expres-

sion. So Thomas Nashe in 1594: "I simpered with my countenance lyke a por-
redge pot on the fire when it first begins to seeth." This etymology suggests an
altogether different home truth: a simmering pot, like a smiling face, can con-
ceal something rather unappealing. It's just as possible to overcook some meats
at the simmer as it is at the boil.

I began thinking about the simmer, and possible alternatives to it, after hearing
recently from Edward Behr, who publishes a handsome and exceptionally in-
formative newsletter called "The Art of Eating." He phoned one day to ask
about a statement that appears in Alan Davidson's books *Mediterranean Seafood* and *North Atlantic Seafood*. According to Davidson, the time required to
heat any object to a given internal temperature is proportional not simply to the
object's thickness, but to the square of its thickness. In other words, if one object
is twice as thick as another, then it will take two squared, or four times as long
to heat its center to the same temperature. So, for example, if it takes 5 minutes
to cook a ½-inch fish fillet to the right doneness, then it will take 20 minutes to
do the same for a 1-inch fillet, all else being equal. Behr said that this didn't
sound right to him or to the cooks he polled; their consensus was that it might
not even take twice as long to cook the thicker fillet. He wondered whether
Davidson's rule was correct. I admitted that I didn't know offhand, and said I
would try to find out.

For a start, I consulted with scientist friends and spent some time in the library. I had assumed that the warming of everyday objects could hardly be esoteric stuff. Well, it might not be esoteric, but it is elusive. Even as some physicists probe the deepest innards of atoms and others scan the outer reaches of the
universe, no one has yet figured out exactly how heat energy makes its way from
one point to another in any solid object, whether a fish fillet or the metal pan it
cooks in. The leading theory of the day is that the energy propagates in waves
from the area being heated. The details are in doubt, and may be for some time
to come.

Fortunately, this ignorance hasn't impeded a practical understanding of
heat conduction. Early in the nineteenth century, the French mathematician
Fourier figured out a fairly straightforward way of approximating the process
by analogy to the diffusion of one liquid or gas in another. While the equations
are straightforward, solving them is quite tedious. But heat conduction is important in so many industries, from food canning to aeronautics and weapons

design, that engineers have done the calculations for certain objects in certain circumstances, and then laid out the answers in the form of graphs. The objects are simple shapes—cubes, spheres, cylinders, infinitely long square bars, infinitely extensive planes—and it's usually assumed that their surfaces jump immediately to a constant temperature at the start of heating. If you can approximate your problem with one of these model situations, then all you have to do is gather a few essential numbers, read another off the appropriate graph, and do some arithmetic. After working through a sample problem in the journal *Food Technology* that involved steaming a large cylinder—a can—of chicken à la king, I was ready to hit the conduction charts.

In the meantime, I had heard from Alan Davidson that his authority for "the square rule" was Nicholas Kurti, professor of physics at the University of Oxford, and latter-day champion of Count Rumford. A less impeachable source it is hard to imagine. Moreover, even my brief acquaintance with the conduction charts was sufficient to show me that the square rule is indeed the rule. Double the thickness of any of the engineers' model objects and you quadruple the time it takes to heat its center to a given temperature. So that was that.

At least on paper. But I had become fascinated by the possibility of applying these military-industrial tools to the home kitchen. Even if frying, roasting, and baking might not immediately raise the entire surface of a food to a constant temperature, cooking in water probably would. So if I could find out three physical characteristics of meat—its density (how much a given volume weighs), specific heat (a measure of how much energy is required to heat it up a given amount), and thermal conductivity (how quickly it conducts heat from one point to another)—then I should be able to predict how long it takes to simmer a cube of beef from refrigerator temperature to a given doneness. I just had to give that a try!

I repaired to the food science literature and found the three numbers I needed. Indeed, I found many candidates for each, since the numbers vary according to the kind of meat and the way the measurement is made. I eventually settled on an average density of 67 pounds per cubic foot, an average specific heat of about 0.75 British thermal units (Btu) per pound per degree Fahrenheit, and a thermal conductivity of 0.25 Btu per hour per foot per degree Fahrenheit. Combined, these numbers yield a thermal diffusivity, or *alpha*, of about 0.005 square feet per hour. For my first prediction, however, I used slightly different figures that gave an alpha of 0.006. All I needed to work with the engineers'

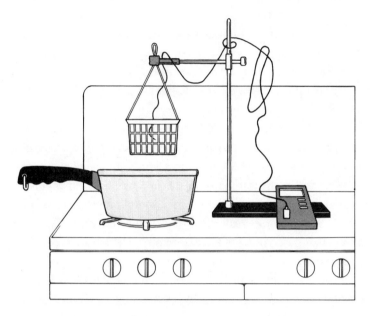

A setup for measuring the temperature of a piece of meat as it simmers.

charts were alpha, the temperatures I was interested in, and the dimensions of the piece of meat. It was a simple exercise to calculate that to heat a 1-inch cube of meat from 50°F to 150°F (10°C to 66°C), or a medium-well doneness, in boiling water, should take 4.1 minutes. Double the dimensions to a 2-inch cube, and the prediction was (2 × 2) × 4.1, or 16.4 minutes.

These figures sounded reasonable. The question was, how close were they to the truth? To answer that, I did the experiment. Because ordinary cooking thermometers are rather bulky and require an inch or two of contact with the object to be measured, I obtained from a scientific supply company a digital thermometer that accepts a variety of plug-in probes. The probe I used was a sphere about a millimeter in diameter, small enough that it would read accurately from just the center of a small cube, and wouldn't create a gaping hole. Then I bought a large chunk of the beef eye of round, which is a single muscle, quite lean and homogeneous, and cut out cubes of different sizes. I placed each cube in the bottom of a plastic berry basket, inserted the probe, and suspended the basket from a chemistry ringstand. I immersed the basket in boiling water, started a stop-watch, and recorded the changes in temperature at the center of the cube.

The charts predicted 4.1 minutes and 16.4 minutes for the 1-inch and 2-inch cubes. (With the alpha I used for the subsequent calculations in this chapter, I would have gotten 4.7 and 18.7 minutes instead.) The moment the thermome-ter hit 150°F, I punched the stopwatch. For the 1-inch cube, 5 minutes; for the 2-inch cube, 17.3 minutes. Startlingly close!

I called Edward Behr back and told him that an eminent physicist, the en-gineers' charts, and my stovetop experiment all backed the square rule, at least for model shapes in model circumstances. I did get somewhat different results in the oven, where the transfer of heat is far less efficient than it is in boiling water, and the calculations therefore more complicated. For cooking in water, however, the question seemed to be settled definitively. End of investigation.

Except that the accuracy of these stovetop predictions was seductive. It held out the promise that I could simulate all kinds of cooking procedures on paper and find out how a food's inner temperature responds to them. I couldn't resist this invitation to play: something unexpected might pop up!* Since internal temperatures are especially important for determining the doneness of meat, I decided to do my playing with pork, chicken, veal, and fish. I ended up working with the conduction charts for hours and taking the temperature of many chunks of meat. Along the way, I found that Edward Behr and his consultants were right to doubt the square rule for a very common, not-so-model cut. And something unexpected did pop up: meats cook, and overcook, very quickly at the simmer. A smiling pot still seems most appropriate for a long-cooked stew. In the case of tender meats, however, there's much to be said for cooking at a lower temperature. What might be called a poker-faced poach.

There are two classes of meat, broadly speaking: the tender and the tough. The tough we cook in liquid for hours to dissolve the source of its toughness, the connective tissue. The tender is dried out and toughened by heat, so with the exception of large roasts, we cook it for minutes rather than hours. Frying and grilling are the usual techniques applied to beef and lamb, which are relatively rich and flavorful. The braise—a short simmer in some liquid, often after an

---

*For readers who would like to play with heat conduction themselves, or who are curious to see what a heat conduction chart looks like, the chart most relevant to stovetop cooking is given in the appendix (p. 315).

initial browning—is generally reserved for pork, veal, and chicken: young, bland cuts of meat that are often low in fat and can use some additional moisture and flavoring. The same preparation is sometimes called a fricassee, or a sauté. Though definitions vary from cookbook to cookbook, poaching seems to be thought of as a gentler operation, perhaps a few degrees below the simmer. The only meats commonly said to be poached are fish, whose flesh is especially delicate, and occasionally chicken.

Braise or poach, the basic technique is nicely versatile. All sorts of liquids will serve, from the usual water and wine to beer, milk or cream or yogurt, vegetable purees, and fruit juices. The range of flavor combinations is tremendous. As it turns out, simmering can also produce considerable variation in the meat's texture, though you'd never know it from recipes that specify just one combination of temperature and cooking time. If you cook the meat to a medium doneness, it will be tender and quite moist. Much beyond that point it will become dry and, in the case of pork, sometimes rather tough as well. After about an hour of simmering, though, pork chops become tender again, and the other meats will begin to fall off the bone, but the texture is dry and disintegrating rather than juicy and firm, much like stewmeat that has cooked for several hours. Now I'm very fond of stews and pot roasts, but to me it seems a waste of tender, choice portions to cook them dry.

One question I thought the conduction charts could answer for me was, How long should it take to simmer an oblong piece of meat or fish to a juicy, medium doneness?

The model shape closest to a chop, fillet, or steak is what the engineers call the "infinite plate." The infinite plate has a defined thickness, but it is endlessly long, endlessly wide. This makes it somewhat longer and wider than our chops and fillets, of course. But it's a good approximation as long as the piece of meat has a thickness that is small relative to its length and width. Heat then reaches the center much more rapidly from the top and bottom than from the sides. Numbers calculated for an infinite plate clearly represent an upper boundary on cooking time. It will take somewhat less time to cook a finite pork chop than an infinite one!

It's possible to take into account heating through the sides of a chop—and so calculate the center temperature in a finite plate—by combining the solutions for infinite plates of the three different dimensions. Chops have a roughly triangular shape, but I found that the average pork and veal loin chop is reason-

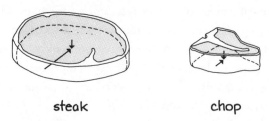

steak   chop

In a broad steak or fillet, heat entering from the sides has a much greater distance to travel (long arrow) *to reach the center than heat entering through the top or bottom* (short arrow). *Heating from the sides therefore has a negligible effect on the cooking time. In a chop or other small cut, however, heating from the sides will shorten the cooking time significantly.*

ably approximated as a rectangle of 2 inches by 3 inches. When I did the calculations, it seemed as though heating through the sides becomes important for these choplike shapes at a thickness of 1 inch. That is, the total heating time for chops 1 inch or more thick is significantly lower than it would be for a cut that is the same thickness, but longer and wider. I therefore calculated one heating time for cuts that are much larger than 2 or 3 inches on a side, and another for a 2-by-3 "chop." I'm not sure how to do calculations tailored to the quarter-moon shape of some fish steaks, but these are usually closer to the dimensions of a chop than to a broad fillet or steak.

In order to calculate how long it would take to simmer meat just to the point of being done, I had to decide what temperature at the center of the meat constitutes "done." Of course, there's no single answer. Different meats seem properly done at different temperatures, and people have different ideas of what a properly done piece of meat should taste like. In the end, I tested several internal temperatures for each kind of flesh, and settled on three.

The lowest internal temperature I chose was 140°F (60°C). Devotees of seafood usually quote this figure, or a few degrees higher, as ideal for fish. I agree; at 140°F fish is fully cooked, its flesh no longer slick, but it is still very moist, and tender enough that words like "melting" come to mind. Veal, pork, and chicken breast are also juiciest at 140°F. However, they're also frankly pink. I enjoy veal this way, but not chicken or pork, which taste thin and raw. Besides, the trichinella cysts that still occasionally infect pork are killed only when the meat reaches 137°F, so 140°F is cutting it close. (If you like very pink pork, you can cook it as little as you want provided you first freeze it for 3 weeks at less than 5°F, or −15°C.)

My next choice was 150°F (66°C), which is the internal temperature of veal, pork, and chicken breast that leaves just an undertone of pink, particularly as slices cool down and sit exposed to the air. (Apparently some of the myoglobin pigment, which turns red when it binds oxygen, can recover from this degree of heat.) A very small patch of dark muscle close to the bone of pork loin chops, and some blood vessels near it, often look redder than the surrounding meat at this temperature, an effect that seems to be due to their higher pigment content. If the redness bothers you, you can either eat around it or cook the meat to 160°F (71°C), which I took as my upper limit. At 160°F pork, veal, and chicken breast are well done, usually with little or no trace of pink. However, they're also noticeably drier. Meat scientists have demonstrated that animal flesh begins to lose moisture at temperatures as low as 100°F (38°C) and suffers most rapidly between 140°F and 160°F. The difference in juiciness between 150°F and 160°F is unmistakable. So if you value juiciness, it's best to aim for the lowest internal temperature you find palatable. If your primary concern is to produce an absolutely safe, microbe-free dish, then you'll have to do without juiciness and heat the meat to 180°F (82°C) or above.

I had figured that the dark meat of chicken would also be best at 150°F or 160°F, but I was wrong. It's still slick and unpleasantly chewy when quickly cooked to those temperatures. I understood why after I poked and probed some thigh and drumstick meat that I had carefully boned and cooked: these parts of the chicken are full of connective tissue. They therefore need to be cooked hotter and longer, so that the collagen can be turned into gelatin. The fibers of the dark meat do get drier in the process, but two things compensate for this: the higher fat content of the dark meat, which supplies a different kind of moistness; and the gelatin formed from the connective tissue, which contributes a certain succulence as well. In any case, the cooking temperature and time for dark meat aren't all that critical. So the timetables apply only to breast meat (which, fortunately, is the chicken part most shaped like a plane).

I began by using the heat conduction charts to calculate the times required to simmer various cuts of meat and fish to 140°F, 150°F, and 160°F at the center. In

Estimated Cooking Time at 200°F (93°C) Simmer for Meat at 40°F (4°C)

For actual cooking, use the timetables at the end of this chapter. "Chop" designates a relatively small cut of meat, about the size of a pork chop; "steak" designates a larger cut.

	To Reach an Internal Temperature of:		
	140°F (60°C) [fish; pink veal]	150°F (66°C) [barely pink veal & pork; chicken breast]	160°F (71°C) [well-done veal & pork]
½-in. chop or steak	2.5 min.	3 min.	3.5 min.
¾-in. chop or steak	6	7	8
1-in. chop	10	11	13
1-in. steak	11	12	14
1¼-in. chop	14	15	18
1¼-in. steak	16	19	22
1½-in. chop	18	20	22
1½-in. steak	23	27	31
2-in. chop	23	26	29
2-in. steak	41	48	55

order to make sure that I didn't underestimate the time, I assumed a low starting temperature and a low simmering temperature. I set the initial temperature of the meat at 40°F (4°C), roughly its temperature a few minutes after it has been taken from the refrigerator. (The initial temperature would be higher and the simmering time shorter if the meat were left out for some time, or if it were browned before simmering.) And I set the cooking temperature at a conservative 200°F, even though water begins to bubble at 208°F or 209°F. When I checked some of my predictions by timing actual pieces of meat, they were pretty close. This was true even when I had only a scant half-inch of water in the pan; complete submersion wasn't necessary. Apparently the vapor in a closed pan at the simmer is hot and dense enough to cook as effectively as the liquid.

I was astonished at how short some of these times are! And at how different they are for different thicknesses. And at how rapidly the central temperature rises, even in a chop 1 inch thick. Turn around at the wrong moment to deal with some small domestic crisis and you can easily overshoot by 20 degrees. By the way, you'll notice that the square rule—double the thickness and quadruple the cooking time—applies to cuts whose length and width are large compared to their thickness. (For the table I rounded most times to the nearest minute, which sometimes obscures the square rule.) But in the case of ordinary chops and similar cuts more than an inch thick, enough heat comes through the sides that a doubling of the thickness has a much smaller effect on the cooking time: more like a doubling than a quadrupling.

Now I've certainly seen recipes that specify a total cooking time of just 10 or 15 minutes, or a 3- or 6-minute poach, or that give guidelines for adjusting the time according to thickness. But they're usually fish recipes. (Notice that the standard rule for fish of 10 minutes cooking per inch of thickness is about right for 1-inch and small 2-inch fish steaks, but too little for larger 2-inch steaks, and far too much for ½-inch fillets.) Meat recipes commonly call for several minutes of browning in a skillet, followed by a half hour or more at the simmer, no matter how thick the meat. Maybe these directions date from the time when meats came from older animals, were therefore somewhat tougher and fatter than they are today, and so were better suited to long cooking. But the numbers in this preliminary table—and many remembered meals—convinced me that when we braise or poach tender meats these days, we're more likely than not to cook them far past their moist, tender best. If we're lucky, we make it all the way to a stewed, dry tenderness. If we're not, our jaws may get a workout. Either way, the quality of the meat has been squandered.

The obvious way to improve our chances of getting juicy meats in a braise is to exploit the predictable relationship between thickness and simmering time. Check the thickness of the meat and choose the cooking time accordingly. (Use the timetable at the end of this chapter; the preliminary version here, with its conservative assumptions about starting and simmering temperatures, could lead to overcooking.) Keep track of the cooking time, including any preliminary browning. If liquid is to be added after browning, preheat it to the boil so that the cooking will be continuous and the time calculable. (Many recipes have us add cold liquid to the browned meat, which interrupts the cooking.) Test the meat on the early side so as not to miss the narrow window of just-doneness. If the liquid requires further reducing to make a sauce, remove the meat first. Such attentions require no great modification of our kitchen routine, and they certainly make a difference. When I've incorporated them into standard recipes, I've gotten moist, tender results more consistently than I had before.

Improvement though it is, this approach to braising does have its flaws. For one, the thickness of the meat is seldom regular. Chops can be 1¼ inch in one place and ¾ inch in another; fish fillets and chicken breasts taper off from an inch or more down to nothing. Furthermore, the dimensions of a raw piece of meat change during the cooking as it shrinks along the grain and bulges up across it. Then there are bones, and skin, and fat, all of which slow the transfer of heat according to their quantity and placement. Even the thermal conductivity of the flesh varies from species to species. And a few degrees' difference in starting or cooking temperatures can translate into a difference of several minutes in cooking time. So while a carefully sculpted test chop may obey the pencil-and-paper predictions quite closely, in practice the predictions are just ballpark figures.

Because most of us are more willing to tolerate overcooked meat than undercooked, we generally heat our foods long enough to make sure that the thickest or best insulated pieces of meat aren't left underdone. By so doing, of course, we necessarily overcook all the rest—including the outer portions of the same thick pieces. If meat is cooking in liquid that is close to the boil, then the outer layers of the meat will exceed the target internal temperature by as much as 50 or 70 degrees, and every minute of excessive cooking will push these drying, toughening temperatures even deeper into the meat. My preliminary table of simmering times demonstrates just how fast this overheating can occur. So attentiveness isn't enough to guarantee the doneness we want in all or even most of the meat in a braise.

Imagine, however, what would happen if we lowered the temperature of the cooking liquid down to the temperature that we want the center of the meat itself to reach. Then the whole piece, from the surface to the center, would eventually be done just right, and it would stay that way no matter how long it sat in the liquid. A cook would have tremendous leeway in the cooking time; we could hardly go wrong. Clearly this would be a more desirable outcome than the rapid overshoot and toughening that can occur at the simmer.

Hoping that I might improve on an improvement, I looked into lower cooking temperatures for the braise. But first I had to be sure that lower braising temperatures would suffice to kill any microbes on the meat that might cause illness. Boiling water is very good at destroying microbes, but what about cooler

Estimated Cooking Time at 180°F (82°C) Subsimmer for Meat at 40°F (4°C)

For actual cooking, use the timetables at the end of this chapter. Cooking times at the 200°F (93°C) simmer are shown in brackets for comparison. "Chop" designates a relatively small cut of meat, about the size of a pork chop; "steak" designates a larger cut.

| | To Reach an Internal Temperature of: | | |
	140°F (60°C) [fish; pink veal]	150°F (66°C) [barely pink veal & pork; chicken breast]	160°F (71°C) [well-done veal & pork]
½-in. chop or steak	3 min. [2.5]	4 min. [3]	5 min. [3.5]
¾-in. chop or steak	7 [6]	9 [7]	11 [8]
1-in. chop	12 [10]	14 [11]	17 [13]
1-in. steak	13 [11]	16 [12]	19 [14]
1¼-in. chop	16 [14]	19 [15]	23 [18]
1¼-in. steak	20 [16]	24 [19]	29 [22]
1½-in. chop	20 [18]	24 [20]	29 [22]
1½-in. steak	28 [23]	34 [27]	42 [31]
2-in. chop	27 [23]	31 [26]	38 [29]
2-in. steak	50 [41]	61 [48]	74 [55]

Note. For reasons of safety, cuts that would cook in 5 minutes or less at 180°F are better cooked at a full simmer.

liquids? A standard handbook of medical microbiology states that effectively all common pathogens are killed when heated for 5 or 10 minutes at 180°F, or 82°C. (Some bacterial spores will survive this treatment, as they may survive boiling, but they aren't a common problem in fresh meats.) It seemed only prudent to adopt this as a minimal treatment that would ensure the safety of the meat's surface. (The interior of healthy muscle is normally sterile, and pork and fish parasites are killed at lower temperatures.) For cooking times much shorter than 10 minutes, it's probably safest to maintain a standard simmer.

Having settled on 180°F as a realistic alternative to the simmer, I calculated new cooking times for the various cuts of meat and fish. As you can see, they're longer than the times at 200°F, but not inconveniently so. The real advantage of having the liquid at 180°F is that there are at least 2 or 3 minutes between most stages of doneness, which takes some of the heat off the cook. For example, it takes just 3 minutes for a large 1-inch fish steak or meat chop to rise from 140°F to 160°F when cooked at the simmer, but a full 6 minutes when cooked at 180°F. So while we continue cooking the meat to make sure that the thickest parts are done through, we won't overshoot the desired doneness in the thin parts as badly. And of course the outer portions of all the pieces will be a good 20 degrees cooler than they would be in a simmering liquid, no matter how long they're cooked. The thicker the piece of meat—the longer it has to sit in hot water— the more it will benefit from that lower temperature.

Numbers, however, are only numbers. The real test is side-by-side stovetop comparisons of the two techniques. I tried quite a few. I did find it easier to hit the doneness I wanted in the slower pot. But timing was still important. Because flesh loses much of its moisture in the range between 140°F and 160°F, over-shooting to an internal temperature of 180°F turned out to be largely indistin-guishable from overshooting to 200°F. Veal and fish ended up very dry, pork dry and sometimes tough. So while cooking with 180°F liquids does give a cook more latitude in timing, it's by no means foolproof.

I now realized that timing is important and tricky, no matter what cooking temperature we choose, with one exception: the temperature we're aiming for the meat itself to attain. I had discarded that exception once I'd found out that temperatures of 140°F to 160°F aren't high enough to kill microbes on the meat's surface. But now I considered the possibility of sterilizing the surface at one temperature and cooking the meat through at another. After all, there are recipes that have us bring eggs or chickens to the boil, and then turn the heat off completely. This two-stage process moderates the initial temperature so that the interior of the food doesn't overcook. Why not adapt it to the braise? First boil the meat briefly to make it safe to eat. Then reduce the temperature to the target temperature, and keep it there until the meat has cooked through.

Because a changing external temperature greatly complicates the calcula-tion of heat conduction in an object, the heat conduction charts that I under-stand don't apply to this technique. However, the timetables I had already worked out helped me estimate how fast the temperature of the cooking liquid would have to fall in order to reach the target temperature before the center of the meat got that hot. Half-inch cuts heat up so fast—to 140°F in less than 3 minutes—that, assuming a minute or two at the boil, you'd have to add ice cubes to cool the liquid temperature to 140°F or 160°F in time. For a ¾-inch cut, you would need to lower the liquid to the target temperature between 3 and 5 minutes after the boiling stopped, and for a 1-inch cut, within 8 or 10 minutes, depending on the target. These numbers sounded more practical.

Back at the stove, I saw that the decline in cooking temperature from the boil varied according to the pan, the amount of liquid, and the quantity of meat. Lighter pans, those made of stainless steel rather than thick aluminum or cast iron, cooled off fastest, as did smaller volumes of liquid. When I used a stainless-steel electric frying pan and 2 cups or less of liquid, it was a fairly simple matter to brown ¾-inch and 1-inch chops for a couple of minutes, add boiling liquid, cover, turn the thermostat down, and have the cooking temperature decline to the desired range before the center of the meat was done. The total cooking time varied from 12 to 25 minutes, depending on exact temperatures and thicknesses. Of course the best thing about this method is that exact timing is irrelevant: once the meat reaches the target, it never gets any hotter. When I let pork chops sit for an hour at 150°F just to be sure, they were still slightly pink and full of juice. After the simmer, what forgiveness!

There's no doubt that temperatures below the simmer offer us a better chance at catching meat before it overcooks. At 180°F we have a few more minutes to work with, and at the target temperature we have all the time we want. Unfortunately, when we descend below the simmer, we trade one set of problems for another. The simmer may not forgive overcooking, but it is easy to find. Lower temperatures are forgiving, but not so easy to find or maintain. We can't just look at the pan and know that the liquid is at 180°F or 150°F. It won't smile, or shiver, or make any other sign except exhale uninformative steam at us when we open the lid.

Because subsimmer temperatures are in a sense invisible, tradition has ignored them. And because tradition has ignored them, our kitchens are not all that well equipped to produce them. An electric skillet with a thermostat does the job best, provided we first test the thermostat markings with a thermometer. But not everyone has or likes an electric skillet, and some recipes require a larger vessel in any case. Ovens and their thermostats are seldom designed to work much below 200°F, so oven braising requires a thermometer and frequent adjustments of a propped-open door. Stovetop braising must also be monitored with a thermometer. The usual culinary thermometers, however, are ill suited for this purpose. In order to immerse the requisite inch or two of the stem in the liquid, it's often necessary to interrupt the cooking and tilt the pan while we wait for the "instant" reading.

Still other complications attend the adaptation of braising recipes to low temperatures. At the simmer, water vapor is sufficiently hot and dense to cook parts of the meat that protrude above the liquid surface. The same is true at 180°F, but at the lower target temperatures, the vapor is less effective. This means that cooking time may be significantly longer for recipes that involve relatively little liquid, unless we heat the entire dish evenly in the oven, or reduce the air space above the pan with foil. Longer cooking times are also necessary for thick braising liquids, which don't heat as evenly or rapidly as thin ones; alternatively, we can thin the liquid for braising and then boil it down after removing the cooked meat. In some recipes, the liquid and vegetables are meant to cook through as the meat does. But starch granules dissolve most rapidly close to the boil, so the sauce may need thickening and the potatoes softening after the meat is done.

There's no question that low-temperature braising can be a fair amount of trouble. Enough, perhaps, that instead of calling it poaching, a neutral term that comes from the French for the "pocket" formed by a cooking egg white around the yolk, we should probably call it coddling.

Coddle or poach, why bother with such eccentric techniques? It depends on how important moist, tender meat is to you—and how much you enjoy exploring new territory. One cook's trouble is another's pleasure. For me, playing with off-the-scale oven temperatures and modifying recipes is great fun; it's like solving a puzzle in a way that wasn't quite foreseen by its inventor. If you're interested in trying the low-temperature braise, you'll find some detailed advice and sample recipes in the summary below. If you do stick with the simmer, remember to take the thickness of your meat into account, and adjust the cooking time according to the table at the end of the chapter. I think you'll find that the added care pays off.

I also wondered whether low-temperature poaching would suit long-cooked dishes like stews and pot roasts. The answer turned out to be no. I tried cooking cubes of beef round at 160°F, 180°F, and at the simmer, around 205°F. The simmered meat was tender after a couple of hours, the 180°F version after a few more, and the 160°F version even later. All the beef cubes ended up tender, and all of them dry. The lower temperatures didn't seem to have any beneficial effect on the meat's texture.

Why not? The key is the combination of temperature and time that is necessary to cook such tough cuts as the round and chuck. Well-used muscles contain greater amounts of connective tissue, which surrounds and infiltrates the muscle fibers to coordinate their action and transmit the force they generate to the bones. Mature connective tissue is much tougher than the muscle fibers themselves, and the older an animal is, the more tightly the strands of collagen—the main connective-tissue protein—are chemically cross-linked to each other. Strands of beef collagen don't even begin to unravel until the temperature exceeds 140°F, and they don't dissolve into gelatin in any appreciable quantity below 180°F. (By contrast, veal collagen dissolves rapidly when a chop is poached.)

Unfortunately, the muscle fibers are much more susceptible to heat than mature collagen. And rather than dissolve these fibers, which are already about 75% water, heat causes them to coagulate. As the proteins of the contractile machinery within the fibers heat up, they're knocked out of their normal arrangements and shapes. They begin to bond indiscriminately with each other, and in the process shrink into a dense mass that has less room for water. So water is squeezed out of the fibers, and the meat gets tougher and drier.

Fiber toughening begins as low as 105°F (41°C), almost before the meat has gotten detectably hot. The great catch in meat cookery, however, is that at least half of the meat's water is squeezed out between the temperatures of 140°F and 160°F, precisely because this is the range in which the tough collagen starts to give way. That is, we can't even begin to dissolve the collagen without drying the meat out drastically. In this temperature range, the highly ordered collagen strands are scrambled and therefore shrink by as much as three-quarters of their original length. But there are still enough intact bonds to hold them together, so as they collapse they exert a new pressure on the fibers that they surround. This pressure compacts the fibers into an even denser mass and also forces much of the remaining free water out of the fibers. In the process of softening the connective tissue, then, we inevitably end up making the rest of the meat exceedingly tough and dry.

With prolonged cooking above 180°F, a modicum of tenderness and moistness is restored to the meat. The collagen network slowly dissolves into gelatin, thus relieving the pressure on the muscle fibers and greatly weakening the attachments between neighboring fibers. As the mass of fibers loosens up and expands, it even reabsorbs some of the fluid from its surroundings. You would never mistake this stewed texture with that of a tender meat cooked just to medium, but for tough meats it's about the best you can hope for.

Low-temperature cooking can't do much for long-cooked stews and braises. Their agenda—hours of cooking at 180°F or above—is set by the connective tissue. Stew at 180°F instead of 200°F and it simply takes longer for the meat to reach a dryly tender texture. The best step you can take to improve the texture of stewmeat is to supply moistness in the form of fat. Either choose a well-marbled cut or lard poorly marbled meat with thin strips of fat.

There is still a good reason, though, not to cook a stew at a full boil. A boiling stew is turbulent; its components are continuously being mixed with each other. This turbulence is used to advantage in the fish stew called bouillabaisse, where vigorous boiling incorporates olive oil into the liquid as a fine emulsion. On the other hand, as Richard Olney has pointed out, turbulence makes it difficult to skim excess fat from the surface of meat stews, because the droplets of fat never sit still long enough to rise to the surface and pool together. The result is a cloudy, sometimes greasy stew. Maintain the liquid at a bare smile instead, and the fat will rise to the surface where it can be removed.

Even if there's no advantage to coddling a stew at 180°F or below, there is one lesson that can be carried over from brief braises to long ones. If you cook the stew in the oven—though, of course, it's much easier to maintain the desired temperature and skim the fat on the stovetop—beware of the oven temperatures that most recipes specify. You may want to begin at 250°F or 350°F (121°C or 177°C) just to get everything hot in a reasonable amount of time, but once the pot begins to bubble, turn the thermostat down to 200°F, or 93°C. (It's always a good idea to check beforehand that the thermostat is accurate.) Cookbooks may call a 250°F oven "slow," but it's well above the boiling point and will churn your stew up just as surely as a "fast" oven will. If you have a clear glass casserole dish, you can verify this just by opening the oven door and taking a look.

In the end, all my calculations and experiments failed to turn up a painless, ideal alternative to the simmer. They did, however, highlight a useful fact that cookbooks generally don't: there's more than one way to braise a chop. You can follow a standard recipe, simmer for half an hour and beyond, and have well-done, dry meat. You can measure the meat's thickness, consult the table of cooking times, begin to check the doneness before the prescribed time, and have a decent chance of getting a juicy medium doneness. You can do the same measuring and consulting, coax your pot or oven to a steady 180°F, and have a better chance. Hover instead over a pot or oven at the temperature you want the meat to reach, and the right doneness is almost guaranteed. Cook's choice.

Maybe one day "smart" stovetops and ovens and thermometers will give us the same kind of control over temperature that we now have over ingredients and cooking times. Meanwhile, despite the added trouble, I've found it easy enough to adapt to shorter simmers and poker-faced poaches. I'm happy to give up smiles on the stove if I can have more of them around the table.

SUMMARY: SIMMERING MEATS

While prolonged cooking close to the boil is necessary to make tough cuts of meat tender, it also dries them out. Tender meats—fish, chicken breasts, pork and veal chops—will take on the same dry, stewlike texture if they're heated much past 160°F (71°C). Many recipes for brief braises almost guarantee a dry result with simmering times that approach an hour.

The time it takes to heat the center of an object depends on the object's dimensions, its original temperature, the internal temperature you're aiming for, and the cooking temperature. The way to obtain moist meat in a braise is to cook it for a period appropriate to the meat's dimensions and the doneness you prefer. When you cook at the simmer, you can overshoot your target temperature for the meat fairly quickly. If you cook at 180°F (82°C), you have a few more minutes in which to check the meat and prevent overcooking. By starting at the boil and then turning the temperature down to the target temperature, you can be sure the meat won't overcook.

If you cook at the simmer or at 180°F, begin by measuring the thickness of the thickest piece of meat. Consult the timetables at the end of this chapter for an approximate cooking time. As you keep track of the actual cooking time, include any initial browning—a minute in the frying pan is about equivalent to a minute at the simmer. Heat the cooking liquid to the right temperature before you add it to the meat or add the meat to it; otherwise the timetables won't apply. Thick liquids may also slow stovetop heating. Somewhat before the estimated cooking time is up, check the thickest piece to see whether it's done; and keep checking regularly until it is. When the meat is done, remove it from the heat.

If the liquid is to be reduced or thickened, or if there are vegetables that remain undercooked, place the meat in a separate dish and do any further cooking without it.

If you cook at the target temperature after an initial boil, check the meat after 30 minutes, and again at intervals of your choosing. Remove the meat when it's done and then finish cooking the sauce or vegetables, if that's necesssary.

If you're not serving the meat immediately, keep it warm or even cool, not hot. Reheat it gently, taking care not to exceed 140°F. If you have well-refrigerated leftovers the next day, boil the liquid separately, turn off the heat, and then add the meat. This gentle treatment will preserve the meat's texture and minimize the development of "warmed-over" flavors. However, if there's any reason to suspect the safety of leftovers, forget about tenderness and boil the whole dish.

Here's an example of a traditional braise that I've adapted to preserve the meat's moistness. One of my favorite recipes is Giuliano Bugialli's *maiale ubriaco*, or "inebriated pork chops," from his *Fine Art of Italian Cooking*. The recipe directs us to chop 10 sprigs of Italian parsley and 1 clove of garlic, mix them with 2 tablespoons olive oil, 1 teaspoon fennel seeds, and salt and pepper to taste, and put this mixture in a frying pan. Four "large" pork chops are then placed in the pan, the pan is set on the heat, and the chops browned 5 minutes per side. We then add a cup of red wine, lower the heat and cover the pan, and "simmer very slowly for 20 minutes, until the wine is evaporated and the pork cooked."

The recipe is simple, which always appeals to me, and the combination of flavors is delicious. But I've had problems with the timing. When the pan is covered and the simmer slow, the wine doesn't evaporate in 20 minutes. If I then turn up the heat and reduce the wine, the chops end up on the dry side, particularly after they've cooled down a bit. I once checked with the thermometer and found that 1-inch chops reach 205°F (96°C) or so at the center. No wonder they seemed dry. Since both the pan and the wine start out cold, we can't compare Bugialli's recipe directly with the timetables. But I would guess that the recipe provides the equivalent of 6 or 7 minutes of real browning and 15 minutes at a real simmer. According to the timetables a 1-inch chop cooked at the simmer reaches well done in only 11 or 12 minutes. The recipe's timing is more appropriate for 1½-inch chops.

Here are three ways of modifying Bugialli's recipe to produce juicy 1-inch chops. I'll explain them in detail so you'll get an idea of how to adapt your own favorite recipes.

To cook inebriated pork chops at the simmer, I look at my timetable and decide that the total cooking time for 1-inch chops should be 10 to 12 minutes. So as not to complicate the timing, I preheat the wine in a separate pan, and heat the pan and herbs until they're sizzling before adding the chops. I brown the chops 3 minutes per side, for a total of 6 minutes cooking time. I then add the hot wine, cover, and simmer for another 3 minutes, turning the chops once to color them evenly. I check the thickest chop. If it's too pink, I simmer for another minute or so, and check again. When the meat is cooked through, I remove it to a warm platter, turn up the heat, and boil down the wine. Then I put the chops back in the pan and turn them to coat them with the herbs and pan juices. The dish is as flavorful as ever, and the chops are still moist.

When I use the 180°F poach instead of the simmer, I alter only two details of the simmering routine. The timetable gives an estimated total cooking time between 15 and 19 minutes, so I start checking for doneness after 7 or 8 minutes of poaching. And I monitor the temperature of the cooking liquid. Since the surface of the hot frying pan is well above the boil, the wine can afford to start somewhat below the boil, though still hot. If the wine exceeds 180°F after I've added it to the pan, I simply keep the cover off and stir it until it cools off. If the wine falls below 180°F, I turn the heat way up. When the liquid approaches 180°F, I turn the heat way down and check it every minute or two until I'm sure it's stable.

The coddled version of inebriated pork chops is easiest done in an electric skillet. I brown the chops for 6 minutes, add wine that is at or near the boil, turn the thermostat down to 150°F or 160°F (66°C or 71°C), and cover the skillet. After a minute, I uncover the pot, turn the chops, and let the liquid cool down by evaporation for a minute or so, until the thermostat lights up just above the target temperature. Then I cover the pot. After another 10 minutes, I turn the chops again. I check the meat for doneness after about 15 minutes of coddling. If it's still quite pink, I turn the thermostat up a bit, and recheck in a couple of minutes. Again, I reduce the liquid only after I've removed the meat.

Though some advance planning is advisable, it's not hard to adapt just about any recipe for a short braise or poach along these lines. The adjustments are fairly commonsensical. (Another: take the breasts out of a *coq au vin* when they've reached 150°F; let the other pieces cook to 180°F or until they're tender.) One less obvious point: thick, viscous liquids aren't as efficient as thin ones at transferring heat, and may therefore require more time than the tables predict.

Finally, some advice on the logistics of poaching and coddling. The easiest way to do either is to use an electric skillet whose thermostat will keep the temperature in the right range. It's a good idea, however, to make sure that the thermostat markings are accurate. Heat up a few cups of water and use a thermometer to check where 180°F, 160°F, 150°F, and 140°F actually fall on the thermostat dial. Don't let the thermometer touch the bottom of the pan, which may be hotter than the water above it.

Because the coddling method begins at the boil and because a pan of hot water cools down slowly, simply turning down the thermostat after the brief initial boil probably won't lower the liquid to your target temperature fast enough. It's usually necessary to remove the lid and allow evaporation to accelerate the cooling. Check the skillet's temperature by moving the thermostat dial until the indicator light comes on. When you get close to the temperature you want, reset the thermostat for the target temperature, replace the lid, and relax.

If you don't have an electric skillet, or if the meat won't fit in a single layer (piggybacking has the effect of doubling the meat's thickness), then cook in whatever pot you have and use a thermometer. This may seem tedious at first, but after a couple of tries you'll get a pretty good idea of how low the burner should be. It's pretty low indeed. I find myself much more likely to let the temperature rise too much than fall too much. Until you're familiar with the behavior of your pot and stove, check on the temperature every 2 or 3 minutes.

Sometimes only a baking dish can accommodate the quantity of meat and liquid you need to cook. Or the cooking liquid may be too thick for predictable stovetop timings. In these cases it pays to explore unfamiliar territory on the oven thermostat. Cookbooks often talk about maintaining a simmer in a "slow" 325°F (163°C) oven: an oven, that is, far hotter than the boiling point! A 325°F oven may *bring* liquid to the simmer slower than a 375°F oven, but once the liquid begins to simmer it will soon reach a full-fledged boil in either oven. Ideally, we would set the oven for 140°F or 160°F or 180°F. Since most oven thermostats aren't marked lower than 200°F, that isn't the simplest thing to do. But it's not impossible either.

For this purpose I find that an old-fashioned, massive meat thermometer with a large dial is more useful than an oven thermometer because its markings are further apart and easier to read. I clip a clothespin on partway down the thermometer's stem so that the stem won't rest on the metal rack (if the air temperature is changing rapidly, the rack will lag behind), and place the thermometer toward the back of the oven, where the temperature is most stable. To calibrate your oven for poaching, turn it on as low as possible, and after a minute or two of initial warmup, prop the oven door open with a rolled-up hot pad. Then, for an hour or so, watch the thermometer dial and move the pad up and down the crack between oven and door. You'll eventually get an idea of the range of pad positions that correspond to temperatures of 180°F and below. It's also possible to heat the oven to 200°F or 225°F, put the dish in, and then turn the oven off; mine loses about 2 Fahrenheit degrees a minute.

When it comes to cooking, I start the oven well in advance so that it has settled down to the right temperature range before I entrust the meat to it. Then I complete the stovetop preparations, put the dish in the back of the oven, and check the thermometer and adjust the door prop every couple of minutes, until the temperature returns to the right range. I keep checking occasionally after that, depending on how stable the temperature is. If your oven is regularly hotter than you want it to be, simply check the meat a few minutes earlier. Since the food is cooking much more slowly than it would at the simmer, you won't overshoot too badly in any case.

BRAISING TIMETABLES

Use the times in these tables (next page) as guidelines, not exact predictions. Measure the thickness of the thickest piece of meat you want to cook and choose the degree of doneness (internal temperature) that you prefer. "Chop" designates a relatively small cut of meat, about the size of a pork chop; "steak" designates a larger cut. Make your first check on the doneness of the meat somewhat before the times shown here. If you brown the meat before braising it, subtract the browning time from the braising time. These tables assume that the meat begins at 50°F (10°C), the temperature it reaches after being taken from the refrigerator and sitting for some time in the kitchen.

Cooking Time at 210°F (99°C) Simmer
for Meat at 50°F (10°C)

	140°F (60°C) [fish; pink veal]	*To Reach an Internal Temperature of:* *150°F (66°C) [barely pink veal & pork; chicken breast]*	*160°F (71°C) [well-done veal & pork]*
½-in. chop or steak	2 min.	2.5 min.	3 min.
¾-in. chop or steak	5	6	7
1-in. chop or steak	9	10	12
1¼-in. chop	13	14	15
1¼-in. steak	14	16	19
1½-in. chop	16	18	20
1½-in. steak	20	23	27
2-in. chop	21	23	26
2-in. steak	36	41	48

Cooking Time at 180°F (82°C) Subsimmer
for Meat at 50°F (10°C)

	140°F (60°C) [fish; pink veal]	*To Reach an Internal Temperature of:* *150°F (66°C) [barely pink veal & pork; chicken breast]*	*160°F (71°C) [well-done veal & pork]*
½-in. chop or steak	*	*	*
¾-in. chop or steak	7 min.	8 min.	10 min.
1-in. chop	11	14	16
1-in. steak	12	15	18
1¼-in. chop	15	18	22
1¼-in. steak	19	23	28
1½-in. chop	20	23	28
1½-in. steak	27	33	40
2-in. chop	26	30	37
2-in. steak	48	58	72

*Since these thin cuts would cook in 5 minutes or less at a 180°F subsimmer—which might not kill all the potentially harmful microbes on the meat—they should be cooked at or near the boil.

The Green and the Brown

Cooking is, among other things, a means of delaying the inevitable decay of plant and animal tissues. It temporarily preserves them by disabling the chemical agents that would otherwise cause them to rot: the active enzymes of the tissues themselves, and of their attendant bacteria and fungi. Cooking prolongs the kitchen life of our foodstuffs by destroying the last traces of biological life in them and on them.

The appeal of salads and other uncooked dishes comes partly from the sense that we are tasting a living thing, fresh and vivid in color and flavor, minimally altered by human hands. Some of these dishes are so fragile that they degenerate visibly in a matter of minutes, long before their nutritional value or safety has been significantly compromised. Lettuce leaves wilt and darken in a vinaigrette; the mashed avocado in guacamole discolors, as do the pulverized basil leaves in pesto. These changes serve as a kind of punctuation: they signify that the brief moment of true freshness is past. In fact, they define that moment, and the value with which we invest it.

A pretty paradox to play with. But not so pretty if the full stop sits before you on a plate. Cooks prize ways of prolonging the appearance of freshness and have accumulated a body of lore for doing just that. Pluck your lettuce leaves apart and you'll do less damage than if you cut them; layer the lettuce with some preliminary oil to protect it from the damaging acidity of vinegar. Keep guacamole from darkening by plopping the avocado pit in its midst. Green up basil pesto by adding a little parsley or cooked spinach as camouflage. As usual, a hodgepodge of truth and fiction! It was obvious what experiments needed to be done in order to sort it all out. Less obvious were some of the results.

Most cut or crushed fruits and vegetables are discolored by some of their own enzymes, which react with the scrambled contents of damaged cells to produce a brownish pigment. This is the fate of both the avocado and the basil leaf. With lettuce, which we keep mainly intact, and which is not especially prone to browning, the problem is different. Of course, dividing the leaves into manageable pieces causes some damage, and you do occasionally see browning along the lighter midribs. Usually, though, the torn or cut edges develop a limp margin of darker green, and a simple dressing of oil and vinegar can raise similar areas all over a leaf.

One longstanding controversy among serious salad-makers is whether it's better to cut lettuce with a knife or tear it with the fingers. Eliza Acton wrote in her *Modern Cookery* of 1845 that "In England it is customary to cut the lettuces extremely fine; the French, who object to the *flavour of the knife*, which they fancy this mode imparts, break them small instead." In modern times, French-trained Madeleine Kamman instructs us to "cut or tear," while all-American James Beard says "Break or tear (do not cut)." The cutters generally don't say much by way of justification. I would say that the knife gives more regular and even-sized pieces, and allows the cook to work on several leaves at once. I have, however, heard one tearer's rationale. Tearing, he suggested, divides a leaf along the boundaries between cells, while a knife cuts right through cells. So tearing does less damage to the leaf than cutting, and therefore prolongs its fresh appearance.

That sounds good. Let the leaf show you where it wants to break. But what if the cell boundary isn't the weak part of the structure? Since the walls of adjoining cells stick to each other, perhaps tearing deforms and pulls open cells all along the tear. And even if you do cut through cells with a knife, a typical leaf cell is microscopic in size, so the damage wouldn't necessarily be prominent to the naked eye. It's true that a blunt knife might bruise a visible swath of cells, but then no one recommends the use of blunt knives.

Plausible microscopic scenarios don't prove anything. Puddings and salads do. I got a few varieties of lettuce, cut some pieces and tore others, and stored them in a plastic bag in the refrigerator for a few days. While delicate leaves like Bibb lettuce showed more darkening than the tougher romaine and iceberg, I could detect no difference between the cut leaves and the torn ones. (Even so, I think that tearing does indeed cause less damage than cutting. When I did the same comparison with basil leaves, which are quite prone to browning, all the cut pieces quickly developed a black edge, while most of the torn edges stayed green.) I then put the pieces into a vinaigrette. Again, the tender leaves darkened fastest, but cuts and tears fared similarly. So we can do what we like; the salad will look about the same.

That result wasn't much of a surprise to me. If it really did matter how lettuce is dismembered, the right way would have won out long ago. I was surprised, though, when I tested the claim in the *Joy of Cooking* that the damaging ingredient in salad dressings is the vinegar. That too sounds commonsensical. Vinegar is highly acidic, and I would expect it to eat away at living cells. Sure enough, when I put a few pieces of lettuce into plain vinegar, they wilted in an hour or so. The pigment in a piece of red leaf lettuce leaked out into the surroundings, a sure sign that the cells had been damaged. So the *Joy*'s recommendation to precoat lettuce with a little oil sounded good. It's also venerable. In *Acetaria*, a treatise on salads published in 1699, John Evelyn wrote that "some, who are Husbands of their Oyl, pour at first the Oyl alone, as more apt to communicate and diffuse its Slipperiness, than when it is mingled and beaten with the Acids."

I then put a few pieces of lettuce into plain oil. In a matter of 10 minutes— much more rapidly than the vinegar had done its damage—the leaves darkened in large patches. After half an hour or so they became limp, and the more delicate leaves turned all but translucent. They had that slick, sodden texture that typifies a salad past its prime. So it seems that the clear and present danger to the freshness of salad greens is posed not by biting vinegar, but by smooth, mild oil. More on the mark than the *Joy of Cooking* were the anonymous authors of *Adam's Luxury and Eve's Cookery*, who wrote of the Sallad in 1744: "the Oil will make it presently soften, and lose its Briskness."

I wanted to get a better view of those dark patches, so I borrowed a low-power (50×) microscope for a few hours. I immersed a piece of lettuce in a drop of oil on the slide. At that magnification, the upper leaf cells looked like tiny medium-green pieces in a jigsaw puzzle. I poked a small hole in the leaf with a tweezer tip. Immediately a much lighter shade of green began to dart irregularly outwards from the hole, following the cell contours. That is, the pieces of the puzzle stayed put, but their color changed. (They turned lighter because they were illuminated from underneath the microscope stage; lit from above, as they would be in a salad bowl, they appear to get darker.) Every few seconds, a bubble would form over the central hole and then pop. Evidently oil was moving into the spongy interior of the leaf and forcing air out through the hole. I

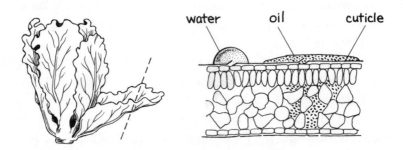

While water tends to bead up on the waxy surface of a lettuce leaf, oil readily spreads over it and penetrates through flaws into the spongy interior of the leaf, causing the leaf to darken and wilt.

saw the same infiltration take place more slowly (and without visible bubbling) along the edges of both cut and torn pieces of lettuce. When I did the same series of tests with water, there was absolutely no visible effect on either wounded or intact leaves.

Why does oil soak into a leaf while water doesn't? Apparently for one of the same reasons that oil is used in salad dressings to begin with. Plant leaves are coated with a protective waxy cuticle, a heterogeneous, water-repelling mixture of chemicals related to fats and oils. The cuticle helps prevent leaves from getting waterlogged in a rain, or from losing too much of their own moisture in dry air. In the kitchen, the cuticle prevents raw leaves from being coated evenly with water; the water tends to bead up and roll off. (Cooking melts and disrupts the cuticle.) Oil, however, gets along well with its chemical cousins in the cuticle and sticks to the leaf surface tenaciously. Oil-based salad dressings like the simple mixture of oil and vinegar are therefore the best at coating lettuce. Water-based sauces like mayonnaise and cream dressings will work, but they must be made thick and viscous so as not to flow rapidly off the leaf surface.

It's exactly this chemical compatibility between cuticle and oil that makes oil an insidious ingredient in salads. That, and its low surface tension compared to water. Water molecules exert such a strong electrical attraction on each other that they tend to minimize their contact with other surfaces: that is, they prefer to form self-contained beads rather than spread out into thin films. Oil molecules are bound much less tightly to each other. So it's salad oil and not water-based vinegar that clings intimately to the outer surfaces of leaves, readily oozes into any breaks in the cuticle, spreads underneath it, and advances into the interior of the leaf.

Despite their thinness, leaves are quite spongy structures. Up to 70% of their volume is empty space. The cells are interlarded with large air pockets that facilitate the exchange of gases during photosynthesis. (Cooking collapses this structure, which is why spinach and other leaves shrink so much on heating.) Lettuce leaves darken when the oil pours into these spaces and displaces the air, the pockets of which had been refracting light and dimming the green of the chloroplasts.

So oil doesn't really damage lettuce, at least initially. It just takes every opportunity to get into it. In so doing, it makes visible any damage that a leaf might have sustained during growth, harvest, storage, or preparation in the kitchen. Squeeze a fresh leaf hard between your fingers or poke it with a fork, and you won't see that much evidence of trauma. But immerse it in oil, and the spot darkens like a developing photograph. Then, as the leaf fills up with oil, its cells are unable to support the added weight, and the leaf begins to go limp. The oil-coated cells then become starved for air and water and begin to die. Eventually we end up with a slick, embalmed shade of a lettuce leaf.

Having recognized all this, I wouldn't bother with any priming coats of oil, which would just start to infiltrate the leaves that much sooner. It's helpful to be as gentle with salad greens as possible, particularly with tender and home-grown varieties. Storebought romaine and iceberg are tougher (and their latex reminiscent of rubber boots). But the cuticle on their outer leaves is sometimes so old and thick that tearing can detach large shreds of it from the underlying cells, and allow those cells to soak up oil right away. It's best to use a knife on such leaves. Dressing the salad should be put off to the very last minute. Tossing with the fingers is probably much easier on the leaves than utensils are, and you can easily feel whether you've added enough dressing to coat the leaves lightly and evenly. Finally, if you're stuck with some battered lettuce, consider a mayonnaise or cream dressing. They have two advantages: their oil is suspended as droplets in water, a form that slows their infiltration into the leaves; and their opacity will help disguise the blemishes.

Oily lettuce apart, the usual culprits in the discoloration of fruits and vegetables are a group of enzymes called the *polyphenol oxidases*. These are protein catalysts that plants employ to modify various phenolic compounds by adding oxygen atoms to them. In an intact cell the enzymes and the phenolic compounds are kept in separate compartments, and the enzymes' activity is strictly regulated. But when the cell is damaged, its highly organized insides are scrambled together, and the enzymes start oxidizing away. The oxidized phenolic products of the enzymes are much more reactive than their parent compounds. If they're produced in sufficient quantities, they combine with each other and with proteins to form large colored aggregates. So if a fruit or vegetable contains enough of both the enzymes and their phenolic targets, it will turn brown when its cellular innards are mixed up and exposed to air.

Because the consequences of their activity are so evident, the browning enzymes were among the earliest enzymes to be discovered and studied. (In 1883 a Japanese scientist, Hikorokuro Yoshida, isolated the compound that causes the lacquer from the lac tree to darken; a decade later G. Bertrand, a Frenchman, extracted the cause of browning in mushrooms.) These proteins turn out to be among life's more ancient inventions. A number of bacteria contain them, and they've been found in almost all plants and many animals. It's also a versatile family of proteins. Amoebas use theirs to envelop themselves in a hard, tough cyst. Lower animals use theirs to accumulate pigment granules for protective coloration. In mammals they are responsible for hair and eye color and for skin color, both innate and acquired: suntans are produced by human browning enzymes.

In plants, though, the function of the browning enzymes remains an enigma. It's possible that the plant enzymes play a role in the synthesis of important compounds. The enzymes' apparent location within the chloroplasts of green leaves and fruits suggests that they may somehow be involved in photosynthesis, perhaps by helping to control the availability of oxygen. So far, their best-documented role is a contribution to the impermeability of some seed coats.

Whatever their role in intact plants, the browning enzymes are most flamboyant in damaged tissue. This fact has led to the theory that they are mainly defensive chemical weapons. Their highly reactive products turn out to be very good at disabling nearby proteins. So, the theory goes, in the event that a plant tissue is invaded and damaged—by a fungus, say—then the mixing of the browning enzymes and phenolic compounds could neutralize the attacker's offensive enzymes and form a protective film against further invasion. This theory—like the defensive system, if it is one—has its weak points. For example, the same reactive products can and sometimes do inactivate the very browning enzymes that make them. And the invading fungi can use their own versions of these enzymes to damage the plant and neutralize *its* defensive compounds. So far there's no clear correlation between a plant's browning capability and its resistance to disease, so the defensive theory remains only a theory.

If the natural role of the browning enzymes remains enigmatic, their place in the kitchen is less so. Sometimes they're actually useful. They contribute to the desirable colors of tea, coffee, and chocolate, and their oxidized products may react with free amino acids in wine to generate aromatic compounds called *aldehydes*. Mostly, however, they cause trouble. They're such an expensive nuisance for the food industry that food scientists have pieced together a good deal of practical information about their distribution and activity.

The level of enzyme activity turns out to vary from plant to plant, variety to variety; from part to part within a single plant, and even within a single part. For example, the blossom end of the avocado browns more rapidly than the stem end; and Red Delicious apples brown more severely than Gravensteins, Gravensteins more than Granny Smiths, Granny Smiths more than Jonathans, Jonathans more than Golden Delicious. Generally speaking, browning enzymes are more active in young tissues than in old. In fruits, they're concentrated in the outer layers, become less active during ripening, but more active during storage after harvest. The content of phenolic compounds—the materials that the enzymes work on—also generally decreases during development and ripening. So mature fruits and vegetables usually brown less intensely than young ones. There are exceptions to this rule. The olive, which has among the highest browning activities of any fruit, turns black as it ripens. Apparently its enzymes are gradually released from an inactive position in chloroplast membranes to become soluble and active. Biochemical stress can also cause the activation of previously inactive enzymes, as is the case when avocados are deprived of oxygen during transport or storage. The same physical damage that mixes together enzymes and phenolics may activate the enzymes as well. And aging fruits and vegetables are often more prone to browning, probably because their biochemical control systems start to fail.

Control is what the cook wants. How the plant controls its browning enzymes is not known, but a combination of long experience and recent experiment has generated a battery of artificial methods. The best-known of these is the use of acid: the enzymes work best in neutral or only slightly acidic conditions. Ascorbic acid, or vitamin C, is an important antibrowning agent not so much because it's an acid, but because it can undo the phenolic oxidation perpetrated by the enzymes. Unfortunately, it accomplishes this by being oxidized itself. So it is used up as it protects, and must be present in large quantities if it is to outlast the enzyme molecules, each of which can oxidize thousands of phenolic molecules. Because oxygen is required for the generation of dark compounds, airtight wrapping can prevent foods from browning. And blanching foods in boiling water will protect them permanently from enzymatic discoloration. (Sufficiently high temperatures will destroy the normal structure and function of any enzyme.)

More esoteric research on the browning enzymes has revealed a couple of other possibilities. Copper ions turn out to play an essential role in the enzymes' activity. Sometimes these metal components can be pulled out of a protein or blocked from productive action. One culinary chemical that may interfere with the copper ions in this way is the chloride ion, which is supplied by table salt. Finally, an inhibitor of browning that's found naturally in tea leaves has been identified by Russian scientists as quercetin, a phenolic compound sold in some "health food" stores as a possible anticancer agent (see chapter 13). It probably works by displacing the usual phenolic compounds, which it resembles in structure, from the enzymes.

Enough biochemistry. Many cookbooks claim that guacamole can be kept from browning by putting the avocado pit into the middle of the bowl. This has always struck me as one of the looniest culinary myths: that emanations from a mysteriously vital seed could keep the dip fresh. For a while I thought that it must be some sport of countercultural cuisine that had outlived its time. But then I came across a cookbook published in Mexico nearly fifty years ago that calls for the pit to be replaced in the sauce. So I decided to investigate further. The use of the pit may very well hark back to the avocado's reputation in its native Mexico and Central America. The fruit's name comes from the Nahuatl for "testicle," which the oblong, rough-skinned fruit supposedly resembles; and the early European explorers described it as a "semen-forming" food that increases the venereal appetite. So the Englishman William Dampier in 1697: "It is reported that this Fruit provokes to lust, and therefore is said to be much esteemed by the Spaniards." Doubtless the seed of this remarkable fruit would be remarkable in its own right. Keeping its surroundings green might not be too much to ask.

It was conceivable to me that the avocado pit could be a source of antibrowning chemicals. Since seed coats often contain large quantities of phenolic com-

Keeping guacamole green: testing an alternative to the avocado pit.

pounds, I wondered whether the avocado seed coat might contain quercetin-like inhibitors of the browning enzymes. And the seed as a whole does inhibit at least some forms of life: it generally kills laboratory animals to which it's fed. Still, I found it hard to imagine how any active molecules could make it from the seed to the margins of the bowl in time to prevent discoloration. The test was simple enough: mash the flesh from an avocado, divide it into two bowls, put the pit into one bowl, and wait. I tried both the Hass and Pinkerton varieties. In each case, the surface of the pitless bowl got detectably gray after about 90 minutes. So did the surface surrounding the pit. Nor was there any gradation of color that might suggest the diffusion of some protective substance from the pit. No sign of any effect whatsoever.

When I removed the pit, however, I found that the depression beneath was still bright green. Perhaps an observation like this was the beginning of the legend! Any guacamole that actually touches the pit stays green. I guessed that the only real service rendered by the pit is to prevent oxygen from reaching the enzymes in the avocado flesh underneath it. So I repeated the experiment, this time replacing the slippery pit with an inert object of about the same size: a 40-watt high-intensity light bulb, whose glass provides a clear window onto the protected flesh, and whose screw base makes a nice handle for insertion and removal. It too kept the avocado underneath it pristine. There doesn't seem to be anything special about the pit.

These days, the better Mexican cookbooks say that the avocado pit helps protect guacamole from darkening only to some extent, and that nothing helps very much. It's true that once you begin serving guacamole, it will eventually discolor. But the outlook isn't all that black. As I discovered by comparing plain mashed avocado with a true guacamole, ingredients like tomatoes and lime juice help lessen the discoloration, probably because their acidity makes the browning enzymes less efficient. In any case, little change is noticeable for between 1 and 2 hours, which is certainly better than pesto lovers have it. (If you know you'll be serving over a longer period, divide the guacamole into several small bowls so that you can start fresh.) And research has shown that some varieties brown much less rapidly than others. The most common California varieties, the Hass and Fuerte, are among the fastest to discolor. The Lerman avocado, which was developed in Israel, takes between 12 and 18 hours to brown badly. So if you're lucky enough to have a choice, you might experiment to see whether one variety ages more gracefully than another.

The experiments with pits and light bulbs did debunk one theory of protection, but they also pointed out a practical alternative: you can keep a batch of guacamole looking fresh for many hours simply by excluding air from its surface. The problem is how best to do this. One recent and otherwise excellent Mexican cookbook claims that guacamole will discolor even if you press plastic food wrap directly onto the surface. Having discovered the different permeabilities of food wraps in my persimmon investigation (see chapter 9), I was ready to bet that the authors hadn't tried one particular wrap. When I pressed films of polyethylene, polyvinyl chloride, and polyvinylidene chloride (PVDC) into three different bowls of guacamole, all of them delayed browning to some extent, but only the PVDC—a.k.a. Saran Wrap—prevented it completely. It did so for 24 hours. PVDC is from 6 to 500 times less permeable to oxygen than the competition, and apparently that margin makes all the difference; the other two wraps simply let too much oxygen through to the enzymes in the avocado flesh. So use Saran Wrap to protect guacamole. If you happen to leave a couple of air bubbles when you press the film into the surface, dark spots will develop, but you can easily spoon out and discard them before serving.

Finally, a word about avoiding the discoloration of avocados even before you cut them open. These semitropical fruit are very sensitive to temperature, and may suffer cell injury—and subsequent darkening—if kept at temperatures much below 50°F (10°C) before they've fully ripened. Most avocado varieties ripen best at between 60°F and 70°F (15°C and 21°C). Above this range they're more likely to develop brown spots, off-flavors, and fungal decay. So a sunny windowsill is not the place for ripening avocados. Once they're soft, and as long as they haven't been bruised, they can be stored in the refrigerator for some weeks.

When it comes to discoloration, the problems of guacamole pale before those of pesto. I've been intrigued by this Genoese sauce, a rich, pungent paste of fresh basil leaves, garlic, olive oil, nuts, and cheese, ever since Colette Hughes introduced me to it in 1974 or 1975. Because we were weekend caretakers at the university botanical gardens then, my wife and I had a large summer garden. Colette was a fellow student of Italian extraction who kept our basil plants well picked; she would leave a note announcing that she had "ravaged" them on her way home from the library.

The flavor of pesto was a revelation—the only fresh herb I had tasted before was parsley—but I remember being impressed as well with how rapidly and deeply its color changed. Within five or six minutes of being mixed with pasta, its original spring green had turned olive drab; eventually it went almost black. By the end of the meal, the noodles were stained like the pages of a book that has been propped open with many cups of coffee. In recent years, I've been puzzled by the fact that while I still see the noodles turn brown, the sauce itself never seems to get quite as dark as it does in memory.

Fresh basil is not an important agricultural commodity, so little or no scientific attention has been paid to its browning enzymes. I've been unable to find a word on the subject. My guess is that the enzymes are abundant and active in basil leaves, their phenolic substrates plentiful, and their work sped by the easy availability of oxygen. When pesto sauce is tossed with noodles, the paste is spread out into a very thin layer, which exposes a tremendous surface area to the oxygen in the air.

I've come across no animistic practices that supposedly keep pesto green, though in an odd counterpoint to the legend of the avocado seed, the Roman naturalist Pliny reported that "pounded basil, if covered with a stone, breeds a scorpion." In his brief and learned disquisition on pesto, Giuliano Bugialli notes that in its native Genoa, the sauce is sometimes supplemented with some parsley to help maintain a fresh green color, and that cooked spinach is used for the same purpose in Tuscany. But the quantity he describes is so small—a teaspoon of spinach in several cups of finished sauce—that I thought these additives could only end up as lonely green shards in a sea of gray.

So I thought until I thought some more, and remembered a way in which spinach or parsley might exert an influence greater than their proportions might suggest. Maybe they're more than camouflage. Maybe they contain active inhibitors of the browning enzymes or their reactions. Was it mere coincidence that spinach contains a fair amount of oxalic acid—a natural inhibitor of the enzymes, according to one report—and that parsley is among the most concentrated sources of vitamin C? (It contains 170 milligrams per 100 grams of fresh herb, or three times the concentration found in orange juice.)

Indeed, mere coincidence it was. I tried adding large amounts of both parsley and spinach to pesto, more than the recipes call for, and I saw no decrease in the rate or extent of browning. So I have no idea why these traditions live on.

Still, the experiment gave me another idea. Maybe parsley and spinach just aren't sufficiently concentrated sources of inhibitors; maybe pure ascorbic acid would do the trick. A quarter-teaspoon of vitamin C granules purchased at my local "health food" store contains 1,250 milligrams, the equivalent of more than a pound and a half of parsley. I dissolved the ascorbic acid in a small quantity of water. I prepared a series of doses—$\frac{1}{32}$, $\frac{1}{16}$, $\frac{1}{8}$, $\frac{1}{4}$, $\frac{1}{2}$, 1, and 2 teaspoons granular ascorbic acid per quarter-cup pesto sauce—by dissolving the additive in a small quantity of water before adding it to the sauce. I smeared some of each batch onto a white plate. After an hour, only the doses of $\frac{1}{4}$ teaspoon and up were still fairly green. After several hours, only the two highest doses were at all distinguishable from the others. And they tasted as sour as a lemon. So unlike their more susceptible counterparts in avocados, the browning enzymes in basil leaves are able to outlast an impressive amount of antioxidant. Vitamin C was not the answer.

Nor did any other antibrowning agents sound promising. Some, like lemon juice and salt, would affect the flavor; and others, oxalic acid and quercetin among them, aren't the best things to consume in any quantity. I could think of only one other possibility, heretical or not: assaulting the enzymes physically, with heat rather than chemicals. I wasn't sure how long a time at the boil would be necessary to disable basil enzymes—published figures for other browning enzymes ranged from a few seconds to minutes—so I started with 60 seconds. I dipped a few leaves into boiling water, timed them, then dunked them immediately in ice water. After squeezing the excess water out, I ground the blanched leaves in a mortar and waited to see whether they would darken. They didn't. Nor did they taste much like fresh basil; the familiar pungency had been replaced by a vaguely sulfurous aroma, and some of the perfume was gone. So I tried 30 seconds. Still no browning after half an hour or so. Fifteen seconds, then 10, then 5. At 3 seconds, the ground leaves became noticeably discolored again. I settled on 5 seconds as the minimum effective treatment.

Next I made a full-fledged batch of pesto with the blanched basil, and dressed some fettuccine with it. It stayed beautifully green for an hour, after which it began to darken just slightly. The blanching water also eventually turned from a light green to brown. So the phenolic compounds in basil leaves appear to be capable of slow, spontaneous oxidation even in the absence of active enzymes. Unfortunately, even 5 seconds of boiling robs the basil of its full pungency and aroma. The sauce still tasted like pesto, but when sampled side by side with the raw sauce, my tasters and I chose the original every time. It simply had more flavor.

The compromise was obvious. Mix a portion of raw basil with the cooked sauce, and thereby restore some flavor to it. So I mixed two parts of a sauce made from cooked basil with one part of a standard raw sauce. It tasted distinctly better. But it also discolored rapidly, and just as darkly as the raw sauce itself! This was a vivid lesson in the power of biochemical catalysts. Each enzyme molecule can attack and modify thousands of target molecules before it itself breaks down. The much reduced enzyme population in the cooked-raw mixture was perfectly capable of taking on all the phenolic compounds from both sets of leaves (boiling doesn't alter phenolic compounds) and funneling them into brown pigments. So there's no point to mixing the raw and the cooked. The traditional raw version will look just the same and taste better.

Since all-out assaults with vitamin C and heat hadn't improved the color of pesto without cost to its flavor, I decided to forget the browning enzymes and concentrate instead on their targets, the phenolic compounds. I started by looking closely at the darkened sauce, really for the first time. I noticed that the fragments of leaf almost always looked dark green and not that unattractive, and that the noticeably brown particles all looked like pieces of a tube. So I got a length of basil stem and some bits of the base that attaches leaf to stem, ground them up, and pressed them on some paper. Within seconds, the ground bits and the paper had turned brown. When I repeated this test with pieces of leaf containing only small veins, the paper became dark green. Evidently the pale vascular stem tissue doesn't have enough chlorophyll to mask the activity of the browning enzymes. So one way to minimize the brown color in a pesto is to remove all the stems and leaf bases from the leaves. Well, at least the stems; pulling off the bottoms of a few hundred leaves isn't practical.

On to the other ingredients. There wasn't much to do about olive oil, garlic, and cheese, all indispensable and unalterable. But there is some leeway in the matter of nuts, which give pesto an added richness and more substantial texture. The traditional choice is the pine nut, but Giuliano Bugialli sanctions walnuts. Some desperadoes have even used sunflower seeds: that's what we did back in our school days, when pine nuts weren't yet readily available. I wondered whether these nuts differed in their susceptibility to browning.

The experiment was a simple comparison. I made small portions of pesto with each of the three nuts, and one portion with no nuts at all. I mixed them with noodles and checked on them every few minutes. After half an hour, the nutless and pine-nut sauces were noticeably lighter than the other two. After an hour, the pesto made with sunflower seeds was clearly the darkest, the pine-nut pesto as light as the nutless one, and the walnut mixture in between. So that's why our recent pestos have never been as black as I remember our first: we can now find and afford pine nuts!

I wasn't able to turn up any precise information on the enzyme or phenolic contents of pine nuts or walnuts. But I did learn that sunflower seeds are notorious in the food industry for their tendency to brown during the extraction of their protein. While the activity of their browning enzymes is only moderate, they turn out to be endowed with impressive quantities—up to 2% of their dry weight—of chlorogenic acid, the same phenolic substance that causes after-cooking blackening in potatoes and possibly in Jerusalem artichokes (see chapter 5). Extraction in alkaline conditions causes rapid and extensive reaction of the phenolic substances with each other and with proteins, and the nutritive value of the extracted protein is thereby compromised.

So it's best to banish sunflower seeds from pesto and stick with the traditional nuts. Even then, the greater the proportion of pine nuts to walnuts, the fresher the sauce will look.

The last frontier was the noodles. I had always assumed that they simply soak up the brown pigments that are generated in the sauce. But noodles are made from wheat flour, flour from the seed of a grass. And the seeds of the sunflower don't just absorb the local color; they actively contribute to it. In the course of my background check on the nuts, I came across the fact that enzymatic browning can indeed be a problem in grain products, particularly in whole grain and rye doughs. Its extent varies according to the variety of grain and the conditions under which it is grown. I found one report that certain wheat strains developed in Mexico were too prone to browning to make acceptable chapatis in India, where the traditional varieties don't darken. In another study, manipulation of the fertilizer regime caused the phenolic content of one wheat variety to change by a factor of four. Durum wheats, from which pasta is usually made, are said to have relatively little browning enzyme activity, and of course any wheat enzymes are destroyed when the noodles are boiled. But if there are phenolic compounds in the noodles, they might still be attacked by the live basil enzymes in pesto, and so add to the discoloration of the dish.

I tested this possibility by spreading some pesto sauce thinly over a plate, letting it sit overnight to brown by itself, then scooping it into a dish, adding a little water, boiling it thoroughly in a microwave oven, and then putting it on noodles. If the noodles were being discolored passively, simply by soaking up brown material from the sauce, then this dark sauce, its enzymes rendered inactive by cooking, would be just as bad an influence as a raw sauce. But if basil enzymes work directly on noodle phenolics, then the cooked sauce would leave the noodles looking white by comparison. The cooked sauce turned out to discolor noodles only slightly. So most of the staining is caused by the attack of basil enzymes on phenolic compounds embedded in the noodle surface.

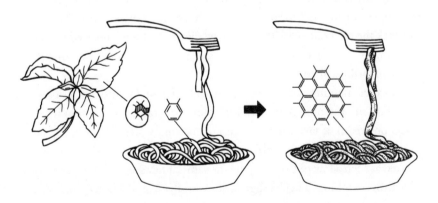

When we toss noodles with pesto sauce, browning enzymes from the basil leaves act on small, colorless phenolic compounds in the noodles and generate large, colored phenolic complexes. The noodles turn a mottled brown.

Since I'd had no luck knocking out the basil enzymes, maybe I could find a way of treating the noodles that would reduce their tendency to brown. I began by looking up the standard method for extracting phenolic substances from plants. It involves a mixture of acid and a semipolar solvent like alcohol; phenolics are largely hydrophobic (water-insoluble) molecules. Unfortunately, the cook's access to concentrated alcohol is limited. I tried soaking some noodles for half an hour in a little lemon juice and vodka, which is 40% alcohol. When cooked they were indistinguishable from ordinary noodles in flavor and texture. They were also indistinguishable from ordinary noodles in their reaction to the pesto—they browned. An overnight vodka bath turned the noodles limp and transparent. (Some of the gluten proteins are also soluble in alcohol.) They took only a minute or two to cook, still had an acceptable texture, and still browned.

As a last resort, I boiled a few noodles in a mixture of 1 cup water, ¼ cup vodka, and 1 tablespoon lemon juice. I reasoned that the higher temperature might accelerate the extraction of the phenolics despite the further dilution of relatively dilute vodka. It worked! This batch of noodles browned very little when sauced. Just to make sure that both alcohol and acid were necessary for this striking effect, I boiled some noodles with lemon juice alone, a tablespoon per cup water. Again, little discoloration! Then I tried a different acid, vinegar, and it worked too, at somewhat higher concentrations. Apparently I wasn't extracting any phenolics. I was just lowering the pH of the noodle surface far enough—from about 6 to about 3—that the basil enzymes were no longer able to attack the phenolics with their usual efficiency. So there's no need to sacrifice anything as expensive as vodka for the sake of white noodles. Lemon juice or cream of tartar will do.

By experimenting with different amounts of acid, I found that a significant reduction in browning requires a minimum of 1 tablespoon lemon juice or 1 teaspoon cream of tartar for each cup of cooking water. That's ¼ cup lemon juice or 1⅓ tablespoons cream of tartar per quart. As you might guess, noodles cooked at such a low pH aren't quite the same. They seem a little more susceptible to overcooking. They're slightly stickier; I've found it best to stir them frequently to keep them separate as they cook, though the sauce does a fine job of lubrication once they're served. And the noodles are noticeably tart when tasted alone. But the strong flavor of pesto pushes this tartness well into the background. I've come to think of it as a good alternative to saltiness, which is the usual flavor we add to noodles during boiling.

What appeals to me about cooking the pasta in acidic water is that it confines the chemical alteration—and so the unavoidable alteration in flavor—to just that portion of the dish where it's most needed: the noodle surface. If we added lemon juice to the sauce itself, the dish would taste sour and uncharacteristic. So I recommend the acid treatment to anyone who's interested in a fresher-looking pesto. Try it once and decide for yourself whether the accompanying changes in taste and texture are obtrusive enough to outweigh the visual improvement.

My experiments did turn up some remedies against food discoloration, but they're all partial and temporary. Yes, it's helpful to know about the acid treatment, about the differences among nuts, and plastic wraps, and salad dressings. Still, once you cut and dress delicate vegetables, herbs, and fruits, there's no way short of cooking to ward off the hues of death and decay.

On the other hand, I'm no longer as put off by some color changes as I was before I got to know them. I will acidify pasta for company, to keep a pesto looking as fresh as possible. Otherwise I often don't bother, because the brown edges have become—well, intriguing. Once a mere indication of staleness, they now also signify the ruggedness of life's vital parts. Hours, days, even months after the obliteration of the cells that constructed and housed them, the browning enzymes go doggedly about their work, finding their materials where they can: in the remains of their own leaf, in a pulverized tree nut, on the surface of a noodle made from the seed of a grass.

The persistence of the browning enzymes is remarkable. So is their virtuosity. The discolored noodle is a token of the cunning economy of natural selection, which, making much from little, has fashioned microbes and basil leaves and humans from many of the same basic parts. The animal cousins of the browning enzymes, the tyrosinases, give our skin, hair, and eyes the shadings that so define our physical identity. They help many of our fellow creatures to attract mates and to escape the notice of predators. They even, as it happens, help some of our fellow cooks to startle and impress us with intentionally darkened pasta. Noodles will turn virtually black when they are made with an exotic ingredient rich in tyrosinase and its melanin pigments: the defensive ink secreted by the squid.

All this may sound like a somewhat demented appreciation. There's a story in Boccaccio, retold by Keats, of a woman whose lover is killed by her brothers. Lisabetta finds Lorenzo's body, severs his head, and hides it in a pot of basil, over which she grieves. The plant grows lush and odorous on her tears and the unusually fertile soil. Pathetic as it is to become obsessed with a flourishing pot of basil, maybe it's sadder still to be intrigued by the decay of its leaves.

Let me hasten to say that I still recognize an old brown sauce as an old brown sauce. It doesn't taste any better than it did before. It's just that brown is a rich color. The next time you see a food darken before your eyes, consider it—for a moment—as a sign of life, of life's power of chemical transformation. A power that is also the essence of the cook's art.

SUMMARY: SALADS, GUACAMOLE, AND PESTO

Blemished lettuce leaves darken more rapidly in a salad than leaves with intact surfaces. The tenderest varieties in particular—Bibb, butter, and oak leaf—will look better if they're handled gently. As long as your knife is sharp, it doesn't matter whether you cut or tear the leaves.

Both vinegar and oil harm the appearance of lettuce, but oil acts more rapidly. It seeps through breaks in the cuticle and spreads into the body of the leaf, displacing air, darkening the color, and producing a soggy texture. The lettuce should therefore be dressed at the last minute. Opaque, water-based mixtures like mayonnaise and cream dressings help mask blemishes and slow the infiltration of oil.

Usually, guacamole will not darken noticeably for an hour or more after it is made. Leaving the avocado pit in the bowl will keep green only the guacamole in direct contact with it. The entire surface of the dish can be kept green indefinitely by pressing Saran Wrap into it; other wraps are less effective for this purpose.

Intact avocados darken easily if mistreated. They ripen best at between 60°F and 70°F (15°C and 21°C). Avocados can be stored in the refrigerator after they are ripe, but before then should not be exposed to temperatures lower than 50°F (10°C).

The browning enzymes in basil leaves can discolor several of the ingredients in pesto. The stems and leaf bases of the basil contribute the most obvious brown particles in the sauce; for a greener dish, remove them from the leaves. Walnuts make a darker sauce than pine nuts, and sunflower seeds will turn a pesto nearly black. Basil enzymes also stain the pasta. To minimize this discoloration, cook the pasta with lemon juice (¼ cup per quart water) or cream of tartar (1⅓ tablespoons per quart water). Noodles boiled in acidic water may stick together and cook more rapidly, so check them often.

Taking the Wind Out of the Sunroot

It's strange that among North America's meager handful of contributions to the modern table, two of them should prove to be such mixed blessings. One is the persimmon, whose delights and shortcomings are described in chapter 9. The other is the so-called Jerusalem artichoke. Actually the snappily crisp tuber of a sunflower, this vegetable does develop a mild flavor reminiscent of artichoke heart when it's cooked. After centuries of neglect, it's showing up again in the markets and being grown—or growing itself—in home gardens. Unfortunately, the Jerusalem artichoke surpasses even dry beans in its power to cause flatulence. Not all cookbooks point this out, and those that do offer few preventive tips. I've tracked down a couple of simple procedures that tone down the Jerusalem artichoke significantly. I also found that the usual explanation for this vegetable's peculiar name was demolished decades ago. There has long been a plausible alternative, and the time has come to dust it off.

The French almost certainly introduced the Jerusalem artichoke to Europe from its native America and gave it half of its misnomer. The first Frenchman to describe its qualities was Samuel de Champlain, who encountered it on July 21, 1605, among the Eastern Abenaki Indians on Cape Cod. As he recalled, "We saw an abundance of Brazilian beans, many edible squashes of various sizes, tobacco, and roots which they cultivate, which have the taste of artichokes." A little later, at what is now Gloucester, Massachusetts, he came upon them again and called them "some roots which were good, having the taste of cardoons [a relative of the globe artichoke], which the Indians cultivate."

That the plant is highly productive was noted by Marc Lescarbot, a lawyer who accompanied one of his clients to New France for about a year, returned from Nova Scotia with Champlain in 1607, and who apparently carried the first tubers back to the Old World. Ten years later, they were well established in France. Lescarbot described them as

> a certain kind of root, as big as turnips or truffles, most excellent to eat, tasting like chards [or cardoons], but more pleasant, which when planted, multiplies as it were out of spite, and in such a sort that it is wonderful. . . . We brought some of these roots to France, which have increased so much that today all the gardens are full of them.

Why should such vigor suggest spitefulness? Lescarbot had been in charge of the settlement's garden for a while; perhaps he had had trouble confining the plant. The English gardener John Goodyer was more precise about its remarkable productivity. He wrote in 1621 that the tubers grow "on long strings a foot or more from the root, raising or heaving up the earth above them, and sometimes appearing above the earth, producing from the increase of one root, thirty, forty, or fifty in number, or more."

In the view of at least one contemporary witness, the Jerusalem artichoke's prolific nature led to its rapid fall from grace in England. In 1629, only a little more than a decade after the tubers reached London, the botanical writer Thomas Parkinson noted that they are, "by reason of their great increasing, grown to be so common with us in London, that even the most vulgar begin to despise them, whereas when they were first received among us they were dainties for a Queen." Even the French failed to embrace what they called the *topinambour*. In 1616 it was reported to be grown mainly for livestock.

To my mind, the Jerusalem artichoke's vigor is one of its most appealing qualities. *Helianthus tuberosus* requires practically no attention between planting and harvesting, and the tubers can be left in the ground through the winter, to be dug up a few at a time as needed. Abundance doesn't necessarily breed contempt. I think two other qualities explain the failure of the Jerusalem artichoke to match the success of the potato and sweet potato, the New World's other notable tubers. One is its distinctive flavor, which perhaps is not neutral enough to serve day after day as an accompaniment to many other foods. Indeed, the first Englishman to record an encounter with the tuber rather disliked its flavor. Thomas Hariot met with it in Virginia among the Algonquians, and wrote in 1588 of *kaishucpenauk*: "their taste was not so good to our seeming as of the other [roots], and therefore their place and manner of growing not so much cared for by us."

Yet the initial admiration of the French suggests that the flavor did not repel everyone. It may have been too distinctive for a staple food, but it was still attractive enough for a variety of occasional uses. No, I think that the Jerusalem artichoke flopped largely because most people paid for the pleasure of eating it with subsequent discomfort. The French hardly ever mentioned this; perhaps they are too urbane, or somehow immune. In any case, the Englishman John Goodyer put the matter bluntly. The tuber had not been grown in England until John Franqueville, who had connections with the king's botanist in Paris, received some; he then gave two to Goodyer in 1617. After remarking on the plant's impressive yield, Goodyer described its culinary and physiological properties.

> These roots are dressed diverse ways; some boil them in water, and after stew them with sack [white wine] and butter, adding a little ginger: others bake them in pies, putting marrow, dates, ginger, raisins of the sun, sack, etc. Others some other way, as they are led by their skill in cookery. But in my judgement, which soever way they be dressed and eaten they stir and cause a filthy loathsome stinking wind within the body, thereby causing the belly to be pained and tormented, and are a meat more fit for swine, than men; yet some say they have usually eaten them, and have found no such windy quality in them.

Goodyer wasn't alone in his harsh assessment of the vegetable. In his book on how to live a long life, Tobias Venner said in 1622 that "It breedeth melancholy, and is somewhat nauseous or fulsome to the stomach, and therefore very hurtful to the melancholic, and them that have weak stomachs." And Robert Brooke, writing critically of the English church in 1649, found in the plant's spiteful increase and digestive effects a rich metaphor: "Error [is] like the *Jerusalem-Artichoake*; plant it where you will, it over-runnes the ground and choakes the Heart."

So roundly disparaged was this vegetable that the only dish it inspired in England over the ensuing three hundred years was Palestine soup, which is itself all but forgotten today. Restaurants in France were known to use it as a cheap, off-season imitation of artichoke hearts. There was a promising period early in the twentieth century when it looked as though the starchless, glucose-poor Jerusalem artichoke could be recommended to diabetics. But physicians found that their patients couldn't tolerate the gastrointestinal side effects.

The modern comeback of the Jerusalem artichoke has been powered by an interest in indigenous and novel foods. This revival is likely to be a brief one as well, unless a way can be found to reduce its heart-choking powers. An opportune moment for some research.

Jerusalem artichokes and beans cause flatulence for the same reason: both contain carbohydrates that we can't digest or absorb. Animals possess only a limited repertoire of digestive enzymes, which break down the major components of their food into usable raw materials. The troublesome molecules in beans and Jerusalem artichokes have never been a sufficiently important part of our diet for us to have evolved enzymes to digest them. And lacking such enzymes, we're unable to tolerate large quantities of these molecules in our diet. When we eat beans or Jerusalem artichokes, the intact carbohydrates go unabsorbed and pass into the lower regions of our digestive tract, which are inhabited by versatile, opportunistic bacteria. When the sudden charge of carbohydrate comes along, the bacteria quickly shift metabolic gears to take advantage of it. They thrive and multiply, and in the process generate copious quantities of carbon dioxide. Gas.

Beans are nevertheless a popular and important food. They contain large amounts of starch or oil and protein—energy reserves for the plant embryo—which we can digest. Their offending molecules, three-, four-, and five-unit sugars made up of sucrose and galactose, are present in relatively small quantities: some 10% or 15% of the bean's dry weight. The Jerusalem artichoke, in contrast, contains no starch or oil, and little protein. Its offending substances are themselves the tuber's main energy reserves, accounting for 50% or more of its dry weight.

Like the potato, the Jerusalem artichoke is a carbohydrate reserve for the next season's sprouts. But where the potato strings together molecules of glucose into long chains that we call starch, the artichoke lays down fructose in chains known as *inulin* (the English chemist Thomas Thomson gave it this name because he extracted it from roots of the elecampane, *Inula helenium*).

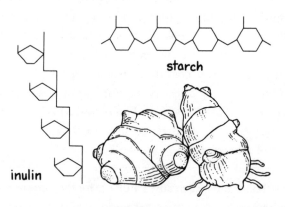

The Jerusalem artichoke stores its energy not in starch but in inulin, a chain of fructose molecules. The human body has no enzymes that can digest inulin into absorbable sugars.

Unlike starch, which is made up of many thousands of sugars and is deposited in the cell in solid granules, the inulin of Jerusalem artichokes is on average about thirty-five fructose units long, and is somehow kept dispersed in the cell's vacuole, despite the fact that it's not soluble in cold water. The Jerusalem artichoke also contains an assortment of shorter fructose chains, all the way down to three units; these are known collectively as *fructosans*. Inulin and the fructosans are common minor constituents of many plants—wheat flour is about 1% fructosans by weight—but they're rarely a major form of carbohydrate. The notable exceptions to this rule are the Jerusalem artichoke, the true globe artichoke, onions and garlic, salsify, and chicory and dandelion roots.

Taming the Jerusalem artichoke is thus a question of removing or altering its inulin and fructosans. The first thing that occurred to me was to treat the tuber as we do beans: boil it in copious amounts of water to leach out the carbohydrates, and then discard the cooking water. This would surely work with the shorter fructosans as it does with the short sugar chains in beans. But I was less sure about inulin. Fortunately, it turns out that inulin is readily dissolved in hot water. And unlike the starch in potatoes, it's already dispersed in the cell's storage vacuoles, not packed into solid little granules.

While reading around in historical accounts that mention the Jerusalem artichoke, I discovered that there was nothing new about my idea. It had just been forgotten. The evidence that hot-water extraction is effective is nearly two hundred years old! In May 1801, a fur trader of the Northwest Company named Alexander Henry learned that a settlement near the site of Winnipeg was starving and surviving only on "esquebois" (from the Cree *askipaw*), "the wild potato or pomme de terre of this country." Henry noted in his diary: "When boiled [it] is tolerably good eating. They are also eaten raw, but are then of a windy nature, and sometimes cause a severe colic. I have known people to suffer much after eating a moderate quantity." One hopes that the settlement at Portage la Prairie had sufficient water, firewood, and experience.

Of course, it would be difficult—and not very pleasant—to collect accurate data on the relative wind-provoking powers of foods. And people react differently to foods. Some, by virtue of native intestinal flora and digestive physiology, can apparently tolerate the Jerusalem artichoke, as even John Goodyer admitted. So a direct test of hot-water extraction isn't really feasible.

Still, there's no doubt that 10 or 15 minutes of boiling in copious amounts of water does extract both inulin and fructosans from the Jerusalem artichoke. You can see this in the kitchen if you boil down the cooking water until it gets syrupy, let it cool, and add a dollop of gin or vodka. A fine white precipitate will cloud the liquid. Much of the precipitate consists of inulin, which is insoluble in alcohol. The fructosans are soluble in both alcohol and water and not visible, but they are mainly responsible for the thickness of the liquid.

To increase the effectiveness of boiling, we can cut the tuber into slices, which increases the surface area exposed to the water. And because the texture of the Jerusalem artichoke resembles that of a carrot or turnip more than a potato, boiling briefly doesn't destroy its texture. The boiled slices can be roasted, used in soups or salads, even fried or deep-fried, with excellent results. If you want to use the tuber raw, as in a salad, or almost raw, as in a stir-fry, the best rule is to make the Jerusalem artichoke a distinctly minor ingredient.

Hot-water extraction certainly helps to make the Jerusalem artichoke more tolerable, but it doesn't remove all the indigestible inulin and fructosans. By boiling a measured weight of sliced tubers, evaporating the water, and weighing the powdery residue, I was able to estimate that 15 minutes of cooking draws out between 40% and 50% of the indigestibles. That still leaves behind double the proportion that dry beans start out with. So I was delighted to come across some information that suggested a supplementary technique. The Jerusalem artichoke is something of a celebrity among plant scientists because its carbohydrate composition changes dramatically during storage. This was discovered over a century ago by the French alcohol industry, which had been advised by the chemist Anselme Payen to try using the tuber as a carbohydrate source for fermentation by yeast; the resulting "beer" could then be distilled to yield pure alcohol. The distilleries had no luck until they noticed that the time of year was critical. Tubers harvested in September or October were almost worthless, but those taken in March and April did indeed provide the yeast with prodigious amounts of fermentable carbohydrate. It turns out that as the tuber winters in the ground, it slowly breaks down some of its inulin into shorter fructosan chains, and some all the way to one- and two-unit sugars. In other words, the wintering Jerusalem artichoke predigests its own carbohydrates.

The details of this transformation were worked out in the 1960s by a British biochemist, Jack Edelman, and several colleagues. Cold temperatures, just above freezing, are necessary. A number of enzymes do the work of breaking down the inulin in such a way as to generate a relatively even distribution of fructosans with from four to eight or ten fructose units. The major common sugar produced is sucrose, which nearly triples in concentration over the course of six or eight weeks in cold storage. Over the same period, the inulin content decreases by half.

No one knows for sure why the Jerusalem artichoke and a few other roots—chicory, dandelion, salsify—do this kind of thing. In the family to which these plants belong (the Compositae), inulin is found mainly in the roots of perennial plants: plants that must survive the winter and sprout up again on their own. The breakdown of inulin may increase the roots' resistance to freezing, since it raises the concentration of dissolved carbohydrates, and this in turn lowers the freezing point of the cell's storage vacuoles. That it's not a mere quirk of evolution is suggested by the fact that fructose polymers are most commonly found in plants of the two most successful and advanced families, the Compositae and the grasses, or Gramineae. (The sweetening of potatoes in cold storage, on the other hand, probably is just a biochemical quirk. Low temperatures apparently weaken the membrane surrounding the starch granule, which allows more sugar to be liberated from the granule than the tuber actually needs to live on. When the potato is brought back to room temperature and its metabolism quickens, the excess sugar disappears.)

At first, chilling sounded like an ideal solution to the gas problem. If left to sit for a few weeks, either in the cold ground or in the refrigerator, perhaps the tuber would clean up its own act. I even came across evidence that the usefulness of such "curing" might have been noticed long ago. In 1726 Benjamin Townsend wrote in his *Complete Seedsman* of the Jerusalem artichoke: "It is a root fit to be eat about Christmas when it is boiled." Because the tubers can be harvested in late fall, this sounds like indirect advice to let them sit for a month or two before using them.

   A closer look, however, showed that cold storage could be of only limited help. Because most of the inulin is broken down into fructosans, not digestible sugars, chilling, by my calculation, reduces the total quantity of offending substances by only some 15%. It had once been thought that perhaps the shorter fructosans could be broken down into sugars by the concentrated hydrochloric acid in our stomach. But in 1988 researchers at the University of Lund, in Sweden, showed that human gastric juice is not very efficient at digesting even short three- or four-sugar chains, at least in the test tube and at normal body temperature. In one hour, even at its most acid, a pH of about 1, human gastric juice broke down only 15% of the three-sugar chains and 9% of the chains longer than eight sugars. At a pH of 1.5, these numbers dropped to 5% and 4% respectively. It's unlikely that digestion goes any better in the stomach, since when we eat a meal, our gastric juices are diluted and buffered by the foods that mix with them. All told, we would probably be lucky to break down 5% or 10% of the fructosans we ingest.

   Cold storage helps a little, then, but boiling, because it extracts both inulin and fructosans, makes the bigger difference.

Nonetheless, very few modern recipes for the Jerusalem artichoke call for an initial boiling. The only one I've come across is the gratin in Elizabeth Schneider's *Uncommon Fruits and Vegetables*. She says that precooking the tuber in milk and water "seems to minimize the effects of a vegetable that 'doth provoke wind,' as the early cookbooks put it." But such a treatment was once quite common for vegetables. John Goodyer said of the Jerusalem artichoke that "some boil it in water, and after stew them," and early French recipes frequently specify precooking. The 1738 edition of La Varenne's *Cuisinier françois* calls for cooking *taupinambourgs* initially "in a braise: then, being well cooked, peel and cut into slices, fricassee with fresh butter, an onion, salt, pepper, and vinegar; serve with nutmeg." And in 1774, Menon wrote in *La Cuisinière bourgeoise* of *topinambours*: "they are highly esteemed; those who wish to eat them should cook them in water, then peel and put in a white sauce with mustard." As I've mentioned, it's better still to slice the tubers before boiling.

My own experiments with precooking brought to my attention another oddity of the Jerusalem artichoke. Once cooked by almost any means, the tuber often, over the course of an hour or so, turns from a bright ivory to a dull gray. The change in color is especially evident if you boil the slices and then set them aside for a while; but it also takes place when the whole raw tuber is baked in the oven, and even when raw slices are covered with boiling pickling solution (water, vinegar, salt, and spices). It's not a particularly attractive characteristic.

This discoloration can be prevented. It's also the sign of a remarkable nutritional virtue. The Jerusalem artichoke is a prodigious storehouse of iron. According to the U.S. Department of Agriculture, the Jerusalem artichoke contains 3 milligrams of iron per 100 grams (about a quarter pound), or five times the figure for the potato, and fully comparable to the iron content of meats, our main source of this mineral. It also happens that together with one other culprit, iron is responsible for "stem-end blackening," a discoloration that becomes evident in some potatoes after cooking.

In the 1960s British biochemists found that when a potato is cooked and its cellular organization destroyed, its iron is oxidized from the ferrous (Fe^{2+}) to the ferric (Fe^{3+}) state, and reacts with a phenolic substance, chlorogenic acid, to generate a dark-colored complex. The standard remedy for stem-end blackening is to add cream of tartar either to the cooking liquid or to the cooked potatoes when they're mashed. The tartaric acid binds to the iron and interferes with its ability to form the dingy complex.

The same cream of tartar treatment does the trick with boiled slices of Jerusalem artichoke. So does lemon juice, whose citric acid is also good at binding metals. Even vinegar will help; its acetic acid doesn't affect the iron, but it raises the acidity of the tuber's flesh and so reduces the amount of chlorogenic acid that is chemically capable of reacting with iron. Adding a small quantity of acid to the cooking water keeps the tuber white—provided, of course, that the acid penetrates throughout the flesh. Once again, slicing helps speed the process.

The use of acid in the cooking water in turn raises another consideration: that of texture. What is especially noticeable with dry beans is also true of the Jerusalem artichoke: acid in the cooking water inhibits the extraction of the structural carbohydrates that strengthen the cell walls, and so dramatically slows the softening of bean or tuber. It may also slow the extraction of undesirable carbohydrates. If you want to preserve something of the tuber's crispness, add the acid at the start of boiling. If you want a softer texture—say in a gratin, or during oven-roasting alongside a leg of lamb—add the acid only for the last five minutes of the boiling, when it will fix the color and texture.

There turns out to be another, not so ordinary method for reducing the inulin content of Jerusalem artichokes, one that also gives the artichoke an entirely different character. I would never have come across it without a tip from Charles Heiser of Indiana University, and Nancy Turner of the Royal British Columbia Museum shared with me the research that she and others have done on the subject.

A number of other inulin-rich, poorly digestible tubers and bulbs have somehow been put to use as staple foods in various parts of the world. One of the best documented is the bulb of the camas plant (species of *Camassia*), a member of the lily family, which was eaten by North American peoples from the Rocky Mountains to the Pacific Northwest. The usual method of preparation in North America was pit-cooking, a technique that the Neanderthals used 100,000 years ago; the New England clambake and the Polynesian luau are two of its vestiges. Lewis and Clark saw camas being cooked in this way on their expedition to the Northwest. In the summer of 1806, Meriwether Lewis set down in his journal the procedure used by the Nez Percé.

> When they have collected a considerable quantity of these roots . . . they dig away the surface of the earth forming a circular concavity of 2½ feet in the center and 10 feet in diameter; they next collect a parsel of split dry wood with which they cover this bason in the ground perhaps a foot thick, they next collect a large parsel of stones of about 4 or 6 lbs. weight which are placed on the dry wood; fire is then set to the wood which birning heats the stones; when the fire has subsided and the stones are sufficiently heated which are nearly a red heat, they are adjusted in such a manner in the whole as to form as level a surface as possible, a small quantity of earth is sprinkled over the stones and a layer of grass about an inch thick is put over the stones; the roots . . . are now laid on in a conical pile, are then covered with a layer of grass

about 2 or 3 inches thick; water is now thrown on the summit of the pile and passes through the roots and to the hot stones at bottom; some water is allso poared arround the edges of the hole and also finds its way to the hot stones; as soon as they discover from the quantity of steem which issues that the water has found its way generally to the hot stones, they cover the roots and grass over with earth to the debth of four inches and then build a fire of dry wood all over the connical mound which they continue to renew through the course of the night for ten or 12 hours after which it is suffered to cool two or three hours when the earth and grass are removed and the roots thus sweated and cooked with steam are taken out, and most commonly exposed to the sun on scaffoalds untill they become dry, when they are black and of a sweet agreeable flavor. These roots are fit for use when first taken from the pit, are soft of a sweetish taste and much the consistency of a roasted onion.

The recipe was much the same in the Pacific Northwest, except that the cooking time was more often 24 to 36 hours. The bulbs were then used to sweeten other foods, or eaten alone as a confection.

Camas bulbs, like Jerusalem artichokes, aren't sweet when raw. The traditional long, slow cooking must therefore break down some of their inulin into digestible fructose. Sure enough, researchers at the University of Michigan School of Public Health found that 48 hours of pit-cooking transformed essentially all the inulin in camas into fructose; a Belgian chemist reports that 24 hours of boiling will do the same to pure inulin in distilled water. So prolonged pit-cooking appears to be much more effective than a few minutes of boiling at improving the digestibility of inulin-rich foods.

Of course, I had to give pit-cooking a try! The technique is easy enough to simulate in the modern kitchen. I put a half-inch or so of water in the bottom of a casserole dish, piled some artichokes onto a rack above the water, covered the dish tightly with foil, and put it in a 200°F (93°C) oven. I checked every few hours to make sure that the dish hadn't baked dry. After 24 hours, the artichokes had undergone quite a transformation. Their skin had turned almost black; their flesh was brown and almost translucent, like a cloudy aspic. And they had developed a sweet, distinctive flavor: something like caramel, but with a difference. Some of my tasters didn't like the difference; some did. I myself find the flavor a pleasant and interesting one.

What can you do with sweet Jerusalem artichokes? The simplest thing is to serve them as is, or skinned, along with a roast. I've also been pleased with a couple of other experiments. One was to treat them like sweet potatoes: puree them, enrich with cream, flavor with ginger or with lemon or orange peel, top with a few pecans, and bake. Another approach, a modification of the Nez Percé sun-drying method, is to slice the artichokes lengthwise into thin strips, place them on a rack, salt them lightly, and bake them in a 200°F oven for a couple of hours, until just dry. They come out crisp and richly flavored, something like very well browned potato chips.

I leave it to more creative cooks to explore other possibilities for long-cooked Jerusalem artichokes. However, you may find as I did that even 24 hours of cooking doesn't render them completely digestible. Perhaps 48 hours would do it, but that's a long time to keep the oven on. Clearly the problem deserves further research.

Finally, the matter of this vegetable's peculiar names: *topinambour* in French, Jerusalem artichoke in English. Here I rely entirely on an article published in 1940 by Redcliffe N. Salaman, author of the classic book *The History and Social Influence of the Potato*. As far as I can tell, Salaman's article has never been bettered, and it has been utterly forgotten. About *topinambour* Salaman repeats the story that had been pieced together by others. In the spring and early summer of 1613, or about six years after Lescarbot and his party had brought the tubers back to France, Paris was excited by the arrival of six natives from a Brazilian island. They were members of a tribe known as the Topinamboux. Queen Marie de Medici received them, and her son Louis XIII was godparent at their baptism. Four years later, Lescarbot wished in print for "a plague on those who caused the hawkers in Paris to call [the tubers] Topinamboux." It seems as though significant quantities of the new tubers arrived in Paris at about the same time as the Brazilians, and the street vendors simply exploited a New World name that was on everyone's lips anyhow, a name more intriguing than the principal alternative at the time, "Canada" or "truffle of Canada." *Topinambour* stuck so well that for nearly three centuries it was widely assumed that the tuber came from South America.

As for *Jerusalem artichoke*, only the "Jerusalem" needs explaining; "artichoke" no doubt comes from the impressions of Champlain and his companions. The oft-repeated story begins by noting that the vegetable is the tuber of a kind of sunflower. In Italian the sunflower is *girasole* (meaning "turn-to-the-sun"; the flower may track the course of the sun through the sky). The English then corrupted *girasole* to "Jerusalem." This derivation was suggested by the botanist J. E. Smith in 1807. But Smith's credibility is not bolstered by his naming the plant's home as Peru. Nor does his theory bear much linguistic scrutiny, as Salaman documented. The word *girasole* had been in use long before the sunflower was brought to Europe in the late sixteenth century. It signified a number of plants that move with the sun, as well as opals and other fiery stones. The first dictionary to give "sunflower" as one meaning for *girasole* is dated 1729: more than a century after the English started calling the vegetable the Jerusalem artichoke. (The most common Italian names for the tuber have been *tartufo bianco* [white truffle], *tartufo di Canna*, and *topinambur*.)

Smith's theory has the great appeal of being very plausible on the surface, and that no doubt explains its posthumous life, sprouting up again and again like the plant it concerns. It also takes less explaining than Salaman's alternative theory, which originated with Salaman's friend, the botanist David Prain. Prain thought it likely that the tuber would have been introduced to England as a commodity not from Italy, but from the Netherlands, which had been supplying vegetables to England for many years. A Dutch book of 1618—four years before the first documented appearance of "Jerusalem artichoke" in English—records that on February 28, 1613, a gardener named Petrus Hondius planted at least one shriveled tuber, and that he was astonished by the bumper crop he harvested on November 13. (Hondius later devoted several stanzas of a long poem to the praise of *artichocken onder d'eerde*, "subterranean artichokes.") The same book says that on account of Hondius's pioneering success, the tuber was known in his country as the "artichoke-apple of Ter Neusen," Terneuzen being the town in which Hondius lived. It's therefore quite possible that the Netherlands supplied England with its first commercial quantities of what were called Terneuzen artichokes. Because "Terneuzen" (pronounced "ter-noozen") would have meant little to the London street vendors selling this Dutch novelty, Prain speculated that they had transformed it into the more exotic, appealing, and memorable sound-alike "Jerusalem."

Prain's theory can't be proven, of course. But it is certainly more plausible than the *girasole* story. Still, as Salaman points out, it's unfortunate that Europeans didn't adopt the name given to the vegetable by the people who domesticated it. Thomas Hariot reported that the Algonquian term was *kaishucpen-*

auk. According to a linguist of the last century, J. H. Trumbull, this is a compound of words for "sun" and "tubers." I wonder whether the Algonquians made a strict distinction between tubers—technically underground stems—and storage roots. "Sunroot" it should have been.

SUMMARY: JERUSALEM ARTICHOKES

The Jerusalem artichoke is the crisp tuber of a sunflower, *Helianthus tuberosus*. When cooked, it develops a mild flavor reminiscent of artichokes. The plant almost grows itself and is very productive.

Like dry beans, the Jerusalem artichoke contains indigestible carbohydrates that can cause flatulence and discomfort. The quantity of these carbohydrates is somewhat reduced during cold storage, a month or more in the cold ground or in the refrigerator. About half of the remaining indigestibles can be removed by boiling the sliced tubers in a large volume of water for 15 minutes. A larger proportion can be broken down to the sugar fructose by cooking the whole tubers for 24 hours. It's best to make raw or quickly cooked Jerusalem artichokes a distinctly minor part of a meal.

Because they contain a remarkable amount of iron, Jerusalem artichokes sometimes turn gray after cooking. To prevent discoloration, add ¼ teaspoon cream of tartar or 1 tablespoon lemon juice per quart of water for the last 5 minutes of boiling; for crisper tubers, add the acid at the start of boiling.

Marinated Jerusalem artichokes. Marinated Jerusalem artichokes are reminiscent of artichoke hearts and can be used in salads as an alternative to the raw tuber. Boil the sliced Jerusalem artichokes for 15 minutes or until the texture seems right; drain and marinate in a vinaigrette. These will keep for several days in the refrigerator if the slices are covered by the vinaigrette. For a supply that will keep several weeks, pack the boiled slices into a quart jar with several crushed cloves of garlic. In a saucepan, heat 1 cup water, 1 cup white wine vinegar, and 1 teaspoon salt. When the liquid reaches the boil, pour into the jar to cover. Screw the lid onto the jar, and let cure in the refrigerator for a week. Serve in salads.

Pickled Jerusalem artichokes. Crisp pickled Jerusalem artichokes are good with sandwiches and as an appetizer. I like Narsai David's quick recipe in *Monday Night at Narsai's*, which uses raw tubers, but I've had trouble with some slices turning gray. Boiling the slices in a vinegar solution for 5 minutes prevents the discoloration and removes some of the indigestibles, though at some cost in crunchiness.

Fill a 2-quart jar with sliced Jerusalem artichokes. In a saucepan, heat 2 cups white wine vinegar and 2 cups water. When this mixture reaches the boil, add the artichoke slices. Return to the boil, and cook 5 minutes. In the last minute, add 3 tablespoons sugar, 1½ teaspoons salt, 1 tablespoon pickling spice, a dash of hot pepper flakes or Tabasco sauce, and 6 crushed garlic cloves. Spoon the sliced artichokes and garlic cloves into the jar; pour in the boiling liquid. Cover and keep in the refrigerator.

Oven-roasted Jerusalem artichokes. For an unusual, slightly sweet alternative to potatoes, boil sliced artichokes for 15 minutes, then drain and pat dry. Place on an oiled baking sheet in a 350°F (177°C) oven. Turn after 15 minutes or when bottom has browned. Remove when second side has browned in another 10 or 15 minutes.

Deep-fried Jerusalem artichokes. Thin raw slices taste like sugary potato chips when deep-fried; preboiled and cut slightly thicker, they're more like cottage fries. Boil sliced artichokes (⅛-inch to ¼-inch thick) for 15 minutes. Blot dry. Fry in oil at 350°F (177°C) until golden brown.

Long-cooked Jerusalem artichokes. Long, slow cooking makes the artichokes more digestible and more flavorful. Put the whole artichokes on a rack in a casserole dish with a little water in the bottom, cover tightly with foil, and cook in a 200°F (93°C) oven for 24 hours, checking every few hours to replenish the water if necessary. Use as you would boiled sweet potatoes. Or slice lengthwise into thin strips, lightly salt, and dry on a rack in a 200°F oven for two hours, or until just crisp.

Beurre Blanc: Butter's Undoing

When my book *On Food and Cooking* was first published, it was sent out to a number of cooking authorities in the hope that they would respond with a few quotable words. Some were more than kind; others were never heard from, or for various reasons declined to comment. One response in particular was a puzzler. A widely admired writer and teacher had been troubled by the omission of *beurre blanc*.

Quite true; not a word about it. But then what was so interesting about *beurre blanc*? To my recollection it was simply butter flavored with vinegar and herbs. I'd had it with fish a few times but never made it myself; the occasional garlicky aïoli aside, I prefer a lighter accompaniment to seafood. A quick check in a few cookbooks confirmed my memory: it's traditionally served with fish in the Loire valley, and the herb is the shallot. It's also a relative newcomer. Neither Escoffier nor the early-twentieth-century edition of *Larousse Gastronomique* mentions it. At the same time, my curiosity was roused. There was something odd about the recipes. As it turns out, *beurre blanc* is a remarkable sauce indeed.

Beurre blanc, literally "white butter," consists of three main ingredients: butter, vinegar and/or wine, and shallots. The vinegar and chopped shallots are boiled together until the liquid is much reduced. Solid butter is then added to the pan over low heat and beaten in to form an emulsion with the consistency of heavy cream. That's it. It's like the other emulsified sauces, hollandaise and so on, but without the egg yolk. Pretty straightforward.

Except for a couple of things. First of all, I had thought that egg yolk was absolutely essential to maintain the emulsion. Emulsified sauces are thick because a small amount of water, a few tablespoons, is forced to accommodate a large amount of oil—a cup or more—in the form of tiny droplets. The oil droplets are packed together with a thin layer of water in between. And the only thing that keeps the oil droplets from coalescing into a separate pool of liquid is the emulsifiers in the egg yolk: substances that coat the oil droplets and repel them from each other. (See the drawing on p. 119.) No emulsifiers, no thick sauce. Just a layer of oil floating over a layer of sour water. Yet *beurre blanc* contains no egg yolk.

The other suspicious thing about *beurre blanc* was the variation in proportions from recipe to recipe. There's a limit to the amount of oil that a given amount of water can accommodate. Mayonnaise is said to be close to the limit, around 3 or 4 parts oil to 1 of water (as we'll see in chapter 8, that's a gross underestimate). Butter sauces like hollandaise, because they have to be warm for the butter to be liquid, are even less stable; Julia Child recommends that about half as much butter be used per egg yolk compared to the vegetable oil used in mayonnaise. But the *beurre blanc* recipes were all over the map. At the low end, Jacques Pépin calls for 4 or 5 parts butter per part added water. At the high end, Raymond Sokolov says anything between 12 and 24 works just fine! Any emulsion that full of droplets would be as stiff as week-old Jell-O. There was something fishy here, and it wasn't just Loire pike. As Richard Olney puts it in his *Simple French Food*, "The utter simplicity of the thing, the paucity of elements, the absence of a binder have engendered a wariness, distrust, or disbelief, than which there are no solider foundations on which to construct a myth."

Clearly it was time to repair to the kitchen and investigate. I stocked up on butter—sweet, because that's what the recipes call for, and because salt might complicate things—and translated several recipes into the equivalents for using half a stick, so as not to waste too much. Despite the common statement in many recipes that the acidity of the vinegar reduction is essential, I began with plain water and omitted the shallots, again to simplify things. A few teaspoons of hot water, a few pieces of butter, a small saucepan, and a small whisk over a low flame: that was the setup.

It took only an hour or so to figure out what was going on, and it was quite a surprise. First I tried to emulsify a half stick of butter, or 4 tablespoons, in 1 tablespoon of water. These are the approximate proportions called for by Jacques Pépin and Madeleine Kamman. With a little care to begin with very small pieces of butter, it worked just fine, producing an emulsion with the consistency of heavy cream. Next, I tried using just 1 teaspoon of water—the rough equivalent of Sokolov's lower limit. By tilting the pan to collect the water and cutting the butter even finer, I got that to work as well. Next, ¼ teaspoon of water, or a butter-water ratio double Sokolov's higher limit. And that worked! So I kept adding more butter, piece by piece, to that ¼ teaspoon of water and watched it melt into the creamy, light-yellow liquid. Half a stick; one stick; one and a half. Two. Still the butter went in, and the consistency stayed nice and creamy. Why hadn't I perpetrated a yellow oil slick? It was time to turn off the burner and think.

Two things were puzzling. First, a stable emulsion was formed without the addition of any emulsifiers. Second, the sauce seemed capable of absorbing an infinite quantity of butter without getting any thicker, and the initial amount of water required seemed minimal. It was as if the butter alone contained the seeds of its own transformation. As if it were a sauce waiting to be made.

Of course! Butter is not just fat. A textbook analysis of unsalted butter gives these figures: 81% milk fat by weight, with an average of 18% water and 1% milk solids (salted butter is about 2.5% salt, 16% water, and less than 1% milk solids). Because milk fat is less dense than water, a given weight of milk fat takes up proportionally more space. So all in all, a stick of butter, or 8 tablespoons, is 1.2 tablespoons water and milk solids dispersed in 6.8 tablespoons fat. And several emulsifying substances occur naturally in butter: about 0.2% of butter's weight is phospholipids, including lecithin; 0.25% is cholesterol; and a similar proportion is monoglycerides and diglycerides. Somewhat over half of the milk solids are proteins (the rest are the milk sugar lactose and some minerals). All these substances help stabilize oil droplets; in fact, they're all found in higher concentrations in egg yolks and account for the yolk's great emulsifying power.

So butter really is a sauce waiting to be made. It contains all the necessary elements: the water base, the oil to be dispersed in droplets, and the emulsifiers to coat the droplets. The ratio of oil to water, 5.7 to 1, is just right for forming a creamy, slightly thick mixture. And a portion of the oil—somewhere between 2% and 50%, depending on how the butter is made—already exists in the form of microscopic droplets coated with emulsifiers, which probably contributes to the ease with which *beurre blanc* can be made.

Butter comes by these remarkably convenient properties thanks to its birth and parentage. Butter is made, of course, by churning cream, which is about 60% water, 40% fat, and 1% or 2% protein. The fat is in the form of globules a few ten-thousandths of an inch in diameter, each coated with a membrane of phospholipids, cholesterol, glycerides, and protein, much of which originated as the membrane of the cow's mammary cell that produced and secreted the fat. When the cream is churned, the fat globules are forced into each other under conditions that cause many of the protective membranes to be disrupted. The semiliquid fat from the exposed globules fuses together into lumps that grow larger and larger, at the same time trapping little pockets of the liquid and the membrane components, as well as some intact fat globules. Most of the liquid, and with it most of the emulsifying material, is drawn off as buttermilk, so that the ratio of oil to water increases from 0.7 to 1 in cream to 5.7 to 1 in butter. What began as an oil-in-water emulsion becomes a water-in-oil emulsion. In the parlance, the original emulsion has been "inverted": the dispersed phase has become the continuous phase, and the continuous the dispersed.

This genealogy helps us realize that when we make *beurre blanc*, we transform butter back into cream: that is, we re-invert the water-in-oil emulsion into an oil-in-water emulsion. No wonder the result inspires an adjective like "creamy"! Depending on how much of a vinegar/wine reduction you begin with, the resulting sauce is the equivalent of a cream with a 67% to 80% fat content. For comparison, the richest cream you can buy, heavy whipping cream, is 40% fat. The reason that the sauce is "white," or at least lighter than the color of the butter, is that the yellow fat has been redivided into droplets so tiny that they reflect light rather than absorb it, just as they do in cream and milk.

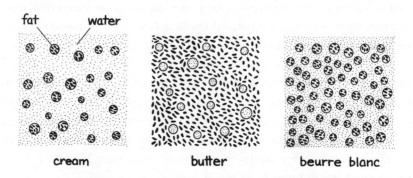

Cream consists of milk-fat globules dispersed in a water solution. When cream is made into butter, the two phases are reversed: droplets of the water solution are now embedded in a mass of milk fat. When we make butter into beurre blanc, *we form an especially rich version of the original cream.*

Beurre blanc, then, is ingenious and downright elegant. Begin with a small amount of warm water. Add a small piece of butter. As the continuous mass of fat melts, it releases its own little pockets of water and emulsifiers, which are ready once more to coat the naked fat droplets as they're formed by the whisking. The whisk is assisted by the presence of many original intact fat globules, which act like a screen to mill large blobs of fat into smaller droplets. Now you have the equivalent of a light cream. Add another piece of butter, which contributes more emulsifiers and more water along with its fat. And so on. The sauce thickens somewhat with each new addition of butter but can never exceed the fat-to-water ratio of the butter itself, or 5.7 to 1. The butter regulates its own transformation, releasing emulsifiers and water as it melts.

The reason, then, that recipes for *beurre blanc* can vary so widely in the amounts of reduced liquid per stick of butter is precisely that, in physical terms, the initial amount of water is almost irrelevant. No matter how much water you begin with, once you start adding butter you begin to approach the oil-to-water proportions of the butter itself. Of the various recipes I checked, Jacques Pépin's recipe gives a final ratio of about 2 to 1; Madeleine Kamman's, 2.3 to 1; Richard Olney's, 2.8 to 1; Raymond Sokolov's, between 3.3 and 3.9 to 1; and Julia Child's, 3.6 to 1. When I incorporated 2 sticks of butter into ¼ teaspoon water, I managed a ration of 5.5. to 1. I could have added another 10 sticks, and reached 5.6 out of a possible 5.7. The differences from recipe to recipe are slight variations in texture and taste. The more butter you add to a given initial amount of acidic liquid, the thicker the mixture gets, and the more dilute the flavor of the initial reduction. But these changes are relatively subtle, and the ideal balance a matter of taste.

Butter's self-regulating quality is also what makes it so versatile and handy in confecting delicious last-minute sauces from the pan juices of sautéed meats. If you dissolve the encrustations in a few spoonfuls of wine, reduce the liquid to about a tablespoon, and then swirl in a few pieces of butter, you end up with a creamy, glossy *"beurre brun,"* the color coming from the browned meat juices. There's no need for careful measurements. As long as you have some liquid to start the emulsion, you can add butter until you've got enough sauce for the occasion. Another traditional means of thickening pan juices is the addition of cream. But butter produces a thicker sauce faster because it has twice the concentration of fat. Heavy cream has to be reduced by boiling in order to reach the same texture.

Madeleine Kamman, who has devised many variations on the basic recipe, suggests convincingly that *beurre blanc* may have arisen as a refinement of butter-enriched pan juices. In her book *In Madeleine's Kitchen*, she describes the way her Loire valley relatives have always cooked fish. They place it in a buttered dish with chopped shallots and wine and bake it, then reduce the juices and thicken them with more butter. As she says, "What is that if not a *beurre blanc?*" This tradition is quite venerable, as the accompanying recipe sampler demonstrates. Fowl and fish dishes were treated thus in England from the time of Shakespeare, and by 1850 *beurre blanc* existed in all but name and particulars of seasoning.

Having figured out the workings of the transformation from butter into sauce, I became curious about how far those workings could be pushed before the system collapsed. Could I make a thicker *beurre blanc*, perhaps something more like a hollandaise, by clarifying part of the butter? Clarified butter is made, of course, by melting the butter and separating the oil from the white residue, which residue contains the water and most of the emulsifying proteins and phospholipids. If you start by making a *beurre blanc* and then begin adding clarified butter, you are now adding nothing but oil, so that neither the emulsifiers nor the water receive significant reinforcements. The sauce should get thicker, but also more fragile.

I did the experiment, again using small quantities so as not to waste more materials than necessary. I made a *beurre blanc* with ¼ teaspoon water and ¼ stick butter, which makes about 2 tablespoons sauce. Then I began to add clarified butter a few drops at a time. The sauce absorbed about 2 tablespoons before breaking at a fairly low temperature, around 90°F (32°C). By this point, with the oil-water ratio just under 10 to 1, it was slightly thicker than ordinary *beurre blanc*, more like a thin batter; it clung to the spoon rather than just coating it. This version was clearly too fragile to be useful. The texture at one tablespoon clarified butter, or a ratio of 7 to 1, wasn't significantly different from that of the original sauce, so it's hardly worth going to the trouble to clarify the butter and add it with care.

No new recipes came out of that experiment. But it does indicate how far from the limits we're operating when we make *beurre blanc*. However much you've made—a cup, say—you could add half again that volume of clarified butter and not tax the emulsifying powers of the sauce. It also demonstrates that the often-cited theoretical maximum ratio for a stable emulsion of 3 parts oil to 1 part water is meaningless in practice. That ratio was arrived at by considering

Historical Precursors of Beurre Blanc

An excellent way to boil chickens. If you will boil chickens, young turkeys, pea-hens, or any house fowl daintily, you shall, after you have trimmed them, drawn them, trussed them, and washed them, fill their bellies as full of parsley as they can hold; then boil them with salt and water only till they be enough: then take a dish and put into it verjuice, and butter, and salt, and when the butter is melted, take the parsley out of the chickens' bellies, and mince it very small, and put it to the verjuice and butter, and stir it well together; then lay in the chickens, and trim the dish with sippets, and so serve it forth. [Verjuice is the sour juice of unripe grapes; sippets are small pieces of bread.]

Sauce for pigeons. The best sauce for pigeons, stockdoves, or such like, is vin-egar and butter melted together, and parsley roasted in their bellies, or vine leaves roasted and mixed well together.

Gervase Markham, The English Housewife (1631)

Pike ragout. Cut it into pieces, put in with some white wine, a bouquet and very fresh butter; season it well with capers and mushrooms; then the sauce being much reduced and well bound, serve with slice of lemon and pomegranate.

Bream ragout. Gut and place a bouquet in the body; melt and rub on some butter, and place it on the grill; when it is roasted, make a sauce with fresh but-ter, capers, parsley and chopped green onions; simmer the sauce well with vinegar and a little bouillon; when the sauce is well bound, serve.

Lotte ragout. Scrape them in hot water until they are white, gut them and place them in some white wine, fresh butter, salt, pepper, onion and capers; simmer, and don't let the sauce turn, that is become oil; garnish with mush-rooms and roe, then serve.

Pierre François de la Varenne, Le cuisinier françois (1651)

Norfolk sauce, or rich melted butter without flour. Put three tablespoons of water into a small saucepan, and when it boils add four ounces of fresh butter; as soon as this is quite dissolved, take the saucepan from the fire, and shake it round until the sauce looks thick and smooth. It must not be allowed to boil after the butter is added.

Water, 3 tablespoonsful; butter, 4 oz.

[As the title suggests, English melted butter was a sauce made by heating water and flour together to thicken, and then adding butter to enrich.]

Eliza Acton, Modern Cookery for Private Families (1855)

how close together you can pack spheres of identical diameter; the spaces in between add up to about 25% of the volume. But if you have a variety of droplet sizes, then the smaller ones can fill up the space between larger ones. My two-stick, quarter-teaspoon sauce was 85% fat, compared to the 75% theoretical maximum; when I added clarified butter, I got up to 91%. Such mixtures can even be fairly stable when they're emulsified by egg yolk.

So *beurre blanc* is probably as close as you can get in the kitchen to a foolproof recipe. There are, however, two ways to sabotage it. Most writers emphasize one of them. Richard Olney: "The sauce will break only if the heat is too high." Raymond Sokolov: "The trick, if there is one, actually consists of nothing more than exercising extra care to keep the heat low and remembering to start with well-chilled butter." Madeleine Kamman, most precise of all: "It is *imperative* that the temperature of the butter not rise above 130°F [54°C]." In my own experiments, I found that the emulsion always began to fail around 136°F (58°C), so Mrs. Kamman's figure sounds exactly right.

Why 136°F rather than something a little more drastic and easily avoided, like 212°F? Thanks to recent biochemical studies of the membrane that surrounds the fat globules in milk, we now know the answer. Researchers at Purdue University found that when the membrane is heated, an irreversible change occurs at exactly 136°F: and that change is the denaturation of the major protein component of the membrane, which has been named *butyrophilin* (from the Greek for "butter-loving"). Butyrophilin is certainly present at the surface of the intact globules from the original cream, and is probably present in smaller quantities on the droplets newly formed when the sauce is whisked, where it migrates from the small amount of buttermilk trapped in the solid butter. When the sauce is heated to 136°F and the butyrophilin begins to lose its normal shape and properties, the protective membranes are badly weakened and spill some of the fat they contain, probably when they collide with each other.

So far, little is known about the natural role of butyrophilin in milk, though stabilizing the fat globules is surely part of the story. For the cook, butyrophilin is simply the chink in the armor of the fat globule. By comparison, the emulsifier lecithin is tough; it can take temperatures close to the boil without suffering noticeable damage.

Still, what dire fate befalls the sauce if you overshoot a little to, say, 150°F

(66°C)? It develops yellow streaks and patches—little pools of oil that are formed when breached droplets leak their contents. An attractive characteristic of *beurre blanc* that generally goes unmentioned in recipes is that a broken one is often easily refurbished. If your attention wanders and you mildly overheat it, simply let the sauce cool down to 110°F or 120°F (43°C or 49°C) and then whisk it for a few seconds. The streaks and puddles disappear and it's practically as good as new, though with time you may notice that small amounts of free fat solidify like little scales at the cool surface. Depending on the oil-to-water ratio established by the recipe, *beurre blanc* can take pretty severe mistreatment. I made a sauce with 1 tablespoon of liquid per stick butter, which translates to a 3 to 1 fat-to-water ratio, and left it on a low flame until it frothed at the rim. That meant that part of the sauce was boiling, and a thermometer immersed in it hit 195°F (91°C). I let it cool down, added half a teaspoon of water to make up for evaporation, and whisked it into a decent sauce that was stable up to 128°F (53°C).

So even when it's overheated, *beurre blanc* is well behaved compared to the other emulsified sauces, which can develop curds of coagulated protein and turn irretrievably oily. This tolerance to abuse results from the fact that butter contains relatively little protein, and that the other important emulsifiers—the phospholipids and glycerides—aren't as easily damaged by high temperatures.

Surprisingly, one of the worst things you can do to a *beurre blanc* is let it slowly cool down to room temperature. That may not sound like culinary abuse—more like benign neglect—but it does make the sauce quite intolerant to reheating. What happens is that as the milk fat solidifies, around 85°F (30°C), the sauce thickens and develops a coarse, grainy texture. This is a sign that the fat from separate droplets has somehow fused together into large crystals. Perhaps the newly formed droplets are so weakly emulsified that they actually stick to each other when the temperature falls and their movements slow down. And once the fat has crystallized, reheating results in a broken emulsion which, unlike the overheated sauce, cannot be rescued simply by whisking.

The same goes for refrigerated or frozen sauce, which doesn't develop such large fat crystals but nevertheless separates when reheated. It's known that freezing destabilizes membranes and layers of emulsifiers. And the trouble with grainy room-temperature and refrigerated sauces is that they've really been turned back into butter: large quantities of fat surrounding little pockets of water. So when you reheat them, just as when you heat butter, the liquid that forms in the pan is a water-in-oil emulsion: melted butter, not *beurre blanc*. The easiest thing to do with a cold *beurre blanc* is to whisk it at room temperature until it smooths out to the consistency of mayonnaise, and then use it as what it now is: a soft flavored butter.

If, however, you're intent on resurrection, there are two options. The first is to start all over again with a spoonful of hot water and a piece of butter to form the initial oil-in-water emulsion, and then slowly add very small portions of the cold moribund sauce. The easier and more effective procedure is to begin with a spoonful of cream, which is a ready-made emulsion of about the same concentration as that formed by the water and butter, and which has the advantage of carrying with it a great abundance of emulsifiers in the form of the casein and whey proteins that normally float about in milk. These proteins are relatively unaffected by heat alone, and will migrate to the surface of fat globules when the globule membranes are disrupted by the denaturation of butyrophilin. The same proteins make it possible to boil cream down to half its original volume, giving a fat-to-water ratio equivalent to butter itself, without the fat globule membranes being torn apart and unleashing millions of tiny torrents of oil. My impression is that a sauce rescued with cream is more stable, less "leaky" than one rescued with water and butter.

It may even be a good idea to follow Jacques Pépin's example and use a couple of tablespoons of cream in the initial emulsion. In addition to providing more intact globules to mill the butterfat into fine droplets, the cream might also contribute enough surplus emulsifiers to make the sauce more stable at high temperatures and more easily revived from low ones. The best idea, though, is to keep the sauce warm.

So there was something interesting after all about *beurre blanc*, this sauce that springs forth fully formed from a spoonful of water and a stick—or two or three—of butter. Among all the elaborate concoctions with which we dress our victuals, it's unsurpassed in the elegant simplicity and aptness of its transformation.

SUMMARY: *BEURRE BLANC*

The vinegar, wine, and shallots are mainly flavorings and diluents; their water content is their only contribution to the physical structure of the sauce.

Because the butter contains water, you can add any amount of butter to the initial liquid without causing the sauce to thicken drastically and break. However, if you exceed about 1 stick per tablespoon liquid, the sauce will be somewhat more vulnerable to overheating.

You'll have no trouble at all if you keep the temperature between 100°F and 130°F (38°C and 54°C).

An overheated sauce can be rescued by cooling, adding a bit of water if necessary to correct for evaporation, and whisking until the oily streaks disappear.

A solidified sauce is most easily salvaged by being served at room temperature as a soft butter. Otherwise, it must be re-emulsified, ideally in a spoonful of cream.

For cholesterol watchers: margarine never was cream, and can't be transformed into a creamy *beurre blanc*.

Two kinds of pans are less than ideal: stainless steel with an aluminum or copper sandwich bottom but thin sides, and any nonstick pan. In the first, heat concentrates at the junction between bottom and wall and overheats the sauce locally. In the second, the polymer surface is more congenial to fat than to water, and encourages the formation of an oily film along the bottom and sides. An uncoated aluminum pan is also to be avoided, since it can discolor the sauce.

An easy basic recipe: to make ½ cup of *beurre blanc*, start with 1 tablespoon of flavored liquid and whisk in 1 stick of sweet butter. To make a larger quantity of sauce, multiply these proportions.

Simplifying Hollandaise
and Béarnaise

Legends about the origins of notable dishes often involve an eminent personage and the element of accident. This insight comes from the British sociologist Stephen Mennell, and it applies well to the supposed invention of *beurre blanc*. According to the *Larousse Gastronomique*, "it is reported that a cook of Nantes named Clémence, who wished to make a béarnaise to dress a pike for her master the marquis de Goulaine, forgot to put in the eggs. The sauce was nevertheless a success. As a result Clémence opened a small restaurant at la Chebuette, near Nantes; it was there that 'Mother Michel' learned the secret of *beurre blanc* before she opened her famous restaurant on the rue Rennequin, in Paris." Richard Olney dined at la Mère Michel's before she retired, and describes her standing just inside the small kitchen, "whisking up *beurre blanc* after *beurre blanc*, each impeccable, in a small, chipped, and battered saucepan of the trashy, enamelled variety. I believe that she was quite proud to be able to exhibit this bit of hardware, for it lent force to the legend of her magic wrist (about which much was written in those years)."

As explanations go, the Clémence story is neat enough. Béarnaise sauce is made by beating butter into a mixture of an acidic reduction, shallots, and egg yolks. Omit the egg yolks and you have *beurre blanc*. The trouble is that whereas neatness—elegance—counts and convinces in scientific matters, in matters historical it raises suspicion. Surely it couldn't have been that simple. Madeleine Kamman has come across a local magazine article lamenting the decline of traditional Brittany country dishes, including *beurre blanc*, that was published in 1924. This evidence alone would seem to do in the Clémence theory, if one of her students was still to be found at work in the 1950s. As we've seen, historical recipes support Kamman's own guess that *beurre blanc* derives from the thickening of cooking juices with butter.

I'm sure that accidents have played a part in the discovery of culinary possibilities. But the romance of luck, inspiration, and the magic touch shouldn't discourage us from purposeful exploration, from some occasional basic research into the workings of a traditional dish. The story of Clémence is useful because it suggests an interesting question: If you can make an emulsified butter sauce without egg yolks, then why bother with the egg yolks in the first place? After all, they're what make béarnaise, its close relative hollandaise (which differs only in details of seasoning), and their tribe tricky. If the egg gets too hot, it can coagulate irreversibly into little lumps, and you may have to start over with fresh ingredients. In fact, one of the earliest versions of hollandaise I've found, "*sauce à la hollandoise*," in the 1758 edition of François Marin's *Dons de Comus*, calls only for butter, flour, bouillon, and herbs: no yolks at all.

It may be especially useful to understand the role of the yolk these days, when we're being told that the eggs in hollandaise and béarnaise sauces can pose a threat to our health. In the late 1980s, both Europe and the U.S. experienced outbreaks of food poisoning that were traced to raw or mildly cooked eggs. Further investigation demonstrated that intact, clean, Grade A chicken eggs can harbor large numbers of salmonella bacteria. Carelessly prepared feed is infecting some laying hens, but others have already been infected before they even emerge from the egg. Certain strains of salmonella are so well adapted to chickens that they colonize the animals' ovaries or oviducts without causing obvious symptoms. The infected hens then deposit the bacteria inside their eggs as they lay them. Breeding hens thus produce infected laying hens, and the laying hens produce infected eggs. Eggs contaminated with salmonella are still rare in much of the U.S., and improved husbandry may eventually eliminate them. But in the meantime health authorities are recommending that eggs be cooked until they're solid throughout: advice that has cast a shadow over the gently heated hollandaise and béarnaise sauces.

So what is the egg yolk doing in hollandaise and béarnaise? And can these sauces be prepared safely? My investigation turned up some surprising facts, and some alternatives to the standard recipes that deserve to be better known.

The egg yolk obviously imparts an eggy richness to its sauces. But most cookbooks either say or imply that the yolk is actually essential to the emulsification of the butterfat, that is, to the thickening and stabilizing of the sauces. This is true in the case of mayonnaise, whose vegetable oil contains no emulsifiers of its own. Yet *beurre blanc* proves that butter is perfectly capable of emulsifying itself. And the ratio of fat to water is no higher in hollandaise and béarnaise than it is in *beurre blanc*, so there's no obvious need for greater emulsifying power in those sauces. Does the yolk really have anything to do with their architecture?

The answer is yes, but the emulsification of oil droplets is secondary. The large quantities of emulsifiers in the yolk do make hollandaise more tolerant than *beurre blanc* to cooling, for example; the droplets are coated heavily enough that they don't coalesce into large crystals, and so are easier to reheat successfully. Much more important is the fact that the yolk makes possible a sauce of notable thickness and body: characteristics that *beurre blanc* can never attain. The yolk owes this talent mainly to its own proteins and to the layer of albumen proteins that always adheres to it when we separate the two parts of the egg. By weight, an egg yolk is about 50% water, 34% fats and related substances, and 16% protein. The large protein molecules, together with even larger yolk particles composed of both fats and proteins, obstruct the movement of water molecules in the liquid, and so make the liquid yolk itself seem thick and viscous.

It's this inherent thickness of the yolk that is largely responsible for the thickness of the yolk-based sauces. Think of the difference between *beurre blanc* and mayonnaise, both emulsions of fat (or oil) droplets dispersed in a water base. *Beurre blanc*, the sauce whose water base consists of thin buttermilk and vinegar, pours like thick cream, while mayonnaise, with its viscous yolk base, is too thick to pour. Generally speaking, the consistency of an emulsion depends on two factors: the consistency of the base, or the continuous phase, and the crowding of the dispersed droplets in the base. In my experiment with adding clarified butter to *beurre blanc*, I crowded 10 parts of oil into 1 part of water, and still the sauce was no thicker than a thin batter. A mayonnaise is already much thicker than that by the time only 2 parts of oil have been dispersed in 1 part of water. It's the viscosity of the yolk that makes the difference.

In the case of the butter-and-yolk sauces, there's a complication: unclarified butter contains water. As we discovered in chapter 6, this is an advantage for the making of *beurre blanc* because it keeps the oil-to-water ratio relatively constant. In a hollandaise, however, the continuous addition of water dilutes the

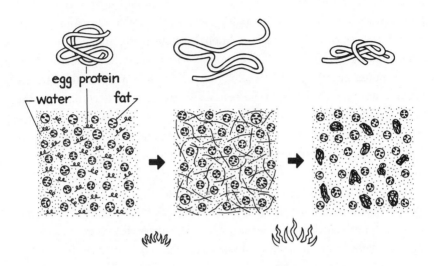

egg protein

water   fat

As we heat a hollandaise or béarnaise sauce, the initially compact egg yolk proteins (left) unfold, tangle with each other, and impede the movement of the water molecules and fat droplets (center). At this point the sauce is nicely thick. If it is overheated, then the proteins will bond tightly to each other and the sauce will thin out again (right).

viscous yolk base—that is, thins it out—and the result can be a consistency not much thicker than that of *beurre blanc*. The most obvious way of getting a thicker hollandaise or béarnaise is to use clarified butter. Some cooks do just that. But many recipes call for whole butter.

How do cooks get away with using whole butter and thinning the yolk base, and still produce a sauce with some body? By exploiting another property of the yolk: it can be made thicker and thicker, even to the point of solidifying, simply by heating it. Again, the proteins are the key. As the temperature of a protein solution rises, these long but intricately folded molecules begin to unfold; and because they're now less compact, they're much more likely to get tangled up with each other. The more tangled they get, the less freely liquid can move around them, and so the more viscous the mixture becomes. If the temperature rises high enough, the tangled proteins coagulate into a solid mass.

Nearly all modern recipes for hollandaise, béarnaise, and their relatives call for the yolks to be precooked, often with some sort of acidic liquid, until they thicken to the consistency of heavy cream. This technique can be traced back to Marie-Antoine Carême, chef to Talleyrand and the Rothschilds, and the first great systematizer of the French tradition. In about 1828 Carême advised that when making a hollandaise, "One must take care to cook the eggs before adding the butter piece by piece." Cooking the yolks simply increases the viscosity of the water phase in order to compensate for the dilution to come when the butter is added. Contrary to what Carême implies and some modern writers assert, it has nothing to do with the emulsification of the butterfat droplets; if anything, cooking the yolks probably has a somewhat deleterious effect on the emulsifiers themselves.

This adjustability of texture is very handy. On the other hand, it's also responsible for most failures and frustrations in the making of emulsified sauces. Thick yolks too quickly become scrambled yolks, especially when we're cooking just a yolk or two in a one-pint saucepan whose corners exclude the most diligent whisk. Ruination can come very fast. Surely it would be handy to know some way of ensuring against it.

There are several ways to minimize the risk. One is to make the yolk base with vinegar, lemon juice, or wine. Acid conditions, it turns out, interfere with coagulation of the egg proteins. All recipes for béarnaise sauce include an acidic reduction, but some for hollandaise make lemon juice optional. So if you have trouble with hollandaise, remember that the more acidic you make the sauce base, the less danger there is of scrambling the yolks.

Though it has no sanction in tradition or from guardians of the public health, a second conceivable way of avoiding overcooked yolks is not to cook the yolks at all. Instead, we can replace whole butter with clarified butter. By melting the whole butter over a low burner or in a microwave oven and then pouring the fat off of the milky dregs, we leave behind the water that would otherwise thin the yolk base. So there's no longer any need to thicken the base by cooking it. I produced a nice hollandaise when I clarified 1 stick of butter, beat it into 1 egg yolk kept just warm (between 100°F and 130°F, or 38°C and 54°C) in a pan over low heat, and adjusted the flavor and thickness with lemon juice and water along the way.

(Microwavers beware: an extremely messy explosion is quite likely if you don't monitor melting butter carefully. The cleanup of a careless meltdown gave me plenty of time to hone my hindsight into this phenomenon. Butterfat, like all fats, is less dense than water; that's why the watery buttermilk collects at the bottom of the container as the lighter fat melts. Microwave energy is much more efficiently absorbed by water than by fat [water molecules are electrically polar, fat molecules nonpolar]. If you continue to pump microwaves into butter that has already separated, the small volume of water at the bottom is quickly heated to the boil, at which point it vaporizes, expands greatly and suddenly in volume—and propels the fat above it out of the container and onto the walls of the oven. So keep an eye on things.)

That's one scramble-proof method for hollandaise, and it's easily adapted to béarnaise and related sauces. Another way to make a hollandaise dispenses with both cooking the yolks and clarifying the butter. This too is untraditional, and may strike some cooks as downright perverse. Instead of precooking the yolks, you prefreeze them! It turns out that egg yolks stiffen up when they are frozen, and stay stiff even after thawing. (This fact has been exploited by mayonnaise manufacturers for decades; I'll go into more detail in the next chapter.) You can either freeze the lightly beaten yolks with an equal volume of water for 24 hours, or freeze them with an equal volume of lemon juice or vinegar reduction for 8 hours. The thawed mixture will have the consistency of soft custard. Put this into a pan over a very low burner, and incorporate the butter piece by piece, using 1 stick per yolk. Adjust the flavor with lemon juice and the thickness with water.

Until salmonella bacteria have been eliminated from eggs, these two scramble-proof techniques, which don't cook the yolks at all, won't really be practical alternatives. Fortunately, a somewhat safer method for emulsifying whole butter without precooking the yolks has been described by some very eminent writers, including Escoffier and Elizabeth David. I'm surprised that it's not better known. Rather than first cooking the egg yolks and then emulsifying the butter, we can do the reverse: incorporate the butter into barely warm yolks and then cook the whole sauce until it thickens. As Escoffier explains in his recipe for hollandaise, the "cohesion" of the sauce is ensured by "the progressive cooking of the yolks."

What's the difference between cooking the yolks and cooking the whole sauce? Basically, it's much easier to control the heating of a cup or two of sauce than to monitor a few tablespoons of yolk. The temperature of a large mass rises very slowly compared to that of a small mass over the same flame. And the slower the cooking process, the more opportunities you have to adjust the heat before the mixture overcooks. Meanwhile the yolk proteins unfold at the same temperature in the made sauce and have the same ultimate effect: they give the sauce body.

I've found one minor drawback to this technique. Sometimes the sauce will separate just as it thickens, which happens at about 160°F or 170°F (71°C or 77°C). You get masses of custardy material floating in a pool of butterfat. Fortunately, you can usually revive the emulsion by adding a teaspoon or two of water and whisking vigorously. If that doesn't work, then start with a teaspoon or two of water in a new bowl and, beginning drop by drop, slowly whisk the broken sauce into the water. The sauce will be somewhat thinner than before, but stable. The same advice, by the way, applies to an overheated hollandaise or béarnaise made with cooked yolks.

In an attempt to figure out why the late-thickened sauce should break during thickening, and why it's so easily revived, I found that I could mimic the whole process using nothing but oil, water, and lecithin. "Health food" stores sell capsules of oil that contains lecithin extracted from soy beans. I made a "model" of a sauce by mixing the lecithin oil with some vegetable oil and then whisking the mixture into some water. When I heated it in a saucepan, at a certain point it too separated into a custardy mass and a pan of oil. I inferred from the reduced volume of this mess that most of the initial water had evaporated. Sure enough, when I added more water and reheated it, the "sauce" was stable even at the boiling point—for a time, and then it separated again. I could also break the emulsion by adding sugar, which binds water as it dissolves.

Based on these experiments, my guess is that the late-thickened sauce breaks during thickening because the gradually unfolding proteins somehow take much of the sauce's water out of circulation. Perhaps the greater surface area that they expose to the solution has more water-binding sites; perhaps the resulting meshwork of proteins traps pockets of water molecules, leaving the oil droplets crowded into a smaller volume of liquid. Simple evaporation is probably also involved. In any event, when there's insufficient moisture to provide a protective shell of water molecules around each oil droplet, the emulsion fails. Supply some additional water, re-form the emulsion, and all is well. I do find that a sauce is less likely to break during the thickening if for each yolk I've added at least ½ tablespoon of lemon juice or vinegar and 1 tablespoon of water.

The nice thing about the "beat now, cook later" method is that it's entirely adaptable to your own favorite recipe. Recipes for hollandaise in particular vary a great deal in the quantity and kind of acidic liquid—lemon juice or vinegar—and in the relative proportions of egg yolk and butter. No matter which recipe you prefer, all you have to do is skip the initial cooking of the yolks and save it for the whole sauce. Of course, the yolks and liquid have to be warm in order to melt and emulsify the butter, but that's quite easy to do without coming anywhere near a scramble.

Equally adaptable to your favorite proportions is the streamlined hollandaise of Canadian cooking teacher Philippa Monsarrat, which Roy Andries de Groot reported on a few years ago. Monsarrat's "5-minute fail-proof hollandaise" calls for the cook to keep all the ingredients very cold until the last minute, with the butter cut into small pieces and put on freezer-chilled plates at the back of the refrigerator. The vinegar and lemon juice, egg yolks, all the pieces of butter, and seasonings are put together into a heavy enameled frying pan, the heat turned on medium-low, and the cook begins stirring. Period. In five minutes, the sauce is done. No precooked yolks; no emulsification of the butter piece by piece, or drop by drop.

This works just fine, and for the same reason that *beurre blanc* works. The lemon juice and egg yolks provide the water phase, and the slowly melting butter releases the oil at an easily emulsifiable rate at the same time that it supplies some supplemental moisture. In fact, you can simplify the procedure even further. (There's nothing like doing a dozen experimental hollandaises in one morning for finding the shortcuts!) The temperature of the ingredients is not all that critical. There's no need to freeze plates or fight your way to the back of the refrigerator. Everything can be at room temperature, as long as you're careful to melt the butter gradually and don't overload the water phase with a lot of oil all at once; and as long as you beat the mixture constantly to disperse the heat and butterfat as evenly as possible.

So here's the ultimate simplification of your favorite hollandaise or béarnaise recipe. Throw all the ingredients into a saucepan (doing the reduction of the vinegar beforehand, if that's called for), turn on the heat, and start beating. Stop when the sauce reaches the desired consistency.

If you're interested in experimenting, then you might also want to play with the standard proportions. It's quite easy to make a hollandaise or béarnaise using fewer egg yolks per stick butter than is usual. Most recipes these days call for 2 yolks per stick; some call for 3. You can easily make do with 1, though there is some difference in consistency; the less yolk, the thinner the sauce. Still, I made a sauce using half a yolk per stick that was noticeably thicker than a yolkless *beurre blanc*. So you can treat the hollandaise family as a continuum of sauces, from the relatively thin and buttery to the relatively thick and eggy. Some of the intermediate formulations might be worth exploring.

Finally, the matter of safety. Nowadays pristine-looking eggs can actually be contaminated with salmonella bacteria. So do we risk food poisoning if we make and eat yolk-based sauces? In early 1990, an update from the U.S. Centers for Disease Control reported that "when eggs are heavily contaminated, standard cooking methods for many egg-containing foods (including Hollandaise and Bernaise [*sic*] sauces, meringue, and scrambled and soft-boiled eggs) may not kill all *Salmonella*." The CDC therefore recommended that "in regions where egg-associated salmonellosis has been identified"—so far, mainly the Northeast and the mid-Atlantic states—"the public should be advised to not eat raw or undercooked eggs."

How much cooking is sufficient to render egg dishes salmonella-free? Unfortunately, there's no single answer: it depends on the numbers of bacteria in the eggs, the rate of heating, and other factors. One benchmark is the common recommendation that intact eggs should be cooked at least to 160°F (71°C), the point at which the yolk hardens. This is also the temperature at which yolks thicken during saucemaking. If lemon juice or vinegar has been added, the thickening may even be delayed to 170°F (77°C). So you might think that a normally thickened, standard hollandaise or béarnaise sauce is as safe as a barely hard-boiled egg. In Britain, where outbreaks of salmonella poisoning have occurred nationwide, public health researchers have shown that even when salmonella are present in an egg in the millions, effectively all of them are killed when the intact egg is boiled long enough to raise the yolk temperature to 160°F. However, when eggs are scrambled to the same temperature in 3 or 4 minutes, some salmonella from a large initial population are able to survive. The key is the difference in cooking times: boiling an intact egg to 160°F takes more than 10 minutes, so it exposes bacteria in the yolk to lethal temperatures for a much longer period of time than does scrambling. Judging from a boiling experiment by Oxford biologist Richard Gardner, the yolk spends 3 or 4 minutes getting from 140°F (60°C), the temperature used in one standard method of pasteurization, to 160°F.

When we make an emulsified sauce, we spend either a very few minutes cooking the yolks alone to 160°F, or somewhat more time thickening the sauce as a whole. So if the yolks happen to be badly contaminated, precooking them in the traditional way probably isn't adequate to render them safe to eat. We might be able to rid a sauce of salmonella by thickening it at the end, and then lingering around the thickening point for several minutes. But the more time a sauce spends at high temperatures, the more prone it is to thin or break. And it's not clear exactly how long we'd have to linger.

If we want to be as confident as possible that a hollandaise or béarnaise sauce is salmonella-free, we simply have to bring the yolks close to the boiling point. The British scientists found that they could destroy effectively all salmonella by quickly scrambling contaminated eggs to 182°F (83°C). Of course, that temperature destroys emulsified sauces as well, or at least leaves them a thin version of their former selves. I had figured that it would also destroy the yolks alone, would probably turn them into crumbly, useless rubber. But just to be sure, I played around with different ways of precooking them. And I hit on a simple, quick method that gets yolks close to the boil, almost surely rids them of salmonella, and yet leaves them capable of making a decent hollandaise or béarnaise.

There are two keys to near-boiling egg yolks for a sauce: heating the yolks quickly but gently, and making it difficult for them to curdle. I began by taking a clue from the fact that acid ingredients hinder the coagulation of the egg proteins. By trying various combinations of water and either lemon juice or vinegar, I came up with proportions that give a custard-like consistency to yolks at temperatures within a few degrees of the boil. As for the cooking itself, after years of owning a microwave oven, I finally found a task that it alone can accomplish well. On the stovetop, it's very difficult to control the near-boiling of thick yolks. A double boiler takes so long that the yolks dry out, and direct heat causes local overcooking. The microwave, on the other hand, heats a small portion of food rapidly and from all sides, and the food won't exceed the boiling point unless it begins to dry out.

Apart from the microwave oven, the cook needs just three or four tools to near-boil egg yolks for the emulsified sauces. One is a small glass bowl, with a capacity of 2 cups or so, that allows observation of the cooking and confines the yolks in a small, manageable area. The others are two or three small whisks. The yolks must be beaten several times during the cooking; and if the same whisk were to be used every time, it would recontaminate the cooked mixture with traces of the original uncooked yolks. True, you can wash the whisk after the initial beating, but once you start cooking there won't be time to wash it again. So keep several whisks on hand.

You might think that a thermometer would be necessary as well. But standard cooking thermometers aren't much good at measuring the temperature of such a small volume of liquid. Nor is it possible to prescribe an exact cooking time that will be right for all microwave ovens and all yolk mixtures. Fortunately, the visible signs of boiling are unmistakable, and make a reliable guide for most cooks. (Because the boiling point of water drops nearly 2 Fahrenheit degrees for every 1,000 feet of elevation above sea level, high-altitude cooks should probably prolong the apparent boiling of the yolk mixture to compensate for its lower temperature.)

The catch with relying on our eyes is that a thickening liquid heats somewhat unevenly, so that only portions of the yolk mixture may actually be at the boil when it becomes visibly agitated. It's for this reason that I prescribe a second heating period after the agitated mixture is beaten together and its temperature evened out. It's also for this reason that I call the technique *"near*-boiling." Because we can only beat the mixture together after the heating has been stopped, and beating hastens cooling, we can't be positive that every bit of the mixture makes it all the way to the boil. But we can be sure that every bit gets pretty close to the boil. And given the experimental finding that salmonella are effectively eliminated when eggs are quickly scrambled to within 30 Fahrenheit degrees of the boil, near-boiling should give us a comfortable safety margin.

Here's a description of the technique; for detailed recipes, see the summary at the end of the chapter. To begin, beat together the yolks, water, and lemon juice or vinegar very thoroughly. Pour the mixture into a glass bowl, cover the bowl with a plate, and heat it in the microwave oven at high power until you can see the surface of the mixture begin to heave and bubble: for a 2-yolk mixture, this takes between 30 seconds and a minute in my 600-watt oven. Continue the cooking several seconds beyond this point. Then remove the bowl. The mixture will look quite ugly and curdled. Beat it vigorously, however, and it'll become creamy. At this point, I find that the temperature of the mixture is between 160°F and 180°F (71°C and 82°C): only portions of it have been heated to the boil. Resume heating the bowl until the mixture begins to heave again: maybe another 15 or 20 seconds. Cook several seconds more, then remove the bowl and beat the curdled mixture until it's creamy. Its temperature is now around 200°F (93°C). Cover the bowl and let it sit for 1 minute. All told, the yolks should spend a minute or more above 180°F, which will almost surely leave them salmonella-free. Then beat the yolks again, scoop them into a pan, and whisk in butter to make your sauce.

Not surprisingly, since near-boiled yolks have taken a beating before they ever see butter, sauces made by this method are more fragile than the standard versions; try not to let them get much hotter than 120°F (49°C). And if you examine the coat of sauce on a spoon, you'll see more shards of coagulated protein. But you'll find little trace of the yolks' initial curdiness on the tongue; these sauces come out surprisingly smooth.

Should you bother to near-boil your egg yolks before making a hollandaise or béarnaise sauce? That will depend on the prevalence of contaminated eggs in your part of the country, the vulnerability of the people you're cooking for, and the degree of your general concern about food poisoning. Since it may be some time before egg producers are able to eliminate the salmonella problem at its source, near-boiling at least offers the concerned cook an alternative to indefinite abstention from the yolk-based sauces.

Concessions to safety aside, I suspect that not everyone will welcome simplified alternatives to the traditional recipes for hollandaise and béarnaise. And I sympathize. The careful concentration of the flavorful liquid, the delicate thickening of the yolks, the unhurried incorporation of the butter bit by bit: these elaborate attentions elevate cooking to a kind of ceremony, a tribute to order and distinction. And a certain satisfaction is lost when ritual is replaced with indiscriminate mixing, when a perilous enterprise gives way to a sure thing. Still, how often do we find ourselves with the leisure to savor the ceremonious or disaster narrowly averted?

Beyond convenience, though, there's a deeper appeal to the simpler methods. The complications of traditional recipes often have to do with establishing our mastery over the ingredients. A good emblem of this is the galantine, a duck or chicken whose flesh is boned, mixed with ground meats, herbs, and other flavorings, then stuffed back into its own skin and cooked. We cut, pound, grind, sweat, beat, and force our foods into submission, remaking them to conform to our desires. The simple recipes, whether traditional *beurre blanc* or streamlined hollandaise, still aim to please, but they're more attentive to the inherent properties of the ingredients. Give it a little moisture to start with and butter will almost make itself into a sauce; with a little prodding, a pan of egg yolks, lemon juice, and butter knows just how to assemble into a hollandaise. To me, this is more remarkable than the fact that a cook can make a sauce with much labor. Neither the palate nor the mind is deprived when we work *with* the ingredients as much as we do *on* them.

SUMMARY: HOLLANDAISE AND BÉARNAISE

The primary role of the egg yolk in hollandaise and béarnaise sauces is to thicken them. The yolk's proteins accomplish this by making more viscous the water phase that surrounds the droplets of butterfat.

There's nothing sacred about the traditional ratio of 2 or 3 egg yolks to 1 stick of butter. A fraction of a yolk per stick will still thicken the sauce noticeably. An innovative cook has plenty of leeway to experiment with balances of flavor and texture in the emulsified butter sauces.

Heat causes the yolk proteins to unfold and increase the yolk's viscosity, so cooking a yolk-based sauce will thicken it—up to a point. If heated much beyond 160°F or 170°F (71°C or 77°C), the sauce will abruptly thin and separate into custardy masses and a pool of butterfat. A separated sauce can usually be rescued either by adding a teaspoon or two of water and whisking vigorously, or by starting with a teaspoon or two of water in a fresh bowl and beating the separated sauce into the water drop by drop, then more rapidly as the sauce reforms. A rescued sauce is always noticeably thinner than the original sauce.

The trickiest step in making the yolk-based sauces is the preliminary cooking of the yolks. This thickens the yolks and compensates for the subsequent thinning caused by the moisture contained in whole butter (clarified butter, whose moisture has been removed, will make a distinctly thicker sauce). Unfortunately, it's easy to scramble the yolks when they're cooked alone. There are several ways of adapting standard recipes to avoid this step. The simplest is to delay the thickening of the yolks until after all the butter has been incorporated.

Streamlined late-thickened hollandaise or béarnaise sauce. Assemble the ingredients called for in your favorite recipe for hollandaise or béarnaise sauce. If you're making a béarnaise, then prepare the flavored acidic reduction and let it cool. Cut the butter into 1-tablespoon chunks. Place the egg yolks, liquid ingredients, and seasonings in a cold saucepan, and beat together thoroughly. Add the chunks of butter, place the pan over moderate heat, and begin whisking gently. Control the heat so that the butter melts gradually and evenly into the yolk base. Once all the butter has melted, continue heating and whisking until the sauce just thickens, when it will be between 160°F and 170°F (71°C and 77°C). Turn the heat down and hold the sauce around 120°F (49°C) until serving.

Recently it's been discovered that apparently pristine Grade A eggs can harbor salmonella bacteria, which cause food poisoning. If the yolks are badly contaminated, then cooking a hollandaise or béarnaise sauce until it thickens may not eliminate all bacteria from the sauce. Higher temperatures, on the other hand, will ruin the sauce. If you have a microwave oven, a small glass bowl, and at least two whisks, you can render the egg yolks almost certainly safe at the same time that you prethicken them. The resulting sauce is somewhat more fragile than usual, but otherwise it's indistinguishable from the traditional version. Use this technique if contaminated eggs have been found in your region, if you're cooking for someone who is especially vulnerable to food poisoning (the very young, the elderly, the chronically ill), or if you simply want to be as confident as possible that the sauce is safe to eat.

Hollandaise sauce with near-boiled egg yolks. This recipe makes about a cup of sauce. Whole butter produces a moderately thick texture. For a thicker sauce, start by clarifying 1½ sticks, or ¾ cup, unsalted butter. (Gently melt the butter in a saucepan, in a slow oven, or in the microwave oven. Skim away the froth and pour the butterfat off of the watery dregs.) If you want to make a larger volume of sauce, cook the eggs in 2-yolk batches; it's hard to get more than 2 yolks at a time to cook evenly.

The timings are based on my experience with a 600-watt microwave oven. I strongly recommend that you start by experimenting with a few egg yolks to get an idea of how your own oven behaves. If you have a cooking thermometer, try to confirm that the mixture is close to the boil after the second heating period.

Have two or three small whisks at hand. Separate 2 egg yolks, using the sharp edges of the shells to cut away the thick cords of egg white, the chalazae. (If you want as lumpless a sauce as possible, roll the yolks on a small plate covered with cheesecloth, which will pull off most of the adhering albumen. You can also strain the cooked yolks, or the whole sauce.) Then place the yolks in a small glass bowl, around 2 cups in capacity, and beat them until homogeneous.

(A much larger bowl will allow the yolks to spread out, which makes it that much harder to heat them evenly.) Add 2 teaspoons lemon juice or vinegar and beat again. If the eggs were U.S. Large, add 2 tablespoons water; if Extra Large, 2 tablespoons plus 2 teaspoons. Beat the mixture again. Throw the whisk in the sink or wash it with hot, soapy water.

Cover the bowl with a plate, place it in a microwave oven, and heat on high power. Stand several feet away from the oven (to avoid exposing your eyes to any stray microwaves), and watch for the point at which the surface of the yolk mixture begins to heave. If you have trouble seeing through the oven door, then open the door and check every 10 seconds or so, beginning after about 30 seconds of cooking. Once the mixture is visibly agitated, let it continue to cook while you count off 8 or 10 seconds; then remove the bowl and beat the yolks vigorously with a clean whisk until they're smooth. Throw the whisk in the sink; you won't have time to wash it. Quickly return the covered bowl to the oven and heat on high until the yolks begin to heave again. Count off another 8 or 10 seconds of cooking; then remove the bowl and beat the yolks vigorously with a clean whisk until they're smooth. At this point, the temperature of the mixture should be around 200°F (93°C). Cover the bowl and let it sit for 1 minute.

In the meantime, wash the whisk in hot, soapy water, and unless you've already clarified the butter to make a thicker sauce, cut 1½ sticks (¾ cup) unsalted butter into thick slices. Even if you'll be adding clarified butter, beat 1 or 2 slices of solid butter into the yolk mixture to cool it down and loosen it up. Scoop the yolk mixture into a small saucepan. Add a pinch of salt and whisk it in. (Never add salt before cooking the yolks; it causes curdling.) Turn the heat on low, add the butter slices, and beat slowly until all the butter has melted into the sauce. If the butter is clarified, add a fraction of a tablespoon at a time to begin with, and work more rapidly as the sauce thickens. Finish by correcting the seasoning with salt and lemon juice or vinegar. Don't let the sauce get any hotter than about 120°F (49°C).

Béarnaise sauce with near-boiled egg yolks. This recipe deviates from the recipe for hollandaise only in the details of seasoning and the proportions of liquid added to the yolks. Begin by boiling together ¼ cup white wine vinegar, ¼ cup dry white wine, 1 tablespoon chopped shallots, 1 tablespoon chopped fresh tarragon or ½ tablespoon dried tarragon, and a few grinds of pepper, until the liquid has been reduced to 2 or 3 tablespoons. Strain the liquid into a small bowl and let it cool. Free 2 egg yolks from as much of the adherent albumen as possible, and beat them in a small glass bowl. Carefully measure 2 tablespoons of the acidic reduction, making up the volume with water if necessary, and add them to the yolks. Beat the mixture. If the eggs were Extra Large, add 2 tablespoons water; if Large, 1½ tablespoons water. Beat the mixture thoroughly. Throw the whisk in the sink or clean it in hot, soapy water. Cover the bowl with a plate.

Proceed with cooking the yolks and incorporating the butter as for hollandaise sauce; see above. Finish by correcting the seasoning and adding 1 tablespoon of finely chopped fresh tarragon to the sauce.

Mayonnaise: Doing More
with Lecithin

Mayonnaise is a remarkable sauce in two obvious ways: it's produced without the application of heat, and it forms the base of many variations that can be served with a wide range of cold dishes. This "beautiful shining golden ointment," as Elizabeth David has called it, is made by emulsifying a quantity of oil in raw egg yolks. Lemon juice or vinegar, salt and pepper, and sometimes mustard provide the basic seasoning, but mayonnaise can be imbued with many different flavors depending on the dish it's meant to accompany, which might be an hors d'oeuvre, eggs, meat, fish, vegetables, or a salad. One list of optional ingredients from the French classical tradition includes *fines herbes* (parsley, tarragon, chives, chervil), tomato, cress, garlic, capers, gherkins, truffles, curry powder, anchovies, and caviar.

While mayonnaise is a wonderfully adaptable sauce, many recipes for it are rather rigid and forbidding, with their intimations of a runny mess if you barely exceed the yolk's capacity for oil. Still more forbidding nowadays is the possibility that even when it's prepared carefully with the freshest ingredients, homemade mayonnaise could cause food poisoning. Salmonella bacteria have been found lurking in the yolks of some intact, Grade A eggs; and since mayonnaise isn't cooked at all, a contaminated yolk is bound to produce a contaminated sauce. (The acid ingredients can kill off bacteria from the yolk, but this process takes anywhere from several hours to several days.) The U.S. Centers for Disease Control have therefore advised against eating raw eggs in any form, especially in areas where outbreaks of food poisoning have already been associated with eggs. (For more details on the current salmonella problem, see p. 101.)

I was happy to discover that the yolk of an egg is also adaptable, much more so than we usually give it credit for. There's more than one way to make mayonnaise. There's even a way of making a mayonnaise that's almost surely safe to eat, contaminated egg yolks or not. These alternative methods may seem heretical to those who hold to a strict definition of mayonnaise. But there is historical precedent for taking liberties with the standard sauce. And if, like me, you don't relish the prospect of a life without the occasional thick, silken, homemade mayonnaise, pedigrees will matter less to you than the quality and safety of the sauce that any given method allows you to make.

In the New World, mayonnaise seems to have caught on around the turn of the twentieth century, well after its obscure, probably eighteenth-century invention in France. Americans used it primarily as a salad dressing, as witness the Waldorf salad, first made around 1895 with apples and celery; or, more baroque, the "Golf Salad" transcribed by Laura Shapiro in her book *Perfection Salad*: "hard-boiled egg yolks mashed with mayonnaise, formed into balls and rolled in cottage cheese." Whereas the French experimented mostly with the flavor, Yankee ingenuity altered the emulsifier itself, and even the kingdom of nature from which the oil comes. An article in the May 1925 issue of *Good Housekeeping* called "Possibilities in Mayonnaise" and labeled "Results of Department of Cookery Research" suggests the following materials as alternatives to the egg yolk: whole egg, egg white, evaporated milk, condensed milk, gelatin, and mashed potatoes. (Fannie Farmer had offered the last in 1896 with the comment that "by the taste one would not realize eggs were not used in the making.") Most appallingly, Vivian Z. Teeter remarks that "those who are trying to reduce will be interested to know that upon the advice of their physician what is known as mineral oil may be used in making mayonnaise. . . . A dressing which has practically no fuel value may be made with gelatine and mineral oil."

As it turns out, commercial research of the time discovered something of genuine interest and usefulness about egg yolks and mayonnaise: egg yolks stiffen on freezing. This fact helps manufacturers produce a quart of mayonnaise with only one or two egg yolks. It also allows the home cook to develop some interesting variations on the traditional recipe, as we'll see.

The possibility of alternative recipes suggested itself one day when I did a simple experiment to determine the maximum amount of oil that a single egg yolk could emulsify. I had been surprised to find that the small amount of emulsifying material in butter was sufficient to stabilize a *beurre blanc* unaided. The egg yolk is much richer in these materials, so I wondered whether its emulsifying power hadn't been somewhat underestimated.

Somewhat indeed! Most recipes for mayonnaise peg the limit at about ¾ cup oil per U.S. Large yolk, and recommend that novices stay well below that. The figure I came up with for that same ordinary yolk was on the order of *100* cups. Something more than 6 gallons of oil! Of course, I didn't just add the oil straight, gallon by gallon; that would have been a waste of oil and work. After adding a certain amount of inexpensive soybean oil, I took a small portion—around a teaspoon—of the mixture and then added more oil to just that portion. I repeated this subdivision several times more, periodically adding water to prevent the emulsion from breaking solely on account of crowding. When all the additions and multiplications were done (if a portion containing one-tenth of the yolk absorbs 1 tablespoon oil, then the whole yolk would have absorbed 10), that astonishing figure emerged: 1 yolk, 100 cups of oil. It seemed impossible, so I did the whole experiment again from scratch. There were some differences, but the result was of the same order of magnitude. There can be no doubt that the egg yolk is a prodigious emulsifier.

I then sat down with a pocket calculator and a few numbers from chemistry books and found that this experimental result could easily have been predicted. By weight, an egg yolk is 50% water, 16% protein, and 33% fats and related substances. Of the last, about two-thirds is fat proper, while 5% is cholesterol and a whopping 28% is phospholipids, the potent family of emulsifiers to which lecithin belongs. A single large yolk contains 2 grams of phospholipid and 3 grams of protein (by comparison, a tablespoon of butter contains 0.02 gram phospholipid and 0.1 gram protein).

The properties of phospholipids have been studied for many years, especially once they were discovered to be the main structural material of the membranes of living cells. It's known that the "head" of the lecithin molecule, the part that projects from the surface of an oil droplet and protects it from other droplets, takes up a surface area of about 100 square angstroms, or 1.6×10^{-15} square inches. Now we make a couple of approximations. First, that all 2 grams of the egg phospholipid are lecithin (the true figure is 1.5 grams, but the other

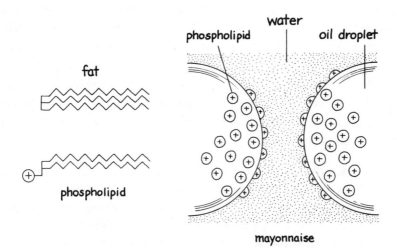

Phospholipid molecules resemble fats and oils in having long hydrocarbon tails, but differ in also having an electrically charged "head" (left). Egg yolk phospholipids stabilize emulsified sauces like mayonnaise (right). Their tails become embedded in the droplets of oil, while their charged heads project from the droplet surfaces and prevent the droplets from coalescing.

phospholipids are chemically very similar). Second, that the average molecular weight of egg yolk lecithin is 825 grams per mole (a mole is defined as 6×10^{23} molecules). The number of phospholipid molecules in a single yolk is then

$$(2 \text{ grams} \div 825 \text{ grams/mole}) \times (6 \times 10^{23} \text{ molecules/mole})$$

or about 1.5×10^{21} molecules (1.5 times 10 raised to the 21st power, or 15 followed by 20 zeroes, or 1,500 billion billion). So the total droplet surface area protected is that number of molecules times 100 square angstroms. It comes out to 1,850 square yards, or nearly a third of the proverbial football field. From roughly 1 tablespoon of egg yolk.

That may seem impossibly large. But two considerations make it sound more reasonable. First, although the area taken up by one molecule is infinitesimal, we're dealing with a tremendous number of molecules. And in essence they're being spread into an infinitesimally thin layer, just one molecule thick.

Pull a piece of any material that thin and it will extend over a very large area. In fact, one of the earliest such experiments was done by Benjamin Franklin, and it gives graphic support to our calculations. Franklin's inspiration was his observation, in itself not original, that when a cook tosses greasy water overboard during a sea voyage, the ship's wake is smoothed (hence the phrase "pouring oil on troubled waters"). And as we now know, because oil can't mix with water and is also less dense, it will spread on water into a surface film one molecule thick (if the area of the water is large enough). One windy day around 1770 at a pond in Clapham, near London, as Franklin later wrote,

> I fetched out a Cruet of Oil, and dropt a little of it on the Water. I saw it spread itself with surprising Swiftness upon the Surface. . . . I then went to the Windward Side, where [the waves] began to form; and there the Oil tho' not more than a Tea Spoonful produced an instant Calm, over a Space several yards square, which spread amazingly, and extended itself gradually till it reached the Lee Side, making all that Quarter of the Pond, perhaps half an Acre, as smooth as a Looking Glass.

Half an acre is about 2,400 square yards; and the eighteenth-century teaspoon held about half as much as a modern one. Franklin's simple experiment demonstrates quite vividly that our calculations are in the right ballpark.

So our egg yolk has about 1,850 square yards of emulsifying power. The question now is, What volume of oil does that droplet surface area correspond to? The answer depends on the droplet size; the smaller the droplets, the more of them there are in a given volume and the greater their total surface area. From various studies it seems that a droplet diameter of 10 micrometers, or about 4 ten-thousandths of an inch, is about average for mayonnaise. Now brace yourself. With that figure, it turns out that when you beat 1 tablespoon of oil into a mayonnaise, you break up that single dollop of liquid into 30 billion individual droplets with a collective surface area of about 8 square yards. The phospholipids in a single egg yolk should therefore be able to coat some 7 trillion droplets produced from 230 tablespoons—15 cups—of oil.

Let's stop for a moment to contemplate these numbers. Say you begin with an unbroken mass of ¾ cup oil and 1 egg yolk. After a few minutes and some exercise of the wrist, you have a mound of some 300 billion oil droplets. These days, astronomers estimate that there are about 100 billion stars in the main body of our galaxy, the Milky Way, which like all spiral galaxies appears to have been stirred around once or twice. In the past cheesemaking has served as a metaphor for Creation; perhaps saucemaking deserves a look. Genesis begins with the division of undifferentiated Chaos into day and night, earth and sea, and division is what beating oil and egg yolk is all about.

Back to our calculated capacity of 15 cups oil per yolk. That's not quite in the 100-cup neighborhood I entered when I tested an actual yolk, but it's some 20 times the limit cited in most cookbooks. Our calculation also ignores the contribution that the egg proteins and cholesterol certainly make to coating the oil droplets, so it's a conservative figure. The bottom line for the cook is this: When you're making a mayonnaise, the last thing you have to worry about is exceeding the emulsifying capacity of the yolk. In most recipes there's a huge safety factor built in. So don't take the dire warnings in recipes too seriously. Still, there is one reason not to stray too far from the standard proportion of ½ to 1 cup oil per egg yolk. If you have only 1 yolk but need 2 cups of sauce, the yolk can certainly emulsify 2 cups of oil. The problem, as we'll see in a moment, is that in order to keep the sauce from separating, you would have to supplement the volume of the yolk with water; and water thins the sauce out. The real virtue of the usual proportions is that they produce a thick, weighty, dignified mayonnaise.

To the experimentally minded cook, the 15-cup and 100-cup figures suggest the possibility of developing a very different mayonnaise recipe, one that contains a fraction of the usual amount of egg yolk. Because the yolk contributes an eggy note to the traditional mayonnaise, perhaps such a recipe would produce a lighter flavor, in which the oil and seasonings would be more prominent. To find out, I embarked on a new round of experiments.

Sure enough, I readily succeeded in making a stable mayonnaise from just a fraction of a yolk. The average Large yolk is about 1 tablespoon in volume. I took ½ teaspoon of yolk, or about one-sixth of the whole, added ½ teaspoon of lemon juice, and beat in about 2 tablespoons of pure (refined) olive oil to reach the consistency typical of mayonnaise. I thinned it out with another ½ teaspoon lemon juice, and added 6 tablespoons oil. I then thinned out this half a cup of very thick sauce with 1 teaspoon water, and added another 4 tablespoons oil. All in all, my sixth of a yolk emulsified ¾ cup of oil—the limit, according to most cookbooks, for a whole yolk. And it was still well below its actual limit. The ivory-colored sauce was stable, and certainly had less of an eggy flavor. Compared to a traditional mayonnaise made with the same amounts of oil, lemon juice, and water, the new version was distinctly more tangy and the flavor of the olive oil was more prominent.

However, two disadvantages to the new formulation were immediately apparent to me. First, it's not easy to get an emulsion started with such a small volume of yolk. Half a teaspoon isn't really enough to work with at all, and when you add the same volume of lemon juice, the mixture is thinner and so less efficient at breaking the added oil into droplets. In the standard recipe, the injunction to beat the oil in drop by drop is unnecessarily conservative, as we'll see; but when the amount of starting material is so small, such caution is essential. The second problem was the consistency of the final sauce, which was less full-bodied, more fragile than traditional mayonnaise. Because it contains less yolk and relatively more water, its water base is thinner. And since the thickness of an emulsion is determined by both the thickness of the base and the crowding of droplets into the base, the sauce is thin as well. In one experiment I found that simply diluting 1 yolk with 1 tablespoon water meant that I had to add half again as much oil to reach the consistency of a sauce made with an undiluted yolk. Now there may be something to be said for a creamy, almost pourable mayonnaise—as a salad dressing, for example—but my aim for the moment was to make as robust a sauce as possible.

It turned out that both problems had the same solution. Having noticed that the color of my thin, low-yolk version was like that of bottled mayonnaise, I took a closer look at the labels of several brands. All of them claimed a cholesterol content of about 6 milligrams per tablespoon of sauce. Since all the cholesterol comes from egg yolks, I calculated that there was about a third of a yolk per cup of bottled mayonnaise, which is substantially less than there is in the homemade version. Yet bottled mayonnaise is, if anything, stiffer than homemade. Hoping to find a way to bolster the body of my lower-yolk sauce, I began reading up on commercial practices.

I soon found that the low proportion of yolk to oil had been common in manufacturing as far back as the 1920s, or shortly after a new way of handling the yolks came into general use. A bit of technological history. Late in the nineteenth century and early in the twentieth, large quantities of egg albumen were used in Europe and the United States as a coating for photographic paper and in dye printing. This caused the accumulation of stocks of egg yolk, which was bought in bulk by bakers and leather makers, among others. So efforts were made to find methods of preserving the yolks, as well as albumen and whole eggs. Salt, alcohol, and other chemicals were the principal means until around 1900, when the freezing of egg products was pioneered by Herbert J. Keith, first in St. Paul and then in Boston. The problem with freezing, though, was that it caused an irreversible thickening of the yolks, which took on the consistency of a gum eraser when thawed. Keith discovered that he could prevent the yolks from seizing up if he mixed them with the whites and a certain amount of salt and/or sugar. Later, others found that just salt or sugar alone would do the trick, though the yolks were still much more viscous after thawing than they had been fresh.

The mayonnaise and dressing business boomed during the 1920s. According to the *Business Week* of January 13, 1932, it was propelled by the "growing recognition of vitamin-supplying salads as a necessary part of human diet." And sometime during the late 1920s, the mayonnaise manufacturers recognized that frozen egg yolks were quite adequate, perhaps even preferable to fresh, for making mayonnaise. Apart from price, their advantage was a simple one: their thickness. The more viscous the continuous phase of the emulsion is, the more readily the added oil breaks into small droplets, and the thicker the final sauce is. Frozen-thawed yolks thus smoothed the manufacturing process and reduced the proportion of yolks required to stiffen a given volume of sauce.

Ever since, most commercial mayonnaise has been made with frozen yolks, about one-third yolk per cup of sauce. The chemistry of yolk thickening is still something of a mystery. The current theory is that freezing deprives the yolk's emulsifier-protein particles of their protective layer of water by solidifying the water into ice crystals, and this causes the particles to bond to each other. In any event, it's an extremely simple trick. What's surprising is that chefs and home cooks never got wind of it. The frozen yolk makes possible a wide range of variations on the traditional recipes for emulsified sauces.

I did a quick set of experiments to establish the best practice for the home kitchen. In separate containers I froze for 24 hours a whole yolk, a plain lightly beaten yolk, a salted beaten yolk, a yolk diluted with an equal volume of water, and a yolk diluted with an equal volume of lemon juice. When thawed, the whole yolk could be cut into pieces with a knife; it was much too solid. The lightly beaten yolk was like a thick set custard; the salted version was somewhat less thick. Neither was easily mixed with water: an important deficiency, since liquid must be added during saucemaking. Of the two diluted samples, the acid version was noticeably more cohesive; the plain-water version had the easy smoothness of a stirred custard. Even after dilution, these thawed yolks were much thicker than a fresh undiluted egg yolk. When I shortened the freezing period to about 8 hours, the whole yolk was still largely solid, the beaten yolk like a thick mayonnaise already, the water-diluted yolk like a very thin custard, and the lemon-diluted yolk just right, like a thick stirred custard. The whole yolk was properly thickened by a period of 4 hours in the freezer.

So the home cook isn't constrained by the practice of commercial operations, which must add a substantial amount of salt to the yolks to prevent overthickening during the long period of cold storage. Depending on how far ahead we're thinking—and if we can be confident that our eggs aren't tainted by salmonella—we do best simply to dilute the beaten yolk with water and freeze it for 24 hours, or add lemon juice or nothing at all and freeze for 8 hours, or freeze the yolk whole for 4 hours. These are only very general guidelines, and they can be modified according to your own preferences in flavor and workability.

The use of frozen egg yolk can make a substantial difference in the consistency of a low-yolk mayonnaise. I made two low-yolk sauces, one with fresh yolk and the other with frozen, using identical proportions of yolk and water. The frozen yolk formed a thick mayonnaise at an oil-to-water ratio of 6.6 to 1. At the same ratio, the fresh-yolk sauce had the consistency of thick cream; it dripped from the whisk. Even at a ratio of 16 to 1, when it was unstably overcrowded with oil droplets, the fresh-yolk sauce was soft and quivering rather than stiff. The frozen yolk, then, makes it possible to achieve a thick sauce with relatively little yolk and a normal, stable proportion of oil.

Here's a basic low-yolk recipe for mayonnaise that can be modified in many ways. It makes about a cup. Again, try it only if you're reasonably sure that your eggs are salmonella-free. Eight hours before you plan to make the sauce, thoroughly mix 1 egg yolk with 1 tablespoon lemon juice, and freeze. (For some reason, yolks frozen with vinegar often fail to produce a stable emulsion.) Once you've thawed the mixture, take ½ tablespoon and place it in the bottom of a bowl. Add a little salt and white pepper, and beat lightly. Have ready a little less than 1 cup of the oil you prefer: olive, soy, corn, canola, or some mixture. For the most stable sauce, one that can be refrigerated for a day or more, make olive oil a relatively minor component of the mixture (more on this detail in a moment). Slowly beat in the oil, about ¼ teaspoon at a time, until the emulsion becomes noticeably thicker; then beat in the rest more rapidly. As you go, correct the thickness and flavor with lemon juice, vinegar, or water. You should add at least 1 tablespoon of liquid altogether; 2 tablespoons will give a more stable sauce.

Compared to a cup of mayonnaise made with a whole yolk, this quarter-yolk version is lighter in color, and lighter and clearer in flavor as well. The oil, acid, and seasonings stand out. Perhaps this characteristic will prove to be amenable to new combinations of oils, vinegars, and other tart fruit juices. Despite the danger of awful innovations—things like "low-cholesterol cherviled pecan-oil mayonnaise with *fraise de bois* vinegar"—something interesting might come of experiments along these lines. I find that even the standard combination of olive oil and lemon juice or vinegar is attractively different in itself, perhaps better suited than egginess for cold summer dishes of fish or chicken.

These low-yolk mayonnaises are interesting variations on the standard sauce. However, like the standard sauce, they'll be on the blacklist of the Centers for Disease Control as long as salmonella bacteria continue to show up in eggs. It wasn't until early 1990, some time after I had put aside the emulsified sauces for other subjects, that I realized just how widespread the concern about salmonella had become. And when I saw national food columnists calling for commercial mayonnaise where once they would have given directions for homemade, I decided to return to the sauces. This time around I hoped to make egg yolks safe for hollandaise and aïoli.

Since the cook's only reliable weapon against salmonella is heat, I began with the butter sauces, which already require some cooking. In chapter 7, I've described how we can use a microwave oven to heat egg yolks nearly to the boil, thereby effectively ridding them of any salmonella they might have contained, and then use them to make a successful hollandaise or béarnaise sauce. When the yolks are first diluted with a little water and acidified with lemon juice or vinegar, they become resistant to curdling, and remain capable of giving body to the warm butter sauces even after being heated to a temperature that would break the sauces themselves.

That may be fine for cooked sauces. But the yolk in a traditional mayonnaise is never cooked. However, as I worked out the near-boiling method for the butter sauces, I was struck by the thick consistency that the diluted, acidified yolks took on when they were cooked: a consistency which sometimes reminded me of the diluted, acidified, frozen yolks, and which suggested that they might be able to produce a thick mayonnaise. The real question, I thought, was whether near-boiled yolks would still be capable of emulsifying large quantities of oil. The heat must alter the proteins drastically, and could conceivably reduce the availability of lecithin for emulsifying duty.

It was easy enough to find out, so I did the experiment. I mixed one Large yolk with a tablespoon each of lemon juice and of water. (I used proportionally more lemon juice than I did for the butter sauces because mayonnaise recipes often call for a tablespoon of acid per cup of sauce. Acid conditions also damage salmonella bacteria and reduce curdling. These high-acid yolks come out smoother than the low-acid versions.) I microwaved the mixture until it became agitated, stirred it, and microwaved it again to the bubble. I let it cool, stirring occasionally to break up loose curds. Then I added a little salt and started whisking in some soybean oil. I ended up with a cup of reasonably thick mayonnaise. By using only ½ tablespoon of another yolk mixture, I then made a thinner but stable cup of sauce with just one-fifth of a yolk. Near-boiled egg yolks do pretty well!

We can thank the yolk's tremendous emulsifying power for this success: even when reduced by heat, it's still sufficient to handle a cup and more of oil. And we can thank the yolk's relatively mild flavor for the fact that the near-boiled yolk isn't all that obtrusive in the finished sauce; the strong, sulfurous odor that we associate with cooked eggs comes mainly from the white. Nor does the texture of the mayonnaise seem to suffer very much. I usually see a few tiny lumps in the finished sauce, but I'm seldom able to detect them on the tongue.

In the course of making a few dozen mayonnaises with cooked yolks, I did find one disadvantage to this technique. It's an intriguing one, and it has baffled my efforts to overcome it. Like a frozen yolk, a near-boiled yolk has some trouble handling olive oil. When I use extra virgin oil, the sauce forms successfully but begins to slacken in a matter of minutes, and almost always breaks after a few hours in the refrigerator. Pure olive oil makes a thicker mayonnaise, but it seldom keeps more than a day.

Though the labeling of olive oils isn't completely reliable, "extra virgin" olive oil is likely not to have been refined with solvents, while "pure" olive oil is mainly solvent-extracted oil, with a small proportion—5% or 10%—of extra virgin oil added for flavor and color. I've tried three or four brands of extra virgin oil, and all of them produce a slack mayonnaise with near-boiled yolks, as do unrefined corn and wheat-germ oils. None of the refined oils I've tested causes this problem. And I can make a more stable sauce by diluting extra virgin olive oil with canola or soy oils. So I suspect that the unrefined olive oil contains trace substances that somehow compromise the layer of yolk emulsifiers that surrounds each oil droplet: trace substances that have been partly removed from refined olive oil. I notice now that raw-yolk mayonnaises made with extra virgin olive oil are also less stable than sauces made with other oils; they'll often break after a day or two of refrigeration. Apparently a minor, slowly developing problem in raw-yolk mayonnaise becomes an immediate problem in frozen-yolk and cooked-yolk sauces, probably because the treated yolks are less efficient emulsifiers.

If olive oil does contain substances that interfere with emulsification, then perhaps further research will determine exactly what they are, and what alternatives we might have to diluting the oil when we make mayonnaise with cooked yolks. Still, unrefined olive oil can be fairly potent in flavor, and most traditional mayonnaise recipes already call for the more neutral refined oils or for a blend. The sauce that stands to lose the most by such dilution is aïoli, whose garlic is set off so well by a strong olive flavor. I find that when I blend equal volumes of olive oil and a neutral refined oil, my cooked whole-yolk mayonnaise is stable in the refrigerator for about a day. For longer keeping, a more reliable formula is one part olive oil to three or four parts refined oil. (If a mayonnaise does turn, you can revive it by working the sauce gradually into another yolk, or into a small amount of water and mustard.)

So the salmonella problem doesn't mean that we have to give up homemade mayonnaise. If you have any doubts about the wholesomeness of your eggs, if you just want to play it safe—or if you like to experiment!—then give cooked-yolk mayonnaise a try.

Enough about alternative recipes; now some general words about mayonnaise technique, no matter how you've treated the yolk. All cookbooks emphasize the importance of adding the oil very gradually at first so that the yolk isn't overwhelmed. If you work too fast, you end up with egg yolk in oil rather than the reverse. However, the universal injunction to go "drop by drop" is unnecessarily tedious. I've found that you can add the oil in doses up to a third of the volume of the yolk itself—not counting added liquid—and incorporate it satisfactorily. For a whole yolk, that's a teaspoon at a time. However much you add, it's handiest to have the oil in a container that pours evenly and delicately; spooning it in is messy and tiresome.

Most cookbooks also tell you to add some liquid to the egg yolks before you begin incorporating the oil. It's actually much preferable to begin emulsifying with the undiluted yolks, and to add the liquid occasionally as you go. The reason is that the emulsification process—the process of breaking a large drop of oil into microscopic droplets—is much more efficient in a viscous material than in a thin, runny one. An egg yolk thinned out by the addition of lemon juice, vinegar, or water offers little resistance to the movement of an oil drop, and the drop can squirm out of the way of the whisk. But oil drops in a thicker undiluted yolk move more slowly, so each drop can be trapped and battered into bits by the whisk and the local areas of the yolk that whisking propels at high velocity. So don't add any of the acidic liquid until you've got the sauce well under way. You'll find that the early stages of whisking go faster and more easily. The final sauce will also be thicker than it would have been otherwise, because you'll have broken the oil up into smaller droplets, at least on average, and small droplets pack together more tightly than large ones.

There's one ingredient it *is* good to add to the yolks at the beginning, and that's a pinch of salt. Try it next time, and observe carefully what happens as the salt dissolves. You'll see two changes: the yolk gets distinctly clearer and noticeably thicker. Both changes have the same cause. Most of the protein and emulsifiers in yolk are held together by electrical forces in aggregate particles called granules, which are about a micrometer (40 thousandths of an inch) in diameter. Like the similarly sized oil droplets in milk and cream, they reflect light and thus make the yolk opaque. Added salt dissolves into positive sodium and negative chlorine ions, and these disturb the electrical environment of the granules, which fall apart into components a tenth or so their original size: below the limit at which they can reflect light. So the yolk clears up as the salt dissolves. At the same time, because the many smaller particles also bind a shell of water molecules to their surfaces, and because their collective surface area is much greater than that of the larger aggregates, there's less free water left in the solution to lubricate things. So a pinch of salt thickens the yolk and thus makes it more efficient at breaking up the oil drops.

Finally, a piece of conventional lore not to bother with. Most mayonnaise recipes tell us to finish the sauce by adding a dollop of boiling water, which they claim will stabilize the emulsion. I've traced this idea back as far as Escoffier in the first decades of this century. He said that the hot water is used "to ensure that the emulsification holds if the sauce is to be reserved for later use." In many recipes, this measure of water far exceeds any liquid added at the beginning or during the course of the saucemaking! From my own experience, it seems clear that the important thing is not the temperature of the water, or when it's added. The important thing is that there be enough water in the sauce to accommodate the amount of oil you've beaten in. The consistency of the sauce will tell you that; if it's getting as stiff as paste and sweating drops of oil, then it's clearly in need of a drink. And in any case, a tablespoon or two of boiling water in a cup or more of room-temperature sauce is not going to raise its temperature enough to do anything useful. It's fine to adjust the flavor and texture at the end, but there's no need to put the kettle on.

Traditionalists may look at my suggestions for cooked-yolk, frozen-yolk, and low-yolk sauces and be appalled that I could call any of these concoctions "mayonnaise." Shades of Vivian Z. Teeter and evaporated milk, mashed potatoes, and gelatin! Let me hasten to say that these ideas are meant not to usurp the proper place of the classic sauce, but simply to make homemade mayonnaise safer and to expand the cook's range of choices in consistency and flavor. However, both Mme Teeter and I can cite an unimpeachable authority for using a variety of emulsifiers, cooked and uncooked, in mayonnaise: namely, Marie-Antoine Carême, great codifier of sauces in the French tradition. In his *Cuisinier parisien* of 1828, Carême gives three recipes for *magnonnaise blanche*. The first calls for raw egg yolks, tarragon vinegar, oil of Aix, aspic jelly, and at the end a few drops of *cool* water to whiten the color. The second, instead of egg yolks, calls for some butter and a ladleful of velouté or béchamel sauce, which are thickened on the stove with flour. This *magnonnaise*, he says, "yields in no way to the first that I described." And his third recipe replaces the yolks with white gelatin, which is obtained by extracting veal meat and bones in simmering water and then boiling the liquid down. Elsewhere he maintains that the sauce made with gelatin "is to be preferred" to the others.

So what exactly does "mayonnaise" signify? The origins of the name remain obscure. It makes its first appearance late in the eighteenth century, and early in the nineteenth it's variously given as *mahonnaise*, supposedly commemorating the taking of Port Mahon in 1756, *bayonnaise*, perhaps from the city of Bayonne, and *mayonnaise*, which has been connected with *moyeu*, an old French word for egg yolk. Says Carême, however, with his characteristic assuredness, "I admit that these words are used by vulgar cooks; but as for me, I protest that in our great kitchens (it is there that the purists reside) these three words are never cited, and that we always denominate this sauce by the epithet of *magnonnaise*." The true root word, according to Carême, is *manier*: to work, to manipulate. "It is only by force of working together these liquids . . . that one finishes by obtaining a velvety sauce, very soft and appetizing, and unique in its kind, because it in no respect resembles the other sauces that are obtained only by the reductions of the stove." The presence of raw egg yolks, then, is incidental; for Carême, the definitive characteristic of such a sauce is the working of oil into an emulsion without the aid of heat.

Well, the last century and a half has seen egg yolks win out over gelatin and the vulgar *mayonnaise* over the purist's *magnonnaise*; nor has Carême's etymology been taken seriously. On the other hand, the standard story that the name commemorates the taking of Port Mahon is not much trusted either. The most recent educated guess, from the lexicographer Pierre Guiraud, derives *mayonnaise* from the old verb *mailler*, meaning to beat, crush, or grind. It may not be Carême's particular root word, but it amounts to very much the same idea. Perhaps it's time to think of mayonnaise as a sauce that doesn't have to be entirely raw or noticeably eggy. On that thought, I'll hold it.

SUMMARY: MAYONNAISE

A single raw egg yolk is capable of emulsifying many cups of oil. You can disregard cookbook warnings not to exceed ¾ cup oil per yolk, as long as you're sure to provide the additional oil droplets with enough water to prevent overcrowding. Each cup of oil will need a total of 2 or 3 tablespoons of water, depending on the consistency you prefer. A Large yolk contains about ½ tablespoon water; the rest can be supplied as plain water, lemon juice, or vinegar.

If you use only a fraction of a yolk per cup sauce—half a yolk or less—the flavors of the oil and seasonings will be more prominent. But the sauce will also be noticeably thinner in consistency, because the viscous yolk is diluted by proportionally more added water.

You can make a thick low-yolk sauce by thickening the yolk in the freezer. The results are best if you freeze an intact yolk for 4 hours, a yolk lightly beaten alone or with an equal volume of lemon juice for 8 hours, or a yolk lightly beaten with an equal volume of water for 24 hours. The advantage of the diluted yolks is that you can begin the saucemaking with a larger volume of the yolk base.

Basic low-yolk mayonnaise. For 1 cup of mayonnaise made with the equivalent of ¼ egg yolk per cup: freeze for 8 hours 1 yolk beaten with 1 tablespoon of lemon juice. Put ½ tablespoon of the thawed mixture in a bowl and beat lightly with a little salt. Measure out about a cup of oil, with unrefined or olive oils at most a quarter of the total. Slowly beat in the oil about ¼ teaspoon at a time until the mixture thickens and then more rapidly. As you go, correct the consistency and flavor with small amounts of lemon juice, vinegar, or water; the total amount of added liquid should be between 1 and 2 tablespoons.

The recent discovery that salmonella bacteria can be present in intact shell eggs means that eating homemade mayonnaise carries some risk of food poisoning. The egg yolks in the traditional sauce are never cooked, so a contaminated egg will almost certainly produce a contaminated sauce. (Commercial mayonnaises are made with pasteurized eggs.) However, cooks who want to ensure the wholesomeness of a homemade mayonnaise can heat egg yolks close to the boil, thereby effectively ridding them of any salmonella, and then use them to produce a stable, reasonably thick mayonnaise. The one disadvantage of the precooked yolks is that they're unable to accommodate extra virgin olive oils, which appear to contain a substance that interferes with emulsification. You can make a stable sauce with these unrefined olive oils by mixing them with other oils.

Basic mayonnaise with near-boiled egg yolks. This recipe makes about a cup of sauce. The microwave timings are based on my experience with a 600-watt oven. I recommend that you start by experimenting with a few egg yolks to get an idea of how your oven behaves. If you have a good cooking thermometer, try to confirm that the yolk mixture is close to the boil after the second heating period. If you want to make more than 1 cup of sauce, you can simply multiply the proportions for the yolk mixture, but the oven timings will be very different. Again, experience with your own oven will be the best guide.

Have two or three small whisks at hand to avoid recontaminating the yolk once it's been cooked. Separate 1 egg yolk, using the sharp edges of the shells to cut away the thick cords of egg white, the chalazae. (If you want a sauce as lumpless as possible, roll the yolks on a small plate covered with cheesecloth, which will pull off most of the adhering albumen. You can also strain the yolk mixture after cooking it, or the whole sauce at the very end.) Then place the yolk in a small glass bowl, around 2 cups in capacity, and beat it until homogeneous. (Large bowls make it harder to cook the yolk evenly.) Add 1 tablespoon lemon juice or vinegar and beat again. If the egg was U.S. Large, add 1 tablespoon water; if Extra Large, 1 tablespoon plus ½ teaspoon. (Reducing the water to 1 teaspoon will produce a thicker sauce, but also makes it easier to curdle the yolk.) Beat the mixture again. Throw the whisk in the sink or clean it with hot, soapy water.

Cover the bowl with a plate, place it in a microwave oven, and heat at high power. Stand several feet away from the oven (to avoid exposing your eyes to any stray microwaves), and watch for the point at which the surface of the yolk mixture begins to heave. If you have trouble seeing through the oven door, then open the door and check every 5 seconds or so, beginning after about 15 seconds of cooking. Once the mixture is visibly agitated, count off 5 seconds; then turn off the oven, remove the bowl, and beat the mixture vigorously with a clean whisk until it's smooth. Throw the whisk in the sink; you won't have time to clean it. Quickly return the covered bowl to the oven and heat on high until the mixture begins to heave again. Count off 5 seconds; then stop the cooking, remove the bowl, and beat the mixture vigorously with a clean whisk until it's smooth. Cover the bowl and let it sit for 1 minute while you wash the whisk in hot, soapy water. Then place the bowl in a shallow pan of cold water and stir the yolk mixture occasionally until lukewarm.

Add a pinch of salt and whisk briefly. Measure out between ¾ cup and 1 cup oil. Keep unrefined or olive oils to half or less of the total volume, a quarter or less of the volume if you want the sauce to last in the refrigerator for more than a day. Beat the oil into the yolk mixture a teaspoon at a time to begin with, more rapidly after you've emulsified several tablespoons. If the sauce gets very stiff, add a few drops of water. Once all the oil has been incorporated into the sauce, adjust the flavor with lemon juice or vinegar. Adding at least ½ tablespoon liquid will thin the mayonnaise noticeably but will also make it more stable.

Low-yolk mayonnaise with near-boiled egg yolks. This recipe makes a cup of somewhat thinner sauce. Prepare, cook, and cool the yolk mixture as in the previous recipe. Remove ½ tablespoon of the mixture and place it in another bowl. Add a pinch of salt and whisk briefly. Measure out about 1 cup of oil, with refined vegetable oil predominating. Beat the oil into the yolk mixture, adjusting the flavor and texture as you go with lemon juice, vinegar, or water. For the most stable sauce, add a total of at least 1 tablespoon liquid.

Four general guidelines for making any kind of mayonnaise:

You don't have to add the oil drop by drop, but don't exceed one-third the volume of the yolk itself in any of the first several additions. For whole Large yolks, that's about 1 teaspoon per yolk.

Don't add any of the acidic liquid to the yolk until after you've formed the initial emulsion; the less dilute the yolk, the more easily the emulsion will form.

Do add some salt before you begin to beat in the oil; the salt increases the thickness of the yolk.

Don't bother to boil any water that you might add at the end. Water (or lemon juice or vinegar) of any temperature will thin the sauce to some degree as well as make it somewhat more stable. Use whatever liquids you like to make the final adjustments in consistency and flavor.

Persimmons Unpuckered

The persimmon is notable among the edible fruits for a peculiar trait: it's unbearably astringent until it has ripened nearly to the point of liquefaction. The North American variety inspired memorable passages of gastronomical prose from two of the first Europeans to taste it. Captain John Smith encountered the *Putchamin* in Virginia around 1607, and later wrote that it is "red when it is ripe: if it be not ripe it will drawe a mans mouth awrie with much torment; but when it is ripe, it is as delicious as an Apricock." In 1610 or so, William Strachey tried the Virginia *pessemmins* and noted that "when they are not fully ripe, they are harsh and choakie, and furre in a man's mouth like allam [alum], howbeit, being taken fully ripe, yt is a reasonable pleasant fruict, somewhat luscious."

The word *persimmon*, like Smith's and Strachey's versions, is an approximation of the Algonquian term, which may have meant "dried fruit." Drying could very well have been the preferred treatment for a fruit that was otherwise edible for only a very short time. While traveling along the lower Mississippi River fifty years before Smith's first taste, the Spaniard Hernando de Soto was presented with a gift of what his chronicler described as "loaves made of the substance of prunes, like unto brickes." Later explorers also wrote of the Indians making dried persimmons into "breads" or "cakes."

The natural range of the native American persimmon tree, *Diospyros virginiana* (*diospyros* means something like "grain of the gods"), runs from Arkansas through the lower Midwest and South, and up the Atlantic states to New England. It is little cultivated, and its fruit seldom seen in markets. This neglect is almost certainly due to its persistent, puckery astringency, which no doubt has discouraged many novices from attempting a second taste. More sought after is the tree's very hard wood, which has been put to use in the heads of golf clubs, in shoe lasts, and weavers' shuttles. The persimmon happens to be one of the few temperate members of the mostly tropical ebony family.

The Oriental or "Japanese" persimmon, *Diospyros kaki* (*kaki* is its Japanese name), is actually a native of North China. It has been found in Han tombs dating to around 100 B.C., and was introduced during the eighth century A.D. to Japan, where only citrus fruits and apples are now more popular. In distinct contrast to Smith and Strachey in Virginia, early European travelers in the East made no mention of astringency in the Asian species, perhaps because they never encountered unripe fruit. According to the Italian Jesuit Matteo Ricci, who wrote around 1600, the Portuguese named the persimmon the "Chinese fig" because "this particular fruit can be eaten only after it is dried." The Portuguese Jesuit Alvarus de Semedo named four northern provinces in China that "dry enough of them to serve the whole kingdom. When they are dry, they are better than our dried figs, to which they have a kind of resemblance." And Engelbert Kaempfer, a physician who accompanied a Dutch mission to the Far East in 1690, noted that the *kaki* grew plentifully throughout Japan, and that "it is no less commendable for its great fruitfulness, than it is for its extensive use, for the fruits of it dried afford a pleasant and agreeable food for rich and poor. The Chinese preserve them with sugar." Kaempfer had also managed to taste the raw fruit, since in a botanical treatise he described the Oriental persimmon as "of a translucent flesh, reddish, soft and somewhat pulpy, edible, very pleasantly honey-like in flavor."

Several of the many varieties developed by the Japanese were brought to the United States late in the nineteenth century, and California now produces a modest amount—some 2,000 tons annually, as compared with 450,000 tons in Japan—as a specialty fruit. The Oriental persimmon is also grown in many yards of California and the South; the tree has a pleasantly open shape and is especially picturesque in the fall, when the fist-sized, orange-red fruit hang among its bare, dark boughs. Japanese production is now dominated by several nonastringent cultivars, notably the Fuyu, which can be eaten hard, like an apple. More commonly seen in this country are the varieties Hachiya and Tanenashi, which are much larger than their American cousins, but like them remain astringent until the "water-balloon stage," when the insides have practically liquefied.

The Oriental persimmon hasn't lived up to the expectations of its early champions in this country. It had been planted here as early as 1828 and was introduced by the new U.S. Department of Agriculture (USDA) in 1863. The department's official agricultural explorers, who were also responsible for establishing durum wheat and date palms in North America, were impressed by the persimmon's prominence in China and Japan and believed that it could be an important addition to our fruit basket. But it has never really caught on. One reason may be the relative characterlessness of the Oriental persimmon. It has a sort of generically fruity flavor, plenty sweet—it's quite high in sugar and a good source of vitamins A and C—but otherwise a little insipid. Kaempfer was right on the mark in likening it to honey, which is a useful ingredient but of limited interest on its own.

Of course, what I call characterlessness might also be called delicacy. Jane Grigson has recently quoted a wonderful appreciation of the Japanese persimmon written in 1931 by Junichirō Tanizaki, who, until a journey to the western countryside of Japan, had never eaten the naturally ripe fruit: "A large, conical persimmon with a pointed bottom, it had ripened to a deep, translucent red, and though swollen like a rubber bag, it was as beautiful as jade when held up to the light." Its insides were a "semiliquid sweet as nectar," of "penetrating coolness." "I filled my mouth with the Yoshino autumn."

The American palate may simply be less responsive to such subtle qualities. Raymond Sokolov, who hunted down the native American persimmon in southern Indiana, pronounced it much superior in flavor to the Japanese, "powerfully fragrant," reminiscent of dates. But it's also seedy and the size of a walnut. With the current interest in novel fruits and vegetables, maybe plant breeders will come up with a good hybrid, a fruit whose amplitude of flavor matches its girth.

Surely another strike against the persimmon was its persistent astringency. Early on, the USDA recognized the need for some way of making the Oriental varieties edible before they became what one agricultural explorer, David Fairchild, called "mushy and mucilaginous": "for, until the persimmon can be pared and eaten without a spoon it will probably never hold the position it deserves in our estimation." And the fruit could only be shipped to market while it was firm and therefore inedible, a fact that many consumers probably learned the hard way. It turned out that there are indeed ways of removing the astringency from firm persimmons, and USDA scientists figured out how they work. To no avail: the growers were probably reluctant to invest in special equipment for a fruit little in demand, and tongue-furred consumers disinclined to give the fruit another chance.

So the Oriental persimmon was a commercial bust in the U.S. Still, every fall I see the handsome fruit dangling in front yards, sometimes uneaten. And I was intrigued by the problem. So I tried to find a way for the individual cook—or lover of fresh fruit—to remove the astringency from persimmons before they've all but dissolved. The advantages would be several: the fruit could be made edible when desired (left to themselves, persimmons can take weeks to soften); they could be prepared in new ways; and they would be somewhat more nutritious (vitamin C is lost as the fruit liquefies). Some cookbooks claim that freezing persimmons will remove their astringency, which is true; what they generally don't mention is that this process takes anywhere from 10 to 90 days. The result, of course, is also pretty mushy. Well, as is evident from all this buildup, I did find a simple, quick way to unpucker the persimmon.

Judging by the variety of folk practices that agricultural explorer F. A. McClure described in 1926, the idea of treating firm persimmons to make them edible goes back centuries. McClure saw four methods of "artificial ripening" used in and around the southern Chinese city of Canton. In city markets, the fruits were immersed in a mixture of water and lime (calcium oxide or hydroxide) for two days to a week or more. Said McClure, "the flesh of water persimmons is firm, slightly juicy to mellow, depending on the stage of ripeness, and mildly sweet." Firm and not astringent! The "smothering" method involved putting the fruit in a covered earthenware jar along with a burning stick of incense. It took a day or two. In the villages, persimmons were placed in jars, surrounded with fresh banyan leaves, and covered for several days. And finally: "The village boys sometimes ripen fruits for their own consumption by burying them in the mud for a few days!"

Notice that these methods for removing astringency have something in common: they all deprive the persimmons of air for a day or more. So too did a Japanese method that had already come to the attention of USDA scientists. David Fairchild had asked a traveler named C. L. Watrous to look into persimmon processing, and Watrous reported back in 1905 on his investigations in Yokohama.

> It appears that they have experimented extensively for many years in this work and have thus far been thoroughly successful in only one way; that is, to take casks in which their beer, called sake, has been stored and have the fruit put in the casks as soon as they have been emptied. The head of the cask must be immediately returned to its

place and the package made air-tight. So treated, if the sake be of very pure quality and not adulterated with alcohol, the fruit, in 5 or 8 or 15 days, according as the weather may be quite warm or less so, may be removed from the package in a firm, sound condition, ready to be shipped long distances, but with the astringency all gone and the flavor fine. They have tried many other ways to cure the kaki but nothing has succeeded except the sake casks, used as above described.

Fairchild sent a copy of Watrous's report to George C. Roeding, a grower in Fresno, California, and in November 1905 Roeding replied with the results of his experiment.

I secured a sake tub from which the liquor had just been emptied and corked it up tight for 11 days, and opened it this morning. It is really astonishing to see how completely the bitterness has left the persimmons, although they are just as hard as the day they were put in.

USDA chemist H. C. Gore then set about to investigate the Japanese treatment, and published his findings in 1911. He found that the secret of the sake barrel was simply its tight seal. First, he confirmed that persimmons would lose their astringency if they were placed in an airtight container with a piece of alcohol-soaked blotting paper. However, some of the fruits so treated became somewhat soft and therefore unfit for shipping. Having read that depriving bananas of oxygen prevented their softening, Gore than tried holding persimmons in containers filled with carbon dioxide alone—no alcohol. After several days, they were nonastringent and still firm. Carbon dioxide—or the lack of oxygen—was therefore sufficient to process persimmons, and it was the oxygen-poor, carbon-dioxide-rich atmosphere produced in the barrel by the fruit themselves that accounted for the success of the Japanese method.

Nothing much ever came of Gore's discovery in this country, where demand apparently has never justified the added expense of processing, or in Japan, where nowadays persimmons are sprayed with an alcohol solution and sealed in plastic-lined cartons for processing during shipment. However, the Japanese have devoted considerable research to determining exactly how the astringency of persimmons is generated and modified; and the Israelis, relatively recent persimmon producers, have adopted and refined the more sophisticated carbon-dioxide treatment. Their work helped me devise a convenient kitchen version of the sake barrel and the mud bath.

Persimmons are astringent because they contain large amounts of *tannins*, a loosely defined group of phenolic chemicals that have in common the ability to bind protein molecules together. It is this property that makes the tannins useful in consolidating the structure of animal hides, or "tanning" them, and that gave them their common name. The Japanese put the otherwise obnoxious persimmon tannins to good use when they clarify sake by adding the juice of unripe persimmons, which precipitates any suspended protein. Teas, red wines, and other astringent foods create a dry, puckery sensation because their tannins crosslink the proteins on the surface of our tongue and palate and in our saliva, which causes the surfaces to constrict and their lubrication to fail. A number of other fruits, including peaches, bananas, and dates, are astringent until they're ripe; this presumably discourages animals from eating them until the seeds are mature. When tannins are present in large quantities, as they are in hard persimmons, this puckeriness is carried to the furry, tormenting extreme that Smith and Strachey described.

As Burton J. Howard of the USDA documented in 1906, the tannins in persimmons are localized in special storage cells, which in Japanese varieties are cigar-shaped and quite large, as much as a millimeter long. (Similar cells are found in the skin and core of bananas and in the flesh of peaches.) You can see these storage sites if you set aside a small amount of ripe pulp and add a pinch of baking soda; in a few hours hundreds of little black rods will appear at the surface, where the tannins have been oxidized and bound to each other in large, light-absorbing complexes. Howard also noted that the disposition of tannins in these cells changes as the fruit loses its astringency. The storage cells initially look much like other cells, and if placed in water will absorb water, swell, and burst. In the ripe, nonastringent fruit, the tannin cells refract light more strongly and don't absorb water. This indicates that the tannins are no longer dissolved in the cells' fluids, but have been bonded into a dense, inert mass. So the reduction in astringency during ripening isn't a matter of the tannins disappearing, but of their being sequestered into unreactive little pellets.

A prescient guess as to how the tannins are defused was made in the 1930s by several Japanese scientists, who found that the levels of a chemical called acetaldehyde were much higher in ripe or processed fruits than in green fruits. They hypothesized that the acetaldehyde somehow reacts with the tannins to form the insoluble, nonastringent masses that Howard saw under the microscope. Given the multitude of biochemical changes that occur during fruit ripening, this sounds like a very simplistic view, but it now appears to be correct. A num-

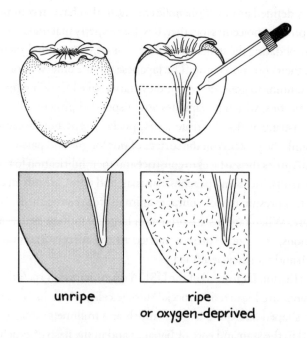

unripe   **ripe**
or oxygen-deprived

The astringent tannins in a persimmon can be revealed to the eye by applying an iron solution to a cut surface. The tannins and iron react to form a black complex. If the persimmon is unripe, tannins are liberated by the knife and spread all over the cut surface. If the persimmon is ripe or has been sufficiently deprived of oxygen, the tannins are confined to scattered storage cells, and can no longer attack the tongue.

ber of Japanese laboratories have shown that extracts of soluble persimmon tannins can be induced to gel—that is, to form a semisolid mass similar to the ones Howard observed in nonastringent tannin cells—by the addition of acetaldehyde, but not alcohol (which also accumulates during the loss of astringency). Another experiment demonstrated that even after boiling, which halts all vital activities in the fruit, an astringent persimmon could still be rendered nonastringent by the addition of acetaldehyde. Still another experiment showed that chemical agents that bind to acetaldehyde inhibit the reduction of astringency in persimmons. So acetaldehyde probably does tame the persimmon tannins.

How does it work? One current guess is that the reaction between acetaldehyde and tannins is similar to the reaction between their respective chemical relatives formaldehyde and phenol, which generates the polymeric structure known as bakelite plastic. The acetaldehyde might act like a kind of glue, bonding the tannin molecules to each other and thereby preventing them from binding to our tongues. And how could this be facilitated by all the treatments that deprive the persimmon of air? It's well known that when plants are forced to do without oxygen for some time, they shift to a pathway of energy production that generates alcohol and acetaldehyde as waste products instead of water and carbon dioxide. An Israeli study has shown that persimmons convert the carbon dioxide in the processing chamber into malate, which is a precursor of acetaldehyde. So the chain of events probably goes like this. When the persimmon is enclosed or immersed, it uses up the remaining oxygen and produces carbon dioxide, which accumulates in and around it. The lack of oxygen then forces the fruit to shift to its acetaldehyde-forming metabolism. The abundance of carbon dioxide helps the fruit make plenty of acetaldehyde. And the acetaldehyde defangs the tannins.

If this explanation is correct, then the presence of alcohol in the traditional Japanese sake cask does make at least a minor contribution to the reduction of astringency. Many fruits, including persimmons, respond to different sorts of stress by producing ethylene gas, which is the plant hormone that stimulates ripening. Alcohol induces the stress response in persimmons. The ethylene they produce in turn induces an increased output of carbon dioxide from the fruit; and the buildup of carbon dioxide in an enclosed cask increases the production of acetaldehyde. The main problem with alcohol processing is that, because it induces the production of the ripening hormone, it also speeds the softening of the fruit. That's fine if you want soft nonastringent fruit; not so fine if you want the fruit to be firm and long-keeping. And because an alcohol-air atmosphere doesn't generate as much acetaldehyde as a carbon-dioxide atmosphere, alcohol processing takes longer.

It may seem as though we've strayed pretty far from the kitchen. Not many of us have domestic carbon-dioxide service, and the alcohol treatment doesn't sound like much of an advance on storing the persimmon in a bag with an ethylene-producing apple or banana to accelerate ripening. But things took a turn toward home in 1986, when Edna Pesis and colleagues at the Volcani Center, Bet Dagan, Israel, published a paper announcing the "Deastringency of persimmon fruits by creating a modified atmosphere in polyethylene bags." These researchers found that when persimmons are simply enclosed in an airtight plastic bag, they generate enough acetaldehyde to eliminate their astringency in four days. Firm, edible fruit in four days, and no need for tanks of carbon dioxide; in fact, the authors reported that the vacuum-packed fruits retain their firmness better than those treated with carbon dioxide. Maybe, I thought, I could get persimmons to create their own unpuckering atmosphere by putting them in a common plastic bag and squeezing the air out of it.

The initial experiments were discouraging. First I tried the thin polyethylene bags that supermarkets provide among the produce bins, and for comparison a sheet of Saran Wrap, which somehow feels more substantial. I wrapped up individual Hachiya persimmons, squeezed the air out, held the swaddling in place with a rubber band, and left them on the kitchen counter. Four days later, both fruits furred my tongue. I then reread Pesis et al. and noticed that their plastic bags were 3.2 mils (0.0032 inch) thick, many times thicker than the flimsy produce bags and a little bit thicker than the thickest freezer storage bags I could find, which were 2.75 mils. I tried one of the freezer bags and, for comparison, two layers of Saran Wrap. Four days at room temperature: awrie again.

Though it was hard to believe, I guessed that the small amount of oxygen left in these wrappings must be interfering with the generation of sufficient quantities of acetaldehyde. Vacuum pumps are not a common household item either, so I reconsidered the possibility of generating carbon dioxide in the kitchen. Of course! We leaven cakes, muffins, and biscuits with the carbon dioxide produced when baking soda reacts with acid. So I took a plastic canister for a roll of 35-millimeter photographic film, poked a hole in the cap, filled the canister with baking soda and cream of tartar, added water and quickly capped the canister, and sealed it in the plastic bag with a hard persimmon. A little messy, sure (the carbon dioxide bomb foams for a while), but ingenious. Also a failure.

At this point I went back to basics. Maybe even my thick plastic bags were too porous; maybe Hachiya persimmons are just very slow metabolizers compared to the Israeli cultivar Triumph, and so don't use up oxygen or put out acetaldehyde at the same rate. I studied up on plastic wraps and found something quite surprising: polyethylene is considered to be a poor gas barrier. Polyvinylidene chloride (PVDC), the generic name for Saran Wrap, is some 350 times less permeable to oxygen and carbon dioxide than low-density polyethylene; and each is 3 times more permeable to carbon dioxide than to oxygen. So I could be losing significant amounts of carbon dioxide from the bags. By calling the consumer information number listed on the package, I found out that Saran Wrap is 0.5 mils thick. Maybe I needed to use several layers of it.

Looking into comparative respiratory rates also turned up valuable information. I couldn't find figures for the Triumph variety; but I did discover that, like apples and pears, Hachiya persimmons are among the moderate respirers. Least active are citrus fruits; ten to twelve times speedier than them are strawberries and raspberries. Interestingly, if you raise the temperature from 68°F to 97°F (from 20°C to 36°C), the metabolic rate of the Hachiya persimmon more than doubles. And elevated temperature is the key to another Japanese method for removing astringency. In a 1971 review of the subject, Saburo Ito described the warm-water treatment: "The traditional method of removing the astringency from persimmon fruits consists of dipping in warm water at 40°C [104°F] and storing for 15–24 hours before use. The product is not of very high quality."

Submerging persimmons in warm water would presumably do two useful things: the water would limit their oxygen supply, thereby causing them to generate acetaldehyde, and the temperature would speed up the chain of events considerably. This may have been a modification of the Chinese lime-water treatment, which took several days. In any case, H. C. Gore at the USDA had experimented with various liquids and found that the thin persimmon skin couldn't prevent the fruit from either bloating or losing juice, depending on the concentration of dissolved material in the liquid. This may be why Ito found the warm-water treatment wanting.

But the idea of eliminating the persimmon's astringency in a day or less was tempting! I decided to try combining the Japanese temperature with the Israeli bag in a warm, dry hybrid treatment. I wrapped the persimmons individually in three layers of Saran Wrap and put them in our gas oven, whose pilot light keeps the interior just at 104°F (40°C). The high temperature, I reasoned, would cause the fruits to use up their oxygen and generate carbon dioxide rapidly, and rapidly convert some of the carbon dioxide to acetaldehyde. I trusted that the three layers of wrap would be effective at preventing outside oxygen from getting in, and inside carbon dioxide from getting out.

This time it worked! After 24 hours in the oven, the persimmons were as firm as before, but their astringency had disappeared. At first, the effect was startling. The texture reminded me of a peach. Not surprisingly, the flavor was stronger than that of the soft-ripe fruits. These oven-treated persimmons had been working very hard and were closely pent up, so all the biochemical by-products of their efforts remained concentrated in the flesh. I would describe the flavor as somewhat alcoholic and strong in the way that slightly overripe fruit can be—perhaps another reason for Ito's low opinion of the warm-water treatment. Those who find the Oriental persimmon rather characterless, however, may find the increased intensity of flavor an improvement.

Having hit on a technique that rapidly eliminates the astringency of Oriental persimmons, I tried a number of variations to find out what materials and times I could get by with. Polyethylene bags of the thin produce variety failed to produce edible fruits even after 72 hours in the oven, but the thick freezer variety succeeded in a little less than 48 hours. A single layer of Saran Wrap did work, but took about 36 hours, while three layers could actually finish the job in 18. By contrast, the same three layers at room temperature had made no detectable difference even after five days. Clearly the process of reducing astringency is tremendously accelerated at the higher temperature, and at that higher temperature there's some leeway in the airtightness of the wrap used.

Since some people may object to the stronger flavor of the oven-unpuckered persimmon, I also tried to find out whether the period of heating could be reduced, and thereby the concentration of alcohol and other volatiles as well. Sure enough, a 12-hour oven treatment followed by 12 hours at room temperature resulted in nonastringent and relatively mild fruit. They reminded my wife of papaya, while to me they were not as perfumed as that—more in the neighborhood of a toned-down mango.

Before I reduce all these experiments to a single procedure, it's necessary to hedge on some of the details. Most of my test persimmons were bought toward the end of the season in California, from the middle to the end of November. They were therefore closer to being naturally ripe than early-season fruit, and responded more rapidly to the unpuckering treatment than some of the early fruit I tried the following year. Conversely, some of the fruit I bought in December developed soft spots when held overnight in the oven. Also, different varieties of persimmon respond differently to carbon dioxide. So you may have to do a little experimenting yourself to find the best treatment for your particular lot. If they're early fruit, give them a few more hours in the oven; if late fruit, a few hours less. Unwrap one fruit and take a test slice; if it's still astringent, re-wrap it and keep the fruit in the oven awhile longer.

Given these disclaimers, here is the basic procedure for unpuckering Oriental persimmons. Wrap the fruit individually in three tight layers of Saran Wrap. Warm them up to about 100°F (38°C) in an old-style gas oven with a pilot light, in a preheated electric oven kept warm by leaving the light on, or in a stockpot full of warm water that you reheat periodically. After about 12 hours, or longer if you prefer a stronger flavor, remove the fruit and let them stand at room temperature for another 12 hours. Then unwrap them, and use immediately or as needed. Treat the firm, nonastringent persimmons as you would a ripe papaya or mango: cut in half and spoon out the firm flesh; cut into wedges and nibble the flesh from the peel; peel and slice, sprinkling with lemon or lime juice; or add to fruit salad.

Can this combination of wrapping and heating also remove the astringency from American persimmons? I couldn't answer that question myself because I couldn't get my hands on any native fruit. But the fall of 1988 brought a pre-liminary answer from southern Indiana, a region where the American persimmon is fully appreciated. At Indiana University, a number of students in Professor Martha Crouch's class on plant biology tested my method. They obtained the best results when the fruit were kept at 70°F or 80°F (21°C or 27°C) for 4 or 5 days, conditions that also caused the fruit to soften. That's actually convenient, since the easiest way to remove the many seeds from the American persimmon is to push the soft pulp through a strainer. So American persimmons aren't as easily unpuckered as the Oriental varieties. It's possible, though, that a little tin-kering could shorten the treatment. If you're interested and have access to some experimental material, try a one-day warm period followed by a day or two at room temperature. And let me know what you find!

Up to this point we've been concerned with tannins as molecules that have an undesirable influence on the flavor—indeed the edibility—of persimmons. It turns out that they can also affect the fruit's texture, sometimes for ill and sometimes for good.

The first clue I had that tannins might influence texture came when I heated a little persimmon pulp in a pan, just to see how it would behave. It behaved miserably. Its flavor flattened out and became slightly astringent; it also got very thick and grainy. Not very nice, and a good argument against cooking this fruit. I didn't make any connection between tannins and the extreme thickening until I read a newspaper recipe for persimmon pudding written by Marion Cunningham. She called for a large amount of baking soda, 2 teaspoons, to be added to 1 cup of persimmon puree, which is then set aside awhile. There followed a parenthetical note: "the persimmon mixture will become quite stiff." That sounded odd, so I tried adding a pinch of baking soda to 2 or 3 tablespoons of puree. Sure enough, in less than a minute it had gelled completely! Marion Cunningham made nothing further of this effect, which was incidental to the pudding recipe as a whole. But it seemed to me that this might turn out to be a useful property, provided one could find alternatives to baking soda, which of course generates a soapy flavor (in the pudding recipe it's later balanced with lemon juice).

I tracked the origins of the baking-soda gambit back to the USDA, where it was thought to reduce astringency. The *Farmers' Bulletin* of October 12, 1915 (number 685), is devoted to a treatise on "The Native Persimmon" by W. F. Fletcher, and ends with a number of recipes for persimmon bread, crumpets, griddlecakes, pudding, preserves, leather, ice cream, and fudge. Fletcher introduces them with this general comment:

> Since heat makes the astringency of the persimmon more apparent, it is always well to add one-half teaspoonful of baking soda (bicarbonate of soda) to each cupful of persimmon pulp in all recipes where the fruit is subjected to heat. Although it has been proved by experiment that the soda may be omitted if the fruit is entirely free from astringency, it is better to use it until one is sure of the quality of the persimmon pulp.

This advice made it into the *Journal of Home Economics* the next month, and eventually became part of received wisdom on the subject. When Fletcher's bulletin was revised in 1942, the antiastringent effects of baking soda were admitted to be minor, and the recommended dose was reduced to ¼ teaspoon per cup pulp.

Does baking soda indeed reduce the astringency of persimmons? In my experience with the Hachiya variety, the answer is: marginally. However, that it has any effect at all is interesting. I found that the addition of enough baking soda to gel the pulp raises the pH to a neutral 7, from the original 5.5 or so (persimmons are not very acid, which I think contributes to their blandness). The nature of the tannins themselves is unlikely to be changed over so short a range, so I guessed that instead the baking soda induces a certain fraction of the tannins to bind with other molecules in the fruit before it can bind to our tongue. Hence the pulp would gel and become less astringent at the same time.

One peculiar side effect of the baking-soda treatment was suggestive of how it might work. Several hours after the baking soda is added and the pulp gels, the surface of the pulp develops little elongated black grains. These are quite obviously the tannin cells; that they turn black only in the surface layer indicates that they're being oxidized upon exposure to the air. This in turn suggests that baking soda might damage the membranes of the tannin cells, thereby giving oxygen access to their contents. It seems plausible that the very same damage could allow still astringent tannins to leak out of the cells, where they would bind with proteins and other constituents of the pulp, thereby gelling the pulp and preventing any subsequent binding to the tongue. The more violent action of heat, on the other hand, might liberate such numbers of tannin molecules that the pulp can't bind them all, so the pulp thickens but gets *more* astringent, not less.

This guess is supported by the results of two experiments in which I made the pulp gel with two very different means of damaging the fruit's membranes. Cell membranes are composed largely of compounds similar to soaps, so that soaps and detergents will disrupt them (soaps are excellent antiseptics for this reason). Sure enough, a mere drop of dishwashing detergent stirred into a few tablespoons of persimmon pulp gelled it in a matter of seconds, without any major change in its pH. Not an alternative that offers many culinary possibilities, but a useful piece of evidence. Cells can also be broken up by simple mechanical force, and my second experiment was simply to whip the pulp in a blender at very high speed, a treatment that liquefies most materials. By contrast, the persimmon puree got so thick that it poured like a rich milkshake.

So I think we have an explanation for the gelling of persimmon pulp: it occurs when the tannin cells are damaged and leak tannins into the pulp, which they bind together. And we have a new quirk of persimmons to play with! Neither heating nor the bicarbonate or detergent treatments are of much practical use. But the high-speed blending has possibilities. For example, I've found that the addition of a couple of tablespoons of lemon or lime juice to a cup or so of ripe, soft persimmon pulp not only balances the fruit's flavor, it actually firms up the texture even more during the blending. Because the blending also aerates, the resulting puree reminded me of a fruit mousse. Denser, yes, and certainly not as rich, since there's no whipped cream in it. But there's a lot to be said for less-rich alternatives to traditional recipes, and there could hardly be a simpler one than this. Forget the whipped cream and the gelatin; just scoop the persimmon pulp into the blender, adjust the flavor, and whip. The relative characterlessness of the Oriental persimmon would even be an advantage if you wanted to incorporate other fruits, either as part of the puree or as pieces folded in afterwards. (There aren't many other fruits around when persimmons are ripe, but persimmon pulp freezes well and can be reserved until the following spring and summer.)

I'm sure others will come up with more elaborate and interesting recipes that exploit the thickening of persimmon pulp, and thereby lend further assistance to owners of prolific trees. However, some words of caution are in order. I mentioned that the influence of tannins on persimmon texture is sometimes for ill, and this can be quite literally true. The Chinese have been aware of the problem at least since 1368, when Chia Ming wrote that "dried persimmons must not be eaten with turtle, for that becomes indigestible and causes blockage." In North America, the Gulf Coast Indians apparently turned the "blocking" powers of the persimmon to medicinal use—astringents have long been used in medicine to stop bleeding, diarrhea, and certain secretions—but the French traveler Le Page du Pratz, writing in 1758, noted the need for great care.

> When it is quite ripe the natives make bread [a cake of dried pulp] of it, which keeps from one year to the next; and the great virtue of this bread, more so than of the fruit, is this, that there is neither diarrhea nor dysentery that it will not stop; therefore it ought to be used only with caution and after purging.

In fact, persimmons are best known in modern medicine as one of the major causes of the *bezoar*, an undigested mass that remains in the stomach and can damage it as well as obstruct the passage of food into the intestine. The word comes from the Persian for "protection against poison"; from ancient times through the eighteenth century, such masses from animal stomachs were thought to be near-magical antidotes. A bezoar stone set in gold is recorded as having been among Queen Elizabeth's crown jewels.

In humans, these obstructive objects are divided into two categories: *tri-*

chobezoars are masses of hair, and *phytobezoars* are masses of plant material. Of the phytobezoars, so many are caused by persimmons that the term *diospyrobezoar* was once proposed as a useful addition to the medical lexicon. The occasion was a classic treatise written in 1938 by a young instructor of surgery and a senior colleague at the Tulane University School of Medicine. The young instructor, later to win wide renown as a cardiovascular surgeon, was Michael DeBakey. DeBakey and Alton Ochsner found that of the 126 reported cases of phytobezoar known to them, 92 (or 73%) were caused by persimmons. All but one of the persimmon bezoars were reported from the United States or Japan. The authors described the typical case history from their own experience:

> The patient usually recounts that his complaints began soon after engorging himself upon persimmons. Not infrequently he was hunting, fishing, or walking through the woods or field and found a persimmon tree with its succulent fruit, which he devoured to appease his hunger. Following this a liberal quantity of water was imbibed to satisfy an insatiable thirst. Within a few hours to a few days following this refreshing but insalubrious repast, characteristically an acute gastrointestinal disturbance of varying intensity develops.

In recent years, it has been found that most people who develop phytobezoars suffer from reduced stomach motility, often as a result of previous surgery, which allows the plant material to congeal undisturbed. Surgery is usually necessary to remove bezoars, though some use is made of enzymes that can break down the cellulose in plant fiber or the protein in hair.

When physicians got around to analyzing the unusual effectiveness of the persimmon in forming bezoars, once again the key turned out to be the tannins. It seems that just as a blender and lemon juice can thicken the pulp, so chewing and gastric acid can, in an otherwise empty and inactive stomach, liberate tannins and encourage them to consolidate the pulp, seeds, and skin. When other foods are eaten at the same time and the stomach is capable of normal peristalsis, the persimmon pulp is diluted and usually can't settle into a monolithic mass.

Bezoars are a relatively rare malady, although a recent report in the *British Journal of Surgery* described an "epidemic" in Israel of seventy-six persimmon bezoars in 1984 alone, a result of the fruit's growing popularity in that country. It's probably a good idea not to engorge yourself on persimmons, whether fully ripe, oven-unpuckered, or pureed, lest the repast prove insalubrious.

SUMMARY: PERSIMMONS

The astringency of persimmons is caused by the natural presence of tannins. As the fruit softens in the late stages of ripening, the tannins are bound up in non-astringent masses, and the fruit becomes edible. An atmosphere rich in carbon dioxide can bring about this reduction in astringency long before the fruit softens.

The Hachiya variety of Japanese persimmon can be made nonastringent by wrapping it tightly in three layers of Saran Wrap (polyethylene will not work), leaving it in a warm (100°F, or 38°C) place for 12 or more hours, and then returning it to room temperature for 12 hours. A gas oven with a pilot light works well, as does a preheated electric oven kept warm with a light bulb, or a large stockpot filled with warm water (check the temperature occasionally and gently reheat if necessary). The longer the persimmon is warmed, the stronger the flavor it will have. The optimal treatment will depend on the variety of persimmon, its maturity, and your own taste.

Use firm, nonastringent persimmons as you would a ripe papaya or mango: cut in half and spoon out the firm flesh; cut into wedges and nibble the flesh from the peel; peel and slice, sprinkling with lemon or lime juice; or add to fruit salad.

Astringency can also be removed from persimmons by freezing them. This procedure takes anywhere from 10 to 90 days, and the resulting flesh is mushy.

Persimmon pulp will thicken considerably when whipped in a blender at high speed (a handheld blender may not be efficient enough). You can make a pleasant alternative to a fruit mousse in a matter of seconds simply by blending persimmon pulp with some lemon or lime juice (1 or 2 tablespoons per cup pulp). Small amounts of other fruits can be added in the blender or folded afterwards into the thickened puree.

When consumed in large quantities on an empty stomach, persimmons can form an indigestible, troublesome mass. It's best not to gorge on them.

Fruit Ices, Cold and Calculated

The diverse multitude of dishes that we call desserts can be sorted into a kind of spectrum. At one end are the elaborate pastries, creams, and chocolate confections that bring a meal to a spectacular, rich climax. At the other end are dishes that provide a pleasant contrast to the meal's elaborations. Prominent among the latter are the plain ices made from fresh fruit, sugar, and water. They blend the unadorned flavor of intense life with a startling, lifeless cold. The combination refreshes: it brings us back to first things, back to earth.

With so little to the ices, you might think that recipes could hardly be simpler or more adaptable to a variety of fruits. That was certainly my assumption when I first contemplated the bounty of our orange, lemon, and pear trees shortly after our move to California. During the first summer I bought one of the new ice cream makers that positively encourage improvisation; they replace the mess of salt and ice with a sealed metal sleeve of coolant, which you prechill in the freezer. As I searched for fruit ice recipes, I was surprised to find that few cookbooks offer more than two or three. General guidelines are rare. And I was especially frustrated by the sparse information about serving. While some ices turned out to be scoopable after a day or two in the freezer, more often they were as inviting as a freezer wall badly in need of defrosting. The recipes gave no hint of this transformation nor of the need for partial thawing in order to undo it. Many a recipe simply ends with the mantra "Freeze in the ice cream maker according to the manufacturer's instructions." Figure the rest out yourself.

A peculiar counterpoint in ice recipes to this vagueness about the freezing process is an intricate, arcane numerology. The texture of an ice depends on its sugar concentration, which can be expressed in several ways. French cook-books often use degrees Baumé or degrees Brix, both in comfortable integers, or specific gravity (density), down to the fourth decimal place. It all sounds quite precise and scientific. Compare recipes, however, and you begin to wonder. Madeleine Kamman describes French restaurant practice: Cook up a concen-trated sugar syrup, and then add enough of it to your fruit mixture to raise the reading on a saccharometer (or hydrometer, a calibrated glass tube that floats in a solution and indicates its density) to between 17 and 18 degrees Baumé, which is a specific gravity between 1.1335 and 1.1425. (This gives a scoopable sorbet.) But the *Larousse Gastronomique* specifies very different gravities: 1.1513 for fruit purees, 1.1697 for fruit juices.

These were two of the few general recipes I came across, and they didn't ex-actly inspire me to rush into the kitchen. (First catch your saccharometer!) Bet-ting that they would take a less Cartesian approach, I consulted the Italians, who introduced ices to the French in the first place. Italian cookbooks limit the num-bers to cups and tablespoons, and their ice recipes to one or two. My desultory search turned up a single general formula, and that was in Sylvia Thompson's recent book *Feasts and Friends*; she attributes it to Tina, the cook at a Tuscan villa she once stayed in. Tina did without a hydrometer, but she probably re-sorted to pencil and paper. For a given volume of fruit, you add an equal volume of sugar syrup—uncooked—calculated as follows: Divide the volume of fruit by 2.5 to get the volume of sugar, and double that for the volume of water. Then for every quart of the fruit-syrup mix, add 7 tablespoons orange juice and 7 ta-blespoons lemon juice, unless the fruit is "blonde," in which case you add 14 ta-blespoons lemon juice. Unlike the French cooks, Tina didn't vary the amount of added sugar according to a fruit's native sweetness. The resulting ices are much less sweet than the French versions, and once thoroughly frozen, must be thawed before they can be scooped.

The simplest ices I've come across are in Stephen Schmidt's *Master Recipes*. No fine adjustments or even syrups here. Schmidt calls for the same amount of sugar and lemon juice to be added to everything from grapefruit to cherries; the only exceptions are lemons, limes, and cranberries. The results are generally about as sweet and soft as the French versions.

This range of approaches, from the finicky to the magisterial, left me befud-dled and provoked. Is it really best to use a hydrometer and adjust the sweet-ening to the fruit, or will a set quantity of sugar take care of all but the sourest?

Why use water to make a syrup, when water simply dilutes the flavor of the fruit, a flavor already diminished by the cold temperature? If you make a syrup, why bother to cook it when you're only going to cool it down immediately and then freeze it? Is there a simple way for the home cook to improvise with any fruit that happens to be available, and come up with an ice of predictable character? How can we predict from a recipe's proportions the texture they're likely to produce? No longer was it a mere matter of oranges and lemons and pears. I was now intent on getting to the very bottom of the dish; I hungered for a Comprehensive Theory of Ices. I went after it with paper, pencil, hydrometer, thermometer, tables of chemical and biochemical data, and a computer. And, of course, a few dozen ices. Here are the fruits of these labors.

Several preliminary questions were best answered by a glance into the past. Fruit ices as we now know them turn out to be a little over three hundred years old. The Italian word *sorbetto*, the French *sorbet*, and the English *sherbet*—and *syrup*—all derive from the Arabic *sharba*, meaning "a drink." Early European visitors to Constantinople frequently described the Turkish *sherbet*, a sweet beverage cooled with snow or ice. The Italians began cooling wine and other drinks in this manner sometime in the sixteenth century. Not long thereafter Italian physicians started to experiment with the use of saltpeter and common salt to cool liquids. And around 1600, by immersing a container of water in a mixture of salts and snow, they succeeded in making artificial ice. Fully frozen versions of the sherbet soon caught on, and spread from Italy to France, from France to England. Much was made of their decorative possibilities; they were usually frozen in large, shaped molds, and sometimes contained whole fruit or flowers. It took a few decades for cooks to learn that by stirring the liquid occasionally as it freezes, they could soften and lighten the texture of an ice. The best were frozen *en neige*, as the French phrased it: into snow.

This bare historical overview was enough to answer one of my questions: Water is an ingredient in many ices because it always has been. The first ices were mainly water to which fruit, spices, or flowers were added for flavor. Whether this kind of mixture actually tastes better than the undiluted fruit is another question. I had a preconceived answer, and was surprised when I got around to making the direct comparison.

A little more history also gave me some idea as to why many recipes prescribe a preliminary simmering of water and sugar for several minutes: some specify five minutes, or even four, which is cutting it pretty fine. The whole business struck me as a little crazy. The amount of sugar involved easily dissolves in water straight out of the tap, given the same four or five minutes of occasional stirring. So why not simply combine water, sugar, and fruit in a single bowl, rather than use an extra pan and extra energy to heat something that must be cooled immediately, and wait for half an hour for the syrup to return to room temperature?

It may be that this is simply a case of professional practice badly translated for the home kitchen. Chefs who must make several ices a day would probably want to use a hydrometer and sugar predissolved into a concentrated syrup, a system that allows them to measure and make rapid adjustments in the sugar content of the mix. And concentrated syrups do require heat to dissolve all that sugar within a reasonable time. But the sugar content of an ice mix is not all that high, so there's no reason to follow the same procedure for an occasional single recipe.

What seventeenth-century recipes I was able to get my hands on seldom called for making a separate syrup, to say nothing of cooking one, though they sometimes directed that the fruit be cooked with water and sugar. But I did find a possible clue to the simmering ritual a couple of centuries later, in Thomas Masters's *Ice Book* of 1844. He included a number of recipes for "water ices," which he defined as being made from "the purest water, flavoured by fruit," and which all involved the use of "clarified sugar." Clarified sugar was made by combining equal quantities of sugar and water and boiling for ten minutes together with some beaten egg white, which was then removed and discarded. Evidently the purpose of the boiling was not to dissolve the sugar, or impart any special character to the syrup; it was to remove the impurities found in nineteenth-century sugar. (The congealing egg white would trap any particles that failed to dissolve.) It may be that cooking the syrup is just an outmoded relic of a bygone era, a habit that survives for no reason other than the conservatism of cookbook writers.

Finally, Auguste Escoffier's venerable *Guide culinaire*, which first appeared in 1904, helped me make sense of the varieties of ice made today. Escoffier divided the fruit ices into three classes. First, the *glace* ("ice"), which most resembles the standard American sherbet, but without the sherbet's added milk or cream. The *glace* was quite sweet and served as a dessert, often molded into a decorative shape. The other two styles of ice were less sweet than the *glace* and "barely frozen." The *granité* (from the Italian *granità*, meaning grainy) was little stirred during the freezing, and therefore coarse in texture. The *sorbet* was finer in texture and somewhat sweeter than the *granité*, served between courses in a consistency "almost liquid enough to be drunk."

Times and terminology change. By 1934, in *Ma Cuisine*, Escoffier lamented that "Sadly, since the bad habit of smoking during the meal has been taken up, the cigarette has dethroned the *sorbet*." Today, the *glace* has all but disappeared, and a sorbet can be pretty much anything. But Escoffier's classification still clarifies the possibilities. The granita is now a relatively low-sugar, granular ice made by pouring the mix into a shallow pan in the freezer and stirring it occasionally as it freezes. Then there are two styles of sorbet, both of them made with rapid freezing and frequent stirring so as to produce a fine texture. One style is made with a moderate amount of sugar and is best served fresh out of the maker; it gets very hard in the freezer. The other is made with more sugar, and can be scooped even after thorough freezing.

So much for what people have made of the fruit ice. Now to understand what makes a fruit ice, it's necessary to shift from history to chemistry. The most important characteristic of an ice mix is its sugar content. This is so not because sugar is sweet, but because it lowers the freezing point of water, as does any other substance that dissolves in water. The dissolved "foreign" molecules simply get in the way of water molecules that would otherwise join up with each other to form a solid mass. So the water must be colder, the forces attracting its molecules together yet more dominant over the motions that knock them apart, in order for it to begin to crystallize. (It's by the same principle that antifreeze compounds prevent a car's engine coolant from solidifying on a cold night and—since the freezing point is also the melting point—salt melts ice on winter streets.) For all practical purposes, the identity of the foreign particles— whether whole sugar molecules, or the sodium and chlorine ions into which salt dissociates—is irrelevant. All that matters is the gross number. In most ices, sugar is simply the most populous dissolved substance, and the only really significant one.

There are several ways to express the sugar content of a solution. Rather than resort to the more exotic and indirect ones found in cookbooks, I prefer to use the percentage of sugar by weight in a mix. For example, 10 grams of sugar in 90 grams of water is 10 grams in a total of 100 grams, or a 10% solution by weight. It's the simplest measure, and the one generally used to describe the chemical composition of fruits. It makes the analysis of any given recipe quite straightforward. Leaving aside fruits for the moment, consider a plain sugar syrup. A tablespoon of granulated sugar weighs about 12 grams, a tablespoon of water about 15, a cup of water about 240. One tablespoon of sugar in a cup of water gives about a 5% sugar solution (12 grams of sugar divided by the sum of 12 grams plus 240 grams). You can then look at a table in the *CRC Handbook of Chemistry and Physics*, a compendium of such information, and find that a 5% sucrose solution freezes at 31.5°F (−0.3°C). If you're using fruit puree instead of water, then to determine the freezing point of an ice mix you find out the sugar content of the fruit, add up the total sugar concentration of the mix, and consult the freezing table.

Now the freezing point of an ice mix is important because it largely determines the texture of the ice. The lower the freezing point, the softer the ice will be at a given temperature. To survey the possibilities, I tried making plain sugar-water syrups into "model" ices and testing their consistency. I figured out how much sugar I would need to add to a cup of water in order to get various sugar concentrations, made up the syrups, froze them in my ice cream maker, and sampled them once they had reached the temperature of my freezer, which is 0°F (−18°C). I found that anything below about 25% sugar (6.5 tablespoons sugar per cup water) ended up ice-hard. Between 25% and 35% (10.5 tablespoons per cup water), the models were stiff but increasingly scoopable with a spoon. Beyond 35%, the dish was filled with noticeable amounts of unfrozen syrup, and the frozen portion was mealy and sticky.

This was my first experimental payoff. There's only a narrow range of sugar concentrations in which an ice will be scoopable right from the freezer and still appealing. Below 25% the mass is impregnable, and above 35% it is too soft and syrupy. Sure enough, Madeleine Kamman's recommended specific gravities fall between 31.5% and 33.5%. Commercial sherbet makers, according to Wendell S. Arbuckle's authoritative tome *Ice Cream*, aim for 28% to 32% (they often use additives to soften the texture). The *Larousse* and Stephen Schmidt approach sticky territory, up between 35% and 39%. Granitas, water ices, and moderately sweet sorbets all turn out to be 25% sugar and below; hence their unsuitability for later scooping.

What is it that makes ices scoopable only above 25% sugar? Ices generally freeze somewhere between 25°F and 30°F (−4°C and −1°C), or between 2 and

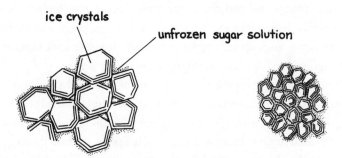

ice crystals

unfrozen sugar solution

If an ice mix contains little sugar, then most of the water freezes into large crystals, and only a small amount of concentrated sugar syrup remains (left). *The texture of the ice is hard and crumbly. If the original mix contains a lot of sugar, then more syrup remains unfrozen and the ice crystals are relatively small* (right). *The fruit ice ends up soft and smooth.*

7 degrees Fahrenheit below the freezing point of pure water. The average home freezer maintains a temperature of between 0°F and 10°F (– 18°C and – 12°C), or far below the freezing point of ices, so you might think that fresh from the freezer, all ices should be hard as a rock. However, only the water in the syrup freezes. As it does, there's less water left in the syrup, so the syrup becomes more and more concentrated. When it reaches around 70% sugar, it will no longer freeze even at 0°F. The more sugar there is in the initial syrup, the sooner it will reach an unfreezable concentration, the more of this permasyrup will remain at freezer temperature, and the softer the sherbet's texture will be. By my figuring, less than 10% of the original water is left unfrozen in a 15% sugar syrup at 0°F, so there's very little lubrication of the ice crystals. Something more than 20% of the water remains from a 30% sugar syrup, and this is apparently about ideal for scooping. But as you exceed this volume of unfrozen liquid, the matrix of ice crystals has an insufficient surface area on which to hold it all. The result is conspicuous, sticky puddles and a mealy texture when you dip a spoon in.

Of course, these experimental sugar syrups are not ice mixes. The main complication introduced by actual fruits is that they usually contain significant quantities of three different sugars: glucose, fructose, and the combined form of the two, sucrose. Table sugar is pure sucrose. Glucose is less soluble in water than sucrose, fructose more soluble. Because their molecules weigh much less, glucose and fructose are much more effective than sucrose, weight for weight, at lowering the freezing point. But at a given freezing point, a mixture of glucose and fructose ends up making harder ices than sucrose does. In short, a mixture of sugars doesn't behave as simply as table sugar alone.

Fortunately, I was able to verify by experiment what the hydrometer method assumes: that we can reasonably account for the effects of the three sugars by treating them all the same. That is, no matter what the distribution of the three sugars, the total sugar content of an ice mix is a good guide to the final texture of the ice. So the all-sucrose model ices do turn out to apply to the real thing. As long as the total percentage by weight of glucose plus fructose plus sucrose is above 30% or so, the ice will be scoopable right from the freezer. I'm not exactly sure why things should work out this way (the viscosity of the unfrozen syrup may be as important for ice texture as the freezing point), but I'm grateful that they do. It makes life much easier.

When I analyzed the sugar content of various ice recipes, I found that they matched well with the behavior of my model ices. Granitas generally fall between 15% and 20% sugar. They turn into a coarse slush, and then crystalline chunks if little stirred, small dry crystals if stirred more attentively. The water ices and moderately sweet sorbets, up around 20% sugar and frozen more rapidly, make a fine slush, then a fine moldable mass, then a fine imitation of cement; they must be warmed for re-serving. (You can make such ices softer by supplementing them with beaten egg whites or gelatin, but that's a different story.) The high-sugar ices exceed 30%, and so can be scooped at will.

Having figured out why different recipes produce such different consistencies, I set about to investigate the role of fruit and the advisability of individualized recipes. To begin with, this was a matter of sweetness. The sweeter a fruit is naturally, the less added sugar it will need to reach the ideal scooping level of 30%. Well, leaving aside such obvious outliers as lemons and bananas, is there really a significant variation in sugar content among common fruits? A few hours in the library gave me the answer. Strawberries, raspberries, and blackberries have a sugar content around 6% by weight. Cherries, apples, pineapples, and grapes are double that and more. So say you're trying to make a scoopable sorbet. Add 7 tablespoons sugar to a cup of strawberry puree and you'll be right around 31%; add the same 7 tablespoons to a cup of cherry puree, and you'll be verging on the syrupy at 35%. Get the cherry right with around 5 tablespoons sugar per cup, and the strawberry will be at a crusty 25%. Even if next-day consistency isn't important, it's evident that one universal proportion of sugar will produce some ices that are much sweeter than others. And acidity, which provides an important balance to sweetness, varies even more, from 0.1% in the pear to 5% and up in the lemon and lime.

There's an important qualification to be made about these figures. They're approximations at best. The sugar content of a given piece of fruit depends on the particular variety, the conditions under which it was grown, the age at which it was picked, the length of time it spent in storage, and its ripeness. Still, we can pretty much count on strawberries being less sweet than cherries, melons less tart than kiwi fruit. Regardless of the large uncertainties involved, I think it's worth trying to tailor ice recipes to the characteristic sweetness and acidity of the fruit.

How can a recipe respect the differences among fruits and still be comprehensive? Professionals often rely on the hydrometer. But the hydrometer has a few disadvantages. It isn't all that easy to find, it's fragile, and it's inconvenient to use unless you cook up a concentrated syrup. A somewhat less effective technique, but an elegantly simple one, is to use the same quantity of sugar for all fruits, and to moderate the variation in sugar content by diluting the fruit purees or juices with some water. For example, Sylvia Thompson's Tuscan recipe for water ices turns strawberries and cherries, which are 7% and 14% sugar respectively, into mixes of 18% and 21%. But this dilution of a fruit's eccentricity in sweetness is purchased with an attendant dilution of its flavor. To me, that seemed a high price to pay.

The obvious alternative was to come up with individual recipes. Since there aren't that many common fruits, and their biochemistry has been studied for decades, I thought I could easily find the relevant numbers and calculate proportions for each fruit. And I did. I'll spare you most of the details. Suffice it to say that I located figures for the total sugar content and acidity of several dozen fruits, and then calculated recipes for the different styles of ice. Ice making is one of the very few culinary operations that come right down to arithmetic. There are only four significant ingredients: the fruit puree or juice, table sugar, water, and lemon juice to boost the acidity. For a given fruit and desired degree of dilution, sugar concentration, acidity, and volume of mix, there's just one combination of these ingredients that will fit. I found the formulas for that combination by dusting off my high school algebra, starting with two simple equations that add up the separate contributions of the ingredients to the sugar content and acidity of the mix, and solving them for the quantities of added sugar, water, and lemon juice.

Just to give you a taste, here are the equations for bringing one cup of undiluted fruit puree to the desired levels of sugar and acid. In these equations

d = the density of the fruit (grams per milliliter)
s = the effective sugar content of the unsweetened fruit (fraction by weight)
S = the final effective sugar content of the mix (fraction by weight)
a = the initial acidity of the fruit (fraction by weight)
A = the final acidity of the mix (fraction by weight).

First, to calculate how many tablespoons of lemon juice to add, we have

$$\text{Tbs lemon juice} = \frac{237 \times d \times [A - a + (a \times S) - (A \times s)]}{[0.78 \times (1 - S)] - (13.88 \times A)} .$$

Now, if we use T to represent the number of tablespoons of lemon juice, then the number of tablespoons of sugar to be added is

$$\text{Tbs sugar} = \frac{\{237 \times d \times [(a \times S) - (A \times s)]\} + \{T \times [(0.78 \times S) - (1.72 \times A)]\}}{12 \times A} .$$

These strings of symbols aren't especially beautiful in themselves. And yet, as they emerged under my pencil from the flotsam of more complicated expressions and crossings out, I felt a mixture of satisfaction and delight: satisfaction at finding the solutions that I knew were buried in the initial equations; delight that the behavior of a food can be described and predicted by a few scratchings of graphite on wood pulp.

And predict they do. All they require is that you choose a fruit, a target sugar concentration, and an acidity. Then you simply plug in the numbers and do the arithmetic. For example, a cantaloupe has an effective sugar concentration of 7%, which means that its puree has a density of about 1.01, and an initial acidity of 0.2%. If we want a scoopable sorbet at 30% sugar and 0.5% acidity, then the equations prescribe 1.6 tablespoons lemon juice and 7.1 tablespoons sugar. Plug these numbers back into the initial equations for sugar content and acidity, and they check.

Arithmetic is distinctly less wonderful than algebra. And I had hundreds of such calculations ahead of me if I wanted to develop and analyze recipes for each fruit. So I ended up giving my personal computer a chance to do something besides process words. I wrote a program in the elementary language BASIC that does two things. First, it generates recipes. If I specify a fruit, a desired dilution, sugar content, acidity, and volume of mix, the program calculates how many cups and tablespoons of fruit, sugar, water, and lemon juice to use. If instead I wish to analyze a recipe, the program will calculate from the proportions specified in the recipe the final sugar content, acidity, and mix volume. This program made it possible for me to make up dozens of ices on paper, get a feeling for the range of proportions required by different fruits, and then come up with recipes tailored to the unique composition of each fruit.

At this point I had a biochemical profile for each fruit and the means of generating recipes from that profile. Now it was time to decide how to achieve the best flavors and textures for the various kinds of ices. These aren't computable matters; they're determined by prejudices, preferences, and judgments. Time for me to declare mine.

First, the matter of acidity. Commercial sherbet makers aim for citric acid to be between 0.35% and 0.5% of the final mix weight. Given the American sweet tooth, my guess is that these figures are on the low side. By comparison, the citrus ice recipes of Marcella Hazan, Carlo Middione, and James Beard average a shade over 1%. When it comes to the acidity of the fruits themselves, there are really two basic classes: low-acid fruits like the pear, grape, papaya, melons, cherry, and peach, with total acid well under 1%; and high-acid fruits like the citrus fruits, small berries, kiwi, and pineapple, with acidities of 1% and up— and up. I did a few experiments in which I changed the acidity of the mix while keeping the sugar content the same, and became convinced of two things. First, any more than about 1 tablespoon of lemon juice per cup fruit gives the mix an unmistakable lemon flavor. This isn't necessarily unpleasant, but it is an alteration of the fruit's own flavor. Second, low-acid fruits seem too tart when their natural acidity is much more than doubled. So I adopted a conveniently simple rule for low-acid fruits: add 1 tablespoon of lemon juice for each cup of mix. The result is usually a final acidity around 0.5%.

It's hárder to generalize for the high-acid fruits. The highest—lemons and limes, at around 5%—definitely need to be diluted with water to make them tolerable. Kiwi, at 3%, and grapefruit, at 2%, are also pretty powerful, and taste better to me when taken down to 1%. The small berries, apricot, and pineapple are already pretty close to 1%, especially after the added sugar in the mix is taken into account, and I find that they don't need any adjustment one way or the other. So: for naturally mild fruits, adjust acidity with lemon juice up to around 0.5%; for naturally tart fruits, dilute acidity with water down to 1%. Moderately tart fruits can be left alone.

This rule highlights an interesting point about the balance between sweetness and acidity in fruits and in ices. The ratio of sugar content to acid content runs from less than 1 for the lemon or lime to 100 for the pear. By comparison, sweet scoopable ices made with low-acid fruits will end up around 60, in the vicinity of natural honeydew and banana, while high-acid ices end up around 30, roughly the normal balance of cantaloupe and cherry. So these confections don't strain the natural balance of sweetness and acidity in fruits, even though their sugar content is generally greater by a factor of two or more.

Then there's the question of making water a major ingredient in the mix, even for fruit whose acidity needs no lowering. I was prejudiced against this tradition for two reasons: it's usually associated with the archaic ritual of cooking a syrup, and it dilutes the flavor of the fruit unnecessarily. However, I soon found that there are two important advantages to the inclusion of water in ice recipes. When I generated sample recipes with and without water, the numbers made obvious a fact to which I'd been oblivious: dilution with water makes a little fruit go a long way. You can make a quart of ice with two cups or less of fruit. Simple economy is probably no mean part of the water ice's continuing appeal.

The second advantage to using water came as a big surprise to me: it often makes the ice taste better! I had assumed that the coldness of an ice would diminish the fruit's flavor to begin with, that water would only diminish it further, and that intensity of flavor is always to be prized. I was right on two out of three. The undiluted fruit does taste more intense, but it doesn't necessarily taste better. A straight pear ice was almost like eating the fruit itself, frozen, while the water ice was more interesting because more subtle and elusive. A straight cantaloupe ice somehow emphasized the cucumberlike, vegetable flavors of the melon, while the diluted version highlighted the fruity perfume. I'm not sure

Sugar and Acid Content of Fruits Used in Ices

	Sugar Content (% of fresh weight)	Acid Content (% of fresh weight)	Ratio of Sugar Content to Acid Content
Lime	1%	5.0%	0.2
Avocado	1	0.2	5
Lemon	2	5.0	0.4
Tomato	3	0.5	6
Cranberry	4	3.0	1
Red Currant	6	1.8	3
Grapefruit	6	2.0	3
Guava	7	0.4	18
Cantaloupe	7	0.2	35
Strawberry	7	1.6	4
Raspberry	7	1.6	4
Blackberry	8	1.5	5
Papaya	8	0.1	80
Apricot	9	1.7	5
Watermelon	9	0.2	45
Peach	9	0.4	23
Black Currant	10	3.2	3
Pear	10	0.1	100
Honeydew	10	0.2	50
Orange	11	1.2	9
Plum	11	0.6	18
Blueberry	11	0.3	37
Gooseberry	11	1.8	6
Passion Fruit	11	3.0	4
Prickly Pear	11	0.1	110
Mango	11	0.5	22
Pineapple	13	1.1	12
Pomegranate	13	1.2	11
Apple	13	0.8	16
Cherry	14	0.5	28
Kiwi	14	3.0	5
Persimmon	14	0.2	70
Fig	15	0.4	38
Grape	16	0.2	80
Banana	17	0.3	57
Litchi	17	0.3	57

how to explain this effect. Perhaps the frozen straight fruit is sometimes too much like itself, its flavor merely coarsened and simplified by the cold. If so, then water might help by interposing a certain distance, leaving the fruit flavor more remote and reduced to its essence. In any case, I'm a late convert to the water ice. But cooks should be able to make the choice for themselves. I still prefer undiluted strawberry and raspberry ices, and others may like vegetable flavors: I've actually seen a nineteenth-century English recipe for cucumber ice cream! I therefore include proportions for both styles of ice.

Finally, a few words about the particular numbers in the recipe tables. My computer program gave me proportions down to tenths of a tablespoon, and a slightly different set of proportions emerged for each fruit. But I've rounded off and simplified the recipes, guided by two principles. First, there's no point in being fussy. As I mentioned earlier, the figures for the original sugar content and acidity of the fruits are only approximations, given their natural variability. In addition, the sugar content of an ice mix is critical only for the soft ices, which need to be between 30% and 35%; otherwise, there's plenty of leeway. And perceptions of the balance between sweetness and acidity are quite subjective; the same amount of lemon juice may seem flat to one person and too tart for another. So fractions of a tablespoon are nothing to get worked up about.

My second guiding principle has been convenience for the cook. Too many ice recipes yield odd or unpredictable amounts of mix, which can be a problem when your ice cream maker has a fixed capacity that you would like to exploit to the full, but not to the overfull. And cup measures are the easiest to keep track of. So I begin with even measures of fruit, and give proportions that will make one pint—two cups—of mix, give or take a tablespoon or two. Simply double these proportions to make a quart, triple them to make a quart and a half, and so on. If you'd like to combine two fruits, just make up half the mix volume with the proportions for one fruit, half with the other, and you'll end up with the right sugar concentration and acidity.

Time now for the recipes themselves. Since there are three dozen fruits done five ways, I've put the proportions into tables. Here are some comments about how the different styles should be made.

First, the granita, or granité, which is supposed to be coarse and crunchy. It's made slowly with only occasional stirring in an open pan in the freezer. This technique favors the production of relatively few, large crystals. The ice cream maker is actually too efficient to make a granita; the mix in contact with the container freezes almost instantly into a rock-hard layer that can completely immobilize the dasher blade. Traditional granitas are made from the citrus juices and water infused with coffee; other versions use tea or herbs.

If you want to make a granita from a noncitrus fruit, strain the juice first, since any small particles will detract from the sensation of crystals melting to nothing on the tongue. Even then, juices from small berries and very pulpy fruits make a better granita when diluted with a comparable volume of water. They are rich in pectin, a carbohydrate constituent of cell walls, which does a superb job of interfering with water crystallization: so much so that sherbet manufacturers like to add it as a stabilizer, since it inhibits the formation of grainy crystals during storage. The consistency of a granita made with straight raspberry juice, for example, is overly fine, almost mushy. Dilute it with water, however, and you get distinct ruby crystals.

Granitas can be made within a fairly broad range of sugar concentrations. Carlo Middione and the *Larousse* both give figures approaching 20%, which is about the same as ices best eaten fresh. On the other hand, Marcella Hazan's orange granita works out to around 13%, her lemon granita 10%, and her coffee granita, at one tablespoon sugar per cup, is a mere 5% sugar. The difference is a matter of texture as well as flavor: the less sugar in the mix, the coarser the crystals. I find that anything between 15% and 20% sugar works well for fruit granitas. The proportions for 20% can be read directly off the chart for the moderately sweet water ices. If you prefer a less sweet flavor and coarser crystals, cut the proportion of sugar on the chart by half, and you'll be close to 15%.

Cookbooks are often vague on exactly how to serve a granita. Occasionally we're advised to serve it fresh, when it's still slightly slushy, or in large chunks, or scraped into shavings. I discovered another possibility. If you stir these low-sugar ices every few minutes toward the end, they will eventually become "dry": that is, they form separate crystals or small aggregates. These can be stored for days in plastic bags with only some coarsening in texture (caused by repeated thawings and freezings as the freezer cycles on and off), and served—even poured!—directly from the freezer. This is an unusual presentation. Sprinkled to cover the bottom of a chilled dish, these "dry" granitas can make a contrasting bed on which to serve formed balls of the other sorbets.

Next, the moderately sweet ices. These are made rapidly in an ice cream maker, or else by the granita method but with more frequent stirring. The aim is to produce a finer, smoother consistency than that of the granita. The traditional sorbet of this type is a water ice: that is, water makes up a substantial fraction of the mix. It's also possible to make an ice without much, if any, added water; the resulting flavor is more intense, sometimes oddly so. I include formulas for both so that you can experiment for yourself. When you make water ices, remember that there's no need to cook the sugar and water into a syrup— unless you need a hot syrup to extract flavor from the skin of citrus fruits, or from herbs or flowers. Otherwise, simply combine water, sugar, and fruit in a single bowl.

The fruit itself can be handled in different ways. Certainly you get a smoother, more refined ice if you strain the puree of all fibrous material, skin, and seeds. But you also lose a fair amount of the fruit that way. And I think you lose a certain textural interest that comes with small particles of fruit embedded in the frozen juice. Straining also takes time. So with the exception of berries whose seeds are big and numerous enough to be a real distraction (a half-pint basket of raspberries contains several thousand!), and large fruits with thick, easily removed skins, I use whole puree.

Moderately sweet ices become impenetrable when they freeze thoroughly. They're best served within a few hours of the making, or else thawed until they become bright with interstitial fluid and slightly mushy. Thawing can be done over the course of an hour or two in the refrigerator, a fraction of an hour at room temperature, or in a few minutes in the microwave (alternate progressively briefer heating periods with breaking up and stirring the mass). The exact timing will depend on the quantity of ice, the kind of container, the temperatures of refrigerator and room, and the power of the microwave.

Then there are the soft ices, which should need little if any thawing before being served. In the neighborhood of 35% sugar, they are, of course, much sweeter than the 20% ices. They also seem surprisingly colder. It turns out that the heat capacity of sucrose—the energy required to raise its temperature a certain amount—is more than five times that of water. So it takes much more heat from our mouth to melt a spoonful of soft ice than it does the same portion of granita at the same temperature. To my taste, the intense cold and sweetness of the soft ice are best balanced by the flavor of undiluted fruit. But the traditional *glace* is made with a syrup. So again I present two sets of proportions for the soft ice, one including water, the other not.

There's a particular advantage to using undiluted fruit puree. The pectins and other cell wall debris that force us to water down many granita mixes are great benefactors for the soft ice. They contribute to the softness by separating the ice crystals from each other and helping to lubricate them. The texture of a straight apricot ice is almost velvety. And they help make the unfrozen syrup phase—which, you'll remember, is what makes soft sorbets soft in the first place—so thick that it doesn't easily leak out of the crystal matrix into sticky puddles.

The possibility of a sticky, syrupy texture in a soft sorbet makes the choice of a target sugar concentration somewhat tricky. There's a fine line between enough unfrozen syrup to render the sorbet scoopable, and enough to cause visible puddling. Puddling usually occurs in sorbets made with diluted or otherwise thin purees—those from melons, for example—and the citrus juices. Pectin-rich fruits that make thick or cloudy purees aren't as susceptible. I've gotten good results by aiming for 30% in the thick purees; because some of their water is trapped within particles of fruit and so can't be part of the sugar solution, their effective sugar concentration is close to 35%. In the case of the juices and thin purees, I've shot directly for 35% or slightly below.

The recipe tables give proportions for the simplest, most basic ices, those made only with fruit, sugar, lemon juice, and water. Of course recipes in cookbooks often include other ingredients. Among the most common are liqueurs, fruit preserves, and honey. All of these help intensify the flavor; and preserves, with the pectin they contain, will smooth the texture. (Madeleine Kamman has created several soft ice recipes made basically with fruit and jam alone; she says they don't even need to be stirred during freezing.) But such ingredients also affect the freezing point of the mix because they contain either a great deal of sugar, a great deal of alcohol, or both. So if you'd like to modify a basic recipe with any of these ingredients, you may want to compensate by reducing the sugar: especially if you're making a soft sorbet. By measuring how jam and honey lower the freezing point of a plain sugar solution, I've determined that a tablespoon of jam is the equivalent of about 1 tablespoon sugar, a tablespoon of honey about 2.5 tablespoons sugar.

The effect of alcohol on ices is more complicated. Some ices, in fact, are made of nothing more than wine, sugar, water, and lemon juice. Like sugar, alcohol lowers the freezing point of water, and in fact is much more effective at it, weight for weight. Ethyl alcohol molecules weigh about an eighth as much as sucrose molecules, so a given weight of pure alcohol contains close to eight times as many molecules as the same weight of sucrose. A 10% alcohol solution will have the same freezing point as a 40% sucrose solution. The typical table wine is around 10% alcohol by weight (12% or so by volume). I've seen claims that you can make an emergency dessert by pouring a bottle of sweet wine into an ice cream freezer.

Well you can, but the resulting slush has a consistency as thin as its taste. The reason is that while the dissolved sugar in a syrup makes the syrup thick and helps hold an ice together, alcohol imparts no body or cohesiveness at all to water or to an ice. And at such low temperatures, the sweetness of a sweet wine doesn't make much of an impression. So you need to add both sugar and water to wine in order to make an ice: the sugar to give the ice body and flavor, and the water to dilute the alcohol somewhat so that the mix will freeze at a temperature high enough to produce at least a thick slush. Similarly, the addition of wine or liqueur to a fruit ice will make it softer, but you don't want to omit their full equivalent in sugar, because the consistency will get too thin.

There are so many different strengths and sweetnesses of wine, liqueur, and liquor that it would take many more pages to cover the possibilities. Instead, let me offer a few guidelines for any experiments you might care to undertake. Liqueurs and spirits, both around 35% alcohol by weight, are useful for making softer, often scoopable medium-sweet ices. Add 3 or 4 tablespoons to a pint of medium-sweet mix. Wine will do the same thing, in larger quantities. Refer to the table for medium-sweet water ices, and simply substitute wine for the volume of water specified. Wine ices can be made by treating the wine as a fruit. Use the proportions for the moderately sweet water ices, and add 8 or 10 tablespoons of sugar for each cup of wine. The delicate flavor of a wine ice deteriorates rapidly in the freezer; try to finish it while it's still fresh.

Some Comprehensive Theory of Ices! Whatever rules and regularities I uncovered threaten to be buried by all the exceptions and complications. Still, buried rules are better than no rules at all—certainly better than spurious rules— and a few first principles can be more valuble than a lot of last words. The stripped-down tables of proportions that follow will give you good basic ices from three dozen fruits. They're not a replacement for your favorite recipes, but if you want to play with new combinations and variations, they'll get you in the right ballpark and minimize the guesswork. At the end of the chapter I give a few of my own recent inventions as examples.

SUMMARY: FRUIT ICES

Basic fruit ices are made with fruit pulp or juice, sugar, lemon juice, and water. They can be coarse or smooth, hard or soft, depending on the proportion of sugar in the mix and the speed with which the mix is frozen. The tables below give proportions for five different styles of fruit ices. Here's how to make each style.

The *granita* is an intentionally coarse, grainy ice. The amount of sugar shown in the table can be cut by as much as half to produce even coarser, less sweet crystals. Fruit purees should be strained to remove seeds and other particles that would interfere with the sensation of crystals melting to nothing on the tongue. Mix the ingredients together, stir occasionally until sugar is dissolved, pour into a shallow pan, and place in the freezer. After the mix begins to freeze around the edges, commence stirring every 15 minutes to break up the larger pieces. Stir more frequently as the whole mass freezes, and according to the texture you want. Small, separate crystals can be obtained by mashing with a spoon or fork until the crystals no longer stick to each other. In a chilled dish, serve freshly made as a grainy slush, or after more thorough freezing as chunks, scrapings, or separate crystals.

The *medium-sweet water ice* has a finer, smoother texture than the granita, but a similar flavor. Strain purees of distracting seeds. Mix the ingredients together, stir occasionally until sugar is dissolved, and chill in the freezer until quite cold. Freeze in an ice cream maker. Serve fresh in a chilled dish, or let the ice sit for 2 or 3 hours in the freezer so it will hold its shape longer once served. This water ice becomes very hard when thoroughly frozen, and must be partly thawed before it can be scooped again. Thaw gradually by placing in the refrigerator or on a counter and checking occasionally, or rapidly by heating for 15 or 30 seconds at a time in the microwave oven, then jabbing with a fork or spoon. To make a softer medium-sweet ice, replace the water with wine, or add 3 or 4 Tb liqueur or spirits to each pint of mix.

The *medium-sweet fruit ices* have the same balance of sugar and acid as the medium-sweet water ices, but water is added, if at all, only to moderate a fruit's

Granitas and Medium-Sweet Water Ices
(Proportions for 2 Cups Mix)

	Fruit Juice or Puree	Sugar	Lemon Juice	Water to Make 2 Cups (approx.)
Apple	1 cup	6 Tb	2 Tb	¾ cup
Apricot	1	7	1	¾
Avocado	1	8	2	¾
Banana	1	5	2	¾
Blackberry	1	7	2	¾
Black Currant	¾	7	0	1
Blueberry	1	6	2	¾
Cactus Pear	1	6	2	¾
Cherry	1	5	2	¾
Cranberry	¾	8	0	1
Fig	1	5	2	¾
Gooseberry	1	6	1	¾
Grape	1	5	2	¾
Grapefruit	1	7	0	¾
Guava	1	7	2	¾
Kiwi	¾	6	0	1
Lemon	½	8	0	1¼
Lime	½	8	0	1¼
Litchi	1	5	2	¾
Mango	1	6	2	¾
Melon*	1	6	2	¾
Cantaloupe	1	7	2	¾
Orange*	1	6	2	¾
Papaya	1	6	2	¾
Passion Fruit	¾	7	0	1
Peach	1	6	2	¾
Pear	1	6	2	¾
Persimmon	1	5	2	¾
Pineapple	1	5	2	¾
Plum	1	6	2	¾
Pomegranate	1	5	2	¾
Raspberry	1	7	2	¾
Red Currant	1	7	1	¾
Strawberry	1	7	2	¾
Tomato	1	8	2	¾
Water**	1	8	(3)	¾

*Melon and orange granitas can be made with undiluted juice, if you prefer; use proportions in the following chart.
**Use to make plain water infusions of coffee, tea, or herbs. Some infusions may be best with little or no added lemon juice. Adjust according to taste.

acidity. Highly acid fruits are omitted from the table because they require substantial dilution. The flavor of the fruit is stronger when little diluted, though this may not always be an improvement. Compared to the water ice, the fruit ice requires substantially more fruit per pint. To make, follow the preceding directions for the medium-sweet water ice.

The *sweet water ices and fruit ices* contain sufficient sugar to remain somewhat soft even when stored in the freezer, and require little or no thawing before they're served. With about double the amount of added sugar of the other ices, they are intensely flavored and feel colder in the mouth. A little goes a long way. Citrus juices, watery pulps, and purees diluted with water are more likely to develop puddles of syrup. Thick, undiluted purees—including apricot, raspberry, and strawberry—make the smoothest sweet ices. (Acidic fruits are omitted from the pure fruit ices because they require substantial dilution.)

To prepare, strain purees of distracting seeds. Mix the ingredients together, stir occasionally until the sugar is dissolved, and chill in the freezer until quite cold. Freeze in ice cream maker. Serve in chilled dishes.

Here are some sample recipes that show how you can put the tables to use.

Rose Water Ice. The proportions I've listed for water-based infusions can be used to make flavors of all kinds. The table for medium-sweet water ice calls for 1¾ cups water, 8 Tb sugar, and up to 3 Tb lemon juice. Heat the water and sugar together until the sugar is dissolved and the solution close to the boil. Remove from the heat and add a large handful of petals from red, aromatic, pesticide-free roses; I use three Mr. Lincoln roses from my garden. Leave the petals in the hot syrup for several hours until the syrup is pink and odorous. Remove the petals and add ½ to 1 Tb lemon juice according to taste (a full 3 Tb would overwhelm the delicate rose flavor). Chill in the freezer until quite cold; then freeze in ice cream maker.

Blackberry-Pear Ice. To combine two fruits in one mix, make a half recipe for each flavor and then combine them. For a medium-sweet water ice, the proportions for pear are 1 cup fruit, ¾ cup water, 6 Tb sugar, 2 Tb lemon juice. For blackberry, 1 cup fruit, ¾ cup water, 7 Tb sugar, 2 Tb lemon juice. Don't worry about fractional tablespoons. Since the proportions for these two fruits are almost identical, you can just mix ½ cup pear puree, ½ blackberry puree, ¾ cup water, 2 Tb lemon juice, and 6 or 7 Tb sugar. Stir ingredients together until the sugar is dissolved; chill in the freezer until quite cold; freeze in ice cream maker.

Medium-Sweet Fruit Ices
(Proportions for 2 Cups Mix)

	Fruit Juice or Puree	Sugar	Lemon Juice	Water*
Apple	1¾ cups	3 Tb	2 Tb	
Apricot	1½	6	0	4 Tb
Avocado	1½	7	2	
Banana	1¾	2	2	
Blackberry	1¾	6	0	2
Blueberry	1¾	4	2	
Cactus Pear	1¾	4	2	
Cherry	1¾	3	2	
Fig	1¾	3	2	
Grape	1¾	3	2	
Guava	1¾	6	2	
Litchi	1¾	1	2	
Mango	1¾	2	2	
Melon	1¾	5	2	
Cantaloupe	1¾	6	2	
Orange	1¾	4	0	
Papaya	1¾	6	2	
Peach	1¾	5	2	
Pear	1¾	5	2	
Persimmon	1¾	3	2	
Pineapple	1¾	4	0	2
Plum	1¾	5	1	
Pomegranate	1¾	4	0	2
Raspberry	1¾	6	0	2
Red Currant	1½	6	0	4
Strawberry	1¾	6	0	2
Tomato	1¾	7	2	

*These mostly minor adjustments of acidity are a matter of taste, and can be omitted.

Sweet Water Ices
(Proportions for 2 Cups Mix)

	Fruit Juice or Puree	Sugar	Lemon Juice*	Water to Make 2 Cups (approx.)
Apple	1 cup	11 Tb	2+ Tb	½ cup
Apricot	1	12	2	½
Avocado	¾	14	2+	¾
Banana	1	10	2+	½
Blackberry	1	12	2	½
Black Currant	¾	13	0	¾
Blueberry	1	12	2+	½
Cactus Pear	1	12	2+	½
Cherry	1	11	2+	½
Cranberry	¾	13	0	¾
Fig	1	10	2+	½
Gooseberry	1	12	1	½
Grape	1	10	2+	½
Grapefruit	1	13	0	½
Guava	1	12	2+	½
Kiwi	¾	12	0	¾
Lemon	½	14	0	1
Lime	½	14	0	1
Litchi	1	10	2+	½
Mango	1	12	2+	½
Melon	1	12	2+	½
Cantaloupe	1	13	2+	½
Orange	1	12	2+	½
Papaya	1	12	2+	½
Passion Fruit	¾	13	0	¾
Peach	1	12	2+	½
Pear	1	12	2+	½
Persimmon	1	11	2+	½
Pineapple	1	11	2+	½
Plum	1	12	2	½
Pomegranate	1	11	2+	½
Raspberry	1	12	2	½
Red Currant	1	13	1	½
Strawberry	1	12	2	½
Tomato	1	13	2+	½
Water**	¾	14	2+	¾

*If you add more than 2 Tb lemon juice, the ices will have a noticeable lemon flavor. Adjust to your own taste.

**Use to make plain water infusions of coffee, tea, or herbs. Some infusions may be best with little or no added lemon juice. Adjust according to taste.

Sweet Fruit Ices
(Proportions for 2 Cups Mix)

	Fruit Juice or Puree	Sugar	Lemon Juice	Water*
Apple	1½ cups	9 Tb	2 Tb	
Apricot	1½	10	0	2 Tb
Avocado	1½	13	2	
Banana	1½	7	2	
Blackberry	1½	11	0	2
Blueberry	1½	10	2	
Cactus Pear	1½	10	2	
Cherry	1½	8	2	
Fig	1½	8	2	
Grape	1½	8	2	
Guava	1½	11	2	
Litchi	1½	7	2	
Mango	1½	9	2	
Melon	1½	11	2	
Cantaloupe	1½	12	2	
Orange	1½	11	1	
Papaya	1½	11	2	
Peach	1½	10	2	
Pear	1½	10	2	
Persimmon	1½	8	2	
Pineapple	1½	8	1	
Plum	1½	10	2	
Pomegranate	1½	9	1	
Raspberry	1½	11	0	2
Red Currant	1½	12	0	2
Strawberry	1½	11	0	2
Tomato	1½	13	2	

*These mostly minor adjustments of acidity are a matter of taste, and can be omitted.

Pineapple-Avocado Ice. Avocado adds a wonderful richness to fruit ices without overwhelming their flavor—it's the plant world's equivalent of cream. But if avocado makes up half or even a third of the fruit in a sweet ice, I find the result too heavy, almost like a super-premium ice cream. At a quarter of the fruit, avocado gives just the right body, and its flavor is quite elusive. I like to add avocado to lemon, lime, and kiwi ices, which are all short on texture-softening pectins and fiber. It also gives a nice smoothness to pineapple.

The sweet-ice tables call for 1½ cups pineapple, 8 Tb sugar, and 1 Tb lemon juice; for avocado, 1½ cups fruit, 13 Tb sugar, and 2 Tb lemon juice. To make avocado a quarter of the fruit, multiply the avocado proportions by a quarter, and the pineapple proportions by three-quarters. This is easier to do if you convert the cup measures to tablespoons: 1 cup = 16 Tb. For 2 cups mix, the final proportions are 1 cup plus 2 Tb pineapple, 6 Tb avocado, 9 Tb sugar, and 2 Tb lemon juice.

Here's how you can predict the consistency that a particular ice recipe is likely to produce. If the recipe calls for little if any added water and ½ cup or more of sugar in 2 cups of mix, then you'll probably get a sweet ice that remains fairly soft in the freezer. If the recipe calls for less than ½ cup of sugar in 2 cups of mix, or if it calls for about ½ cup but includes a significant volume of water, then the result will probably be a medium-sweet ice that hardens in the freezer. Ices that include egg whites, gelatin, or alcoholic liquids turn out softer than their sugar content would suggest.

If you're interested in experimenting with ice textures, here are some useful numbers. For recipes in the neighborhood of 20% sugar, the level typical of the medium-sweet ices, adding or subtracting 1 tablespoon sugar will change the sugar concentration by about 2%; adding or subtracting 1 tablespoon water, by 0.5%. For the sweet ices, around 35%, 1 tablespoon sugar will change the sugar concentration by about 1.5%; 1 tablespoon water, by 1%.

If you need to calculate mix volumes, simply remember that a given volume of granulated sugar contributes about half that volume when added to a liquid. For example, 4 tablespoons sugar will increase the volume of the mix by 2 tablespoons.

The Pleasures of Merely Measuring

Two hundred years ago, Count Rumford discovered something fundamental about how the world works. His inspiration? Apples. Not falling from the tree, but steaming on the table.

> When dining, I had often observed that some particular dishes retained their Heat much longer than others, and that apple-pies, and apples and almonds mixed (a dish in great repute in England), remained hot a surprising length of time.
>
> Much struck with this extraordinary quality of retaining Heat which apples appeared to possess, it frequently occurred to my recollection; and I never burnt my mouth with them, or saw others meet with the same misfortune, without endeavoring, but in vain, to find out some way of accounting in a satisfactory manner for this surprising phaenomenon.

Eventually another chance observation set Rumford on the right track. He had heated an alcohol-filled thermometer, one with a four-inch bulb, and happened to set it in a sunny window. The bright light enabled him to notice swift currents in the alcohol, currents that died only when the thermometer had fallen to room temperature. Rumford guessed that such circulation might be responsible for the movement of heat within a liquid: hot particles would be carried to cool regions near the liquid's boundaries, and cool particles to hot regions. To find out whether this was true, he deliberately interfered with the currents in a container of hot water by dissolving starch in it; a second container he stuffed with eiderdown. As he expected, each of these mixtures took significantly longer to cool down than water alone. So it was that Rumford discovered in liquids what we now call *convection*: the transfer of heat in a fluid by the movement of the fluid's own atoms or molecules. (Convection in air had been discovered in the seventeenth century by Carlo Renaldini. In solids, whose atoms and molecules aren't free to move from one place to another, heat transfer takes place by means of "conduction," which is still something of a mystery. See chapter 3.)

And the injurious apples? Rumford deduced that although stewed apples consist mainly of water, they retain heat longer than dishes of a thinner consistency because their convection currents are slowed by dissolved substances (sugars, starch, pectin), which make the liquid more viscous, and obstructed by solid particles (fiber). The outer regions of the dish do lose heat to the air, but they can't mix well with the hot interior. So a spoon that penetrates much beyond the deceptively cool surface may bring up a scalding mouthful.

I doubt that there are any basic principles of nature left for modern-day Rumfords to discover in the kitchen. But there are still plenty of kitchen principles waiting to be revealed—or repealed—by experiments as simple as those Rumford used to follow up his hot lead. In this chapter I'll conclude my own investigations with a handful that were quickly resolved by a few measurements of temperature, time, or weight. Some of the questions are trivial indeed! Yet I found that stopping to consider them left me better acquainted with the foods and techniques concerned, however familiar they already were. And the simple act of measuring brings its own pleasures. The satisfaction of pinning down a vague impression with a number, for example, or the contentment of being confirmed in a preconception, or—most stimulating of all—the surprise of being jolted out of one.

First, a question inspired by Rumford's burned tongue. How much good does it do to blow on a hot spoonful of soup or a cup of coffee? This seems to be a nearly universal reflex, one that's learned early. I remember our children imitating us with puffed-out cheeks long before they'd graduated from the high chair. Does blowing actually accelerate the food's cooling, or is it just something to do while the food cools on its own? For that matter, what kind of heat can our mouths tolerate?

I answered the last question first, by measuring the temperature of water that was as hot as I could stand to allow past my lips. In fact, my lips were more sensitive than my mouth. A spoonful of water at 170°F (77°C) was tolerable once it had gotten inside. I'm sure that everyone has a slightly different threshold, and that an individual's threshold varies from one occasion to another, but it's probably going to be in the same neighborhood. In any case, I used 170°F as the target temperature in subsequent cooling experiments.

I started with spoonfuls. To simulate the dinner-table situation in a reproducible way, I suspended a soupspoon in mid-air (the air was 66°F, or 19°C) using a laboratory ringstand and a clamp. I took the digital thermometer I had obtained for my earlier experiments in meat cookery and fixed its conveniently small temperature probe in, but not touching, the bowl of the spoon. Then I boiled some water, poured it into the spoon, started a stopwatch, and stopped it when the thermometer had fallen to 170°F. I did this for twenty different spoonfuls of boiling water. The first ten I left alone. The last ten I blew on continuously, pausing only to take breaths, and being careful not to spill any water.

The results were unequivocal. The unaided spoonful of boiling water took an average of 45 seconds to cool down to 170°F. With a headwind, the average time was 21 seconds. Evidently fast-moving air carries heat from a hot surface more efficiently than still air. It does this in large part by encouraging evaporation from the water surface, a process that requires heat and therefore cools off the liquid that remains. So blowing isn't just busy work. It cuts the cooling time by half: probably somewhat less if you're also engaged in conversation.

At least that's the case for thin broths and the like. But what about hearty, thick dishes with impeded convection currents, like Rumford's stewed apples? Blowing will cool the surface, but might the spoonful's interior stay hot even so? I repeated the experiment with a thick soup. To help other investigators compare their results, I chose a commercially available, standardized reagent: Campbell's split pea soup. Since the thicker soup took substantially longer to cool, I did only three trials in each of the two ways. A spoonful of split pea soup spent an average of 103 seconds cooling down to 170°F on its own. With assistance, it took 66 seconds: not half the time, but about two-thirds the time. The thicker a dish's consistency, the less help blowing will be.

We can't really do anything to improve the convection in a single spoonful of thick soup. But when presented with a scalding bowl, many of us practice artificial convection: we scoop spoonfuls from the bottom to the surface. This action exposes more of the soup to the cool air, and mixes hot and cool masses of

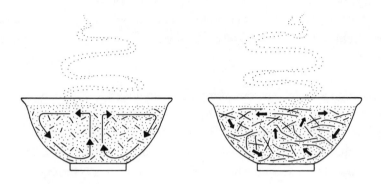

In a thin liquid like broth or coffee (left), *convection currents* (arrows) *rapidly mix hot interior areas with surface areas that have been cooled by evaporation, and the container as a whole cools down rapidly. In a thick soup* (right), *large carbohydrate and protein molecules prevent the liquid from moving as freely, so while the surface cools, the interior stays hot.*

soup together. I tested its effectiveness by pouring a measured cup of boiling soup into a fairly broad bowl, and seeing how long it took for the middle of the bowl to fall to 170°F. When left alone, two bowls of pea soup took an average of 6 minutes. With continuous scooping, two others took 90 seconds. By contrast, bowls of hot water took 2 minutes and 80 seconds respectively when left alone and scooped. Artificial convection is clearly an excellent supplement to the real thing.

Then there are cups of tea and coffee. I had the vague impression that blowing cools the surface, which is where we sip from anyway, but that it doesn't have much of an effect on the rest of the cup. When I timed a 10-ounce mug of boiling water, I got a lesson in just how efficacious convection is. Left alone, the mug took about 5 minutes to reach 170°F. With near-continuous blowing, it took between 2½ and 3 minutes. And it didn't matter whether I placed the temperature probe at the bottom of the mug or barely below the surface; the readings were the same. The water circulates so rapidly that surface and bottom temperatures were indistinguishable.

So blowing and scooping are effective and—though a slight giddiness can accompany the former—safe methods for cooling down excessively hot liquids. There's a corollary to this finding: the cook who prefers a calm atmosphere in the dining room may want to serve soups 20 or 30 degrees below the boil.

Evaporation is useful when we want to cool liquids off, but it can be counterproductive when we're trying to heat them up. Over years of setting pots of water to boil, I had come to wonder whether covering the pot saves anything much in time or energy. Putting the lid on minimizes evaporation and the cooling it causes, but is the difference significant? The answer is yes, especially for large volumes of water. Raising a gallon to the boil from 58°F (14°C) on a gas burner took 23 minutes with the lid, and 35 minutes without it: or half again as much time and gas. A half-gallon in a smaller saucepan took only a fifth again as much time when uncovered: 18 rather than 15 minutes. I found that the uncovered pots began to fall behind the covered ones when the water reached around 150°F (66°C) and evaporation became noticeable. Below that temperature it doesn't matter whether there's a lid or not. This settled another question for me and for others with disorganized cabinets. Go ahead and put the pot on the flame, then return to the cabinet and search for the right lid. You've got a while before it's needed.

Evaporation may be the culprit in some mysterious problems we've had with baked potatoes. I've always made a point of coating potatoes with oil before I bake them. For some reason, my wife usually didn't bother, so comparison of the two methods was inevitable. Unoiled skins turn out rather light and flabby, just as they do when the potato is "baked"—actually, steamed—in foil. I much prefer the crisp, dark skin that oiling produces. The differences in texture and color indicate that oil helps raise the skin temperature well above the boiling point. The high temperature drives moisture out of the skin, and the water-repelling nature of the oil prevents the skin from absorbing new moisture from the body of the potato. The skin therefore dries out, gets hotter than it otherwise could, and begins to brown.

Oil turns out to have another effect. We generally cook several medium-sized potatoes at a time, usually the red- or yellow-skinned "waxy" varieties, in a rickety toaster oven. At 400°F or 425°F (204°C or 219°C), they're always done in an hour. At least when I cook them. My wife has often baked potatoes for an hour and found them badly underdone, almost crunchy inside. Another quarter-hour is sometimes enough, sometimes not. When I finally noticed the correlation between tardiness and oillessness, I decided to measure the internal temperatures of potatoes with and without oil as they baked in a standard gas oven. I found that potatoes consistently heat through faster when their skin is oiled. The oiled potato generally reached 200°F (93°C) about 10 minutes before its unoiled partner. As was the case with the pots of water, the heating rates began to diverge between 140°F and 160°F (60°C and 71°C). And the difference in doneness is exaggerated when the potatoes are baked in the relatively inefficient toaster oven.

I first interpreted these figures to mean that the unoiled skin continuously absorbs moisture from within the potato and allows it to evaporate, thereby slowing the cooking, while the oiled skin acts as a somewhat waterproof barrier, reducing evaporation and any consequent slowdown in heating. The difference is more obvious in the toaster oven because it has less of a heat reservoir with which to overcome the cooling effect. However, this theory suggests that potatoes should lose moisture more slowly when they're oiled. And they don't really seem to. With or without oil, half-pound potatoes generally lose 15% or so of their weight in an hour. Perhaps, then, the oil doesn't prevent water vapor from escaping, but does minimize the resultant surface cooling by keeping the potato skin well above the boiling point. Or maybe the oil layer simply makes the transfer of heat from oven air to potato more efficient. The data haven't yet suggested an obvious explanation to me. But they have had a profound and welcome effect in our kitchen: all our baked potatoes are now crisp-skinned!

One other point. The difference in doneness is most apparent in waxy potatoes. The drier, mealier russets show the same divergence in heating rates, but their texture isn't as noticeably affected. Some purists might question the baking of waxy potatoes in the first place. The russet is indeed the classic baking potato, but I think that's largely because it's so good at soaking up butter and sour cream. The waxy potatoes are moist enough on their own that they offer more of a choice in what we add to them: lots of butter is fine, but so is a little, or some drained yogurt, or a squeeze of lemon and a grind of pepper. I've come to prefer them.

Speaking of ovens: I've spent years under the impression that when opening the oven to check on its contents, I should work as fast as possible so that the oven and food won't cool down too much. My haste has resulted in misadventure more than once, so it occurred to me to check just how badly the cooking is set back when the oven door is opened. I'm now more relaxed. I tried opening the door for a full minute, which is plenty of time to maneuver the most awkward dish. When the oven started at 350°F or 450°F (177°C or 232°C), the temperature fell 100 degrees and more, but made it all the way back up less than a minute after the door was closed. Our gas oven may respond more quickly than an electrical element, though the temperature usually seemed to rebound without the gas coming on, as if the residual heat in the oven's walls was sufficient to heat a new volume of air. Different ovens behave differently, but I'll bet that most cooks can afford to relax. If you tend toward the frantic when you poke at a roast or pie, it might do you good to take the measure of your oven's thermal resilience.

One piece of kitchen lore that has always struck me as finicky to a fault is the claim that fresh mushrooms should be wiped, not rinsed. Mushrooms soak up moisture at the least opportunity, it's said, so don't let them come anywhere near water, or they'll get soggy and lose their delicate flavor. Now it's true that water doesn't bead up on mushrooms the way it does on most vegetables; fungi lack the waxy cuticle that terrestrial plants have. But mushrooms are already 90% water, so what difference could a few drops more make? And rinse water comes in contact with only a small fraction of the mushroom's cells. I've never noticed any difference in flavor. Moreover, mushrooms live in intimate contact with dirt, even if it's some sterile mix concocted by the growers. They're often dirty in the store. And dry wiping is the hard way to remove grit from a soft mushroom.

To test the lore, I weighed out 252 grams of fresh mushrooms on a postal scale, submerged them in tap water for 5 minutes, removed them, blotted the surface moisture, and reweighed them. The mushrooms now weighed 258 grams, which meant that twenty-three mushrooms had absorbed less than half a tablespoon among them, or a sixteenth of a teaspoon each. That's after 5 minutes of soaking. It takes me 5 or 10 seconds to rinse a mushroom, which I now do without the hint of a second thought.

Now to the low end of the temperature scale, and liquids that are at their best when chilled. I regularly forget to refrigerate wine or beer before it's needed, and usually make do with the freezer. But I've never been sure just how much time to allow, or whether the freezer is really that much faster than the refrigerator. So I sacrificed a few bottles and cans to find out.

First, bottles of wine. It's my feeling that white wines and champagnes are often served too cold, so chilled that they have practically no aroma. To choose an appropriate target temperature, I sought the advice of Emile Peynaud, an eminent French enologist and author of *The Taste of Wine*. Peynaud recommends a range roughly between 45°F and 55°F (7°C and 13°C). So I settled on 50°F as a temperature that would be pushing the upper limit, especially after the wine was poured into a room-temperature glass, but that would at least allow a first glass to be enjoyed while the bottle finished its cooling.

To monitor the temperature of the wine as it cooled, I removed the cork from an old, neglected bottle of Blue Nun, pushed a thin nail through the cork, pulled the nail out, and pushed the thin temperature probe through. Then I pulled the probe out the other side for four or five inches, so that it would end up in the middle of the bottle. I placed the cork in the bottle being tested, plugged the lead from the temperature probe into the thermometer, and started measuring.

My tests revealed very little difference in chilling times between ordinary wine bottles and the substantially thicker champagne bottles, nor between dry and sweet wines. The results, then, should apply to whatever bottles you have on hand. When a wine bottle started between 70°F and 75°F (21°C to 24°C), it took about 2 hours to drop to 50°F in the refrigerator, and about 45 minutes to do the same in the freezer (my freezer temperature is 0°F, or -18°C). So the freezer is indeed much faster.

Still, 45 minutes is a long time to wait. (Thirty minutes gets you close to 55°F.) Refrigerators and freezers cool mainly by means of cold air, which isn't very efficient (only a small portion of the bottle touches the freezer floor). Water, being much denser, is correspondingly more efficient at absorbing heat from an object. So I tried an ordinary ice bath, whose temperature hovered around 40°F (4°C), about the same as a refrigerator compartment. Ice water (two trays of ice and enough water to reach the neck of the bottle) brought the wine to 50°F in 20 minutes, or one-sixth the time required in the refrigerator, and half the freezer time. So if you can remember to keep enough ice on hand, you can cope with warm wine pretty quickly.

The ice bucket is a nice solution for another reason: it chills the wine to 40°F just as fast as the freezer does, in an hour or so, but without the danger of over-cooling. If you happen to forget a bottle in the freezer, the wine will begin to solidify in a couple of hours, expanding as it freezes. After four or five hours, it'll push its cork right through the soft lead capsule and leak slush.

What works for wine works for beer as well. Instead of 3 hours in the refrigerator or 30 minutes in the freezer, a 12-ounce can of beer descended from room temperature to 45°F in 15 minutes or so when mostly immersed in ice water. Bottled beer took somewhat longer, since glass doesn't conduct heat as well as aluminum: 40 minutes in the freezer and 25 minutes in ice water.

Fine beers, like fine wines, aren't at their best when arctic cold. But there are times in life when nothing but an icy beer will do, and those are usually the times when we're most impatient. An ice bath at 40°F just won't get a beer ice-cold, so it's 45 minutes or so in the freezer. Unless we're really desperate, in which case there's brine. Salt lowers the freezing point of water. Add several tablespoons of salt to a tray of ice cubes and a cup of water, and the resulting ice bath will be about 10 degrees cooler than usual. A room-temperature can of beer immersed in this mixture (in a small container; it's important not to dilute the salt with too much water) got down to 45°F (7°C) in 7 or 8 minutes, and to 38°F (3°C) in 20 minutes. Still not exactly ice cold, but close enough to hold us while another gets down to 32°F (0°C) in the freezer.

I also wondered about different ways of serving beers: whether frosted glasses and foam coolers significantly slow the inevitable warming. A frozen glass actually lowered the beer's temperature by several degrees, so that the beer was as cold as or colder than it began for a full 15 minutes. In the same time, beer in an unfrozen glass lost its cold edge, rising from 40°F to 46°F. I left these glasses full throughout; if they were actually being drunk, they would certainly have warmed faster, as they also would on a hot summer afternoon. (I did the experiment when the ambient temperature was about 70°F, or 21°C.) But the cold glass clearly helps a great deal. Similarly, a soft foam cooler kept a full can within 3 degrees of its original temperature for 30 minutes. Over the same time, a naked can rose 7 degrees, and a naked can that I picked up every minute or two rose 10 degrees. Coolers too are valuable aides.

The following low-temperature investigation is offbeat enough to require some preliminary explanation. In the early 1970s I first heard an improbable claim: hot water freezes faster than cold water. That sounded crazy to me. In order to freeze, the hot water would first have to cool down to the initial temperature of the cold water, and during that cooling period, the cold water would have gotten even colder. How could the hot water ever catch up with the cold water? Thinking so far and no further, I dismissed the whole idea.

A few years ago, while thumbing through Jearl Walker's treasure trove of everyday science, *The Flying Circus of Physics*, I found this statement: "In cold regions like Canada or Iceland, it is common knowledge that water left outside will freeze faster if it is originally hot." Walker cites seven articles in physics journals on the subject. From these I was able to trace the "common knowledge" back 2,300 years to Aristotle. He wrote in his *Meteorology* that "Many people, when they want to cool water quickly, begin by putting it in the sun. So the inhabitants of Pontus when they encamp on the ice to fish (they cut a hole in the ice and then fish) pour warm water round their rods that it may freeze the quicker; for they use the ice like lead to fix the rods."

Recent scientific interest in this strange phenomenon was sparked by the observation and tenacity of a novice cook. A Tanzanian high school student, Erasto Mpemba, was in the habit of making ice cream in the school refrigerator. So were many other boys. The usual procedure was to boil some milk, add sugar, let the mixture cool, and then put it in the freezer. One day in 1963, another boy saw Mpemba boiling up his milk and, in order to guarantee himself one of the remaining ice trays, added sugar to his own unboiled milk and rushed the mix into the freezer. Mpemba later recalled: "Knowing that if I waited for the boiled milk to cool before placing it in the refrigerator I would lose the last available ice-tray, I decided to risk ruin to the refrigerator on that day by putting hot milk into it. The other boy and I went back an hour and a half later and found that my tray of milk had frozen into ice cream while his was still only a thick liquid, not yet frozen."

Mpemba had no luck convincing his teachers that hot milk would freeze faster than cold, but he found a more open mind in D. G. Osborne, a professor of physics at Dar es Salaam. Osborne too had his doubts but wanted to encourage "questioning and critical attitudes" in students. "In this case there was an added reason for caution," Osborne explained, "for everyday events are seldom as simple as they seem and it is dangerous to pass a superficial judgment on what can and cannot be." Osborne did some experiments and confirmed Mpemba's observation: Boiling water could take as little as a third the time required by room-temperature water to reach the freezing point. When Mpemba and Osborne published their findings in the journal *Physics Education* in 1969, they were greeted with some disbelief, but also with corroborative experiences. From one correspondent, the memory that the hot washing water his mother threw outside froze faster than cold water. From members of a bird club, the fact that hot water poured in a bird bath on a cold night actually froze faster than cold water. Hot-water pipes in houses apparently freeze before cold-water pipes; in processing plants, warm fish before cold.

How are such things possible? A number of physicists intrigued by the problem have proved Osborne's point about the complexity of everyday events. Several different factors seem to be involved. In the case of hot liquid in the freezer, one stands out: evaporation. Of course, hot water gives off more vapor than cold water. This evaporation gives hot water two advantages over cold water in a race to the freezing point. First, evaporation actively removes water from the container, which reduces the quantity that remains to be frozen, and a small mass freezes faster than a large mass. Second, evaporation creates convection currents in the freezer's air. In a sense, a container of hot water blows over its own surface, and so speeds its cooling by the same means we use to cool a spoonful of soup. The combination of the two effects can sometimes be enough for hot water to freeze faster than cold water.

Sometimes, but not always. Because the rate of cooling also depends on such variables as the shape of the container and the size of the freezing compartment, hot water often takes longer to cool than cold water. Another complication was the fact that the physicists' experiments ended when the water just began to freeze. But the obvious practical question was whether we can freeze ice cubes any faster by using hot water, and ice cubes aren't ice cubes until they've frozen all the way through. So I set out to determine whether the Mpemba phenomenon was at all relevant to ice-cube making.

I poked a small hole in the lip of a plastic ice-cube tray, snaked my temperature probe through the hole so that it would be held in the middle of the nearest well, and used the probe to follow the temperature of the water as it froze. I averaged two trials with tap water at about 60°F (16°C) and two with water that had boiled for 15 minutes. I chose 31°F (−1°C) for an endpoint, since water won't fall below 32°F (0°C) until it has solidified. The results: the cold water in the middle of the well began to freeze after about 25 minutes, the hot water after 43 minutes. Nothing like the Mpemba phenomenon. However, the hot water did a remarkable job of catching up. It solidified after an average of 123 minutes, the cold water after 128 minutes. That was startling enough: the boiling water had to fall 150 degrees further than the cold water, yet they ended up, so to speak, in a dead heat. My guess is that the hot water needs to spend less time in the actual process of freezing because evaporation during the initial descent to the freezing point has diminished its mass, so there's less water there to freeze.

I may have failed to observe any accelerated cooling because our freezer creates artificial convection currents with a blower to keep the compartment frost-free. These currents might be more effective at cooling than any movement induced by the hot vapor, and so might obscure any contribution by that movement. Or perhaps the geometry of ice cube wells doesn't favor accelerated cooling. On the chance that a greater surface-to-volume ratio would help, I ran the same test with wells that were only half full. The times were shorter, but the results were the same: both hot and cold water took about 75 minutes to solidify, with the hot water making up for a 12-minute lag in reaching the freezing point.

Despite Aristotle and Mpemba, then, we can't count on hot water to make fast ice cubes. On the other hand, you might make a fast dollar by betting a friend that trays of hot and cold water will take about the same time to freeze. Just be sure to try it in your particular freezer first.

Finally, some measurements I had made in my experiments on searing and simmering forced me to rethink my idea of what happens when we cook meat. When I looked into simmering times, I found that an inch-thick piece of meat just out of the refrigerator takes about 11 minutes at a 200°F (93°C) simmer to reach 140°F (60°C), or medium rare, at the center. And, as you may recall, I was surprised to find that a minute of browning on one side was the full equivalent of a minute of total immersion in 200°F water. I had thought that since a frying pan heats only one side at a time, it would be only about half as effective as total immersion.

I rationalized my finding by assuming that the higher temperature of frying compensates for the briefer exposure to heat. But then when I fried 1-inch meat slices all the way to medium rare, I anticipated that the cooking times at temperatures higher than the boiling point would be substantially less than 11 minutes. Instead, they were still very close to 11 minutes!

This was true whether or not the meat was seared at a very high temperature, and even when I "seared" the meat for the entire cooking period. In the broiler,

the cooking time was substantially longer. Quicker results did come from grilling the meat quite close to intensely hot coals. The meat surface was partly
charred by the time I was done, but the 1-inch slices reached 140°F in 9½ minutes, 1½-inch slices in 17½ minutes. Strangely, though, boiling the meat took
almost exactly as long as grilling did! In other words, no matter how I cooked
the meat, the fastest it heated up was the rate characteristic of boiling water.

While this may be a convenient fact for estimating cooking times, it contra-
dicts common sense. At least it did mine. Surely high cooking temperatures
should heat food through faster than low cooking temperatures. That's certainly the case for cooking at the boiling point and below; the main advantage
of simmering at lower temperatures is exactly the longer stretch of time between stages of doneness. But beyond the boiling point, it doesn't seem to matter how hot things get; even red-hot coals heat meat through at the same rate as
boiling water. How could that possibly be?

Here's my theory. Remember that meat in the process of being fried emits
steam, which is formed from juices continuously leaking out of the meat and
onto the pan. When the juices hit the pan, they're vaporized: rapidly if the pan
is smoking hot, not so rapidly if it's moderately hot. So the cooking temperature
that the interior of the meat actually feels is not just the temperature of the pan.
At least until the meat becomes well done and dries out, the effective cooking
temperature is determined by the mixture of juice and steam that's continuously replenished in the space between the pan and the meat. That temperature
will be slightly lower than the boiling point of water: so frying turns out to be
much like simmering. In the case of grilling close to red-hot coals, the external
temperature is so high that exiting juices are instantly vaporized: so the effective
cooking temperature doesn't just approach the boiling point, it is the boiling
point. Aggressive grilling is therefore the equivalent of boiling.

There's something else that sets boiling and grilling apart from frying and
simmering. When cooked to an internal temperature of 140°F, simmered and
fried slices of beef are medium rare; but boiled slices at 140°F are more like medium, and grilled slices are quite well done, with just a touch of pink at the very
center. Now it's obvious that boiling will cook the meat through faster than simmering, and get the outer portions hotter as well. But how can grilling heat the
center of the meat at the same rate that boiling does, and yet apparently heat the
rest of the slice more rapidly?

I'm not sure. Maybe as the outer layers of the meat are cooked and lose much of their moisture, the intense heat of the coals forces those layers above the boiling point and penetrates them more rapidly, while the as-yet moist, undercooked areas close to the center still reach only the boiling point. The center would therefore continue to experience an effective cooking temperature of 212°F (100°C). This is just a guess. In any case, the main point is that very hot coals cook meat faster than boiling or frying not because they get heat to the center faster, but because they somehow overload the outer, earlier-cooked areas with more heat. The same internal temperature can therefore signify very different degrees of doneness, depending on the intensity of the heat source.

My measurements of cooking times produced another peculiar fact that needs explaining. Why should a minute of frying on one side be the full equivalent of a minute of simmering both sides simultaneously? Well, it isn't when all you do is cook for a minute or two. But when you turn the meat over and cook it to medium rare, the total frying time does turn out to be the same as the total simmering time. I think that the explanation must be something like this. When you fry the meat on one side, that side gets much hotter than the center. If you then turn the meat, the cooked side immediately begins to cool down; but as long as it's still hotter than the center, it continues to heat the center. So even though only the second side is now in actual contact with the pan, the center continues to feel the influence of the pan on the first side. It's being heated from both sides. Nor does the number of turns seem to matter much. When I flip the meat every minute or two, the center temperature rises smoothly, tracking the simmering temperatures almost exactly. When I flip it only once, after 5 or 6 minutes on the first side, the temperature rises more slowly to begin with, and faster after the turn, but it still gets to a given doneness at about the same time. For similar reasons, grilling times match boiling times pretty well.

What this all comes down to is that the side of the meat facing the heat isn't nearly as hot as I had thought, and the side away from the heat isn't nearly as cool. Which is fortunate. Cooking meat would probably be much trickier if it worked the way I thought it did. Sometimes surprises are all for the best.

SUMMARY: MISCELLANEOUS MEASUREMENTS

Blowing is an effective way of cooling spoonfuls of thin soup and cups of coffee or tea. It's less effective for thick liquids. A bowl of thick soup can be cooled rapidly by scooping and stirring it.

When boiling a large pot of water, you'll save a fair amount of time and energy by covering the pot.

Oiled potatoes bake faster than unoiled potatoes, especially if you're cooking a waxy variety in a toaster oven.

Many ovens return to temperature very quickly after having been opened for a full minute, so it's usually not necessary to rush when you check on the progress of a dish.

Fresh mushrooms can be rinsed without damaging their flavor or texture.

A warm bottle of white wine cools to 50°F (10°C) in about 2 hours in the refrigerator, 45 minutes in the freezer, or 20 minutes in an ice bath. Cooling a can of beer to 45° (7°C) takes 3 hours in the refrigerator, 30 minutes in the freezer, or 15 minutes in an ice bath. A bottle of beer takes 3 hours in the refrigerator, 40 minutes in the freezer, or 25 minutes in an ice bath. A can of beer in iced brine takes 8 minutes to reach 45°F, 20 minutes to reach 38°F. Frosted beer glasses and foam coolers slow the rewarming significantly.

Hot water can sometimes freeze faster than cold water. In my freezer, ice-cube trays filled with hot or cold water take about the same time to freeze.

Meat takes about as long to cook when fried one side at a time as when immersed in barely simmering liquid, about as long when boiled as when grilled close to red-hot coals. The intense heat of a grill doesn't reach the center of a steak any faster than the heat from boiling water would, but it does cook the outer layers more rapidly.

PART TWO

MAKING THE GOOD LIFE BETTER

Cooking and eating owe much of their interest to the fact that we're omnivorous. The range of gastronomical pleasures is great because the human species can learn to like just about anything. An opportunistic palate was a valuable trait in the early peopling of the earth; wherever sufficient numbers of plants or animals were available to support human life, someone could come along and adapt to the local flavors. Since then, the practice of agriculture has narrowed our diet by cultivating only a tiny fraction of the earth's offerings, but even this runs quite a gamut, from root to leaf to seed, fungus to herb to tree, mollusc to quadruped to bird.

Along with the pleasures of a catholic palate, omnivory brings a fundamental problem: the human diet isn't predictable. Our choice of foods can change drastically from generation to generation, or from meal to meal. The body can cope with a great deal of biochemical variability in its food, but it is far from perfect, and our current affluence and long lifespan have exposed some serious flaws. A regimen that seems perfectly healthful for thirty or forty years can turn out to be catastrophic in the longer run.

The human palate accommodated itself first to the earth's offerings, then to the successive innovations of cooking, agriculture, and industry. Now, thanks to the biomedical sciences, we're learning how this useful combination of adaptibility and ingenuity has managed to take a toll on our long-term health. As a consequence, we've begun to guide our adaptability and ingenuity with our intelligence, to accommodate our tastes to the body's limits. And we've begun to appreciate some of the subtle ironies of our condition as earthly creatures who must eat to live.

Fat and the Heart

Fat. That small word has been swollen with significance throughout its long history. Early on, it described a desirable condition of domesticated food animals and meant "fatted": that is well-fed, full-fleshed, and ready for slaughter, either to nourish human beings or to please the gods. With its suggestion of abundance, *fat* came to be applied to fertile earth as well; hence the biblical phrase "the fat of the land," the farming term "fat soil," and, from the Celtic, "Ireland."

The many virtues of animal fats and plant oils were well known in prehistory. They provided our ancestors with steady illumination, with lubrication, and, when boiled with an alkaline substance like wood ash or soda, with soap. In the Near East, they were used to protect the skin against the desiccating desert heat. Perfumers discovered that fats will extract the odors of flower petals and other aromatic materials. Ointments were compounded for medicinal purposes, and anointing was a ceremony of consecration. Judging by the evidence of the papyrus Ebers, frying in fat was known to Egyptian kitchens thirty-five centuries ago. It may even have been recognized that fats are an especially concentrated source of nutriment. For thousands of years of human history, fats were relatively rare and highly valued.

Times have changed, at least in the affluent industrial countries. With our vast herds of food animals relegated to near invisibility on ever fewer farms and ranches, and ritual sacrifice reduced to the occasional backyard immolation of small prepackaged portions, we apply the adjective *fat* mostly to ourselves. And we mean by it not a pleasing abundance of flesh, but undesirable excess. Thanks to modern medicine, the word now bears overtones of disease and death. Large amounts of body fat predispose us to various ailments, we're told. Even if we ourselves are trim, the fat in our foods can plug up the blood vessels and injure the heart.

Despite the warnings, we're probably more besotted with food fat than our ancestors ever were. This once rare commodity is now something we swim in, to the tune of some 20 gallons annually per person, or almost a cup each day. The reason is that fats are responsible for many of the characteristics that appeal to us in foods. Some, preeminently butter and olive oil, and the fat in meats, contribute desirable flavors. As a cooking medium, fats make it possible for us to heat foods quickly and evenly at temperatures well above water's boiling point, and so to create new, intense flavors (see chapter 17). Above all, fats contribute a smoothness of texture, a moistness, richness, and lubricity that seem universally appealing. In the modern baking industry, these qualities go collectively by the bottom-line name *go away*. The proper admixture of fats makes a mouthful of bread or pastry, of meat or potato go down easy, which prompts the desire for another mouthful to sustain the experience. Industrial concoctions, the fast foods that account for a greater and greater proportion of our daily diet, are accordingly crammed with fats. Unfortunately, the mouthful goes away but the fat doesn't. So our palates overrule our reason; and so, if the physicians are to be believed, we ready ourselves for the slaughter, sacrificing years of life on the altar of good mouthfeel.

It's easy to accept the idea that serious diseases are caused by virulent microbes, by the poisonous chemicals in cigarette smoke, and by debilitating deficiencies of essential nutrients. But common, everyday amounts of a common, everyday nutrient, one that our bodies were designed to exploit, and arguably the one that contributes most to the appeal of our foods? Not fair. Also, after decades of basic and clinical research across the globe, not really disputable. It turns out that animal fats and some vegetable oils increase the concentration of cholesterol in our blood, and cholesterol in turn damages our blood vessels. Nearly half of all deaths in the industrialized West—almost a million a year in the U.S.—are attributable to diseased arteries. Of these, it's estimated that about half are caused in large part by fat consumption, and could have been avoided.

To say that the case against fat and cholesterol isn't really disputable doesn't mean that it's not disputed, even by some physicians. Articles like "Diet-Heart: End of an Era" or "The Cholesterol Myth" appear to promise a definitive—and welcome!—disproof of the fat dogma. But their arguments generally boil down to a simple one: No one has proved that changing our diet in midlife will increase our life expectancy. That's true, at least for the moment, and it's probably true for a simple reason. We know that heart disease begins as early as adolescence and takes decades to develop into a life-threatening condition. No wonder, then, that medical studies of altered diets lasting a few months or even a few years fail to find a large reduction in heart attacks or deaths. This doesn't necessarily mean that a low-fat regimen won't slow the development of heart disease. It probably means that diets and patients must be followed for many years before the benefits become evident.

There's some striking evidence that we're at least on the right track. It used to be that the United States trailed only Finland in per capita death rates for heart disease. The U.S. death rate began a dramatic decline in the mid 1960s, and by the late 1980s had fallen 40%, dropping us from second to eighth place. Improvements in medical care, a fall in cigarette smoking, and better control over high blood pressure are apparently insufficient to explain the decline. However, other important changes preceded it by a decade or two. Vegetable shortening and margarine overtook lard and butter in the 1940s; in the 1950s, low-fat milk was introduced and egg consumption dropped. And since then, our consumption of poultry, fish, and unsaturated vegetable oils has risen. It's impossible to prove that this broad dietary shift from saturated to unsaturated fats is directly responsible for the reduction in the death rate. But it almost surely has something to do with it.

On the other hand, the possible benefits of a modified diet are sometimes exaggerated. It's well established that an individual's risk of developing heart disease increases steadily with his or her blood cholesterol level. Even so, a few people with very low cholesterol levels still die of heart attacks. And fully half of the people with very high levels are examples of what Jan Breslow of Rockefeller University has called the "Winston Churchill syndrome": people who have "some sort of natural immunity to cardiovascular disease, despite the worst that the environment—or they themselves—can do." In other words, individuals differ tremendously in their apparent susceptibility to cholesterol. They also differ in the responsiveness of their cholesterol levels to dietary change. So, for a given person, even the strictest low-fat diet is no guarantee of immunity from heart disease. At best, it shifts the odds in his or her favor.

The medical establishment's current preventive approach—recommending lower fat and cholesterol intakes for all adults—is an approximate one. It will do many people some good and others no good at all, though it probably won't do them any harm either. Eugene Braunwald of the Harvard Medical School has called the universal dietary recommendations a "shotgun" approach that "although logical today, is based on our incomplete understanding" of heart disease. The day may come when each of us will routinely have our genetic propensity to heart disease analyzed and our arteries scanned, and we'll be told whether it's worth our while to follow a precautionary diet or take preventive drugs. Until then, we really won't know for sure. At the moment, family medical history is one guide, and blood cholesterol levels are another. There's also the simple prudential wager: to paraphrase Pascal on belief in God, we have more to lose by betting one way than the other.

Those of us who do want to eat prudently can count on newspapers, magazines, and television to inform us of the very latest dietary findings. Unfortunately, being frequently informed is not the same as being well informed. New studies of this or that fiber, this or that oil are reported before any consensus has been reached on their significance, so we ride a rollercoaster, lurching from one craze to another. The ups and downs are seldom balanced by the accumulating, even leaden weight of knowledge about heart disease, which doesn't lend itself to 30-second or one-paragraph summaries. We end up wondering whether anyone really knows anything.

What's usually missing from the public discussion is some sense of perspective: an explanation of what heart disease actually is and why it develops. According to the popular shorthand, "sticky" cholesterol in the blood plugs up the arteries. It sounds almost trivial, a matter of bad plumbing. The reality is more insidious, more evidently cause for concern. It also happens to be fascinating. For as scientists have gone about investigating heart disease, they've unearthed some surprising insights into our nature as creatures with fundamental design flaws, creatures who can either exacerbate or compensate for these flaws by the ways in which we think and eat.

To understand the what and why of heart disease and of fat requires us to delve more deeply than usual into the realm of cells and molecules. Unfamiliar ground, yes. But it's where our health is determined. We should know it better. And like any journey to a new place, the excursion can sharpen our awareness of everyday life, its strange mixture of accident and necessity.

Inward, then, to the arteries.

The heart is the vital muscle that pumps blood, with its oxygen, nutrients, and protective agents, to all cells in the body. It executes between two and three billion contractions in a lifetime. There are many ways in which this amazingly reliable organ can be damaged. The most common is obstruction of the coronary arteries, the arteries distributed around the upper part of the heart. (*Coronary* comes from the Latin for "crown.") These are the vessels that supply the heart itself with blood. If the coronary arteries become blocked, a person experiences a heart attack, a failure of the muscle caused by the death of some of its cells. When a blockage occurs in the blood vessels supplying the brain, the result is a stroke, or the death of brain cells.

If we give any thought at all to our vascular system, the network of blood vessels, most of us probably visualize it as a passive system of tubes, a kind of color-coded indoor plumbing. In fact it's an extremely active tissue, one that continuously responds to and controls the flow of blood, and that must absorb the stresses imposed by the incessantly pumping heart. The aorta, with a diameter of about an inch, and the arteries, on average a fifth that size, have very elastic walls that expand to accommodate the volume of blood ejected at each heartbeat, and then recoil to push most of the blood more gradually and evenly through the rest of the system than the heart could alone. The arteries eventually narrow to the arterioles, vessels about a third of a millimeter in diameter, which are less elastic but contain a large proportion of muscle cells in their walls. By contracting and relaxing, the muscle cells cause the arterioles to constrict or dilate, and thereby control both the pressure of the blood in the vessels, and the amount of blood that flows to the capillaries in different tissues.

The muscular arteriole walls accomplish this carefully calibrated distribution of blood in response to signals from nerves and from the *endothelium*, the remarkable lining just one cell thick that coats the interior of the entire vascular system. The endothelial cells not only register and translate the presence of hormones and other chemical signals from the brain and other organs; they can also sense local changes in oxygen concentration and even blood pressure, and direct the muscle cells in the vessel wall to contract or relax accordingly.

Normal aging appears to affect the vascular system in two ways. First, the aorta and arteries become less elastic, less effective at smoothing each pulse of blood, so the pulse pressure rises. Second, the muscular arterioles become on average less easily widened, so the blood pressure rises and distant tissues aren't as readily supplied when their demand for blood increases. Both of these processes are probably the outcome of natural changes in the composition of the vessel walls, mainly an increase in the proportion of stiffening connective tissue. To some extent, then, a kind of "hardening of the arteries" is inevitable. Fatty obstruction of the arteries, however, is not.

The earliest detailed analysis of diseased blood vessels describes the effects of ordinary aging, not fatty obstruction. Still, it offers an astonishing anticipation of the modern view of heart disease. The anatomist was Leonardo da Vinci. Around 1510 he performed an autopsy on an old but otherwise healthy man he had known in the hospital of Santa Maria Nuova at Florence, in order to determine "the cause of a death so sweet." His conclusion:

> The old who enjoy good health die through lack of sustenance. And this is brought about by the continuous narrowing of the passage of the [blood] vessels by thickening of the coats of these vessels. . . . And this coat of the vessels acts in man as in oranges, in which the peel becomes thicker and the pulp diminishes the more they become old.

Why should the inner layer, or "coat," of the blood vessels thicken with age?

> I consider that a thing which is nearer to that which feeds it increases more; and for this reason these vessels being a sheath of the blood that nourishes the body, it nourishes the vessels so much the more as they are closer to the blood.

Overnourishment of the blood vessels leads to starvation of the heart: Leonardo's penetrating irony remains central to the modern understanding of heart disease. In fact, the ironies have been accumulating. Direct exposure to over-rich blood may well initiate arterial injury. But fat and cholesterol must share the blame for the subsequent, often fatal damage with the body's powers of growth, development, and healing.

The body's contribution to its own disease has become evident over the last decade or so, thanks to detailed anatomical and biochemical investigations in many laboratories. The healthy human artery consists of three layers. The innermost layer is made up of the lining of endothelial cells, which actually makes contact with the blood, and a thin sheet of connective tissue that contains only an occasional muscle cell. Both the amount of connective tissue and the number of muscle cells slowly increase with age, so that, as Leonardo observed, this layer gradually thickens. The outermost layer of the artery is a more substantial sheet of connective tissue containing a few muscle cells. The middle layer is the muscular wall proper. It is contained between two coarse sheets of elastic tissue, and comprises from one to more than thirty concentric spirals of muscle cells, depending on the size of the artery.

The medical term for chronically narrowed arteries is *atherosclerosis*, a compound of the Greek words for "gruel" and "hardening" that describes the characteristically mealy and toughened consistencies of the obstruction. Atherosclerotic injury takes place in the innermost layer of the artery, just under the endothelial lining. It takes the form of a local thickening that progressively grows into the opening of the vessel. The obstruction, or *fibrous plaque*, consists mainly of a mass of muscle cells embedded in a thick, tough matrix of connective tissue. Also present in the plaque are many *macrophages*, a scavenging variety of white blood cell; the word means "big eaters." In the middle of such a mass there may also be a core of fatty material, including the debris of dead cells and solid crystals of cholesterol. The muscle cells and macrophages are often themselves packed with droplets of cholesterol compounds, to the extent that under the microscope they look like pockets of foam. The proportions of fatty and fibrous materials vary, but both intrude on the inner opening of the artery and restrict the blood flow.

In addition to this direct sort of blockage, the irregular surface of the fibrous plaque and the gruely, unstable fatty core, which readily cracks under the pressure of flowing blood, both favor the formation of clots. These may either obstruct the area of the plaque itself or break off and become lodged in a narrower stretch downstream.

The popular caricature of atherosclerosis is a distinct plug of cholesterol sticking to the inner surface of the artery and blocking blood flow. In fact, atherosclerotic injury occurs within the artery's structure and involves the artery's own cells. Somehow large numbers of muscle cells and macrophages and unusual amounts of connective tissue erupt in a normally thin, sparsely populated layer of tissue. Somehow solidified cholesterol accumulates *within* the inner lining of the artery, and only in isolated spots. We still don't fully understand the life history of the atherosclerotic plaque. But we do know the broad outline of the story, and it's a surprising one. The four main actors are the muscle cells and endothelial cells native to the artery wall, and the macrophages and platelet cells that are carried in the blood.

The muscle cells found in the blood vessels—as well as in the digestive tract and uterus—are known as smooth muscle cells. They're specialized to generate the slow, even, involuntary contractions that maintain the tone of these hollow organs. There are two main types of smooth muscle cells in the artery wall. Most cells have an extensive contractile apparatus and do the work of regulating blood pressure and blood flow. A smaller population lacks the contractile machinery but is freer to move from one place to another in the tissue; these cells specialize in the synthesis of connective tissue proteins—*collagen* and *elastin*—that reinforce the structure of the artery. Intermediate cell types also exist, and each type can be gradually "modulated" into the other type by various means.

This versatility, which is extremely rare among mature animal cells, is almost certainly a result of the arteries' need to be able to adapt to changing demands. As the fetus develops in the womb, for example, the blood pressure and patterns of blood flow constantly change, and different parts of the fetal vascular system must be reinforced or muscularized to different degrees. Studies done in Hungary and in New Orleans have shown that even the vascular systems of newborn infants have substantially thickened areas where muscle cells have migrated from the middle layer of the artery to the inner layer, multiplied, and synthesized large amounts of reinforcing material. These thickenings particularly occur near branches and divisions in the arteries, which suggests that they represent a strengthening of the blood vessels in response to especially turbulent or otherwise stressful flow. Such sites also turn out to be the preferred locations for atherosclerotic injury.

What controls whether smooth muscle cells are contractile or synthetic, whether they stay put in the middle layer or migrate to the inner layer and pour out connective tissue proteins? It appears that certain constituents of the normal connective tissue in the artery wall tend to maintain the muscle cells in their contractile form. But a number of other compounds signal contractile cells to become synthetic ones, attract them from the middle layer into the inner one, or induce them to proliferate. Here's where the cast of other cells enters the story.

The endothelial lining of the artery is especially important because it largely determines what substances from the blood are allowed to pass into the artery wall. If an area of the lining is somehow damaged, then the blood itself may come into direct contact with underlying cells. And at least one protein constituent of blood plasma can transform contractile muscle cells into synthetic cells. In addition, damaged endothelial cells somehow induce neighboring cells to become "activated," to begin dividing so as to replace the damaged cells and restore the integrity of the lining. Activated endothelial cells secrete a number of growth-promoting substances. Some of these stimulate the endothelium itself, but some stimulate synthetic smooth muscle cells to migrate and divide. So both the damaged artery lining itself and the blood plasma that leaks through it can cause smooth muscle cells to begin populating the inner wall.

Injury to the endothelium also brings macrophages to the scene. These scavenging white blood cells begin their career as circulating *monocytes* and are attracted into a tissue by biochemical signs of damage. Once they've taken up residence in a wound, they engulf and digest cellular debris and some microbes, and can secrete a number of defensive chemicals that kill other microbes. They also produce growth factors that mobilize the restorative capabilities of the injured tissue by inducing cells to multiply and synthesize connective—that is, scar—tissue. Some of these growth factors can activate smooth muscle cells in the artery wall and set them on the march to the area just under the damaged endothelium.

Finally, there are the blood platelets. These cells are armed with granules of potent chemicals that are released only in certain circumstances. Some of these chemicals are the same growth factors generated by the endothelium and macrophages; others are clotting factors that cause platelets and certain blood proteins to mass together and slow the bleeding from gross injuries to the blood vessels. The inner surface of a healthy artery prevents clotting, but a damaged endothelium or exposed connective tissue will induce platelets to aggregate and release their granules. The platelet growth factors also activate smooth muscle cells in the area.

The lining, muscle, and blood cells evidently make up an organized repair system. When the blood vessels are intact and operating effectively, their muscle cells are maintained in their contractile, quiescent form. When a certain area is put under abnormal stress or injured, then the sensitive endothelial lining and certain blood cells recruit nearby muscle cells to migrate to the weakened area, multiply, and lay down reinforcing connective tissue. Such a sequence of events may well be what causes the normal thickening near arterial branch points, where the blood flow is especially turbulent. Once the stress is relieved or the injury repaired, then all elements of the system settle back into quiescence.

Unfortunately, it's easy to see how this natural repair system can go wrong. Consider, for example, what would happen when an area of endothelium near a branch point, and so already somewhat vulnerable, is subjected to chronic stress from high blood pressure, or a local viral infection, or toxic chemicals from cigarette smoke. The persistent stress causes the endothelium, macrophages, and platelets to remain activated, to recruit ever more muscle cells under the affected endothelium. The artery's inner layer thus gets thicker and thicker, to the point that it may occupy a significant portion of the arterial channel and compromise the flow of blood. Simultaneously, the normally muscular middle layer becomes locally depleted of muscle cells; over time, it may become so weak that it gives way, balloons into an aneurysm, and bursts. So the patch job ends up dwarfing the original, relatively minor injury, and can itself cause death.

Another major complication that frequently arises from chronic stress or chronic injury to the endothelium involves the scavenging macrophage. Proliferating smooth muscle cells and macrophages both have a propensity to accumulate large amounts of cholesterol compounds. The actively multiplying muscle cells probably require large amounts of cholesterol to construct their new membranes. The macrophages have no such need. Instead, one of their scavenging functions is to absorb any cholesterol-containing particles, or *lipoproteins*, that have been chemically damaged—oxidized, for example—or that have become stuck to proteins in the connective tissue. This cleanup activity removes potentially toxic or interfering materials from the wound and creates a local reservoir of cholesterol for the cells that will multiply during the healing process. The upshot, however, is that whereas the average cell strictly controls its cholesterol intake, the macrophage does not. And, it turns out, both activated macrophages and endothelial cells emit powerful oxidizing chemicals that are probably antimicrobial weapons. Unfortunately, these chemicals also oxidize lipoproteins.

Now consider what happens when the arterial repair system is operating continuously in response to chronic stress, at the same time that the blood contains a high concentration of lipoproteins. The more lipoprotein particles there are in the blood, the more likely some will either become attached to the artery wall or be oxidized by all the repair activity. There will therefore be a continuous supply of these cholesterol carriers for the macrophages to scavenge. Eventually individual macrophages will take in more cholesterol than they can tolerate, and become poisoned. Some cholesterol may even precipitate into pure crystals inside them.

As the engorged macrophages die, the cholesterol crystals and droplets of cholesterol compounds are left embedded in the enlarged mass of connective tissue under the artery lining, where they attract yet more macrophages to absorb them. The cycle of macrophage engorgement and death continues, and the cholesterol and dead cells gradually coalesce into a fatty core, a macrophage graveyard. Meanwhile, new generations of muscle cells grow around them, continuously secreting more fibrous connective tissue that can trap more blood lipoproteins. The plaque intrudes further and further into the bore of the artery. If the plaque ruptures, platelets aggregate to form a clot. Eventually the flow of blood becomes inadequate, and part of the heart or brain is damaged.

This is the reality of atherosclerosis, as it's currently understood. The wall of the artery suffers chronic damage. An efficient repair system is set in motion to reinforce the damaged area. But in the presence of plentiful blood cholesterol, the macrophages eat themselves to death and disintegrate within the artery wall, thereby perpetuating the injury and the repair activity that eventually blocks the artery.

So far I've emphasized a secondary role for cholesterol in the development of heart disease. However, it's quite likely that a high concentration of blood cholesterol can itself constitute a form of biochemical stress, can trigger as well as sustain the chain of events leading to arterial blockage. When researchers feed animals a high-cholesterol diet, the first change they see is the attachment of circulating white blood cells to the artery lining. This suggests that the blood cholesterol particles themselves are causing the initial injury to the endothelium. And endothelial cells in the test tube are indeed damaged by oxidatively modified cholesterol particles, which are probaby more common in the blood when cholesterol levels are high. So cholesterol isn't necessarily just an accessory after the fact. It may sometimes be the primary villain in the development of heart disease.

The story of atherosclerosis involves the unfortunate intersection of two separate subplots. The one we've just followed is the body's admirable but imperfect effort to maintain its blood vessels in good working order. The smooth muscle cells and macrophages are just doing their job, but there's no supervisor to prevent them from going too far and making the repair worse than the initial damage. The other plot is the arrival of the blood cholesterol that encourages the re-

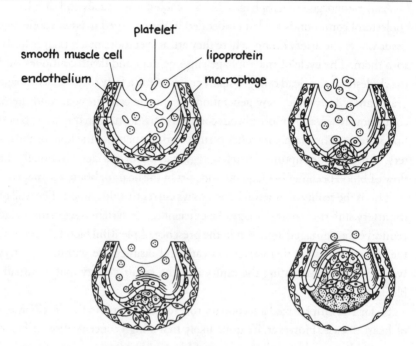

The development of atherosclerosis. Upper left: *Injury to the inner lining of an artery attracts circulating blood platelets and monocytes, and allows lipoproteins rich in cholesterol (dots) to seep into the underlying connective tissue. The monocytes take up residence in the area as scavenging macrophages. The endothelial lining, platelets, and macrophages all release chemical signals to activate the wound-healing process.* Upper right: *In response to these signals, smooth muscle cells from within the artery wall begin to multiply and migrate toward the wound, which they reinforce by producing connective tissue. Meanwhile, the macrophages ingest lipoproteins that have been oxidized or trapped in the wound area.* Lower left: *If the blood contains large quantities of lipoproteins, they will continue to seep into the artery wall, and may even cause further damage to the lining. The macrophages scavenge lipoproteins until they're poisoned by the cholesterol they accumulate. The poisoned cells die, rupture, and release the cholesterol back into the wound. This in turn attracts more macrophages to the wound, and prolongs the migration of the muscle cells.* Lower right: *Over time, the wound grows into a mass of cholesterol crystals, cell debris, connective tissue, macrophages in various stages of engorgement, and muscle cells. This mass can eventually fill the entire bore of the artery and stop the flow of blood.*

pairs to slip out of control. It's here that food comes into the story and that all the cells in the body turn out to be troublemakers. But it's also here that some of the best prospects for preventing heart disease suggest themselves.

The overwhelming case against cholesterol has been built over more than a century, and by scientists throughout the world. In 1843, just three decades after the French chemist Chevreul recognized cholesterol as a distinct substance and gave it a name (from the Greek *chole*, bile, and *stereos*, solid—it was initially extracted from gallstones), a German pathologist, Julius Vogel, described the presence of telltale crystals in diseased blood vessels and identified them by their shape as cholesterol. The fact that certain foods could cause heart disease in animals was discovered in prerevolutionary Russia, at the Imperial Military Medical Academy in St. Petersburg. Between 1908 and 1913 researchers there showed first that eggs and fatty meats cause atherosclerotic plaques to develop in rabbit arteries, and then that pure cholesterol alone, when added to the rabbit's normal vegetable diet, did the same thing.

In the first survey of human populations, C. D. De Langen of the Dutch Public Health Service reported in 1916 that serum cholesterol levels were much lower among the inhabitants of Java than in their countrymen who served as stewards on European passenger ships and ate a European diet. By the 1930s he had evidence of a correlation between the fat content of the diet and the incidence of atherosclerosis. Following each World War, it was determined that death rates for heart disease had declined significantly in European countries that had been forced to ration food and had suffered some degree of malnutrition. During the Korean War, American physicians found in autopsies that an astonishing 77% of their soldiers, of average age twenty-two, had atherosclerotic plaques in the coronary arteries, while very few Korean casualties did. It looked as though the origins of heart disease lay in the habits—probably dietary habits—of adolescence or even childhood.

The early 1950s brought several other key observations. Researchers in Holland and in Oakland, California, demonstrated that saturated fats generally produce higher human blood cholesterol levels than do unsaturated fats. Preliminary epidemiological surveys in a number of countries turned up a correlation between blood cholesterol and the likelihood of developing heart disease. And at the Berkeley campus of the University of California, the initial discriminations were made among the various lipoproteins that transport cholesterol in the blood, and their respective correlations with heart disease.

The metabolism of cholesterol in animals is labyrinthine and still not fully understood. But scientists are now beginning to glimpse the ultimate mechanisms by which diet influences the quantity of cholesterol in the blood. Central to this progress has been the Nobel Prize–winning work of Michael S. Brown and Joseph L. Goldstein at the University of Texas Health Sciences Center in Dallas. Brown and Goldstein scrutinized a genetic disease, familial hypercholesterolemia, whose sole effect is to produce extremely high blood cholesterol levels: up to six or ten times the normal figure. This disease is sometimes called a "natural experiment" because it proves that high blood cholesterol alone is sufficient to cause heart disease. People born with the severe form usually suffer heart attacks in childhood; those with the less severe form, in their thirties and forties. By identifying the genetic defect that causes familial hypercholesterolemia, Brown and Goldstein discovered the primary means by which our bodies remove cholesterol from the blood—or fail to do so. The machinery has turned out to be dizzyingly intricate. Here's a simplified sketch that will help us answer three key questions: Why does cholesterol build up in the bloodstream? Why do people vary so much in their susceptibility to heart disease? And how can some fats actually reduce blood cholesterol levels?

Cholesterol is, among other things, an essential structural component of all our cells. Our cells are therefore able to synthesize their own supply, but they also exploit the presence of cholesterol in the meats, eggs, and dairy products we eat. Once they're absorbed by the small intestine, both fat and cholesterol are transported in the blood in *lipoproteins*, which are microscopic packages of lipids (cholesterol, fats, and their chemical relatives) and proteins. There are several different varieties of lipoproteins, each with a different makeup and function. A single lipoprotein particle contains several thousand molecules altogether. The liver acts as the central packager and traffic controller.

The cholesterol-supply system has three essential features. First there's the shipping and receiving mechanism. The lipoproteins are routed and sorted in the blood by means of a number of proteins. One group of proteins can be likened to delivery trucks: they help hold the fatty substances together in a functioning lipoprotein, and get them to the right destination. A second group of proteins serves as the receiving dock at each cell. These receptor proteins, which Brown and Goldstein discovered, sit at the exterior of the cell, recognize a particular kind of lipoprotein, grasp onto it, and help pull it into the cell. The combination of delivery and receptor proteins determines the destination of a given lipoprotein. Most lipoproteins originate in the small intestine or liver, and after unloading some of their cargo along the way, eventually return to the liver. But cells in the rest of the body can also take in lipoproteins or can ship unwanted cholesterol back to the liver.

A second feature of the cholesterol-supply system is that there's no effective disposal mechanism. Our cells can't break cholesterol down or transform it into some other kind of molecule, and the body doesn't excrete very much. The liver does use cholesterol in the bile to help emulsify fatty foods in the intestine, but the intestines reabsorb much of the bile, and only a small amount of cholesterol is actually lost. So once we ingest cholesterol or our cells manufacture it, the body has to find some place to put it. Most cholesterol ends up in one of four places: in cell membranes, in storage depots within the liver and in other cells, in the bile, and in the bloodstream. The liver apparently maintains separate "pools" of cholesterol for the bile, for circulation to the body, and for storage, so that once assigned to the bile, for example, a molecule of cholesterol probably won't end up in the blood.

The third feature of the system is that beyond a certain point, the more packages of cholesterol there are in the bloodstream, the less willing the body's cells are to take them in. The number of lipoproteins taken in by a cell depends on the number of receptor proteins on the cell's surface. And Brown and Goldstein discovered that the number of receptors deployed by a cell is controlled by the cholesterol level in the cell. The better supplied with cholesterol a cell is, the fewer receptors it makes, and so the less cholesterol it subsequently removes from the blood.

Now let's put all the pieces together. If our food is rich in fat and cholesterol, then our blood fills up with the delivery lipoproteins, and our cells receive plenty. The more cholesterol each cell accumulates, the less it needs: in fact, as we know from macrophages in the artery, too much can kill. So the cell begins to shut down its own production, put the excess into storage, and refuse additional deliveries. The cell thus optimizes its supply of cholesterol.

That's fine for the individual cell. But if we continue to eat rich foods, then lipoproteins keep pouring into the blood. With fewer receptors working throughout the body, more lipoproteins remain in the blood, and for a longer period of time. The arteries then become a kind of cholesterol dump. And the more lipoproteins there are in the bloodstream, the more likely it is that significant numbers will become oxidized, damage the artery lining, engorge scavenging macrophages, and so cause the growth of atherosclerotic plaques. A cholesterol-supply system that works well in the short run for individual cells ends up endangering all cells by disabling the body's vital supply lines.

Long before physicians came to this understanding of cholesterol's role in heart disease, they had noticed that heart disease tends to run in families, and guessed that genetic factors help determine an individual's susceptibility to it. The pioneering work of Brown and Goldstein has made it possible to appreciate just how numerous and subtle the genetic factors may be. Familial hypercholesterolemia turns out to be caused by defects in a major receptor protein, which leaves all cells in the body largely unable to take up cholesterol from the blood. But because a number of packaging proteins and cellular receptors are essential for the proper disposal of the various lipoproteins, defects in any of the corresponding genes could also raise blood cholesterol levels. Other mutations in the packaging proteins might conceivably leave those levels unchanged but increase the affinity of the lipoproteins for the artery wall, or make them more prone to oxidative damage: these effects too could accelerate the development of atherosclerosis. And there are probably other genes that help determine the sensitivity of the arterial lining to stress, and the rate at which smooth muscle cells and macrophages can generate atherosclerotic plaques.

Even this primitive understanding of the genetics of heart disease helps us appreciate how difficult it is to study the influence of diet on blood cholesterol levels, or of cholesterol levels on heart disease. Unlike inbred laboratory animals, people are genetically diverse. The blood cholesterol levels of individuals in any test group will therefore react differently to a given diet, and their arteries will be able to tolerate different levels of blood cholesterol. So inconclusive human studies don't mean that the cholesterol theory of heart disease is wrong. Several other strong lines of evidence remain in its favor. It's just that we still have a lot to learn about the genetic factors that determine what high dietary or blood cholesterol will actually do to a particular individual. The major challenge for heart researchers in the years to come is to find out what genes are responsible for the Winston Churchill syndrome, how people who aren't fortunate enough to be endowed with those genes can be identified early, and how they might compensate by their choice of foods, or by some sort of medication.

Another byproduct of Brown and Goldstein's work on the major receptor protein was the ability to determine the optimal biochemical conditions under which the receptor operates, including the concentration of lipoprotein at which the receptor binds to it most effectively. That concentration turns out to be about what it is in most animals and in human newborns—but less than half of what is considered a "normal" adult level in the Western world today. So it appears that our entire cholesterol-metabolizing system, and the blood vessels that are forced to contain any excess, were designed for a load much smaller than the one we typically impose on them.

From this inference about natural cholesterol levels there follows an obvious prescription: we should eat far less of our fat- and cholesterol-containing foods than we now do. The prescription's major adverse side effect is also obvious: we would essentially have to give up many of our favorite foods, and with them a great deal of pleasure. At the moment, there's some optimism that this side effect can be eased, at least when it comes to manufactured and fast foods. There's a chance that food technologists may succeed in making low-fat foods more acceptable with new fat substitutes, industrial concoctions that have some of the desirable properties of fat but that don't raise lipoprotein levels. We'll have to see just how adequate these substitutes really are. Right now, the more conservative, more palatable course of action is to moderate our consumption of fats and oils, and then try to find other ways to reduce further our risk of heart disease.

For people who are already at high risk, there are medications that lower blood cholesterol levels by interfering either with the absorption of cholesterol in the intestine, or with cholesterol synthesis in the body's cells. And because the lipoproteins appear to do their damage only after having been chemically damaged, substances that protect the lipoproteins from oxidation may protect the arteries as well. One such drug has recently been found to do just that in animal tests.

The pharmacological approach has its own drawbacks. Drugs are expensive, require close medical supervision, and often have undesirable side effects, effects that could be magnified in the decades over which artery-protecting drugs would be taken. So it may be years before preventive medications come into general use. In the meantime, some of our everyday foods, whose long-term effects are somewhat better known, are turning out to have remarkable properties of their own. We may actually be able to use them to intervene in both subplots of heart disease. And not just by replacing fats with other nutrients (a simple reduction in fat intake may be how "fiber" lowers blood cholesterol), but by being smarter about the fats we choose.

It's been known since the 1950s that the saturated fats typical of milk, eggs, and meats tend to produce higher blood cholesterol levels than do the unsaturated fats typical of many vegetable oils. In fact, the nature of the fat in the diet usually influences cholesterol levels more than the intake of cholesterol itself. Any understanding of this peculiar fact had to await the basic understanding of cholesterol traffic that Brown and Goldstein contributed. In just the last few years, scientists have found that individual fatty acids, the building blocks of the fat molecules in our food, have distinct influences on cholesterol's destination in the body.

In one of the more revealing experiments, David K. Spady and John M. Dietschy at Dallas fed combinations of cholesterol and various fats to hamsters, whose metabolism resembles ours in important respects. They supplied cholesterol in doses that are comparable (relative to body weight) with our own daily intake. As expected, adding cholesterol alone to the feed caused decreases in receptor production and cholesterol synthesis, and an increase in storage. It doubled the animals' blood cholesterol levels. When coconut oil (more than 90% saturated fatty acids) was fed along with cholesterol, the liver cut its production of receptor proteins even more, while raising cholesterol synthesis and decreasing storage. This combination of three undesirable trends resulted in an overall *quadrupling* of blood cholesterol levels. Olive oil (65% monounsaturated oleic acid), on the other hand, restored about half of the receptor production that cholesterol alone had cut and further increased liver storage, which left blood levels about where they were on the cholesterol-only diet. Safflower oil (79% di-unsaturated linoleic acid) also restored some production of receptor proteins, but boosted cholesterol synthesis and decreased storage in the liver. Despite two unfavorable trends, safflower oil actually reduced blood cholesterol slightly compared to the doubling on the cholesterol-only and cholesterol-olive oil diets: a pattern suggesting that it may encourage cholesterol absorption and storage elsewhere in the body, or perhaps the diversion of cholesterol into bile.

The results of these animal experiments are still only suggestive of what goes on in the human body, but what a suggestion! Apparently particular fatty acids help to channel cholesterol along particular metabolic routes, some of them more desirable than others when it comes to the health of our arteries. And it isn't just a matter of saturation. Medium-length saturated fatty acids don't raise blood cholesterol; nor does stearic acid, a saturated acid typical of animal fats and cocoa butter (possibly because our body quickly desaturates it to form oleic acid). One particular saturated acid, palmitic acid, the end-product of the fatty-acid synthetase enzyme system and therefore one of the two most abundant fatty acids in land animals, may well be the major cholesterol-raising villain in the fats we eat.

On reflection, it's not so surprising that dietary fats have such distinct effects on cholesterol metabolism. We usually think of fats as an undifferentiated reserve of calories. But their constituent fatty acids originated as essential structural material for cell membranes; and individual fatty acids, with their unique structures, are called on to perform different biochemical tasks. For example, studies of liver cell membranes, bile, and stored cholesterol (every molecule of which is joined to a fatty acid) show that each material contains its own characteristic mix of fatty acids. We still don't know just why each kind of fatty acid has the influence it does. When we do, we may be in a better position to control the traffic of cholesterol through our blood vessels.

So mono- and di-unsaturated fatty acids keep some cholesterol out of the blood by funneling it into cells and perhaps the bile. There's another group of fatty acids that help out in a very different way. The initial clue was a surprisingly low incidence of heart disease among mainly carnivorous Greenland Eskimos. In the early 1970s the Danish researchers H. O. Bang and J. Dyerberg suggested that the penta- and hexa-unsaturated fatty acids peculiar to the food chain in the oceans might somehow protect the arteries. This now appears to be the case, but not primarily because they lower blood cholesterol levels (they may, but some studies have found that they raise them). Whereas some "terrestrial" fatty acids make helpful adjustments in the cholesterol-supply system, the "marine" fatty acids restrain the arterial repair system.

The highly unsaturated fatty acids characteristic of cold-water fish happen to be precursors of molecules called *eicosanoids*. So, it turns out, is the di-unsaturated linoleic acid, the major polyunsaturate in vegetable oils. These fatty acids enter into the membranes of cells in the blood vessels and heart, and are converted by those cells into eicosanoids when necessary. The eicosanoids are a family of important signals in the body's defense and repair systems; different members of the family call forth different responses. The byproducts of linoleic acid encourage a strong one: the attraction and attachment of macrophages, platelet aggregation and clotting, and the constriction of blood vessels. The byproducts of the fish-oil fatty acids generally have the reverse, or at least more moderate effects; they may be signals by which the body shuts down the repair response. They also somehow reduce the heart's tendency to beat irregularly when it's put under stress by constricted arteries.

The human body isn't very efficient at making fish-oil fatty acids for itself, though it can do so from the tri-unsaturated linolenic acid that is found in rapeseed ("canola") oil and (in much smaller quantities) green vegetables. If the diet is poor in linolenic acid and fish oil, then our cell membranes contain mainly derivatives of linoleic acid, and their eicosanoid production tends to produce a strong repair response. A diet rich in fish oil, on the other hand, populates the cell membranes with the parents of moderating eicosanoids, and therefore tends to retard the development of heart disease.

There's still much to be learned about the fatty acids and their remarkable effects on the body. Not all the news will necessarily be good. Highly unsaturated fats like the fish oils and some vegetable oils are prone to oxidation, which can generate toxic byproducts. Suppressing the repair response and rerouting cholesterol may be desirable on balance for our arteries, but not so desirable for other organs or diseases. And given our genetic differences, not everyone will benefit from the helpful fatty acids. So it's too early to stake the future on fish-oil capsules or a particular kind of cooking oil. Still, these discoveries raise the possibility that we may be able to optimize our use of fats, to find a combination that minimizes the dangers of the typical Western diet. For example, food manufacturers might find a way of incorporating a mix of cholesterol-moderating, artery-calming fatty acids into their products. This wouldn't be any great gastronomical advance, but it could make processed and fast foods less harmful to the public health.

There are other, more traditional methods for changing the mix of fatty acids in foods. It's been known since 1900 that the lipid composition of eggs, milk, and meat can be changed by modifying the animals' feed. Chickens fed less grain and more green plants accumulate linolenic acid and its derivatives in eggs. Milk fat is less saturated when the cow is given an energy-rich feed, and beef fat when the meat is taken from a milk-fed calf or an animal over two years old. Simplest of all, the leaner the meat, the more of its fatty acids are contributed by cell membranes. And because animal membranes are generally less saturated than their storage fats, leaner meat will therefore be richer in unsaturated fatty acids. (Of the fatty acids in cattle fat, 30% are palmitic acid, and 1% linolenic acid or its derivatives; in cattle muscle, the figures are 20% and 14%.) Early in this century, most beef came from rangy Longhorns, which gradually gave way to smaller, fatter English breeds. The grain-fattened Angus will continue to provide us with the finest steaks, but for the purposes of everyday carnivory, maybe it's time for the return of the lean, grass-fed steer.

Any of these changes alone would shift the fatty-acid balance of our diet only slightly. Combined, they might add up to a significant improvement. And surely there are other helpful substances yet to be identified. It will be fascinating to see whether we can make our rich foods more healthful by tinkering with the fine points of their chemistry.

So a few quirks of our physiology—our handling of cholesterol and saturated fats, our arterial repair system—are among the primary causes of heart disease. But the quirks aren't just ours. What, after all, is this attractive nuisance called fat, and what is it doing in our foods? Why do we have such a taste for it? Why are some fats more saturated than others? And why should beef and butter cause trouble, not olives and fish?

A little basic chemistry. Fat is a mixture of biological compounds called *lipids*, or molecules composed mainly of carbon and hydrogen. Because they're electrically symmetrical, or nonpolar, while water is asymmetrical, they tend not to mix with water. Each molecule of a food fat, which is solid at room temperature, or an oil, which is liquid, is essentially a combination of three long hydrocarbon chains called *fatty acids* stuck together. It's the intermingling of the long fatty acid chains that produces the appealing characteristics of fat: its viscosity, or full body and smoothness, and its high boiling point, which means a permanent moistness and the potential for cooking temperatures hot enough to cause browning.

A group of compounds related to the fats, usually found in smaller quantities in food, is the *phospholipids*. They're like the fats and oils except that one of the three fatty acids is replaced by a polar, phosphorus-containing portion. The phospholipids can act as an intermediary between the other lipids and water, their tails associating with the lipids and their polar heads with water. The most common phospholipid in nature and so in our foods is probably lecithin. Most of the emulsified sauces are made possible by the abundance of lecithin in egg yolks. Cholesterol belongs to a third, altogether different class of lipids, the *sterols*. These are more compact structures than the fats and phospholipids; they're built on a core of four interlocking carbon rings.

The lipids have played an essential role in the function of living cells from

The structures of some important lipids found in foods. Palmitic acid, a common saturated fatty acid, is a major cause of elevated blood cholesterol levels. Highly unsaturated eicosapentaenoic acid is one of the fatty acids in fish oils that may slow the development of atherosclerosis.

the very beginnings of life. Because they don't mix evenly with water, they're well suited to the job of forming boundaries in a watery environment. They can surround and enclose the water-based contents of the cell and create distinct compartments within the cell, thereby allowing it to separate various biochemical activities. In modern organisms, these functions are performed mainly by the phospholipids, which readily assemble into a two-layered membrane, one set of polar heads facing the watery interior, the other set the watery exterior, and the tails of both sets mingling in between.

In order for this thin, delicate envelope and the proteins embedded in it to function properly, the membrane must be neither completely solid nor so fluid that normal molecular motions disrupt it. Cells optimize the physical properties of their membranes in two ways. One is by controlling the sterol content. Typical membrane sterols are flat, rigid molecules that slip between neighboring fatty-acid chains, packing them more compactly and restricting their motion. The main job of cholesterol in animals is apparently to tighten up their cell membranes.

Cells also control the fluidity of their membranes by modifying the mix of fatty acids in their phospholipids. This is why we and our foods contain both

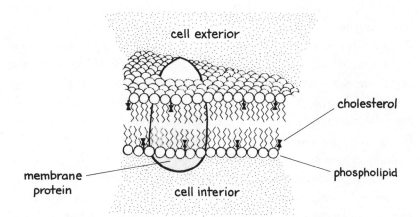

The membrane of a typical animal cell. Phospholipids form the bulk of the membrane; occasional cholesterol molecules give it added stiffness.

saturated and unsaturated fatty acids. In a saturated fatty acid, all the available binding sites along the carbon chain are occupied by hydrogen atoms, and the chain has a highly regular shape. In an unsaturated fatty acid, binding sites on two adjacent carbon atoms are used to form a second carbon-carbon bond, so that the chain contains two fewer hydrogen atoms than it could: and the chain is kinked at the double bond. A *poly*unsaturated fatty acid has two or more double bonds along its length, which result in a curl. These irregular kinks and curls get in the way when the temperature drops and a mixture of fatty acids begins to solidify into an ordered array. Unsaturation therefore tends to lower the melting point of both phospholipids and fats. The exact mix of saturated and unsaturated fatty acids in membranes and fats depends on a number of factors, including the temperature of the organism's environment: the colder the cell, the more unsaturated its lipids must be in order to have the proper fluidity.

If lipids started out as the building blocks of cell membranes, then why are they now concentrated in marbling and belly fat as well? The key is an incidental property of the long hydrocarbon chains that make good membranes. It turns out that these fatty acids also offer large numbers of oxidizable bonds, which means that they generate a large amount of chemical energy when they're dismantled: twice that provided by the same weight of the main energy currencies, carbohydrates like sugars and starch. So at some point in the history of life, certain organisms cultivated the alternative of storing their energy reserves as fats instead of carbohydrate. The economy of storing more calories in less weight would have been especially valuable to the mobile organisms, mainly animals, whose maneuverability could be improved by a lighter energy supply. Similarly, animals obtain more energy from high-fat food than they do from the same weight of a food that is mainly carbohydrate or protein. Surely this basic nutritional advantage is the origin of our abiding hunger for fat.

Animals now store nearly all of their energy reserves in fat. Because plants are stationary and not disadvantaged by the weight of their energy reserves, they still rely mostly on carbohydrates. This is why meats are much richer in lipids than most fruits and vegetables. The average vegetable is around 0.3% lipid by weight, nearly all of which represents membrane phospholipids. Lean meats like chicken and fish, by contrast, are 5% to 10% fat, and a well-marbled steak may be 33% fat.

A final glance at cholesterol. Not only does it stabilize cell membranes: it also stabilizes the membranes of the lipoproteins that transport lipids throughout the body. And relatively small quantities serve as the chemical precursor for making several hormones and vitamin D. Despite a common misimpression, plants do contain cholesterol, particularly in actively growing tissues; but the amounts are insignificant compared to the concentrations found in animals, where it accounts for up to half of the lipid in cell membranes. Plants create a wide variety of sterols for use in their membranes, with cholesterol usually a bit player.

If plants use many sterols in their membranes, then why do animals, particularly the vertebrates, rely so exclusively on cholesterol? There's no obvious answer, but one important factor may have been the emergence of the nervous system. Brain and nervous tissues are exceedingly rich in membranous material and therefore in cholesterol—fifty times more so than muscle or fat. Some biochemists have speculated that particular requirements of the nervous system, together with the necessity of using some sterol to help distribute lipids in the body, and the large quantities needed for both of these functions, put unusual constraints on the range of molecules that would work—and cholesterol emerged as the all-purpose sterol. Whatever the explanation, the centrality of cholesterol in animal chemistry means that whenever we eat meat, eggs, or dairy products, we necessarily take in large quantities of it, and our blood fills up with cholesterol-rich lipoproteins.

So: the fat that gives us such pleasure has its origins in the barriers that protected the delicate chemical organization of life from the forces of dilution and disorder, and fat has helped animals exploit their powers of movement by providing a light-weight energy supply. The versatility of the cholesterol molecule may account for its prominence in the animal body, most notably in the network of cells that allows us to experience such a sensation as pleasure in the first place. These molecules have helped make us what we are.

Some of the same molecules now turn out to unmake many of us. As we've seen, there's hope that some kinds of fatty acids, particularly polyunsaturated linolenic acid and its derivatives, may help us compensate for the flaws in our systems for cholesterol distribution and arterial repair. But why do we have to look to plants and fish for help? Why aren't beef and butter and eggs rich in the fatty acids that might allow us to better tolerate the cholesterol they contain? More evolutionary flukes.

Plants are an abundant source of polyunsaturated fatty acids mainly on account of the peculiar requirements of their photosynthetic apparatus. In fact, the most abundant fatty acid on the planet may be the tri-unsaturated linolenic acid, since it's the major lipid constituent of the photosynthetic membrane in plant chloroplasts. This membrane is packed so tightly in the chloroplast, thus maximizing the amount of surface that can intercept sunlight and convert it into chemical energy, that a square inch of spinach leaf contains nearly four square feet of membrane: about a third of which is in turn occupied by lipids rich in linolenic acid. One of the important steps in photosynthesis, the transfer of an electron from one protein complex to another, depends on the ability of a carrier molecule to move rapidly in the membrane; and the highly unsaturated membrane lipids create a very fluid membrane that accommodates such movement, even at temperatures near the freezing point. In addition, the widely splayed chains of its two unsaturated fatty acids give the membrane lipid molecule an overall conical shape that's especially suitable for making the very tight turns that result when the membrane is folded and packed into the chloroplast.

Linolenic acid everywhere, and barely a drop to drink! Green vegetables are less than 1% lipid by weight, so we fill up on the water and carbohydrate without getting all that much of it. Our main sources of vegetable fatty acids are the storage oils from seeds and fruits. Since the balance of fatty acids in these oils is less critical to the plant's functioning, they range all over the map, from highly saturated tropical seed oils (coconut, palm, cocoa) to mostly monounsaturated fruit oils (olive, avocado) to highly unsaturated temperate seed oils (safflower, corn).

We may not eat enough green vegetables to get much linolenic acid, but we eat plenty of animals that do. Cold-water fish construct their characteristic fatty acids from the linolenic acid supplied by ocean plankton. They elongate and de-saturate linolenic acid even further because their usual operating temperature is close to the freezing point, and their membranes and fats would be too stiff without highly unsaturated fatty acids. Warm-blooded grazers, on the other hand, maintain a relatively high body temperature, so they saturate much of the linolenic acid from their food to keep their membranes and fats from being too fluid. This is one reason that deep-water fish turn out to be better for our arteries than farm animals.

But body temperature is only part of the story. Our beef and dairy products contain very little linolenic acid or its derivatives; they're among the most con-centrated sources of saturated fatty acids in our diet. Yet the fat of pasture-fed horses contains less than two-thirds the saturated fat of the pasture-fed steer, and nearly six times the polyunsaturated fat. Wild game animals may contain an even higher proportion of unsaturated fatty acids.

So why is it that we don't get the benefit of the chloroplast lipids from our beef, lamb, milk, and butter? The answer has to do with why our ancestors do-mesticated cattle and sheep in the first place: that is, because these animals can live on grass, and so provide food for humans without taking any other food out of our mouths. Cattle and sheep are ruminants. In order to make efficient use of their rather dilute food source, they and their close relatives have evolved a multichambered stomach and symbiotic relations with a variety of microor-ganisms, including both bacteria and protozoans. The first chamber of the stomach, the *rumen*, contains a soup rich in microbes that, unlike their host an-imal, can digest cellulose, the main structural carbohydrate of plants. The mi-crobes thrive on the pulverized mass of green matter that enters the rumen, and the animal absorbs the many nutrients generated by the microbes.

It turns out that the rumen microbes actively transform the major leaf poly-unsaturates into stearic acid, the fully saturated fatty acid that is relatively rare outside of ruminants and cocoa butter. They all but eliminate polyunsaturates from the rumen and so from the animal's fat and its milk. Yet the microbes don't appear to make any use at all of the stearic acid they produce. For the moment, the best clue to the purpose of this transformation is the fact that free fatty acids can be toxic to some microorganisms, apparently because they tend to coat microbial surfaces and so interfere with the absorption of nutrients. The more unsaturated the fatty acid, the more toxic it is. (Polyunsaturated fatty acids are also more easily oxidized, and the byproducts of oxidation can be toxic.) So our cattle don't pass on the fatty acids that are good for us because the same fatty acids are probably no good for their digestive partners, who saturate them in self-defense.

Now there's a challenge for the genetic engineers: come up with some rumen microbes that are able to tolerate linolenic acid. However, the resulting meat and dairy products might pose challenges of their own. In the 1970s, dairy scientists got polyunsaturates into beef and milk by feeding cattle encapsulated vegetable oil. Unfortunately, the polyunsaturates were quickly oxidized and generated rancid flavors, though this was cured to some extent by vitamin E supplements. Further experiments along these lines won't necessarily advance haute cuisine, but they might make ordinary eating easier on the arteries.

Back at last to the fatted calf! The road turned out to be pretty long, and not exactly scenic. But all the spelunking through cell membranes and artery walls, livers and rumens, was necessary to trace the various narrow paths of biological adaptation and compromise that intersect in the knot of heart disease. Atherosclerosis results in large part from too successful a pursuit of the very stuff we're made of. Fat, like cholesterol, is an essential part of us, has helped us become habile and smart, so that we can now more than satisfy our abiding hunger for it. But when we do so, fat and cholesterol can end up starving our hearts and brains of blood. Individual cells in the body control their cholesterol content quite effectively by refusing to take delivery on more than they need, but in so doing they turn the bloodstream into a cholesterol dump. When that happens, the arteries' powers of growth and healing can be twisted into generating mortal disease. Our food animals would be better for us if we fed them less assiduously, and if their digestive aides were less sensitive to the lipids of the field.

Biological evolution has supplied us with very effective solutions to immediate problems: getting enough to eat, getting each cell the right amount of cholesterol, patching injuries in our blood vessels. It hasn't done such a great job of coordinating these solutions to avoid the havoc they can wreak in the long run.

Fortunately, what biological evolution has failed to do, cultural evolution appears capable of doing. The medical sciences are finding better ways for each of us to determine our susceptibility to heart disease and, if it's advisable, to control our systems of cholesterol distribution and arterial repair with diet or drugs. True, there's still a long way to go. But even cultural evolution takes time.

Heart disease is often called a disease of affluence or of civilization. That lets nature off too easily. Instead, I would call it one instance of the incongruity between civilization and the quirky biology that gave rise to it. Our mastering of nature has been driven in part by bodily hungers and desires that were formed in the usual condition of nature: namely, scarcity. Now we find that our bodies aren't designed to handle abundance; that although it's more pleasurable, abundance can be just as lethal as famine. Having succeeded at adapting to nature by controlling it, we now need to adapt to the consequences of our success, and answer a different hunger: the hunger for a pleasurable life that's also long and active. Our mind must lend to the arteries and liver and palate a foresight and prudence that they lack. It will take the continuing, civilizing efforts of physicians and biochemists, farmers and cooks, to make the good life better for us.

Food and Cancer

Toward the end of the eighteenth century, a concoction called toast and water enjoyed something of a vogue in England. It was made by toasting a piece of stale bread, then steeping the toast in water until the water had turned brown. The toast was removed and the colored, flavored water taken as a mild restorative. According to food historian C. Anne Wilson, this beverage may have been born around 1700 as a cheap and very approximate imitation of coffee. Fannie Farmer included it among her recipes for invalids as late as 1896.

W. Mattieu Williams, an English writer of popular books on science who published *The Chemistry of Cookery* in 1885, performed some interesting experiments with toast and water. In the process he became one of the first to discover evidence that common foods may be injurious to our health. Williams himself, however, interpreted his findings to mean just the reverse.

> I have often amused myself by watching what occurs when toast and water is prepared, and I recommend my readers to repeat the observation. Toast a small piece of bread to blackness, and then float it on water in a glass vessel. Leave the water at rest, and direct your attention to the under side of the floating toast. Little threadlike streams of brown liquid will be seen descending in the water. This is a solution of the substance which, if I mistake not, is a sort of caramel, and which ultimately tinges all the water.
>
> Some years ago I commenced a course of experiments with this substance, but did not complete them. In case I should never do so, I will here communicate the results obtained. I found that this starch

caramel is a disinfectant, and that sugar caramel also has some disinfecting properties. I am not prepared to say that it is powerful enough to disinfect sewage, though at the time I had a narrow escape from the Great Seal Office, where I thought of patenting it for this purpose as a non-poisonous disinfectant that may be poured into rivers in any quantity without danger. Though it may not be powerful enough for this, it has an appreciable effect on water slightly tainted with decomposing organic matter.

This is a very curious fact. We do not know who invented toast and water, nor, so far as I can learn, has any theory of its use been expounded, yet there is extant a vague popular impression that the toast has some sort of wholesome effect on the water. I suspect that this must have been originally based on experience, probably on the experience of our forefathers or foremothers, living in country places where stagnant water was a common beverage, and various devices were adopted to render it potable.

A curious fact indeed, and just as curious an idea for exploiting it. Williams was astute to observe that caramel suppresses the growth of bacteria, but he may have been incorrect in his assumption that it is "without danger" to higher forms of life. Modern medicine has recently rediscovered the disinfecting properties of caramel and has determined at least part of the basis for those properties. Two research articles published in the 1980s reported on the "clastogenic [chromosome-breaking] activity of caramel and caramelized sugars," and the "genotoxic activity of caramel on Salmonella and cultured mammalian cells." Caramel in fact damages the genetic material—the DNA, or deoxyribonucleic acid—of both bacteria and animals. It must therefore be under suspicion as a potential cancer-causing agent, a carcinogen.

The last several decades have brought much bad news of this sort. Caramel; toast and another traditional restorative, beef broth; raw mushrooms; cured, barbecued, and fried meats—these are just some of the familiar foods that have been stigmatized as possible carcinogens. Meanwhile others, mainly vegetables of the cabbage family, have been recommended as possible anticarcinogenic agents. But the perpetual qualifier "possible" casts doubt on these often dispiriting discriminations, and we seldom hear any rationale for them. Why should brussels sprouts be good and mushrooms bad?

There *is* a rationale for all this, a developing scientific consensus about the nature of cancer and the ways that diet may influence it. Like the consensus on atherosclerosis, it suggests the encouraging possibility that simple changes in our eating habits may significantly reduce the incidence of a fearsome disease, one that currently kills one of every five Americans. An acquaintance with this rationale can help us make sense of the interim reports and dietary recommendations that make it into the news. And like heart disease, cancer turns out to be a window onto our biological heritage. Through it we can glimpse some of the ambiguities and compromises that are inherent in the chemistry of life on earth.

Our realization that foods may cause cancer is very recent, and therefore still sketchy and provisional. The first well-founded suspicion that a form of human cancer could be associated with any agent in our environment was expressed in 1761 by the English physician John Hill, who noticed that heavy users of snuff often developed nasal tumors. A few years later, the surgeon Percivall Pott made the connection between an increased incidence of scrotal cancer in chimney sweeps and their exposure to soot. And beginning in the nineteenth century, a number of cancers were associated with particular industrial occupations, including mining, smelting, and dyeing. It wasn't until the 1930s that the individual toxic components of soot were identified, and around the same time that several industrial chemicals were shown to cause cancer in animals. Several hundred such chemicals are now known. It's our relatively long experience with these prominent manufactured poisons that conditions us to think primarily of industrial chemicals, pesticides, and the like when the word *carcinogen* is mentioned.

The initial indication that our daily bread might not be absolutely innocent came in the 1930s with the discovery that butter yellow, a food coloring commonly used in Europe and the Far East and briefly in the U.S., caused liver cancer in animals. Still, this was a synthetic food additive and cast no suspicions on ordinary home-prepared foods. In 1950 it was found that liver cancer also resulted from ingestion of certain plants of the genus *Senecio* that were used as medicinals in parts of Africa and Europe. This was the first evidence that carcinogenic chemicals exist in living things, but the plants were obscure and not really foodstuffs.

In the 1960s the survey hit home. Fatal epidemics in Idaho trout hatcheries and English poultry farms were traced to aflatoxin, a previously unknown carcinogen produced by a common mold that contaminates grains and peanuts.

Safrole, the principal flavoring component of sassafras root and a valued ingredient in root beer, was found to be carcinogenic in animals and was banned
from use in food manufacturing. Bracken fern, whose spring fiddleheads are
eaten as a delicacy in many parts of the world despite widespread knowledge
that it poisons livestock, proved to be strongly carcinogenic in laboratory animals. Nitrosamines, which had first been associated with human cancer as industrial materials and by-products, were discovered in cured meats and in
cheese.

Spoiled grain, odd plants, processed meats: even these didn't seem to be too
immediate a threat, at least in affluent countries where foods are fresh and various. Unfortunately, 1964 brought more ominous news. Researchers at the Chicago Medical School discovered a potent, well-studied soot carcinogen on the
beloved American charcoal-broiled steak. Nor was it a barely detectable trace:
a single large well-done steak carried the same amount of benzo(a)pyrene as is
generated from the smoking of several hundred cigarettes.

At first it looked as though we could rehabilitate the barbecue simply by taking care to prevent fat from falling onto the fire and undergoing combustion to
hazardous hydrocarbons. For those who craved a smoky flavor, the Chicago
team found that liquid smoke, a tarless water condensate of wood smoke that
can be painted on food, was free of the then-known soot carcinogens. But in the
1970s scientists developed quick, convenient methods for screening possible
carcinogenic substances, and it soon became evident that hydrocarbons were
not the only problem. Takashi Sugimura and colleagues at the National Cancer
Research Center in Tokyo discovered several previously unknown compounds
that are generated when high-protein foods like meats are merely browned,
and whose mutagenic activity appeared to be comparable to that of the most
powerful known carcinogens. Barry Commoner, later a third-party presiden-
tial candidate in the U.S., made headlines in 1978 when his laboratory reported
the presence of DNA-damaging substances in both the ordinary fried ham-
burger and the quintessence of haute cuisine, beef broth (see chapter 16). And
the new tests showed that, tarless or not, liquid smoke is a potent damager of
DNA. Everyday, moderate cooking techniques thus became as suspect as
industrial-scale curing and severe overcooking.

The list of questionable foods has continued to grow. Toast, coffee, chocolate, comfrey tea; on the raw side, mushrooms, basil, parsnips, rhubarb, mus-

tard—all these foods have been found to contain particular chemicals that may be carcinogenic. And here are a few highlights from the literature of the late 1980s: High doses of salt cause cancer in animals. Chlorinated water contains carcinogenic chloroform. Acetaldehyde, the first substance created by the human body as it metabolizes alcohol, damages DNA in the presence of alcohol; and alcohol may increase the potency of other carcinogens. The ingestion of unsaturated vegetable oils, even when unheated, increases the likelihood that laboratory animals will develop certain kinds of cancer. Heated fats and oils accumulate oxidized fatty acids, and many of these cause DNA damage. Carcinogenic nitrosamines form when foods are cooked in ordinary gas ovens (the flame burns the air's nitrogen to nitric oxide, which then reacts with the food). Pyrazines, compounds that contribute to the characteristic flavor of browned foods (see chapter 17), cause DNA damage. And when we eat broiled or fried meats, we expose the cells in our body to between ten and fifty times the quantity of DNA-damaging chemicals that we do when we eat boiled or baked meats instead.

Apart from the dismaying findings, all these reports have one important thing in common: they offer no direct evidence about the actual threat that a given food poses to human health. The experiments were all done on bacteria, cultured cells, or animals. However, the idea that such laboratory results are relevant to human beings began to gain circumstantial support in the 1970s from epidemiological studies, statistical surveys of cancer incidence in particular populations. Cancer rates turn out to vary tremendously from country to country and even within countries. Stomach cancer is more common in Japan than in the United States, and colon and breast cancer less common; but when Japanese migrate to the U.S., the second generation shows the typical American pattern, not the Japanese pattern. This kind of information suggests that environmental factors are more significant than heredity, at least for some forms of cancer. The role of food comes more obviously to the foreground when groups with distinctive diets are compared with others who live in the same place: Mormons in Utah, for example, or Seventh-Day Adventists in California. Members of both these groups consume less meat and alcohol and more fruits, grains, and vegetables than the general population; and members of both groups have lower rates of colon cancer and breast cancer.

In 1981 Oxford epidemiologists Richard Doll and Richard Peto surveyed the vast accumulation of population data in order to assess the relative contributions of different factors to the incidence of cancer in America. They concluded that dietary adjustments could cut the total number of cancer deaths by between 10% and 70%. Stomach and colon cancer might be reduced by 90%; gallbladder, pancreas, breast, and endometrial cancer, by 50%; other forms of cancer, by between 10% and 20%. If we assume an overall reduction of 40%, then our current diet apparently contributes to about as many cancer deaths as does cigarette smoking, to ten times as many deaths as does occupational exposure to carcinogens, and to ten to twenty times as many deaths as does exposure to chemical pollution.

In her landmark book of 1962, *Silent Spring*, Rachel Carson wrote of the modern age of synthetic pesticides: "For the first time in the history of the world, every human being is now subjected to contact with dangerous chemicals, from the moment of conception until death." By 1980 we found ourselves facing the uncomfortable realization that for thousands of years before the advent of the pesticide industry, human beings had subjected themselves to dangerous chemicals whenever they consumed grilled, smoked, or salted foods. And our food plants have been slipping us their own poisons for millions of years. The worrisome chemicals in mushrooms, for example, are hydrazines, which are naturally occurring relatives of rocket fuels and pesticides. Indeed, plants contain a tremendous variety of toxic compounds, the main purpose of which appears to be to defend the immobile plant against animal predators and microbial pathogens. In 1983 Berkeley biochemist Bruce Ames, a pioneer in the development of tests for identifying likely carcinogens, estimated that "the human dietary intake of 'nature's pesticides' is likely to be several grams per day—probably at least 10,000 times higher than the dietary intake of man-made pesticides."

That figure sounds shocking at first. It implies that there's no escape from potential carcinogens. And there really isn't. As we'll see, even our own bodies produce them. But the story of "nature's pesticides" is actually cause for optimism. Despite the plant toxins that we ingest in fruits, vegetables, and grains, these foods are generally associated with good health, and low cancer rates. (There are exceptions, of course, such as plants that are unusually rich in toxins, and some fermented or spoiled products.) The benignity of fruits and vegetables indicates that we don't necessarily need to worry about every trace of every toxin, natural or synthetic, in our foods. This is lucky, since it would be impossible to eliminate them all in any case. Instead, we can concentrate on the possible: choosing mild preparation methods, reducing our consumption of particular foods that are likely to be carcinogenic, and increasing our consumption of foods that have anticarcinogenic properties. As we learn more about the influence of foods on the development of cancer, it may become possible for each of us as individuals to reduce our risk significantly. Given the failure of modern medicine to find reliable cures for most forms of cancer, the prospect of improved prevention is very good news indeed.

Statistics and chemical rosters are useful, and about all the information there is in press reports for the general public. But the perspective they give us is a limited one. In order to understand how chemical culprits are identified and with what certainty, why natural food compounds can be as harmful as synthetic chemicals, and why there is optimism about possibly anticarcinogenic foods, we need to peer into our cells and get acquainted with some of their biochemical machinery. This is where cancer originates and where it's most effectively fought.

Cancer, which comes from the Greek word for "crab," originally denoted an abnormal, hard swelling; it may have been suggested by the pattern of dark veins that sometimes radiate from a tumor. Today, cancer is defined more precisely as the uncontrolled overgrowth of a malfunctioning population of cells, either in an organized tissue or circulating in body fluids. Cancers differ in the particulars of their origin and development, but they also share certain characteristics. Cancer is best thought of as a large family of related diseases.

The normal cells in the tissues of our body behave in a very orderly way. Each cell contains the full complement of genetic information contributed to us by our parents, but each cell makes use of, or expresses, only the small fraction of that information appropriate to its specialized role. Muscle cells express one subset of genes; brain cells, a largely different subset. Generally speaking, the specialized cells of a tissue are unable to divide and reproduce themselves; instead, they're replaced by the carefully controlled division of the tissue's less mature, as yet unspecialized *stem cells*, the progeny of which then undergo specialization. Each tissue has characteristic rates of cell death and replacement. Cells lining the digestive tract are replaced every few days, while nerve, heart, and voluntary muscle cells are seldom or never replaced after birth.

Cancer cells differ from their normal, orderly neighbors in two important respects: they divide at a rate that's inappropriately fast, and they don't perform their specialized duties properly. The result is a growing mass of malfunctioning cells that eventually interferes with the healthy workings of the body. Compared to normal cells, cancer cells adhere less strongly to each other and are more mobile, which is why they're easily transported to other parts of the body and so spread the disease. Because these abnormal cells arise in normal tissues, and because all the descendants of a particular cancer cell inherit the same characteristics, it seems quite likely that cancer begins with a relatively unspecialized cell whose basic library of genetic information—its DNA— has somehow been changed. It's almost an axiom in cancer research that "the" fundamental cause of cancer is a permanent alteration, or *mutation*, of the genetic material that controls important aspects of cell behavior. And mutations arise when the DNA of a cell is damaged.

The major classes of cancer-causing agents known today are ultraviolet radiation, ionizing radiation (X rays, gamma rays), chemicals, and viruses. Each is known to alter the DNA of living cells, either directly or indirectly, and the first three have been doing so ever since life arose. The sun is a powerful source of ultraviolet light, the earth and outer space both sources of ionizing radiation. Oxygen itself, vital though it is for most organisms, in some of its atomic and molecular forms is also a potent damager of DNA.

Even in the absence of external damaging agents, DNA molecules are vulnerable to the ordinary conditions in living cells. The integrity of DNA, like that of any other molecule, is a matter of chemical bonding; and one of the things that makes life possible is the relative ease with which the chemical bonds of organic molecules are broken and formed. If everything were perfectly stable, then nothing would happen, and nothing would live. The DNA in our cells is constantly buffeted by the random motions of surrounding molecules, its bonds constantly being broken and then re-forming. It's also attacked by highly reactive compounds that are generated by the cells themselves during their normal metabolism. A small fraction of cancer incidence may be due to the intrinsic instability of DNA and the essential activity of our cells.

All living things have always had to contend with the vulnerability of DNA and with the ubiquitous presence of DNA-damaging agents. Accordingly, all living cells maintain systems of specialized repair enzymes that continuously monitor their DNA for signs of damage and act to fix it quickly. The human repair systems are remarkably reliable. It's estimated that they manage to handle several thousand episodes of oxidative DNA damage every day in each of the body's 100 trillion cells.

Though astonishingly effective, our DNA repair systems aren't perfect. Some mutations escape repair and subsequently cause disease. This may seem a regrettable flaw in our biochemical machinery, but it's actually a precondition for our very existence. Human beings, like all forms of life on earth, evolved from earlier forms. And evolutionary change, the natural selection of organisms best adapted to their environment, can take place only after changes in the genetic makeup of organisms have generated a diverse population. As biologists say, "mutation drives evolution." However harmful mutation can be to us as individuals, our species wouldn't be here without it.

How does damage to one cell's DNA lead to the development of cancer? There are probably a number of different routes, both direct and indirect. Since cancer is in essence a disease of uncontrolled cell growth, one obvious route would begin with the mutation of a gene that's involved in normal cell growth and multiplication. There are many such genes in every cell; they direct the production of various chemical signals that promote growth and that suppress it, of receptors that detect these signals and initiate the cell's response to them, and of other proteins that help regulate the various stages of cell growth. This route to cancer has been documented in both laboratory animals and humans. To date researchers have identified several dozen genes that, when mutated, are capable of giving rise to cancerous cells. Many of these critical genes were first discovered in cancer viruses, some of which cause the disease by carrying into a cell altered versions of the cell's own growth-controlling genes.

A slightly longer route to cancer could begin with a mutation in the genes responsible for the DNA repair systems. If a cell's repair abilities are compromised, then it becomes more likely that one of the thousands of daily insults to the cell's DNA will be overlooked, and become a permanent defect. A repair mutation might therefore lead indirectly to a growth mutation, and the growth mutation to cancer. That repair defects play a role in human cancer is well documented. Inherited abnormalities in DNA repair have been identified, and they carry with them a greatly increased risk for certain kinds of cancer.

Defective growth genes can also be inherited from one's parents, in which case, like the inherited repair defects, they're present in all cells in the body and confer on an individual an increased risk of developing cancer throughout life. Inherited susceptibility now appears to be an important factor in lung and colon cancer, for example. Or defects may arise in a single cell at some particular instant during life, the result of the body's own metabolism or exposure to a mutagen in the environment. It's not necessary for the mutagen to hit a critical gene directly. If DNA damage occurs while a cell happens to be dividing and so copying its DNA, then the copying process can be disturbed, and errors introduced in genes that are far distant from the original damage.

So far, the path from DNA damage to cancer looks fairly direct. Mutation in a growth-control gene causes uncontrolled growth. But we've only looked at the first step or two along a very long path. Unrepaired DNA damage seldom leads immediately to the development of a tumor. Instead, there's a lag period, which can last decades, before the affected cell gives rise to unmistakable disease. It's mainly this delay, together with our varied diet, that makes it all but impossible to study the dietary causes of cancer directly in individual people. How can we know whether there's any connection between a well-charred steak eaten in 1970 and a disease that manifests itself in 1990?

The first step in the genesis of cancer, the mutation of a gene that controls cell growth, is called *initiation*. The second, lengthy stage is known as *promotion*, and involves an as yet ill-defined set of events that cause the mutated cell to alter its behavior and begin to proliferate abnormally. Promotion may be caused by the same agent that mutated the cell in the first place, or by other substances that don't damage DNA, but somehow encourage such damage to express itself in behavioral changes. Promoting agents probably exert this kind of influence in a variety of ways. Some of them have been shown to interact with signal receptors in the cell membrane, which then set off a series of processes that eventually accelerate cell division. Other promoters may simply be general irritants that damage all the cells in a certain area and allow an abnormal cell to proliferate unfettered by the controls usually exerted by its neighbors. Or they may cause further mutations in the initiated cell. However, unlike the initial mutation of a cell, which is an essentially instantaneous and irreversible event, promotion is a prolonged and reversible process. If a promoting agent is applied for some time and then withdrawn, the tissue can return to a normal condition and the mutated cell fail to progress to a tumor.

Because the greatly increased risk of cancer that accompanies smoking is re-

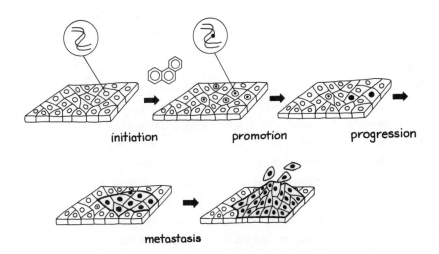

initiation   promotion   progression

metastasis

The development of cancer. In the stage called initiation, *a cell's DNA* (helix in circle) *is somehow altered* (black dot on DNA and in some cell nuclei). *Mutations of DNA can be caused by some chemicals (shown here: a polycyclic aromatic hydrocarbon found in barbecue smoke), as well as by certain kinds of radiation and viruses. These mutations are usually repaired or else fail to cause disease. In the stage called* promotion, *however, a few cells* (shaded nuclei) *are primed for unrestrained proliferation by further genetic alterations or other growth-enhancing influences. In* progression, *the cancerous cells multiply faster than their normal neighbors, and grow into a tumor.* Metastasis *is usually the deadliest phase of the disease, when some tumor cells break away and invade other tissues, where they form new tumors.*

duced again when a smoker quits, it's thought that cigarette smoke is important mainly as a promoter of cancer, not as a mutagen. Among elements of our diet, alcohol and the additives saccharin, cyclamate, and BHT (butylated hydroxytoluene) are thought to be weak promoting agents. A somewhat controversial case is fat. The fatty acids into which fat is digested are chemically similar to detergents, and do appear to irritate the intestinal lining and cause cell proliferation. However, fat may have more important effects as an "enhancer": that is, it may create certain conditions that in turn favor promotion. For example, the consumption of fat increases the secretion of bile into the intestine, and bile acids are thought to be promoters of intestinal cancer. (Some intestinal bacteria also convert bile acids into powerful mutagens.) And to the extent that fat intake contributes to excessive body weight, it also contributes to increased risk for a number of cancers.

Because the initiation of cancer ultimately involves a single chemical event— the reaction of a carcinogen with DNA—whereas promotion involves the prolonged activity of a number of biochemical circuits in the cell, initiation has been much easier to study than promotion. Researchers have compiled a remarkably detailed body of information about this important first step in carcinogenesis. They've shown that some carcinogens remove a group of atoms from exposed portions of the DNA's double helix and replace it with another, while other carcinogens distort the shape of selected components of DNA, and still others insert themselves into the helix and cause a major disruption in its structure. The ultimate effect of all these events is the same: the genetic template is damaged. If the damage is not repaired by the cell, errors or alterations in the DNA are generated and perpetuated when the DNA is copied during cell division. Should the mutation affect one of the genes that control a cell's growth, then cancer may result.

If DNA damage is indeed the underlying cause of most forms of cancer, then it follows that any *mutagen*—any agent that causes mutations—must be under strong suspicion as a likely carcinogen. Because the chemistries of DNA in bacteria and in humans differ only slightly, scientists have developed rapid and inexpensive screening tests that use bacteria and other cell cultures to detect mutagenic activity: sophisticated versions, in a way, of W. Mattieu Williams's experiment with caramel. The most widely used of these tests is the Ames test, named after Bruce Ames, who began developing the method in 1964 as an offshoot of his research on the synthesis of amino acids in bacteria. Ames was inspired, he recalls, by reading the list of ingredients on a package of potato chips and realizing that many chemicals were making their way into our diet without having been tested for any but the most immediate effects on health.

The Ames test uses strains of *Salmonella* bacteria (the species that causes typhoid fever) that have a nonfunctional DNA repair system, and that can't synthesize their own essential amino acid histidine. In these defective strains a gene for one of the enzymes that the bacteria normally use to produce histidine has been mutated. Such bacteria grow perfectly well on a mixture of nutrients that includes histidine, but can't grow in its absence. The original Ames test calls for the bacteria to be cultured in the presence of the chemical to be tested and only a bare trace of histidine. If the chemical does damage DNA, then some of the mutations it causes will restore the ability of the bacteria to synthesize their own histidine, and so to thrive and reproduce despite the limited amount of histidine available. The result: large, visible colonies of bacteria. The number of such *back mutations* from defective to normal growth provides a measure of the mutagenicity of the chemical. Similar tests use other kinds of cultured cells to screen chemicals for the ability to induce mutations.

Chemicals that test positive can then be administered to animals to see whether they also cause cancer—a much more laborious and expensive procedure. The mutagenesis tests appear to be good predictors of carcinogenicity; most chemicals that are positive in the Ames test and that have been tested in animals do cause cancers. For example, the Ames test was responsible for finding that the flame retardant Tris, once widely used in children's sleepwear, is a mutagen, and subsequent tests showed that it causes cancer in animals.

Still, nothing definitive about human cancer is proven by these laboratory tests of a chemical's ability to cause mutations in cells or cancer in animals. For one thing, not all chemicals that damage DNA necessarily cause cancer in animals. Futhermore, a chemical that causes cancer in one species can fail to do so in another, so rat tests may not always be relevant to humans. And because animals are usually given an enormously larger dose of the test chemical than humans typically encounter, a dose that's close to being fatal in its own right, the animals may develop more cancers simply because they're very sick. So apart from a few well-characterized industrial chemicals, even confirmed mutagens and animal carcinogens can only be suspected of involvement in human cancer. We lack direct evidence of their involvement. This is true for the entire list of scrutinized foods that I recited above. Charred meats, mushrooms, toast, and the rest have fallen under suspicion because they contain mutagens or animal carcinogens, but we don't yet know—and we may never know—whether they actually contribute to human disease.

In all studies since about 1973, the Ames test has called for an added ingredient: extract of rat liver, with which the suspected mutagen is mixed before the bacteria are exposed to it. This refinement was necessitated by an intriguing twist in the studies of how carcinogens bind to DNA. It had been known since the

1930s that the hydrocarbon soot carcinogens were chemically inert: an unexpected characteristic for potent poisons! This fact led the English biochemist Eric Boyland and others to guess that the hydrocarbons were converted into a more chemically active form in the body, just as, on the positive side, the body converts dietary beta-carotene into active vitamin A. By the 1950s, this conjecture was widely accepted, and in the 1960s James A. Miller and Elizabeth C. Miller at the University of Wisconsin demonstrated in convincing detail that many chemical carcinogens don't bind to DNA. They're not in themselves mutagenic.

Today we know that *most* chemical carcinogens are relatively innocuous in themselves. They are carcinogens because our bodies make them into carcinogens. Our own cells transform these substances into highly reactive derivatives, and the derivatives then damage our DNA. Much of this transformation occurs in the liver. So Bruce Ames added extract of rat liver to his bacterial test in order to detect otherwise nonmutagenic chemicals that the animal body converts into mutagens.

This conversion is called *metabolic activation*: an inactive "procarcinogen" is transformed into an active carcinogen by the body's own enzymes. The elucidation of metabolic activation was an extremely significant advance in our understanding of cancer. For one thing, it helps to explain why known carcinogens have very little in common to account for their toxicity. They are chemically dissimilar but, as the Millers pointed out in 1969, their metabolic derivatives generally do have one feature in common: a very reactive, electron-deficient site that is especially drawn to complementary electron-rich sites in DNA, particularly nitrogen and oxygen atoms.

Metabolic activation also helps to explain why animal species differ in their susceptibility to carcinogens—differences that greatly complicate the application of animal experiments to humans. We now know that animal species differ in their tendency to activate particular procarcinogens into carcinogens. And within a given species certain organs are more susceptible to cancer than others because they are more likely to activate carcinogens. The liver, where much of the synthesis and breakdown of molecules takes place, plays an especially prominent role in the metabolic activation of carcinogens. The skin, lungs, and digestive tract also have a notable ability to generate carcinogens, and so are prone to developing cancers. Once activated, carcinogens can also be transported to distant parts of the body before they do their damage.

Why should the body contribute to its own undoing by converting various chemicals into carcinogens? This is the ironic effect of an otherwise desirable activity: the defusing, or *detoxication*, of harmful chemicals. It has been known since the middle of the nineteenth century that the body excretes in modified form many of the unusable or "foreign" compounds that it absorbs. Some of these compounds are oxidized; others are *conjugated*, that is, combined with one of the body's own chemicals; still others are both oxidized and conjugated. Toward the beginning of the twentieth century, scientists realized that most of the metabolized forms are less toxic than their originals, and more soluble in water. They came to use the term *detoxication* to designate the body's conversion of foreign, unusable, often poisonous chemicals to forms that are both less harmful and easier to excrete. In the 1950s researchers discovered that much of this activity is carried out in liver cells. We now know that detoxication systems are also present in the skin and lungs, which are directly exposed to the environment, and in the digestive tract, which surrounds ingested materials from the outside world. These tissues constitute our first line of defense against foreign compounds, both chemical by-products of the industrial age and, originally, our planet's impressive complement of natural toxins.

Several different systems of enzymes in the human body cooperate to dispose of foreign compounds. The first phase of the process usually involves the activity of the *oxygenases*, enzymes that insert an atom of oxygen in a nonpolar, water-insoluble hydrocarbon compound; the extra oxygen atom makes one corner of the target molecule more polar, reactive, and susceptible to further modification. The second phase of detoxication calls into service a variety of *conjugating enzymes*, which combine the target molecule, by means of its newly reactive corner, with one of the body's own water-soluble molecules, such as sulfate, glutathione, or glycine. This familiar biochemical tag acts as a kind of passport to speed the target molecule out of the cell for excretion, usually in the urine.

It now appears that one of the major families of detoxicating enzymes, the *cytochrome P-450 oxygenases*, originated several billion years ago in early bacteria as a system for synthesizing and breaking down some essential components of their own cell membrane, the steroids and fatty acids. (Some of these enzymes still help humans to synthesize hormones, bile acids, and vitamin D.) The application of oxygenases to foreign molecules seems to have begun about a billion years ago when certain cells, the earliest members of the animal kingdom, developed the habit of feeding on other living cells. The principal victims of this predation, the earliest members of the plant kingdom, supplied their own nutritional needs from the simple inorganic compounds available in the environment. The plants adapted to animal predation by beginning to synthesize a variety of defensive toxic substances, such things as alkaloids and cyanide compounds. In turn, animals adapted to this chemical warfare by developing chemical defenses: the animals' oxygenase enzymes gradually took on the additional task of disarming foreign chemicals. The new versions of these enzymes performed the same biochemical operations as the original versions did, but on a new class of molecules, the plant toxins.

Animal detoxicating systems may have begun as a defense against plant toxins, but they eventually became responsible for the general disposal of unusable imports. The plant world is remarkable for its biochemical ingenuity and profligacy, which is why its fruits, vegetables, and flowers are so various and appealing as well as occasionally deadly. The molecules that are responsible for their flavors and colors are also foreign to our workings as animals. If we didn't have enzymes to dispose of molecules like these, even they would accumulate in our cells and eventually poison us.

A second important stage in the evolution of detoxication seems to have come a few hundred million years ago, when enough vegetation had accumulated on land to make it possible for lightning or volcanic activity to start large, smoky fires. The combustion of organic matter, whether a green plant or the coal and oil into which it eventually decomposes, generates many compounds with the capacity for fouling up animal biochemistry. So animal enzymes were adapted again to dispose of this class of natural pollutants—long before the coming of factory smokestacks, long before our ancestors first gathered around campfires to broil their meat.

Our detoxication systems, then, are the product of the animal kingdom's long and hard experience with the tremendous variety of chemicals that animals take in but have no use for. But why do these systems sometimes make things worse, why turn mild toxins into powerful carcinogens? The answer is that, given the magnitude of the task, our detoxication systems are of necessity simple and undiscriminating. Most mammals probably have at least a dozen different P-450 oxygenase enzymes that act on foreign chemicals. But even ten dozen enzymes would be greatly outnumbered by the legions of chemicals they must get rid of. It would be an impossible task for an animal to prepare a special set of enzymes for each and every foreign compound it might ingest. So each type of detoxicating enzyme handles a wide range of foreign target molecules. The P-450 oxygenases, for example, process such different structures as chromate ions, sulfur dioxide, alcohol, and 1-, 2-, 3-, 4-, and 5-ring hydrocarbons; any one individual enzyme may handle thousands of different compounds. While most other enzymes are very specific in their activities, the P-450 oxygenases are probably the least specific enzymes known.

In order to provide broad protection in an economical way, the detoxication systems have evolved to perform just a few simple manipulations—oxidation, reduction, conjugation—and to apply them to any compound that doesn't have a role in our normal metabolism. For the vast majority of foreign chemicals, this defense system is perfectly adequate. But in some cases its work is counterproductive. For example, consider how our bodies handle certain polycyclic aromatic hydrocarbons, the initially water-insoluble, inert carcinogens in soot and in tobacco and barbecue smoke (they've also been found in meteorites). Our cells first oxidize the hydrocarbon called benzo(a)pyrene to produce a slightly water-soluble derivative; they then hydrate this derivative, then oxidize it again: and the third product is a powerful DNA-binding carcinogen. The carcinogen can in turn be conjugated with glutathione or further hydrated, and so rendered nontoxic and eliminated through the bloodstream and urine. But the same oxygenase activity that gives the conjugating enzymes a reactive handle on the hydrocarbon molecule also turns that molecule into a potent DNA damager.

The great majority of chemical carcinogens owe their mutagenic properties to just such flaws in the defensive system of detoxicating enzymes. The oxygenases are usually the culprits, although instances of carcinogenic conjugates have also been found. Because the oxygenases have multiple and overlapping duties, it will probably be difficult to single out particularly unhelpful enzymes and block their activity. And once cancer develops, of course, the detoxicating enzymes complicate chemotherapy by disarming anticancer drugs in the malignant cells.

The story of metabolic activation may sound disheartening: the flaws are not just in our foods and surroundings, but in ourselves. Yet the intensive study of metabolic activation has also brought some of the more hopeful news about cancer prevention. By understanding the weaknesses of our detoxication system, we may be able to compensate for some of them.

As is true of most enzyme systems in the body, the detoxication network operates at very low levels until it is actually needed: that is, until cells are confronted with a dose of molecules that must be removed. Current evidence suggests that when the body is challenged, molecules of the foreign substance bind to specific receptors on the surface of or within cells, and this complex then travels to the cell nucleus, where its presence activates the genetic machinery that synthesizes the enzyme system needed to deal with that molecule. The stimulating substance is said to *induce* the various enzymes, the exact mix of which—this or that oxygenase, this or that conjugating enzyme—depends on the nature of the foreign molecule.

The fact that the detoxicating enzymes are induced by the presence of their targets was discovered thanks to the surprising observation in 1951 that the application of one carcinogen to rats could actually *reduce* the toxic effects of a second carcinogen. The Millers at the University of Wisconsin looked into this odd phenomenon and found that the presence of the first carcinogen increased the activity of the enzymes that detoxicate the second. This was interesting, but didn't seem to have any practical applications. Fighting one carcinogen with another isn't an attractive option.

Practical—and exciting—applications became evident in the late 1960s, when Lee W. Wattenberg of the University of Minnesota Medical School studied the induction of rat oxygenase enzymes by various synthetic carcinogens. Curious to try a different class of compounds from the usual polycyclic hydrocarbons, he tested a synthetic flavone—and found it to be a strong inducer. The importance of this finding, Wattenberg realized, was that flavones also occur naturally in plants. In 1968 he showed that two flavones found in citrus fruits have some inducing activity, and that the synthetic flavone reduced the incidence of cancer in experimental animals. These results, he wrote, "open up the possibility that dietary constituents might conceivably alter the response of animals or man to exposure to [benzo(a)pyrene] and other polycyclic hydrocarbons." That is, our foods might contain compounds that would induce protective levels of detoxicating enzymes.

A few years later, Wattenberg noticed that rat intestine and lung tissue appeared to maintain high oxygenase activities even in the absence of carcinogens or other foreign molecules. These high enzyme levels, he discovered, were induced by alfalfa meal in the commercial feed given to the rats. Wattenberg then surveyed a variety of vegetables to see whether other plant materials would induce the detoxicating enzymes, and found that brussels sprouts, cabbage, cauliflower, and broccoli did just that. Further analysis showed that *indoles*, a class of chemicals that includes important plant growth hormones, were responsible for the induction.

Some indoles are also present in coal tars, and others are known carcinogens produced by charring high-protein foods, so it might have been that Wattenberg had simply tracked down yet another natural compound that mammalian bodies work hard to neutralize and excrete. However, he soon found that both pure indoles and ordinary whole brussels sprouts reduce the incidence of chemically induced cancers in animals. Around the same time an epidemiological study of patients with colon cancer reported that the incidence of colon cancer was lower among people who claimed to eat cabbage regularly. Taken together, the laboratory and epidemiological results suggested that indoles and perhaps other plant constituents might offer some protection against cancer for human beings as well as animals.

A new research area was born! Since then, Wattenberg and others have found that a variety of plant constituents reduce the incidence of cancer in laboratory animals. These include fairly widespread phenolic compounds and flavones, the isothiocyanates and indoles of the cabbage family, terpenes that contribute to the flavor of citrus fruits and caraway seeds, and pungent sulfur compounds characteristic of onions and garlic. Many of these cancer inhibitors appear to work by inducing a mix of detoxicating enzymes that actually detoxicates a potential carcinogen rather than activating it. Some plant substances tend to suppress the induction of oxidizing enzymes that cause activation. Others increase the induction of oxygenases, but change their relative activities in a way that minimizes activation. (For example, in the case of the potential carcinogens known as aromatic amines, oxidation of the nitrogen atom activates the molecule into a carcinogen, while oxidations that take place on the carbon ring are harmless.) Still other plant compounds induce more of the conjugating enzymes that bind carcinogens to neutralizing molecules before they can do any damage. This last effect, which is caused most notably by terpenes and by sulfur compounds of the onion family, may be the most desirable of all, since it's probably the safest. In contrast, altering the pattern of oxygenase activity can sometimes increase—rather than reduce—the metabolic production of carcinogens, and raise the incidence of experimental cancers.

As research into dietary anticarcinogens widened, new agents with new modes of action were identified. They fall into several categories. First, there are substances that prevent the generation of certain carcinogens, notably the nitrosamines, in our digestive tract. Vitamins C and E block the necessary chemical reactions, while wheat bran and an amino-acid derivative in codfish bind nitrite, which renders it unavailable for nitrosamine formation. Then there are substances that bind directly to carcinogens, particularly of the aromatic hydrocarbon type, and so prevent them from reacting with DNA. Such "scavengers" that may work within cells include plant phenolic compounds, while in the digestive tract both chlorophyll and fiber may prevent carcinogens from entering our cells in the first place. (Fiber also has other, largely mechanical effects, including the dilution of carcinogens and the hastening of their elimination from the digestive tract.) The highly reactive by-products of a cell's normal metabolism can be scavenged or "quenched" by vitamins E and C and by beta carotene, the orange pigment in vegetables and fruits that the body converts into vitamin A.

Finally, there are substances that somehow suppress the complex, poorly understood process of tumor promotion, the slow transformation of a single mutated cell into an actively growing tumor. In laboratory animals, cabbage-family isothiocyanates and citrus oils have slowed the production of certain tumors, as have both natural and artificial antioxidants. Among the effective natural antioxidants are plant phenolics and flavones; among the artificial ones, the phenolic food additives BHA (butylated hydroxyanisole) and BHT. The trace metal selenium does the same, as do chemical relatives of vitamin A, which somehow induce immature cells to mature and lose their ability to multiply. The same fish-oil fatty acids that help slow the development of heart disease also suppress tumor development, apparently by reducing the levels of signal molecules that encourage inflammation and cell proliferation. And by binding to irritating free fatty acids and bile acids in the intestines, calcium reduces cell multiplication in the intestinal lining.

Some of these substances, in particular selenium and the relatives of vitamin A, suppress tumor promotion only in doses that are substantially higher than those available from our foods, and that in some cases approach toxic levels. They may therefore have to be handled as drugs rather than as dietary components or supplements. Still, antipromotional substances may be the most promising class of cancer preventives. Given the very nature of living cells and the many thousands of chemical mutagens, both natural and synthetic, to which we're exposed throughout our lives, it's impossible to avoid at least some damage to our DNA. Because promotion is the reversible and more extended phase of cancer development, the best strategy may well be to try to slow the progression of that initial damage into active disease.

The unraveling of the nature of cancer, the body's role in creating carcinogens, the existence of anticarcinogens—all of this has made for exciting science, as well as for the appealing prospect of a world in which many kinds of cancer will be prevented by dietary adjustments or supplements. As John Cairns of the Harvard School of Public Health has pointed out, preventive measures against infectious and deficiency diseases were successful in part because improved sanitation, water supplies, and nutrition made life more pleasant for everyone. In the case of cancer, Cairns notes,

> [If] the important factors are the carcinogens, we may be in for a difficult time, because it is not going to be easy to get the inhabitants of the affluent West to alter their habits. If, however, cancer rates are determined by a deficiency of anticarcinogens, the goal of preventing most forms of cancer may actually be attainable.

The optimistic interpretation of the laboratory and epidemiological evidence to date is that we can reduce our cancer risk by eating more fruits, vegetables, and whole grains. Say, for example, that you want to have a dinner of consommé, a nicely charred steak, and hydrazine-rich mushrooms. Then— the optimists would say—add some brussels sprouts, wild rice, a garlicky salad, and apple pie to the menu. The chlorophyll and fiber will bind to hydrocarbons in the digestive tract; the sprouts' indoles will adjust your detoxicating enzymes to minimize the activation of hydrocarbons; the garlic's sulfur compounds will speed the conjugation and excretion of mutagens; the apples' store of ellagic acid, a phenolic compound, will scavenge any remaining activated hydrocarbons before they cause trouble; and the vitamins and antioxidant compounds will prevent any already initiated cells from progressing to active proliferation. If you eat less steak on account of all the vegetable trimmings, so much the better. Even vegetable haters have been accommodated by the so-called health food industry, which has rushed in with capsules of "Citrus Bioflavonoids," "Citrus-*free* Bioflavonoids" (hooray for freedom of choice), and Quercetin (a single flavonoid). Somehow it seems only fair that, having helped get us into this mess by pushing the animal kingdom into detoxication, the plants should help get us out of it.

Unfortunately, this add-a-vegetable optimism is built on shaky foundations. To begin with, the growing mass of direct evidence for natural anticarcinogens derives from animal studies, and the human body may well respond differently to many of these chemicals. Second, the behavior of an individual's detoxication systems is influenced by a number of other factors, including heredity (some people are apparently less vulnerable to cigarette smoke because their oxygenases aren't easily induced), smoking and drinking (alcohol induces the oxygenases), general diet (high-protein diets increase the activity of detoxicating enzymes, high-carbohydrate and high-fat diets decrease it), environmental or occupational exposure to foreign compounds (gas station attendants and anesthesiologists, for example, habitually inhale them), and medication (drugs also induce and are metabolized by the detoxication enzymes). Third, the actual significance for our health of steak or mushroom or toast carcinogens, of apple or cabbage anticarcinogens, is not known. It may be that they're negligible compared to, say, overall fat intake.

Finally, the realities of our everyday diet are much more complicated than the situations studied in the laboratory. We don't limit ourselves to one or two kinds of food, and every food is a mixture of hundreds of components, some helpful, some harmful, and many of which remain to be characterized. Basil leaves owe much of their flavor to estragole, a known animal carcinogen; but they also contain vitamins A and C and phenolic substances. So is pesto good or bad for our health? And single plant chemicals have been shown to tip the balance of detoxicating enzymes to an animal's favor in one situation and to its detriment in another. For that reason alone it's too early to trust capsules containing wildly unnatural amounts of plant flavonoids, which are themselves potentially toxic foreign compounds. The same goes for the artificial food preservative BHT, which has also hit the "health food" stores, and which has shown evidence of being a weak tumor promoter as well as an anticarcinogen.

Several epidemiological studies of dietary supplements are currently under way, and maybe in a few years we'll know whether these chemicals can do us any good. But given the complexities of plant chemistry and animal metabolism, and the difficulty of establishing causal relationships in human cancer, we may never know exactly what to think of foods like basil or mushrooms or cabbage.

Where, then, does this mass of epidemiological correlation, intriguing laboratory findings, optimistic theorizing, and general uncertainty leave us? With an appreciation for how much and yet how little we know about cancer, and about the effects of our foods on the body. With the realization that, given our limited knowledge, choosing a healthful diet nowadays is a matter of trying to shift the percentages a few points in our favor. With good circumstantial evidence to justify a varied diet that deemphasizes fats and oils, cured meats, overcooking, heavy drinking, and overeating in favor of fruits, vegetables, grains, low-temperature techniques like braising, and moderation. With the recognition that cooking is in some ways still a primitive craft, and that we might benefit from a greater awareness of and control over its chemical consequences. With a heightened sense for some of life's fundamental ironies: that genetic change created all of us, and will destroy many of us; that our antipoison defenses can poison us; that food, sunshine, and fresh air—all natural and pleasurable and necessary—may eventually play a role in our undoing. Above all, with a hunger for more information!

Perhaps in a decade we'll begin each meal with what has been called an "inhibitory hors d'oeuvre": say, a glass of juiced brussels sprouts and carrots spiked with selenium, ingredients that will inhibit the formation or action of carcinogens, and probably the appetite as well. Then again, recent studies have shown that chlorine compounds in plain tap water can inactivate some mutagens, and that a few of the components of caramel are antioxidants and do the same. Toast and water, anyone?

Minding the Pots and Pans:
The Case of Aluminum

It's a dazzling story of downward mobility. Barely a hundred years ago, spoons made of aluminum were rare enough to be displayed in the Fifth Avenue window of Tiffany's. At the then new Maison d'Aluminum, according to the Paris correspondent of *Scientific American*, "Buyers are noticed to take up and admire aluminum goods, and to lay them down again the moment the price is mentioned." Yet today aluminum cookware is more common than any other kind, and we discard tons of aluminum foil, cans, and packaging in the trash every year.

This cascade of aluminum through the kitchen was unleashed by the invention of elaborate metallurgical techniques, and is sustained by the element's natural abundance. But metallurgy and economics are only part of the story. Aluminum promised to be the ideal culinary metal come at last! Several more easily purified metals had been made into pots and pans over the centuries, and all of them had the serious drawback of tainting foods that were cooked in them. Sometimes this contamination seemed to improve a food. The Romans valued lead for rendering concentrated grape juice immune to spoilage, and English cooks once recommended copper for the bright green it imparted to boiled vegetables. But the consequences for the diner were generally less desirable. Tin can cause gastrointestinal upset; copper, that and worse. Lead turned out to be an insidious, chronic toxin that may have debilitated many in the Roman elite.

The only trustworthy kitchen metal before the advent of aluminum was iron, which turned out to be an essential nutrient (as did copper, but we need much less copper and are less tolerant of overdoses). Iron's reaction with foods was probably a genuine virtue; cast iron pots may have provided an important mineral supplement for our forebears. However, cast iron can spoil the color and flavor of some foods, and if neglected it will rust in a matter of hours. It's also awkwardly heavy. These inconveniences were solved in the late 1920s with the arrival of the first stainless steel utensils. But stainless steel is a relatively poor conductor of heat, which means that its pans tend to develop hot spots and scorch their contents.

Aluminum triumphed so readily over steel, iron, and the other culinary metals because it is at once an excellent conductor of heat, remarkably lightweight, nearly "stainless," and, in the trace amounts it adds to foods, harmless. Or so the medical authorities said. Early doubts about the safety of aluminum were easily dismissed, but in the 1970s physicians discovered that in certain extreme situations, aluminum can damage the brain. This and other developments led in 1980 to a disturbing speculation in the pages of a prestigious medical journal. Perhaps, it was suggested, the aluminum in pots and pans is responsible for many cases of Alzheimer's disease, a degenerative brain disorder that is thought to be the most common cause of mental deterioration in the elderly.

The conjecture was dismissed by many medical scientists at the time, and never won much of a following. But it has been kept alive for a decade by regular research reports on the possible connection between aluminum and Alzheimer's disease, and many people continue to wonder whether their utensils have been slowly poisoning them. The answer is almost certainly no, even though we ingest more aluminum than we might think, and even though this is unlikely to be doing us any good. There's no doubt that close scrutiny has somewhat tarnished a once flawless reputation. The story of our favorite kitchen metal is a salutary reminder that our pots and pans—and pitchers and cans—deserve more consideration than we usually give them. We generally ignore our utensils, especially if they stay shiny and don't demand attention. Yet any metal container, and even some ceramic ones, will leave residues in food, and metals can indeed have powerful effects on the body's workings, both for good and for ill.

Aluminum is a singular substance. It's by far the most abundant metal in the earth's crust. The igneous minerals feldspar and mica, and their weathered product, common clay, are all mainly aluminum silicates. Clays also contain aluminum oxide, or alumina; other forms of alumina are sapphire, ruby, and corundum, the hardest mineral after diamond. In the earth's crust only oxygen and silicon are more abundant, constituting 50% and 25% of the crust, respectively, with aluminum at 8% and the second commonest metal, iron, at 5%. Yet our ancestors began exploiting copper and tin in about 4000 B.C., the Iron Age began in around 2000 B.C.—and the Aluminum Age not until A.D. 1900. The ancients were unable to lay their hands on the most common metallic element because its oxide and silicate minerals are extremely stable. There are no nuggets or veins of pure metal to be mined; and unlike iron, which can be reduced from its oxide in a simple furnace, aluminum isn't easily smelted from its ore.

The ancients did, however, mine the potassium and ammonium sulfate salts of aluminum, or *alums* (from the Latin *alumen*, meaning "bitter salt"). They used these versatile compounds to fix dyes onto fabrics, to tan animal skins into leather, and, in the gentler form of a medicinal astringent, to tighten up living skin membranes. (Each of these activities can now be taken as ominous foreshadowings.) Alums were apparently the first chemical compounds in history to have been intentionally and effectually purified; in the late Middle Ages, dyers prepared them by successive rounds of dissolving and recrystallization. They've also been used—for many centuries in China, and since about 1700 in Europe—as a means of clarifying murky water. When added to water, the salts dissolve and the aluminum reacts to form largely insoluble aluminum hydroxide. As the hydroxide precipitates from the solution, it adsorbs suspended particles in the water and carries them to the bottom. Today aluminum sulfate treatment is widely used in municipal water supplies, and in some instances elevates the aluminum content of tap water. Alum can be found to this day on the spice shelves of American supermarkets; it's a traditional means of firming the texture of cucumber pickles. Two related compounds, sodium aluminum sulfate and sodium aluminum phosphate, provide a charge of acidity in most commercial baking powders.

The road from alum to aluminum utensils was a long one. The element's existence was deduced around 1810, when the English chemist Humphry Davy named it, but it wasn't until 1854 that the Parisian Henri Sainte-Claire Deville developed a procedure that yielded the metal in quantity, though at high cost. It involved reacting alumina with chlorine gas and ordinary salt to generate sodium aluminum chloride, which was then reacted with molten sodium metal to give pure aluminum.

Owing to its appearance and price, aluminum was initially treated as a cousin of the precious metal silver. One of the first items to be crafted from it was a baby rattle for the newborn son of Napoleon III; jewelry and inlay work were other early applications. The first culinary items—eggcups, spoons, and pans—were inspired by the obervation that, unlike silver, pure aluminum isn't blackened by the sulfur liberated from cooked eggs. (Modern utensils are made of harder alloys, and these are slightly discolored by egg cookery.) Early boosters praised aluminum's relative chemical inertness, and predicted a bright future in the kitchen.

Aluminum became less precious and more useful thanks to the simultaneous and independent efforts of two young inventors: Charles M. Hall of Oberlin, Ohio, and Paul L. T. Héroult, who worked near Paris. In 1886 both hit on a more economical method of extracting pure aluminum: Dissolve alumina in a molten mineral containing sodium and aluminum fluorides, and then run an electrical current through the solution; molten aluminum collects at the bottom of the reaction chamber. In 1888 Hall, a Pittsburgh metallurgist named Alfred E. Hunt, and their backers formed the Pittsburgh Aluminum Company, later renamed the Pittsburgh Reduction Company and finally the Aluminum Company of America, or Alcoa. By 1890 the Hall-Héroult process had dropped the price of aluminum from twenty dollars a pound to about two.

Even at two dollars a pound, aluminum was overpriced for most manufacturing; the exceptions were surgical instruments and such novelty items as combs and tea balls. Aluminum's remarkable lightness—it is a third as dense as steel—and continuing declines in price led to its slow infiltration into military and industrial applications. Teddy Roosevelt carried an aluminum canteen in the Spanish-American War; the Wright brothers' airplane engines contained aluminum parts, as did some early automobiles; electrical transmission lines were made lighter by replacing copper with aluminum. Aluminum foil was introduced in 1913 in the form of leg bands for racing pigeons.

But the first major application of the new metal was, in fact, cookware. Small numbers of aluminum utensils were imported from Europe and manufactured in the United States quite early. The Pittsburgh Reduction Company began casting aluminum tea kettles in 1892, and in 1901 it organized the Aluminum Cooking Utensil Company, originator of the Wear-Ever brand. "The only cooking utensils that will not rust, crack, or burn," one of the first advertisements proclaimed. (The element has a low melting point, however, so that thin, cheap pans get very soft if heated when empty: soft enough that you can poke holes through the bottom with a fork.) By the 1930s, more than half the money spent on cooking utensils went to aluminum ware. That remains true today, despite the introduction of stainless steel cookware in the late 1920s. In 1984, some 175 million pounds of aluminum were made into utensils, and 4 billion pounds into cans, foil, and packaging: altogether, about half of the total poundage that went into buildings and airplanes.

The persistent belief that aluminum cookware causes disease has its roots in the shady reputation of alum, which had been commonly used at least since the eighteenth century as an adulterant to whiten flour, heighten the color of red wines, generate stable heads of foam in beer, and otherwise "improve" foods of poor quality. Somehow alum's involvement in fraud created the general misimpression that it was poisonous. This perception caused legal problems in the 1870s for manufacturers of baking powder who replaced cream of tartar with cheaper aluminum compounds, a practice that's forbidden in Britain to this day.

According to the American Medical Association, business competitors were responsible for spreading the theory of Charles T. Betts, an Ohio dentist, that aluminum cookware was dangerous. The association's journal *Hygeia* asserted in 1929: "Due to the advent of aluminum cooking utensils the sale of other types of ware for this purpose has been greatly injured. As a result there has been considerable propaganda during the past few years that the cooking of food in aluminum was a common cause of cancer. There is no scientific evidence for such statements." In any case, the new cookware was sufficiently appealing to withstand this propaganda as well as the objections of the homeopaths, who blamed aluminum for everything from digestive complaints to rheumatism, migraines, and "the inability to make up one's mind."

As the new cookware caught on in America and Europe, the medical establishment took the position that aluminum was harmless. Only small quantities of the metal were liberated from pans during cooking, and its reactions with food weren't as obtrusive as those of copper, tin, or iron. Experiments suggested that the animal body was unable to absorb aluminum as it passed through the digestive tract. And, in any case, aluminum was naturally present in many of our foods. Eventually, the element was trusted enough to be enlisted as an ingredient in a popular medication. And so it was in the form of a medicine that aluminum first revealed its destructive powers.

Since the 1940s people suffering from a variety of digestive complaints have been treated with aluminum hydroxide gel, which is still the major ingredient in many over-the-counter antacids. Because it was thought that the human digestive tract couldn't absorb aluminum, the dosage was not strictly controlled. People felt free to take and physicians to prescribe huge quantities, sometimes the equivalent of a pound or more of aluminum per year, or more than one hundred times the amount normally provided by our food. Then in 1960 it was reported that some enthusiastic consumers of aluminum hydroxide were developing a bone disease characterized by pain and frequent fracturing. This aluminum-induced degeneration now appears to be the result both of phosphorus depletion in the skeleton and the incorporation of aluminum, which inhibits remineralization. Here was the first clear evidence that the human digestive system can absorb enough aluminum to make a wildly unnatural intake harmful.

A much more serious consequence of medical exposure to aluminum was discovered about fifteen years later in patients with severe kidney disease. Several hospitals in the United States and in Europe reported that some of their regular dialysis patients were developing symptoms of brain damage and dying in a matter of months. Damaged kidneys are very sensitive to the presence in food of phosphates, ubiquitous chemical compounds that normal kidneys filter from the blood. Since phosphates exacerbate kidney damage, doctors had prescribed large doses of aluminum hydroxide gel for these patients. The aluminum forms an insoluble complex with phosphates in the intestine, which prevents the phosphates—and, it had been thought, the aluminum—from being absorbed. At first, this gel was the obvious suspect in the cases of brain damage.

The primary villain indeed turned out to be aluminum: but not the thousands of milligrams taken daily by mouth. In dialysis treatment, a machine does the kidney's job of filtering the blood by "washing" it in a carefully formulated solution of water and salts. In all of the affected hospitals, dialysis dementia was traced to relatively high aluminum levels—around a milligram per quart—in the dialysis water. When aluminum is taken by mouth, only 1% or less of the dose is absorbed by the intestine. That which is absorbed passes first to the liver, where some is excreted immediately in the bile, and only the remainder needs to be filtered out of the blood by the kidneys. Blood and tissue levels are therefore kept consistently low. But the aluminum in the dialysis water went straight into the patients' blood. Once aluminum is in the blood, the main means of excreting it is the kidneys: but the kidneys of dialysis patients are severely impaired to begin with, and the dialysis treatment itself was further loading the blood with aluminum rather than removing it. Regular doses from dialysis treatment therefore caused aluminum to accumulate in the body in large quantities. And in such quantities, the element damages the brain.

Further examination of dialysis dementia has revealed that it can also be caused by oral intake alone. For even after the introduction of deionizers to purify dialysis water, 1% or 2% of all dialysis patients still suffer brain damage, apparently from the aluminum in the phosphate-binding medication. And some kidney patients, particularly young children, develop the symptoms of dialysis dementia without ever undergoing dialysis. Here only the oral intake of aluminum could possibly be responsible.

These have been worrisome discoveries, and physicians now monitor the use of aluminum hydroxide in kidney patients more carefully. However, medication-induced brain damage never seemed especially relevant to the average kitchen. The quantities of aluminum involved in dialysis dementia are gargantuan, and kidney patients suffer the unusual disadvantage of having lost much of their normal ability to excrete aluminum. Their illness may also make them vulnerable to aluminum poisoning in other, more subtle ways.

The suspicion that home-cooked food might cause aluminum poisoning grew out of an accidental discovery made in 1960. When the brain of a rabbit was injected with an aluminum solution, individual cells developed fibrous tangles that were similar—but not identical—to those found in Alzheimer's disease. (No such structures are found in dialysis dementia.) In 1973 neurologist Donald R. Crapper McLachlan and his colleagues at the University of Toronto followed up on one implication of this discovery. They found that the concentration of aluminum in the brains of Alzheimer's patients was greater than normal. This conclusion was disputed in some other studies. In 1979, however, researchers in Vermont used an X-ray microprobe to determine that aluminum was in fact concentrated in the diseased brain cells of Alzheimer's patients. It is now generally agreed that elevated concentrations of aluminum are associated with the visible areas of damage, although the overall increase in aluminum levels among Alzheimer's patients is 1.5- or 2-fold, compared to a 10-fold increase in people suffering from dialysis dementia. The absolute amounts involved are quite small. By one estimate, the average aluminum content of the brain in Alzheimer's disease is about one-thousandth of a gram, or much less than the amount that our foods naturally contain every day.

These arcane developments on the kidney ward and in the laboratory were brought to a focus in the kitchen in 1980, when the *New England Journal of Medicine* published a letter from a young psychiatrist at the Yale University School of Medicine. His avowed purpose was "to call attention to a possible public-health hazard: aluminum-induced organic mental syndromes from corrosible aluminum cookware." As an impecunious student and intern, Dr. Stephen E. Levick had bought and cooked in cheap aluminum pots. He eventually noticed such signs of corrosion as pitting and powdery deposits. Levick explained that corroding cookware has been known to release large amounts of metal into food; the Bantu tribe of South Africa brew a kind of beer in iron pots, and absorb so much iron that their cells become filled with it. This overload of an essential mineral causes a variety of ailments. Levick concluded his letter: "The iron pots of the Bantu people may have their counterparts in the aluminum pots of industrialized nations, with aluminum-induced dementia as the analogous disease. Large numbers of people in our aluminum-using society may be the victims of slow aluminum poisoning from several sources. Corrosible aluminum cookware may be a nontrivial source."

Common experience makes this propositon sound all too plausible. Surely everyone at one time or another has left aluminum foil in direct contact with leftovers in a stainless steel bowl and opened the refrigerator the next day to find patches of foil completely etched away. There's no doubt that utensils leave metallic residues in foods, particularly acidic foods. For example, tomatoes normally contain less than 1 milligram of aluminum per serving. If they're cooked for two hours in an aluminum pot, the same serving will contain about 2 milligrams. Store them in the same pot overnight, and the dose is about 4 milligrams. This certainly sounds like quite an increase.

However, it's less impressive when considered in light of the natural aluminum content of our food. Our average daily intake is on the order of 10 milligrams, most of it from fruits and vegetables that absorb aluminum from the soil. So even in the extreme example of tomatoes cooked and stored overnight, the pot's contribution is only a fraction of what we would normally ingest anyway. And the pot will shed less metal when the food is less acidic, the cooking time shorter, or when it's used only for cooking, not storage.

Nor are utensils the only or even the largest source of extraneous aluminum in our lives. Most household baking powders contain sodium aluminum sulfate as the acidic half of the leavening agent; a homemade cake can contain 5 milligrams of aluminum per serving. Commercial cake mixes use sodium aluminum phosphate, and produce cakes with from 5 to 15 milligrams per slice. Alum has long been used to keep both sweet and sour pickles firm; a medium pickle may contain 5 milligrams. Other aluminum compounds are added to keep table salt and nondairy creamers from caking up in the package. Then, of course, there are the antacid tablets and liquids, buffering compounds in some aspirin tablets, and antidiarrheal medications. One dose of an aluminum antacid can contain anywhere from 35 to 200 milligrams, and the potential daily intake can reach 5,000 milligrams, or five hundred times the amount naturally present in our food.

So even if it's occasionally abused, an aluminum pot makes a fairly minor contribution to our aluminum intake, particularly if we enjoy pickles and cakes and sometimes eat ourselves into indigestion. But this conclusion would be small comfort indeed if aluminum in the diet, whatever its source, were found to cause Alzheimer's disease. The suspicion is not dead. Nor is it flourishing. The consensus among researchers at the moment is that, while aluminum may somehow be involved in some stage of the disease, it's almost certainly not the primary cause.

To date, the origins of Alzheimer's disease remain elusive. As is the case with cancer, the long period over which the disease develops obscures the connection between effect and cause. Moreover, no one has yet identified the precise nature of the damage that the brain suffers in Alzheimer's disease. In fact, there's still no definitive way of diagnosing the disease in a living patient; only after an autopsy can doctors be sure. It only complicates matters that the brain is the least accessible and least understood organ in the body. Nor is aluminum a cooperative suspect. It has no long-lived radioactive isotope, which means that there's no convenient way of tracing its fate in animal or human experiments.

Alzheimer's disease takes its name from Alois Alzheimer, a German psychiatrist and neuropathologist who in 1907 first described a case of dementia associated with the presence of tangled fibers in certain brain cells. The symptoms include severe deterioration in a person's memory, perception, and abilities to use language, solve problems, judge, and learn. These disturbances in the higher mental functions correlate closely with damage to the brain that is very selective. Autopsies show that the damage takes several forms. One is an apparent loss of cells, mainly large neurons. The number of cells is not necessarily very high, but they may be crucial for connecting different areas of the brain and coordinating their activity. There's also a severe reduction in the presence of certain neurotransmitter molecules by which neighboring cells normally communicate with each other.

The two most striking diagnostic hallmarks of Alzheimer's disease, and those with which aluminum is associated, are neurofibrillary tangles and neuritic, or amyloid, plaques. Both structures are readily seen with a microscope in thin sections of brain tissue. The tangles, which Alzheimer discovered, are found within individual neurons. They appear to fill up much of the cell and consist of protein filaments wound together in pairs in the form of a helix. The plaques, which had been observed a decade or so before Alzheimer's work, are masses of protein that have been deposited in spaces between cells (*amyloid* means "like a starch granule"). They often form the focus of a cluster of degenerating nerve cells. Similar deposits are often found in cerebral blood vessels as well. Both aluminum and silicon have been found in high concentrations at the center of amyloid plaques, an arrangement which suggests that these minerals might somehow initiate the plaque's formation. Aluminum is also associated with tangle-bearing neurons.

The actual significance of the plaques and tangles remains unknown. It's conceivable that they cause the symptoms of the disease directly by interfering with the function of cells: the tangles by disrupting the transport of materials within a neuron, and the plaques by blocking communication between cells. However, smaller numbers of both plaques and tangles can be found in the brains of normal elderly individuals. Similar kinds of tangles appear in patients suffering from a variety of other brain disorders. And other species of mammals develop plaques during aging, yet don't suffer from an animal equivalent of Alzheimer's. (This lack of an animal model has also impeded research into the human disease.) The fact that neither structure is unique to Alzheimer's disease suggests that they may be general manifestations of damage to the brain, but not the initial injury itself.

Whatever their actual role may be, the tangle and plaque proteins are at least tangible evidence of trouble. By determining what these proteins normally do and how they end up in tangles and plaques, researchers hope to learn something about the origins of Alzheimer's disease. Proteins can be analyzed in great detail by the powerful modern techniques of molecular biology, but the tangle and plaque proteins have presented some unusual difficulties. Both are insoluble aggregates that must be teased apart before their components can be identified. Great progress has come in just the last few years. The information is still preliminary, but it suggests that both deposits result from specific, relatively subtle alterations in the biochemical activity of brain cells. The major plaque protein appears to be a small piece of a larger protein that may be essential for the development of the nervous system. The plaque may perhaps result from the production of excessive quantities of this protein as part of the brain's response to some kind of injury. And one of the major tangle proteins is a normal component of the cell's transport and structural systems, but it appears to have been chemically modified (phosphorylated) in a particular and abnormal way.

These fledgling biochemical studies of the diseased brain are beginning to mesh with genetic analyses. There is such a thing as a familial, inherited tendency toward early and severe Alzheimer's disease. And Down's syndrome, a birth defect caused by the presence of an extra copy of chromosome 21, or a certain portion of it, afflicts victims who survive into their thirties and forties with an Alzheimer's-like dementia that is accompanied by the characteristic tangles and plaques. Some cases of familial Alzheimer's disease also map to chromosome 21, as does the gene for the parent plaque protein. However, the locations don't exactly coincide; and the gene for the prominent tangle protein is on chromosome 17. So there appear to be several different forms of genetic susceptibility to Alzheimer's disease, and defects in the genes for the plaque and tangle proteins themselves are not responsible. Most likely, other genes somehow cause the abnormal production or handling of these proteins.

Genetics is certainly part of the story. As is true of both cancer and heart disease, one can inherit a predisposition to become ill, or a random mutation in an important gene early in development can generate such a predisposition. But there's more than genetics to cancer and heart disease, and the same is true of Alzheimer's disease. A person's brain can evidently be affected by environmental factors that somehow initiate or accelerate the course of the disease. This is demonstrated most vividly by the case of identical twins who suffered from the genetically transmitted familial form of Alzheimer's disease—one of whom developed it thirteen years before the other.

What might these aggravating factors be? A number of possible culprits are known to cause the development of Alzheimer's-like tangles and varying degrees of mental impairment. Serious physical injury—a strong blow to the head—is the cause of prizefighter's dementia, or the punch-drunk syndrome, which is accompanied by tangles within brain cells; such an injury is the one characteristic that recurs most frequently in the histories of patients with Alzheimer's disease. Certain viruses, among them those that cause measles and influenza, can reach the brain and cause encephalitis and tangle formation. This fact lends some credibility to a recent report suggesting that a slow-acting virus may be involved in some cases of Alzheimer's disease, though several earlier studies failed to find any microbial agent.

Much closer to the kitchen, there's good evidence that diet—more exactly, a severe and chronic mineral imbalance—can also cause the formation of neuronal tangles and a slow degeneration of the brain. This evidence comes from the experience of several isolated populations in Guam, Japan, and New Guinea that had suffered from a high incidence of dementia associated with paralysis, and of amyotrophic lateral sclerosis, a degenerative disease of the nerves that control movement. The symptoms, which can take decades to develop, eventually appeared in some individuals who had left their home islands as early as age eighteen. In addition to the tangles, elevated levels of both aluminum and calcium were found in the brains of victims. Investigators from the United States and Japan found no evidence of an infectious agent, a plant or animal toxin, or a simple genetic pattern. Instead, the key factor appeared to be that many of the affected villages were located in areas whose drinking and garden water, which was taken from shallow wells, was extremely poor in calcium and magnesium and relatively high in aluminum. Beginning in the early 1970s, as deeper wells were dug and foods were supplied from elsewhere, the incidence of the disease declined steeply.

The hypothesis that this western Pacific syndrome is caused at least in part by an inadequate diet is supported by experiments with monkeys, who develop neuronal damage when fed a diet low in calcium and magnesium and high in aluminum. Taken together, the human syndrome and animal experiments have several implications that may be relevant to Alzheimer's disease. First, the brain is sensitive to gross mineral imbalances, and deficiencies could be just as important as excesses. The aluminum levels in the drinking water of the affected Pacific villages were not unusual by the standard of American municipal supplies, so the critical factor is likely to have been the coincident deficiency of two essential minerals, magnesium and calcium. Second, even given extreme dietary imbalances, the brain's sensitivity is determined by genetic or other factors. This would explain why only a fraction of the villagers developed the syndrome. Diet, in other words, may act as a trigger to cause the manifestation of a genetic susceptibility.

A third implication of the western Pacific syndrome is that the effect of mineral imbalances on the brain may be quite indirect. How else could a lack of dietary calcium cause excessive calcium levels in the brain? One interpretation of the syndrome goes like this. The chronically inadequate intake of calcium and magnesium cause an increase in the activity of parathyroid hormone, which enhances the intestinal absorption of calcium—and incidentally of aluminum—and which mobilizes calcium from the bones for use by the rest of the body. The combination of this hormonal imbalance, the unusually high circulating levels of minerals, and some otherwise innocuous genetic abnormality then cause a breach in the *blood-brain barrier*, tightly joined capillary cells that strictly regulate the passage of substances from the blood into the brain. A variety of diseases are known to compromise this important biochemical filter. In the case of the western Pacific syndrome, the blood-brain barrier apparently allows unusual amounts of calcum and aluminum to pass through the brain capillary walls. Thus a diet deficient in calcium can lead to abnormal, possibly damaging concentrations of both calcium and aluminum in the brain.

Genes, head injuries, viruses, hormones, severe mineral imbalances—any or all of these things may contribute to the occurrence of Alzheimer's disease. So what about aluminum itself? There's certainly plenty of incriminating circumstantial evidence. Aluminum is found at the core of amyloid plaques and is associated with neuronal tangles. The story of dialysis dementia proves that aluminum can be a neurotoxin. The western Pacific syndrome suggests that dietary exposure might be hazardous when the diet is also deficient in essential minerals. It seems likely that once aluminum is in the bloodstream, it can enter the brain via transferrin, a protein that normally delivers iron but that also binds aluminum. There's some evidence that aluminum has effects on capillary cells and so might alter the blood-brain barrier. And studies in the test tube have shown that aluminum does react with DNA, enzymes, messenger molecules, and transport molecules. Once it enters the brain, then, it could conceivably influence the formation of amyloid plaques or neurofibrillary tangles.

To date, the case against aluminum has been stated most sweepingly by P. O. Ganrot of Sweden. Ganrot points out that alum has been used for many centuries to tan animal skins into leather, a process in which the metal ions crosslink the skin protein collagen into a dense, water-resistant mass. And like the ancients who valued alum for fixing color to cloth, modern microscopists have found aluminum ions quite useful as a mordant to fix dyes selectively to the DNA-containing nucleus of cells. Both these practices demonstrate the affinity of aluminum for critical biological molecules, and suggest that aluminum could cause trouble by binding brain proteins and DNA into a nonfunctioning kind of leather. In fact, Crapper McLachlan and his coworkers in Toronto have reported finding aluminum associated with the nucleus of tangle-bearing cells, and in concentrations around one-quarter of those typical of metal-tanned leather. (Other investigators, however, have found aluminum to be associated with the protein tangles themselves.)

Ganrot also makes the point that aluminum appears to accumulate steadily in the brain during an individual's lifetime. Since neurons in an adult never divide, they have no opportunity to dilute substances that they're unable to excrete or break down, and so those substances simply accumulate. It has been speculated that one important factor in aging might be a progressive condensation and inactivation of each cell's complement of DNA. Perhaps, Ganrot suggests, aluminum accumulation and its binding to DNA causes part of the degeneration that we consider a part of normal aging, as well as the pathological degeneration of Alzheimer's disease. This might explain why small numbers of tangles and plaques are also found in the brains of old people who hadn't suffered from Alzheimer's disease.

A dispiriting scenario! But Ganrot's argument has its weak points, the main one being its generality. The fact that aluminum attaches itself to all kinds of protein and DNA doesn't explain the very specific pattern of degeneration seen in the diseased brain—only certain groups of neurons in certain areas are affected—or the very specific and peculiar nature of the protein deposits. (Ganrot wrote in 1986, before the tangle and plaque proteins had been identified.) Indeed, the indiscriminate binding of aluminum to a host of different cell molecules could constitute a good defense against aluminum poisoning: the metal ions would be spread among so many different processes that no single one would be severely affected.

Ganrot has met this objection by suggesting that aluminum binds more strongly to DNA than to other molecules, so that it slowly but surely migrates to the cell's nucleus. Such a gradual process of concentration could also explain the long time lag in the development of the western Pacific syndrome and Alzheimer's disease. However, a number of other researchers dispute this binding hierarchy. Preliminary experiments in 1988 led two British chemists, J. D. Birchall and J. S. Chappell, to propose that the preferred destination of aluminum in cells is not DNA, but *phosphatidylinositol*, a molecule in the cell membrane. This relative of lecithin binds metals very avidly because it offers two exposed phosphate groups at adjacent positions of a carbon ring. It's a crucial piece of the mechanism by which cells translate many chemical signals into an appropriate response. Interference with this mechanism could therefore cause a devastating cascade of malfunctions. This scenario also sounds plausible though, like Ganrot's, it doesn't account for the particular patterns of brain injury and protein aggregation seen in Alzheimer's disease.

Yet another theory arises from studies of the anatomy of Alzheimer's disease. Because the degeneration begins in areas of the brain that are directly connected to the outside world by means of the olfactory nerves, several researchers have suggested that the causative agent might gain entry to the brain through the nose. The abundance of aluminum in rock and clay means that the dust we breathe could be a source of aluminum in the brain. Regardless of whether clay minerals actually cause Alzheimer's disease, one eminent student of the western Pacific syndrome, D. Carleton Gajdusek, has proposed that the aluminum and silicon found at the center of amyloid plaques constitute claylike particles of aluminum silicate, and that these particles actively catalyze the aggregation of amyloid protein into the plaques that surround them. This is a gloomy parody of the idea that, early in the evolution of the living cell, terrestrial clays may have acted as inorganic catalysts to promote the copying of complex molecules. If clay helped fashion our one-celled ancestors and therefore us, it may also help unfashion us.

So a number of highly speculative hypotheses make aluminum out to be a cause of Alzheimer's disease in one way or another. But none is supported by direct evidence. And there is substantial evidence to the contrary. Most damaging to the case against dietary aluminum is one basic fact: despite the correlation between Alzheimer's disease and the presence of aluminum in the brain, there does not seem to be any correlation between the disease and the overall intake of aluminum. The levels of aluminum in the blood and in tissues other than the brain are not elevated in Alzheimer's patients, which suggests that they haven't been chronically exposed to unusual quantities or absorbing more than normal from their food. Moreover, brain aluminum levels similar to or higher than those characteristic of Alzheimer's disease are found in people suffering from a number of other ailments, including cancer and liver disease; this suggests that high brain aluminum may be only a general indication of damage to the blood-brain barrier. Down's syndrome victims have plaques that contain aluminum and silicon despite only three or four decades of normal exposure to aluminum. To date, epidemiological studies have failed to find an association between the development of Alzheimer's disease and either occupational or medicinal (antacid) exposure to aluminum. And despite universal exposure to aluminum through our food, drinking water, and air, Alzheimer's disease is the fate of only a minority (though a sizable minority) of the elderly.

While we're still too ignorant to be sure, it now seems unlikely that aluminum is a primary cause of Alzheimer's disease. Perhaps an accessory, an agent that causes some damage after something else goes wrong with the body's metabolism of minerals or control of brain chemistry. Or perhaps aluminum is just an innocent indicator that something has indeed gone wrong. But not a master villain that should be avoided at all costs. This is fortunate, because the costs would be very high indeed. In order to reduce our aluminum intake significantly, we would have to restrict our consumption of many grains, vegetables, and fruits, as well as tea, coffee, and wine.

The clay-in-the-brain theories may turn out not to explain Alzheimer's disease, but they do call to mind another curious fact about aluminum. It's the most abundant metal by far in soil and rock, and yet no living thing appears to have any use for it. In contrast, iron, magnesium, copper, zinc, and a half dozen other metals are essential to our health. In fact, the human body does a superb job of excluding aluminum from its workings: we normally absorb less than a hundredth of what we ingest, and we excrete most of the rest. Why? The answer lies in the peculiar nature of the metallic elements in general, and of aluminum in particular.

Some four-fifths of the 107 known chemical elements are classified as metals. A metallic element has only a loose hold on its outer electrons, which are therefore somewhat free to move around. Mobile electrons are what make metals good conductors of heat and electricity, good reflectors of light, and malleable materials; they also guarantee that in solution, metals exist as positively charged ions. About ten metals have an essential role in the workings of human beings. At the same time, double that number are known to be toxic. Even with the essential metals, the margin between an adequate intake and a poisonous one is quite narrow, often a matter of just a few milligrams. Living things have an edgy relationship with the metals; we can't live without them, but we can't live with very much of them either.

Metals are indispensable to life in one major respect: they provide a source of positive electrical charge in a chemical environment otherwise dominated by strongly negative oxygen groups and by nonpolar bonds involving carbon, hydrogen, nitrogen, and sulfur atoms. Positively charged particles have many different uses in living things. One is the maintenance of electrical and osmotic balance between cells and their fluid surroundings, and another is the generation of electrical signals; here the main resources are potassium and sodium. Some metal atoms give up two or more electrons and yet readily take one back. Cells use these versatile atoms to transfer electrons from one molecule to another in a number of essential metabolic reactions. Iron and copper are preeminent in this role, followed by molybdenum, manganese, and cobalt. Iron and copper are also used to handle oxygen and its highly reactive compounds.

Metals also contribute to the structure of living things, and at a variety of levels. Vertebrates build up their rigid skeletons by depositing phosphate salts of calcium, but even individual molecules of DNA, RNA, and protein have intricate twisted and folded shapes that are often stabilized by metal ions. The positively charged ions bond to and bring together negatively charged portions of these molecules that would otherwise repel each other. Magnesium is the principal stabilizing metal (the potassium ions in a cell also affect the electrical environment and thereby the structure of large molecules). By virtue of the temporary changes it can induce in the structure—and thereby the function— of some proteins, calcium is put to use as a signaling ion in the machinery that turns various cellular processes on and off.

The ability of many enzymes to modify other molecules depends on the participation of metal ions. They are especially useful when it's necessary for the enzyme to bind a negatively charged portion of the target, or when a source of positive charge can strain a bond in the target and make it more vulnerable to attack by the enzyme. Metals may help either as an integral part of the enzyme, which is usually the case with copper and zinc, or as a free-floating "cofactor"

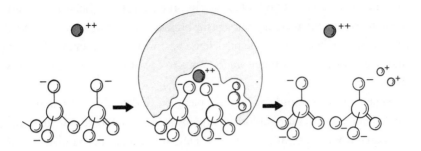

Metals help our cells carry out the essential work of building molecules up and break-ing them down. By distorting some electron-rich bonds, a positively charged magne-sium ion helps an enzyme and a water molecule to split one phosphate group from an-other: an important reaction in a variety of cellular processes.

that reacts simultaneously with the target, the usual role of magnesium. Mag-nesium also chaperones the omnipresent phosphate group, a cluster of one phosphorus and several oxygen atoms that is a part of DNA and RNA, of the phospholipids that make up cell membranes and pass signals, and of ATP (adenosine triphosphate), the common coin of energy transfer in living cells. By tugging the electrons away from their atoms and exposing the phosphorus atom to attack, magnesium makes it much easier for a host of enzymes to work on the phosphate group and so carry on the biochemical business of life.

Thus metals have an importance out of all proportion to their small quan-tities in the body (2 ounces or less of magnesium, 0.2 ounce of iron, and 0.004 ounce of copper). And small amounts of the wrong metals, or the wrong amounts of the right ones, can seriously disrupt our biochemistry in many ways. Not enough of an essential metal will impair the function of enzymes that de-pend on it; too much will spill over into other reactions and interfere with them. This is why the iron beer pots of the Bantu people cause them trouble. There's also a genetic tendency, *hemochromatosis*, that causes the body to absorb just a milligram or two a day more iron than it loses; by middle age, the accumulated excess is sufficient to damage the liver and the heart. (In earlier, more marginal times, hemochromatosis was probably an asset rather than a disease.) And the wrong metals can displace the right ones from their proper place or otherwise obstruct vital processes. Lead inhibits hemoglobin synthesis and so causes anemia; mercury starves the body of oxygen by preventing hemoglobin from binding it; both lead and mercury damage the brain by interfering with a variety of processes. The body's first line of defense against metal poisoning is the remarkably low efficiency (on average, about 10%) with which the gut absorbs them.

Where does aluminum fit into this picture? To date, there's no indication that it is an essential nutrient for any organism on earth. So exposure to significant quantities is generally undesirable. Despite aluminum's abundance, most organisms are only quite minimally exposed to its ions. In neutral ground waters, most of the aluminum is bound up in insoluble hydroxides. When ground waters become acidic, however, large quantities are released into solution. In the tropics, where soil acidity is high due to the rapid decay of vegetation, free soil aluminum is the single most important factor limiting crop productivity, mainly because it binds up essential soil phosphates and can be toxic to plant cells. It now appears that pollution-generated acid rain kills freshwater fish primarily because it releases aluminum ions in concentrations (0.3 milligrams per quart, similar to some drinking waters) sufficient to coagulate the mucus proteins in their gills. Aluminum poisoning may also be involved in forest damage caused by acid rain. Species that are tolerant to aluminum are few and far between; they tend to be acid-loving plants like the blueberry, cranberry, and tea bush (a cup of tea contains about a milligram). (The variable flower color of the hydrangea is caused by aluminum, which forms a blue complex with the otherwise red pigment in acid conditions.)

A peculiar physical characteristic of aluminum may explain its absence from the biochemical machinery of living things. In solution, any positively charged ion attracts the somewhat negatively charged oxygen atoms in neighboring water molecules, which therefore gather in several layers around the ion. This shell of water interferes with the ability of other molecules to reach the ion and react with it. One indication of the rate at which an ion can react with other molecules is the rate at which water molecules move in and out of the inner, most tightly bound layer. The smaller the ion or the greater its charge, the stronger the force it exerts on the water molecules, and the slower they are exchanged from the inner layer. The magnesium ion, one of the workhorses in assisting enzymes, has an exchange rate of around 100,000 per second. Ferrous iron, copper, and zinc are even faster, and calcium is so fast—100 million ex-

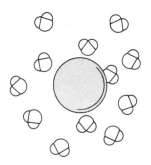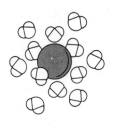

In solution, the magnesium ion (left) *and other large ions of low charge attract a relatively loose assembly of water molecules. The small, highly charged aluminum ion* (right) *attracts a very tight assembly that slows its reactions with other molecules.*

changes per second—that it's put to use as an all-purpose trigger for biochemical processes. The aluminum ion is both smaller and more highly charged than all these essential ions. Its exchange rate is about 1 per second—the slowest of all the common metals. Aluminum is probably too sluggish to be anything but a monkey wrench in the machinery of life.

The comparison with magnesium is a telling one, because there's evidence that aluminum can interfere with magnesium-aided processes, particularly those involving phosphates, to which aluminum binds much more strongly than magnesium. For example, both magnesium and a phosphate-containing molecule are required for the assembly of *microtubules*, structural proteins that are important in cell transport and division and that are continually being assembled and disassembled according to the cell's needs. In the test tube, a moderate deficiency of magnesium allows even small amounts of aluminum to participate in microtubule chemistry. The microtubules assemble correctly, but their disassembly becomes more difficult, and the cell's usual magnesium-mediated control over the process is lost. Other experiments have shown that aluminum also inhibits a variety of enzymes.

So aluminum appears to be incompatible with our biochemistry. It can't keep up with our enzymes, and it has an unfortunate tendency to bond strongly and unproductively to the essential phosphates. We can probably thank this phosphate binding for the fact that aluminum isn't acutely toxic except in huge doses. Much of the aluminum we ingest binds to phosphates in our food and is never absorbed, and the small quantities that do make it into our cells are probably spread over a variety of molecules, so that no one process is severely impaired. But even if we tolerate it remarkably well, no amount of aluminum—or of any other inessential metal—does us any good. Simple common sense would suggest that we avoid turning our bodies into junkyards for nonbiodegradable scrap metal.

How can we minimize our intake of aluminum? The biggest source for many people is antacid medication, and here, unfortunately, there's no good alternative at the moment. Sodium bicarbonate, calcium carbonate, and magnesium hydroxide aren't nearly as effective as "aluminum hydroxide gel" (actually a complex mixture of aluminum oxides and hydroxides). Aluminum-based antacids are ideal because they raise the pH in the stomach to between 3 and 4, and maintain that level for about an hour. In contrast, both sodium bicarbonate (baking soda) and calcium carbonate induce a pH greater than 5—an extreme change in stomach acidity that can cause a "rebound" overproduction of acid—and maintain a desirable acidity for only a few minutes. Magnesium hydroxide is intermediate in its properties, but has the disadvantage of being a laxative. And large doses of sodium, calcium, and magnesium can cause their own problems.

Aluminum-based antacids also have side effects. The standard daily dose doubles the normal blood aluminum concentration of most people, but in some people the increase is tenfold. And because aluminum bonds with phosphates, which prevents both from being efficiently absorbed in the intestine, prolonged use of aluminum antacids can deplete the body of phosphates and cause a weakening of the bones. For both these reasons, antacids are best used in moderation.

Of the aluminum in our diet, there's little to be done about the 10 milligrams or so a day that we ingest from grains, fruits, and vegetables. Drinking water is not a major source; aluminum sulfate treatment can actually reduce the levels in waters that are naturally high in aluminum, and finished waters rarely exceed 1 milligram per quart. Nor do aluminum cans raise the levels in soft drinks or beer. The most notable quantities of aluminum come from baking powders that contain sodium aluminum sulfate or sodium aluminum phosphate. These compounds are widely used because they're better than other leavening agents at producing a delayed charge of gas during baking (the "double action"). However, monocalcium phosphate powders are available, and some bakers prefer them, particularly in recipes that tend to expose the bitterness of the aluminum compounds.

Then there are aluminum cooking utensils. We could eliminate their small contribution to our mineral intake by throwing them out. But I doubt that such a sacrifice of inexpensive, light, even-heating utensils is worthwhile, particularly if it means switching to inexpensive stainless steel pans that develop hot spots and increase the amount of charred material in our food, which is probably no good for us either (see chapter 13). Instead, cooks can apply a little common sense and choose the best utensil for each job.

Here are a few simple guidelines. No metal from a pan will get into foods that are steamed. Very little metal is released during frying, cooking nonacid foods like grains and pastas, rapidly boiling nonacid vegetables (beans, peas, carrots) in large amounts of water (particularly when little or no salt is added), or boiling sugar syrups for preserves and candy (glucose and fructose inhibit the oxidation of the metal atoms). Naked metal pans of the usual sorts, aluminum included, are fine for such everyday preparations. But for making stocks, sauces, stews, soups, and other long-simmered or acidic foods, avoid using a plain aluminum pan, which might boost the food's aluminum content by a hundredfold or more. Instead, use a less reactive surface: an enameled or a nonstick pan, or stainless steel. For storage in the refrigerator, glass or plastic containers are preferable to the pots and pans in which the foods have been cooked. If you use a stainless steel bowl, don't let a covering of aluminum foil come in contact with the food; an electrolytic reaction between the two metals will cause the foil to dissolve onto the food.

The alternatives to plain aluminum cookware have their own limitations. Anodized aluminum has a very hard, protective oxide coating that prevents direct contact between food and raw metal. However, the coating is only a few thousandths of an inch thick and therefore vulnerable to wear. Enamel and nonstick coatings are also subject to wear, and nonstick fluorocarbon materials will decompose and emit noxious vapors if heated much above 500°F (260°C).

Some of the most attractive pans combine two materials: a highly conductive layer of copper or aluminum under a stainless steel cooking surface. Unfortunately, the most common design limits the conductive metal to a plate in the pan's bottom, which tends to concentrate heat at the junction of bottom and wall and cause charring. And even culinary stainless steel, an alloy of iron, chromium (18%), and nickel (8% or 10%), is not perfectly inert. Its permanently bright surface belies the fact that it too is corroded by acid and salty foods; we never see any rust or tarnish because a film of chromium oxide is formed first, and that film is clear. The average stainless steel pan, though, loses perhaps a tenth or less of the metal that an aluminum or nickel-plated pan does, and most of this loss is iron, an essential mineral. However, one brand tested in the late 1970s released more nickel into an acidic liquid than was deemed healthful: over 400 milligrams per quart. Neither nickel nor chromium has been proved to be an essential mineral for humans (each may be required in tiny quantities), nor are they known to be toxic when ingested in small amounts with food. But nickel is a common cause of contact dermatitis, which oral ingestion can exacerbate.

While cooks should be aware of the hidden flaws in cookware and know how to work around them, we also have to realize that containers have been contaminating food ever since they were invented. The corrosion of metals is inevitable, especially in the harsh environment of the kitchen. It's simply their natural tendency to revert to the original oxidized condition from which we extracted them. True, there have been times when the corrosion of cookware caused widespread and serious illness. The Romans adored the sweet, long-keeping syrup (long-keeping because a gram of lead per quart rendered it inhospitable to life of any kind!) that resulted when grape juice was boiled down in a lead-lined pot, and the American colonists suffered from pewterware of high lead content. But those times are long past. Cookware has never been safer than it is today.

In fact, metal poisoning is now much more likely to come our way from other sources. Handcrafted pottery can be hazardous if it is made with lead-containing ceramic glazes, which produce beautiful earthenware at relatively low firing temperatures. Improperly manufactured pitchers and mugs still poison and even kill people who have used them to store or serve fruit juices, soft drinks, cocktails, wine, and coffee. Lead also escapes from the solder still used to close some "tin" cans (actually tin-plated steel); because the seam in an opened can is especially vulnerable, leftovers should be transferred to another container for refrigeration. Tin itself can reach emetic concentrations in canned fruits and vegetables, particularly when these foods contain unusually high levels of nitrate or sulfur compounds and are stored after opening in the can. Early-morning patrons of vending machines have suffered from drinking acid beverages that sat in a copper pipeline overnight. People have become ill after barbecueing on a refrigerator grille that contained cadmium, and after leaving party food in zinc-galvanized tubs.

The lesson is obvious. We should choose our containers with the same kind of care that we give to the food we put in them. In general, it's best to avoid pottery of unknown or amateur manufacture, and any but the standard stovetop metals.

Aluminum to zinc, hypothetical to proven—this has been some litany of corrosion and poisoning! But to my mind, the story is cause not so much for anxiety as for attentiveness. It comes down to a basic conflict of interests. Metals are invaluable to the cook because among all the earth's resources they are the best conductors of heat, are easily shaped into tools and containers, and are practically indestructible. On the other hand, metals are both essential and hazardous to all living things because they are versatile, powerful chemical reactants. Some consideration of their chemical nature should inform the cook's choice and use of utensils. Otherwise, in however minor a way, we may incidentally corrupt the living vessels we mean to nourish.

PART THREE

REFLECTIONS

Beyond supplying practical advice on dietetic and culinary matters, science also deepens our understanding of cooking and eating. This is not news; Jean Anthelme Brillat-Savarin explored the idea well over a century ago in The Physiology of Taste. *Strangely, the physiology of his* Physiology *has been neglected by his admirers, so I begin with a belated appreciation of the science in this gastronomical classic. Then on to osmazome, the essence of meat flavor, which the chemists of Brillat-Savarin's day thought they had captured. They were mistaken, but the story illustrates the close affiliation of biochemistry and cookery. Finally, some news: a hint as to why the human animal has come to enjoy the flavors of cooked foods. Recent chemical and biological findings offer an intriguing glimpse into the nature of gastronomical pleasure and its abiding mystery.*

The Physiologist of Taste

Jean Anthelme Brillat-Savarin is remembered today mostly for a handful of epigrams. "Tell me what you eat, and I will tell you what you are." "A dessert course without cheese is like a beautiful woman with only one eye." "One can learn to cook, but one must be born knowing how to roast." "The discovery of a new dish does more for human happiness than the discovery of a star." These lines come from the first two pages of his *Physiology of Taste: Or, Meditations on Transcendental Gastronomy*, which he published privately and anonymously in 1825, which has since gone through many editions in a variety of languages, and which might fairly be called the classic book on the pleasures of the table. M. F. K. Fisher's English translation, which I'm quoting from with only a few small changes, is a classic in its own right, still going strong after forty years.

The renown of *The Physiology of Taste* is richly deserved, but it should rest on more than a couple of the book's several hundred pages. In fact, taken as a whole, this is a very unlikely book to have become a gastronomical classic. The title promises a certain attention to scientific matters, and they're often not of the most appetizing sort. "Physiology"! Imagine opening an issue of *Gourmet* or *Food and Wine* and finding detailed descriptions of the tongue's movements during eating, or of the remarkable arrangement of tissues that prevents us from choking when we swallow, or of the fate of food in the stomach. Discussions of exhaustion and death. Speculations on embalming. Brillat-Savarin's meditations encompass all these things. But over time, this side of his book has been largely forgotten. It says a great deal about our watered-down image of Brillat-Savarin that the current edition of *Bartlett's Familiar Quotations* tries to

Jean Anthelme Brillat-Savarin.

credit him—or discredit him—with the cheery slogan, "A meal without wine is like a day without sunshine."

The physiology in *The Physiology of Taste* was largely ignored even by the many writers who imitated its title and eclectic mixture of aphorism, anecdote, and exposition. Balzac, who wrote an admiring biographical essay on Brillat-Savarin, published *The Physiology of Marriage* in 1829, and less notable scholars dilated in succeeding decades on the physiology of the opera, the cafe, the umbrella, billiards, and "the ridiculous," among other things. In this short-lived genre, *physiology* was reduced to a synonym for *character* or *portrait*. These books aspired only to the form and fame, not the substance, of *The Physiology of Taste*.

Brillat-Savarin may have been responsible for a temporary change in the word's meaning, but he himself used *physiology* literally, to mean a scientific analysis of the workings of living beings. Roughly a third of his book is devoted to the chemistry and physiology of food and eating. Delightful as the aphorisms and anecdotes are, *The Physiology of Taste* would be a lesser book without its attention to science. Like the astringent tannins in a red wine, this element lends the whole a certain solidity and dimension, and has helped it age well.

The brief biographies that accompany most editions of *The Physiology of Taste* string together the same facts: Brillat-Savarin was born in Belley, a town lying between Lyon and the Alps, in 1755. He became a lawyer, fled the Revolution, spent two years in New York teaching languages and playing violin in a theater orchestra, returned to France, eventually became a judge on the Court of Appeals in Paris, and died in 1826. Now we don't need any particular explanation for why a lawyer came to write about the pleasures of the table. Everyone eats, and some people give it a good deal of thought. But why the *physiology* of taste?

As is evident from the book, Brillat-Savarin had a lifelong fascination with science and medicine. He mentions in passing in meditation 22 that while studying law at the University of Dijon, he was also taking a course in chemistry from Guyton de Morveau, who was in the vanguard of the new chemistry, and another in "domestic medicine" from an expert in public health, Hugues Maret. He describes himself in one anecdote as a *"pharmaconome,"* or connoisseur of medicines; another passage shows him to be well versed in the theory of phrenology. And he admits in the preface that he greatly enjoyed being mistaken for a physician:

> I am above all a lover of doctors (*"médecin-amateur"*). It is almost a mania with me, and one of the happiest moments of my life was when, as a guest, I entered the amphitheater with the professors to listen to Dr. Cloquet's presentation of his prize thesis, and heard a murmur of curiosity run through the audience. The students had mistaken me for a distinguished foreign professor, honoring the gathering with his presence!*

In a sense, *The Physiology of Taste* is the culmination of Brillat-Savarin's amateur scientific career. Having once been mistaken for a distinguished professor, he is now able to bestow the title on himself by publishing his book as the work of an anonymous "Professor, member of many learned societies," and referring to himself throughout as "the Professor." He gives a medical cast to much of his material; his anecdotes are often case histories, his recipes prescriptions. The Professor delivers a formal lecture to his cook on the theory of frying, since "the phenomena which take place in your laboratory are nothing other than the ex-

---

*Brillat-Savarin probably heard Dr. Jules-Germain Cloquet hold forth in 1819 on the subject of abdominal hernias, but he may also have known Jules-Germain's brother Hippolyte, also a doctor, who published a treatise on smell, *Osphrésiologie*, in 1821.

ecution of the eternal laws of nature." And he writes with doctors and scientists in mind: "I was carried along by a laudable curiosity, by a fear of lagging behind the times, and by a desire to be able to hold my own with the men of science with whom I have always loved to associate."

Among his learned associates was Brillat-Savarin's closest friend, Anthelme Richerand, a physician who left his mark on the book in both evident and not so evident ways. Richerand was also a native of the town of Belley. Some twenty-four years younger than Brillat-Savarin, he made his reputation at the age of twenty-two, in 1801, when he published the popular *New Elements of Physiology* (Brillat-Savarin quotes extensively from a later edition on the subject of death). It was at Richerand's country house that Brillat-Savarin began writing his book and that the anecdote of the huge turbot is set; in the dialogue that follows the opening aphorisms, it is Richerand who convinces him to publish.

Knowing that the two were good friends and then reading their books side by side leads one to imagine that Brillat-Savarin and Richerand must have had regular and lively debates on gastronomical physiology and honed their arguments on each other. It's clear that Brillat-Savarin relied on Richerand's *New Elements of Physiology* for his basic definition of food and description of digestion; yet he vigorously disputes the idea, duly reported by Richerand, that animals can have a more acute sense of taste or smell than man (though his grounds are notably unscientific).

On the subject of gourmandism itself, it appears that each felt his friend to be in need of instruction. In his book of 1810 *On Popular Errors Regarding Medicine*, Richerand wrote:

> The art of the Apiciuses, under the name of gastronomy, has in our time made advances that are as disgraceful as they are surprising. At the risk of passing for a disciple of Sancho Panza, I cannot excuse myself from citing to those who thus debase human nature, "that the gourmands dig their grave with their teeth," and that "rather than live to eat, one should eat to live."

This is the voice of the practicing physician, and it's still audible in the edition of *New Elements of Physiology* published in 1825: "Man is of all the animals perhaps the one whose taste has the most delicacy, as long as he does not enfeeble his sensitivity early by means of strong drink, spiced ragouts, and all the refinements that are contrived every day by the extravagance of banquets." To such remarks, which he may well have inspired, Brillat-Savarin replied succinctly, and with a dash of his own brand of physiology:

> No matter how gourmandism is considered, it deserves praise and encouragement.
> Physically, it is the result as well as the proof of the perfect state of health of our digestive organs.
> Morally, it is an implicit obedience of the rules of the Creator, who, having ordered us to eat in order to live, invites us to do so with appetite, encourages us with flavor, and rewards us with pleasure.

Of their good-humored set-tos there is a taste in the dialogue early in Brillat-Savarin's book, where he accuses, with "oratorical rage," his "horrified" friend of a "habitual vice, which all my exhortations have not corrected": "You eat too fast!"

Among Richerand's influences on *The Physiology of Taste*, it's quite likely that he introduced Brillat-Savarin to a book that provided him with a model and a title for his own. In 1820 Dr. Jean-Louis Alibert, a colleague of Richerand's at the Paris School of Medicine, published a book that tried to explain such human feelings as hope, fear, pride, resentment, and love by means of the basic "instincts," or "primordial laws of the sensitive [animal] system," of self-preservation, imitation, relation, and reproduction. Brillat-Savarin quotes twice from Alibert and calls him "a doctor as witty as he is wise." The title of his book was *The Physiology of the Passions: A New Doctrine of the Moral Sentiments*.

Though the books are quite different (Alibert's is soberly systematic), Brillat-Savarin and Alibert shared a confidence that complicated human behavior can be elucidated by reference to our nature as animal creatures. The times were congenial for such attempts to apply science to everyday life, and for an amateur like Brillat-Savarin to take an interest in the sciences. The "new chemistry" was in full stride, and books on the chemistry of agriculture and industry, and on the physiology of human disease, were being written for the general educated public. As for the science of food, the year 1821 brought the publication in England of Fredrick Accum's *Culinary Chemistry*, with French excerpts appearing in 1825 in A. M. Verry's *Cuisinier des cuisiniers* (*Cook of Cooks*), a book that Brillat-Savarin recommends to his readers.

There's no doubt that Brillat-Savarin's own interests and the influence of his friends led him to view medicine and the sciences as the backbone of his project. He says in the preface that in order to do justice to the pleasures of the table, which "are so everpresent and so necessary, and . . . have such a direct influence on our health, our happiness, and even on our occupations," "it was necessary to be a physician, chemist, physiologist, and even a little erudite." Quite a transformation for a lawyer! And evidence of a remarkable, syncretic view of human experience. Others had written about cooking, about food, about gastronomy, food chemistry, and alimentary physiology. But no one else had asserted that the refinements of gastronomy are grounded in chemistry and physiology, or that an account of the pleasures of the table required a consideration of the effects of heat on foods, of foods on the senses and health, of body on mind. To this day, *The Physiology of Taste* remains unique among books on food in its scope and penetration.

Driving Brillat-Savarin's transformation into a triple-threat amateur scientist was a great gusto for the pleasures of analysis, experiment, and theorizing. One manifestation of this delight was his charter membership in the Society for the Encouragement of National Industry, headed for many years by Jean Antoine Chaptal, a noted chemist whose book on agricultural chemistry Brillat-Savarin cites. (Chaptal once discoursed learnedly on "the etiology of the formation of soup"; his name survives today in the winemaking term *chaptalization*, the addition of sugar to the crushed grapes prior to fermentation.) In the same breath as his medical masquerade, Brillat-Savarin recalls the day he presented his own invention to the society's fellows: the "irrorator," a pocket-sized compression pump that sprayed perfume in the air. And at another point, thinking of possible applications for the new abundance of sugar created by the fledgling French sugar beet industry, he suggests that sugar might be put to good use in embalming. As one commentator, Roland Barthes, has exclaimed: "*cadavre exquis: confit, candi, en confiture!*" ("exquisite corpse: conserved, candied, in preserves!").

Another sign of Brillat-Savarin's delight in inventiveness and speculation is his refreshing embrace of the future. In his day, restaurants were a recent innovation; such New World delicacies as coffee, chocolate, vanilla, and the tomato were still novelties of a sort; and chemists were discovering new elements and compounds every year. Thus the human race seemed to Brillat-Savarin "still very young," and he imagined, over and over, that time would bring new insights, new powers, new dishes, even fundamentally new pleasures. Chemistry, he believed, would be the discipline to reveal the ultimate nature of taste and smell, and would conquer the heretofore "unruly" gases to obtain "new substances and effects which will enormously enlarge our powers." From explorers and scholars he expected more discoveries of foods and spices that would bring new sensations and new dishes. Noting that our sense of hearing was enlarged by the discovery of harmony, Brillat-Savarin anticipated the day when the sense of touch may "open us to a new source of happiness." Certain dreams convinced him that European culture had not yet reached the limits of human pleasure, and he hoped that physiologists could bring us bliss "at will." And in the climactic "historical elegy," a lament for the limitations on gastronomical pleasure imposed by historical circumstance, from the cookless Garden of Eden to his own time, Brillat-Savarin gave way to ritual weeping for the gastronomes of 1825, who

> will not live to revel in the discoveries which the sciences prepare for the year 1900, delicacies born from rocks, perchance, or liquors resulting from the pressure of a hundred different vapors; you will not see the things which travelers who are not yet even born will bring from that half of the globe which still waits for our discovery, our exploration.

It must be admitted that Brillat-Savarin was not much of a prophet. True, science has done wonders with gases, including the control of fruit ripening and the packaging of various manufactured foods. But scientists are still somewhat mystified by the "chemical senses," taste and smell. No new foods of particular note have emerged from explorations since 1825. The sense of touch hasn't been much advanced, even by the notorious experiments of the late 1960s. Perhaps the generation of bliss at will has been achieved, but only at great cost to those who become addicted. And I doubt that mineral-oil mayonnaise and petroleum-derived food colorings are what Brillat-Savarin had in mind as rock-born "delicacies."

Today, Brillat-Savarin's predictions, like the details of his outdated physiology and chemistry, have only an antiquarian interest. Still impressive, however, is the overall effect of his speculations and explanations, which range from past to present to future, outlining immediate and remote causes and consequences, foregrounds and backgrounds, to generate a sense of the whole. The opening words of this concise but spacious book are "*L'univers*": "The universe is nothing without the things that live in it, and everything that lives, eats." They place all of creation before us in a way that makes the activity of eating essential to its meaningfulness. The details of nineteenth-century French gastronomy are embedded in a matrix that extends from the cosmic to the microscopic, from the dawn of history to a future century.

This comprehensiveness would be dull if it were systematic. Instead, it takes the form of those surprising leaps from one subject to another that are one of the characteristic delights of *The Physiology of Taste*. Brillat-Savarin often draws back from particular foods and sensations to place them in the larger scheme of things. The subject of fish brings up the theory, then "none too orthodox" but now generally accepted, "that the ocean was the cradle of everything that exists; that mankind itself was born in the sea." For a philosopher, Brillat-Savarin observes, fish are "an endless source of meditation and of astonishment":

> The varied forms of these strange creatures, the senses which they lack and the restriction on those which they possess, their diverse means of existence, the influence upon this of the places in which they must live and breathe and move about: all these things extend the world of our ideas and of the limitless modifications which spring from matter, from movement, from life itself.

This is looking at fish afresh!

The gastronome too provides Brillat-Savarin with the occasion for meditation. The physiology of the senses reminds him that "the destiny of man, considered as a sentient being," is "the preservation of the individual and the continuation of the species." Alcohol and its effects lead him to propose that a love of strong drink and a fear of the future are two "distinctive attributes of man, that masterpiece of the last sublunary revolution." This last phrase in turn leads into meditation 10, "On the End of the World." In our day, when similar scripts are being suggested to explain the extinction of dinosaurs and to predict the climatic effects of nuclear war, it's an especially peculiar sensation to read Brillat-Savarin's description of a cometary near-miss and the subsequent generation of temperatures sufficient to cook all flora and fauna on earth (this is based on an outdated view of comets, but never mind), his seven questions covering the effects on the physical world and on human society, and his decision not to share his own conclusions with his readers: "I do not wish to deprive them of the plea-sure of doing it themselves."

The cumulative effect of these excursions is to foster a sense that food and eating, however fundamental and delightful, are only part of our experience, and that they gain in interest and significance when they lead us on to insight into the natural world and human experience. The same implication arises from one particularly grim theme in Brillat-Savarin's divagations. It's there to some extent in the cometary roast, but more noticeably in meditation 14, "On the Pleasures of the Table," which begins startlingly: "Man is incontestably, among the sentient creatures who inhabit the globe, the one who endures the most pain." It is the fear of this suffering "which makes man throw himself, without even realizing it, toward the opposite extreme, and give himself com-pletely to the small number of pleasures which Nature has permitted him."

To introduce the pleasures of the table as a means of partial, inadequate compensation for all the ills the flesh is heir to, from toothache to warfare, is to attribute to them both a certain emotional dignity and a certain futility. Simi-larly, meditation 26, "On Death," begins: "The six most important necessities which the Creator has imposed on mankind are to be born, to move about, to eat, to sleep, to procreate, and to die." The point of this meditation is to show that, just as fulfilling the other necessities is accompanied by feelings of plea-sure, so too is death. But to place dining in this company is to affirm at one and the same time its relative prominence and its ultimate insignificance. In the light of such passages, gastronomy appears to be an effort to make the best of a bad situation; and two of the opening aphorisms stand out in stark relief:

> The Creator, while forcing man to eat in order to live, tempts him to do so with appetite and then rewards him with pleasure.
>
> The pleasures of the table . . . can be a part of all his other pleasures, and they last the longest, to console him when he has outlived the rest.

The sixth-century Roman statesman and scholar Boethius, awaiting execution, wrote about the nature of happiness and suffering and called his book *The Con-solations of Philosophy*. The somber theme that runs quietly throughout *The Physiology of Taste* might be designated "the consolations of gastronomy."

It's interesting that Brillat-Savarin's faith in progress didn't extend to medi-cine and the alleviation of suffering. Physiology provides an explanation for the workings of the human body, but promises no cures for gout or the diseases of

society. If it eventually brings us bliss at will, bliss would only balance, not eliminate, human pain. Suffering and death are inevitable; fine dining is compensation, not a cure. In this, *The Physiology of Taste* is very much a book of the Old
World. Within a decade of its publication, Sylvester Graham roused into life
the American willingness to believe that certain foods can bring salvation.

The Physiology of Taste is quite a mosaic indeed. Brillat-Savarin cobbles together human physiology and food chemistry, high gastronomy, eschatology,
and thanatology. He combines a faith in progress with a fatalism about the human condition: "Mankind would be much unhappier if it could see into the future," he says of the beginnings of obesity. His love of doctors alternates with
disapproval of their methods. Aphorisms, detailed scientific explications, dia-
logues, anecdotes, "sermons," histories, poems, meditations, reveries—some
jambalaya.

What binds the book together, rounds it into such a satisfying whole?
Mainly, I think, the professorial yet jocular voice with which Brillat-Savarin delivers his analyses. Meditations on "transcendental" gastronomy. To gratify a
weak appetite "takes more genius, more deep thought, and more hard work
than it would to resolve one of the most difficult problems in the geometry of
the Infinite." For a deliberation on the erotic properties of truffles, the Professor
convenes his experts "in a committee, in a tribunal, in a senate, in a sanhedrin,
in an Areopagus, and we have rendered the following decision, to be com-
mented upon by writers of the twenty-fifth century: 'The truffle is not a positive
aphrodisiac; but it can, in certain situations, make women tenderer and men
more agreeable.'"

Balzac describes the tone of Brillat-Savarin's book as one of "pontifical solemnity," with pronouncements being handed down like the Ten Command-
ments or Kepler's laws of planetary motion. Yes, except that the Professor
outLords the Lord. The effects of this kind of voice are complicated. It gently
mocks the pretensions of all learned treatises, the claims of both author and
subject to high seriousness. But it also reflects on the work at hand. There's no
doubt that Brillat-Savarin believes the subject of food to be worthy of serious
discussion, but he also knows that gastronomy can be overdone. For true pontifical solemnity, just skim some of the food writing of our own day, where
abound adjectives like "astonishing," "ravishing," "devastating," "compelling,"
"supernal," and "sublime."

The modern French savant Roland Barthes has interpreted the ironic tone of *The Physiology of Taste* as a sign of "timidity": Brillat-Savarin doesn't have the courage of his convictions, so he makes his book into a long joke. Yet perhaps even savants can profit from such jokes. Brillat-Savarin's professorial persona works in concert with the book's loose structure and miscellaneous content to capture an elusive and heterogeneous subject. Like an orbiting satellite, Brillat-Savarin circles around his subject, approaching it not directly but tangentially, always at a distance, always seeing the rest of the universe just over the horizon. No single perspective lasts for very long; there's always another view.

"Transcendental chemistry," the Professor says, teaches us that a piece of chocolate should not be ground before it is added to hot water; rather, it should be allowed to melt in the water. The joke is that such chemistry is nothing if not mundane. It does not dig very deep into the nature of things. What makes "transcendental" an appropriate epithet is that the investigation does bear on what can be a transporting experience: the intense, fleeting pleasure that a food can provide. The materials and actions—food and eating—are in themselves ordinary. It's the way we respond to them, the meanings and connections we supply, that dignify them.

The emblem of this double nature is the muse Brillat-Savarin invents for gastronomy: Gasterea. The name sounds like a parody of Astrea, the Roman goddess of justice, in whose service Brillat-Savarin labored much of his life. *Astrea* derives from the Greek word for "star," a distant, pure beacon of illumination, and *Gasterea* from "belly," one of the least idealizable portions of the human anatomy. Gasterea stands for the ennoblement of the belly by the mind. As much as taste itself, or history or philosophy, physiology and chemistry are means by which this transformation can be accomplished.

What sets *The Physiology of Taste* apart is the diversity of its perspectives on cooking and eating. "An intelligently planned feast is like a summing-up of the world," Brillat-Savarin said—and so is his synoptic banquet of a book.

The Saga of Osmazome

As an avid student of the new chemistry and its implications for good eating, Brillat-Savarin was especially impressed by a discovery that seemed to offer a grasp on the very source of gastronomical pleasure. His description of it fills the opening pages of meditation 5, the first section of *The Physiology of Taste* devoted to food, and he later returns to it several times. This great discovery, which was given the sonorous name *osmazome*, was a remarkable extract of meat: in it was concentrated the essence of the meat's flavor. Fittingly enough, osmazome was found by means of new chemical techniques that had first been used to cook foods; in turn, it became the first instance in which chemistry influenced the thinking, if not the practice, of cookbook writers and their public. Its career was brief, but as we'll see, the students of osmazome were indeed onto something important.

Here is Brillat-Savarin in praise of osmazome.

> The greatest service rendered by chemistry to alimentary science is the discovery or rather the precise knowledge of osmazome.
>
> Osmazome is that eminently savory part of meat that is soluble in cold water, and that is distinguished from the extractive part in that the latter is soluble only in boiling water.
>
> It is osmazome that gives merit to good soups; when caramelized, it forms the brown sauce of meats; by it is formed the brown crust of roasts; finally, from it comes the special flavor of game.
>
> Osmazome is found above all in adult animals with red or brown

flesh, which we call mature flesh; one never or hardly ever finds it in lamb, suckling pig, chicken, or in the white meat of the largest birds. It is for this reason that true connoisseurs have always preferred the thigh; among them the instinct of taste had anticipated science.

It is also the foreknowledge of osmazome that has caused the dismissal of so many cooks who had been persuaded to turn away from tending their basic stock: it made the reputation of the monasteries' bouillon-soaked bread and cheese, caused the adoption of toast in bouillon as a restorative in medicinal baths, and inspired Canon Chevrier to invent marmites locked with a key (this is the same man to whom spinach was never served on Thursday without having been cooked since Sunday, and put on the fire every day with a new dollop of fresh butter).

Finally, it is to husband this substance, although as yet unknown, that the maxim has been introduced that, in order to make a good bouillon, the pot should only *smile*: a very distinguished expression for the country from which it came.

Osmazome, discovered after having delighted our fathers for so long, can be compared to alcohol, which intoxicated generations before it was known that one could strip it naked by distillation.

When meat is boiled in water, osmazome is followed by what one means especially by extractive matter: this last product, reunited with the osmazome, makes up the juice of meat.

A remarkable find indeed! One single substance that is responsible for the special qualities of meats and any foods made with meat. And responsible not for such relatively abstract, intangible qualities as nutritional or medicinal value, but for flavor itself: a quality essential to the immediate pleasure we take in eating. Brillat-Savarin might very well have said that without osmazome, gourmandism would be a mere shadow of itself. For one thing, he explains, osmazome provided our distant ancestors with their first taste of the advantages of cookery. When, in his recounting of culinary history, he reaches the discovery of fire and so the first cooked foods, he argues that

Once fire was known, the instinct for improvement led us to apply it to meats, at first to dry them, and then we put them on the coals to cook them.

Meat treated thus was found to be much improved: it takes on greater firmness, is more easily chewed, and the osmazome, when browned, becomes aromatic and gives it that aroma which has never ceased to please us.

The chemistry of osmazome gave us the original pleasure of the table, and it also gives us the table's highest possible pleasure. Osmazome is especially responsible for the taste of game, which Brillat-Savarin feels "provides most of the highly flavored dishes that constitute transcendent cooking." Just as alcohol, the essence of wine and "water of life," intoxicates us, so osmazome, the essence of meat and therefore of cookery in general, transports us to a higher realm.

So what exactly is this marvelous stuff? How was it discovered? And what has happened to it? Why aren't our modern cookbooks filled with paeans to its glory, our gourmet shops stocked with expensive vials for making *sauce à l'osmazome*, with which Brillat-Savarin dresses early asparagus in the ultimate of his gastronomical tests?

Osmazome was the product of new chemical techniques that were gradually taking hold in the late eighteenth century, and that brought chemistry back to its roots in the kitchen. In the generation before Brillat-Savarin's, the most common means of analyzing the chemical composition of a substance was by distillation, a relatively high-tech procedure that derived from medieval alchemy. Its great popularity resulted not so much from its true usefulness as from a handful of great successes and so the promise of others. And it accorded well with the accepted theories of chemical composition.

In order to distill a substance, the chemist heats it until it begins to give off a vapor, and then collects that vapor, whose composition will vary according to the temperature and the duration of heating. The distillation of wine and beer produces a vapor rich in alcohol because alcohol is more volatile than water. Similarly, the "essential oils" that give certain plants their distinctive aromas are volatile and so concentrated by distillation. In its early days, distillation was primarily a pharmaceutical technique for capturing the "essences" or "spirits" of plants that were used as drugs. The obvious increase in effectiveness brought about by the distillation of wine into alcohol, which became known as *aqua vitae*, or "the water of life," was reason enough for the technique to flourish.

Gradually, the alchemists, who were interested not so much in medicine as in understanding and controlling the transformations of matter, began to use distillation as a way of dissecting the composition of things. They found that when plant or animal tissues were put in the retort and gradually heated, five products were obtained. The first vapor was a volatile "spirit" analogous to alcohol, and it was followed by a "water" and an "oil." At the end of the process, the original material was reduced to a blackened mass that could be separated into various mineral salts, and an irreducible "earth," which was also known as *caput mortuum*, or "death's head." By studying the relative quantities and properties of these five elements, the alchemists and early chemists hoped to learn something of the nature of living things.

But they didn't learn much. The same five elements were found with little variation in all distillations. And the more critical practitioners, among them Robert Boyle in the late seventeenth century, argued that the very process of distillation might be responsible for producing these elements: they may not have existed in the original material, but could have been formed by the action of heat.

Early in the eighteenth century, an alternative method of analysis came into prominence. It too had venerable roots in pharmaceutical practice, and involved extraction by means of various liquids. The essential oils of plants could be drawn out by soaking them in a quantity of neutral oil or fat, while other principles would dissolve in water. Around 1700 the French chemist Simon Boulduc studied two varieties of the medicinal root ipecacuanha by distillation and by double extraction in water and alcohol, and was able to distinguish between the two varieties by the extraction technique. Around mid-century, the German chemist Andreas Marggraf used extraction in alcohol to discover sugar in beets (and thereby laid the foundation for the beet sugar industry).

As extraction gradually caught on as an analytical technique, the old classification of elements gave way to a more modern vocabulary based on the solubilities of substances in various liquids. Brillat-Savarin would have heard this new classification propounded in the chemistry course he took from Guyton de Morveau in Dijon in 1776. The book based on that course explained that the difficulties caused by distillation "determined modern chemists to use it only to decompose [vegetable or animal] bodies, and only after exhausting the action of more gentle solvents capable of attracting to themselves some constituent part without destroying the totality of the mixture. They extract with water the mucous or gummy matter; the resin is separated by alcohol or ether, and acids precipitate some earths and fixed salts."

It wasn't lost on the modern chemists that their new "infusions" and "decoctions" of organic materials had everyday counterparts. These procedures essentially meant making a soup stock—a water extract—and then further studying the liquid. In 1730 Etienne Geoffroy published what is probably the first study of meat bouillon. It was a traditional medicinal for invalids, and Geoffroy wanted to estimate how much of the meat's substance was extracted by cooking. His conclusion: enough to be nourishing. Several decades later, the great French *Encyclopédie*, which classified "bouillon" as a term of "medicine" rather than "cookery," summarized Geoffroy's work in detail.

The pioneers of the discovery of osmazome were Hilaire-Marin Rouelle and Pierre Thouvenel. Unfortunately, on this point I must take the word of later chemists. Rouelle published very little of his work; all we know of his famous courses comes from several surviving manuscript sets of lecture notes taken by his students. Thouvenel, on the other hand, published several "medico-chemical" treatises, but they're quite rare, and the two I've obtained make no mention of bouillons. I suspect that the source referred to by later writers was his *Mémoire sur les corps muqueux* (*Report on Mucous Bodies*) published in Montpellier in 1770. In any case, Thouvenel, who served as inspector of mineral waters in France and physician to Louis XVIII, is credited with having mentioned Rouelle's experiments with water extractions of flesh, and extending his results.

We can reconstruct Thouvenel's achievement from the admiring testimony of several eminent colleagues. In his *System of Chemical Knowledge* (1801), the great French chemist Antoine de Fourcroy (a patron of Brillat-Savarin's friend Dr. Richerand) said that

> the physician Geoffroy described the effect of water, and the amount of soluble matter that it liberates during boiling from a great number of different meats, in connection with the nutritional part contained in each. This work was of some value only relative to dietary properties. Thouvenel was the first who tried to understand the diverse principles, or rather the constituent materials of muscles. For this he employed several procedures that were unused before him, and that allowed him to give a somewhat more positive notion of the nature of these organs.

Fourcroy goes on to describe Thouvenel's procedure for analyzing the chemical composition of meat:

> Modern chemists treated muscle as they did a vegetable material, mixed of many different substances, which they attempted to separate from each other, at first by mechanical means, then by chemical pro-

cedures. Since this organ is filled with blood and lymph vessels that contain liquids, the force of a press served to separate them for Thouvenel. The fluids that he obtained were treated successively by heat, which coagulated the albuminous matter and crystallized the salts by evaporating the water; and by alcohol, which dissolved away several salts, and also a particular extractive substance which this chemist believed peculiar to muscles.

The interesting thing about this extractive substance was the fact that it was viscous, like the jelly that can be extracted from soup bones and meat, but could be separated from that jelly: and most remarkably, it appeared to account for the flavor of the meat.

Thouvenel's finding was also noted by Jean Antoine Chaptal—the head of Brillat-Savarin's pet Society for the Encouragement of National Industry—in his definitive three-volume *Elements of Chemistry* of 1794:

> M. Thouvenel, to whom we are indebted for interesting researches on this subject, has found in flesh a mucous extractive substance, soluble in water and in alcohol, possessing a peculiar taste which jelly has not; and when this substance is very much concentrated, it assumes an acrid and bitter taste. Fire develops an aromatic flavor in it.

To my knowledge, it was Chaptal who first saw that these new chemical procedures and results had direct relevance to the work of the cook. After observing that chemists had divided flesh into a handful of "principles"—insoluble fibrous matter, coagulable lymph, jelly, salts, fat, and Thouvenel's extractive matter—Chaptal inserts into his technical treatise on basic chemistry a remarkably detailed analysis of the making of soup. With some allowances for outdated ideas and the contemporary translation, it's not a bad description:

> From these principles we may give the etiology of the formation of soup, and follow the successive disengagements of the principles we have spoken of.
>
> The first impression of the fire, when a soup is made, is the disengagement of a considerable scum, which is taken off until it no longer appears. This scum arises merely from the disengagement of the lymph, which coagulates by the heat. It assumes, by the impression of the fire, a red color, which it does not naturally possess.
>
> At the same time the gelatinous part is disengaged, which remains dissolved in the soup, and congeals only by cooling. It forms on the sur-

face of the cold soup a body more or less thick, according to the nature of the substances, and the age of the animals; for young animals afford a larger quantity than such as an old.

As soon as the flesh is penetrated by heat, flat round drops arise, and float at the surface of the fluid, in which they are not afterwards dissolved, but congeal by cooling, and exhibit all the characters of fat.

In proportion as digestion [cooking] proceeds, the mucous extractive part separates: the soup becomes colored, assumes its peculiar odor and taste; and it is more particularly to this principle that its properties are owing.

The salt which is dissolved at the same time takes off the insipidity of all the before-mentioned principles: and at this period the soup is completely made.

According to the nature of the several principles which are disengaged, and the order in which they appear, it is evident that the management of the fire is not a matter of indifference. If the boiling is hastened, and a proper time is not allowed for the disengagement of the mucous extractive matter, the three inodorous and insipid principles are obtained. This is observed in soups made by cooks who are hurried, or who have not allowed time to pay due attention to their work. When, on the contrary, the digestion is made over a slow fire, the principles separate one after the other, in order; the skimming is more accurately performed; the aromatic flavor which is disengaged combines more intimately, and the soup is of an excellent flavor. These are the soups of the good women who perform better with a small quantity of meat, than professional cooks with their usual prodigality, and in their case we may say that the appearance is more valuable than the substance.

The heat must not be applied too long; for the great evaporation, by concentrating the principle of smell and taste at the same time with the salt, renders them acrid and bitter.

It had been observed earlier, by Rouelle, for example, and even by Menon, author of a cookbook published in 1756, that cookery is a chemical operation. But no one before Chaptal had given such attention to a particular dish. Notice that he makes no effort to reform soupmaking, nor claims any special importance for his analysis. In this case, chemistry has simply explained the underlying rationale for a traditional recipe.

Thouvenel's analysis of the flavorful component of flesh and Chaptal's application of this and other insights to practical cookery were carried a step further by Fourcroy in the ninth volume of his *System of Chemical Knowledge*. Fourcroy goes into some detail on the making of not only bouillons, but also the more concentrated version, or consommé; the ultimate in concentration, the solid *tablettes de bouillon*, or "portable soup," the eighteenth-century precursor of bouillon cubes; and the roast. And he was probably the first to draw a connection between the flavoring of the bouillon and the intensification of flavor that accompanies roasting. The connection, of course, is provided by Thouvenel's extractive material.

> One procures the extractive matter that is removed from muscle by boiling it in water and then washing with alcohol the product of the bouillon evaporated to the consistency of thick honey. This reagent does not affect either the gelatin nor the majority of salts contained in the product. When the highly colored alcohol is evaporated, one obtains a reddish-brown material, of piquant flavor and even bitter, of a particularly aromatic odor. When one heats it a little more strongly than just to dry it, it boils and bubbles, and takes on the odor of caramel and its sugary flavor. It appears that this extractive matter is what forms on roasted meat the glistening brown, highly-flavored glaze that is called *rissolé*. This extract remains soft in the air and gives their melting properties to bouillon tablets. . . . It remains to be determined whether this kind of extract is fully formed and contained in muscular flesh, and that it is not produced by the decomposition of fibrous tissue, brought about by the aid of the action of heat.

That last qualifying sentence is the sign of a thorough chemist. It raises a good, and ultimately fatal, question about the genuine identity of the flavorful extract.

The substance that Rouelle or Thouvenel discovered by treating beef soup with alcohol, that Chaptal included in his etiology of soupmaking, and that Fourcroy connects with the savoriness of roasts: this substance is clearly identical with what Brillat-Savarin celebrates as osmazome two decades later. It was given this odd name by a collaborator of Fourcroy's who, strangely, claimed to have discovered the substance in 1806. At least among gastronomes and chefs, the name extended the life of this extract beyond its useful years.

The baptizer of osmazome was Louis Jacques Thenard, who attended the

Louis Jacques Thenard.

public lectures of Fourcroy and his collaborator Nicolas Vauquelin and succeeded Vauquelin at the Collège de France in 1804. In that same year, at the request of Fourcroy, Thenard investigated a recently described "zoonic acid," which was a distillation product supposedly unique to meat. In this first of his forays into meat chemistry, Thenard showed that the substance in question was actually impure acetic acid. He went on to distinguish himself as an analytic chemist, and is best remembered for having discovered hydrogen peroxide. In 1832 he succeeded Chaptal as head of the Society for the Encouragement of National Industry, to which he had belonged all his professional life. It's quite possible that he had been showered with the perfume from Brillat-Savarin's irrorator.

The word *osmazome* first appeared in print in 1806, when the *Bulletin of the Faculty of Medicine* of the University of Paris published a summary of a report given to the faculty by Thenard. Perhaps because of his critical work on zoonic acid, Thenard had again been asked by a senior colleague, this time the director of the faculty, Michel-Augustin Thouret, to reexamine a matter of meat chemistry. In 1803 Antoine-Alexis-François Cadet de Vaux had published a *Report on the Gelatin of Bones*, which claimed that soup made from bones was identical to soup made from meat, and so should be employed for feeding the poor and the sick. Thouret, however, was bothered by the differences in taste, odor, and color between bone and meat bouillons. And so he invited Thenard to study the issue at the Hôtel-Dieu, a venerable charitable hospital in Paris.

Thenard found that whereas a bone soup produced large amounts of jelly when concentrated, meat soup produced much less, and its jelly seemed to be a mixture of gelatin and other substances. He then extracted the cold meat jelly with alcohol for several hours and passed the mixture through a filter, which retained the gelatin and passed "a peculiar substance." This substance could also be obtained by extracting raw flesh with cold water and alcohol. The report continues:

> This material, unknown until now, plays a remarkable role in bouillon. It has its odor and flavor to a very marked degree. M. Thenard proposes to name it *osmazome*. Osmazome is different from all other animal materials. . . . It is to osmazome that meat bouillon owes its odor and flavor; in flesh, the proportion of this substance to gelatin is about one to five. It does not exist at all in bones, which explains the difference between bouillon made with them, and bouillon made with meat.

It's more than a little strange that Thenard claims his discovery to be a novel one, given the attention paid only five years earlier to the "extractive substances" by his own patron Fourcroy, who quite likely introduced him to meat chemistry in the first place. But Thenard could certainly claim to have improved on the extraction procedure, since he went to the trouble of filtering out the gelatin and so presumably ended up with a purer extract.

Thenard's great coup was to give this now middle-aged extract a catchy name. *Osmazome* is a compound of two Greek words, *osme* meaning "odor" and *zomos* meaning "soup." It's quite likely that Thenard owed his inspiration to Fourcroy, although this time rather indirectly. In 1804 Fourcroy and Vauquelin had been scooped by an English chemist, Smithson Tennant, in the discovery of a new metal. The French chemists admitted the inferiority of their work in a paper of 1806, and their colleagues were sure to have known and shared in their disappointment. Tennant, meanwhile, had named the new element: "A pungent and peculiar smell . . . arises from the extrication of a very volatile metal oxide; and, as this smell is one of its most distinguishing characters, I should on that account incline to call the metal *Osmium*." So *osme* was much in the air at the Collège de France, and Thenard seized on it for his own "new" odorous substance.

In any event, *osmazome* is a wonderful coinage, its ruminative alliteration suggestive of savoring. And it gave an immediately distinctive identity to what had until then been a vaguely defined mixture that accounted for a vaguely defined sensation. This specification of the pleasure principle in soups and meats gave the extract a new life. Not so much among the chemists—in 1821, for example, Joseph Proust devoted an entire article to this "quintessence in the art of cooking" without mentioning either Thenard or osmazome—but among the then-new tribe of scribes, the writers on gastronomy.

Osmazome first infiltrated the gastronomical world through the efforts of a nephew of Cadet de Vaux who was also a student of Fourcroy's, one Charles-Louis Cadet de Gassicourt. Like Brillat-Savarin, young Cadet had trained in and practiced law, but he abandoned that career in his early thirties for pharmacy, an applied form of chemistry. He had very likely met Fourcroy and Lavoisier in his own home, since his legal father, Louis-Claude, a student of Rouelle's and apprentice of Geoffroy, was himself a noted pharmacist. (Cadet's natural father was Louis XV; his mother, a descendant of Louis XIV's physician.) Cadet eventually became pharmacist to Napoleon and was an influential figure in French science. He was also a prolific writer in a wide range of genres, from technical papers to one-act comedies, light verse, travelogues, and political tracts.

In 1809 Cadet published "On Osmazome and Its Use," a pharmaceutical paper in which he noted that osmazome "is not at all nourishing and assimilable like [gelatin]; but it excites the digestive organs with its flavor, and disposes them to absorb the nourishing principles. It could therefore be of great aid in medicine, to revive the appetite of convalescents without burdening their stomachs." In the same year he published, anonymously, *A Course in Gastronomy: Or the Dinners of Manant-Ville*. Manant-Ville, whose name means "city boor," is a provincial nouveau riche who wants his son to be instructed in the ways of the world, and so hires Victor Fage, a "phagotechnician," or specialist in the lore of fine dining. The book is a series of conversations between the students and their various teachers. While Cadet's book contains a great deal of information, it's awkwardly packaged in stiff dialogue, with little of the grace and wit of *The Physiology of Taste*. On the other hand, Cadet's learned book in praise of gastronomy predates Brillat-Savarin's classic by fifteen years. And Cadet provided the first popular account of food chemistry, anticipating Fredrick Accum by a decade. In the chapter "Culinary Chemistry," occasioned by Manant-Villes's indigestion and subsequent curiosity about the subject, the adjunct professor Oxigenius discourses on the proper preparation of soup. A footnote appended to the word *color* reads: "This extract, named *osmazome* by the celebrated Thenard, also contains all of the savory portion of the meat."

With Cadet's *Course in Gastronomy*, Accum's *Culinary Chemistry* of 1820—which elevated osmazome from footnote to center page as the cause of "the peculiar grateful flavour of animal food"—and Brillat-Savarin's paean, the savory extract of meat had been thoroughly introduced to the general reader. Henceforth, and for decades to come, cookbook writers, especially in France and England, did not omit to mention osmazome and the importance of retaining it during the preparation of meat dishes.

Perhaps the ultimate tribute to osmazome's currency was its acceptance by two very different characters, Marie-Antoine Carême and Isabella Beeton. Carême was the first of the great celebrity chefs—chef to Napoleon, the Rothschilds, and Talleyrand—and a prolific and impassioned writer. He begins his *Art of the Chef in the Nineteenth Century*, published in 1830, with a slashing criticism of earlier writers, who had ignored the analysis of the pot-au-feu, the mainstay of the laboring class—"Oh ignorance! What darkness surrounds you!"—and goes on to give much the same analysis as Chaptal, Brillat-Savarin, and Accum. "By the means of moderate heat, the pot-au-feu gently forms a scum; the osmazome, which is the most savory part of the meat, dissolving little by little, gives an unctuousness to the bouillon; and the albumin . . . mounts to the surface of the pot in a light scum. . . . *Voilà* the advantageous results of this entirely chemical operation." Carême also appeals to the action of osmazome in his directions for brown sauce and for consommés.

Then there was Isabella Beeton, wife of an English magazine publisher, who compiled a massive *Book of Household Management* from 1859 to 1861. Four years later, she died after childbirth at the age of twenty-eight, but some version of her book has been in print ever since. Whereas Carême's books were written for the professional chef and those who appreciated his art, Mrs. Beeton wrote for the middle-class housewife. She devotes a full three pages to "The Chemistry and Economy of Soup-making," giving paragraph 100 over to osmazome, and concludes her description: "By roasting meat, the osmazome appears to acquire higher properties; so, by putting the remains of roast meats in your stockpot, you obtain a better flavour."

Osmazome was thus one of the most notable accomplishments of the new chemistry, which did a fairly good job of explaining the events in meat cookery by reference to the handful of substances it had discovered in flesh. This chemical explanation left its imprint on cookbooks of the time, and osmazome was invoked for decades after Brillat-Savarin eulogized it.

Unfortunately, even as Brillat-Savarin and Carême introduced osmazome to all levels of the culinary world, chemists were already doubting its existence. Fourcroy had questioned the simple identity of the extractive material in 1801, before Thenard had even given it a name. And before *The Physiology of Taste* appeared, several chemists had suggested that osmazome was really a mixture of salts, acids, and "animal matter," or even "fibrin"—the fibrous protein— "slightly altered by being boiled in water and dissolved in that liquid." By 1837 a French dictionary of *materia medica* noted that osmazome had been found in blood, brains, kidneys, oysters, mushrooms, dahlia roots, and ginger, and also seemed to be developed "in the act of torrefaction," or browning. The editors suggested that a return to a more general name, "extractive matter of bouillon," was in order because osmazome did not appear to be a "simple immediate principle," but rather a complex mixture.

How complex, and how interesting, would only become clear in the twentieth century. A degree of heat high enough to brown a food creates hundreds of new flavor components. When the French chemists cooked their bouillon down to a thick concentrate, they were browning it. So rather than being the essence of meat flavor, osmazome was the essential residue of prolonged, intense heating. Had Thouvenel, Brillat-Savarin, and the others known this, I doubt they would have been disappointed. I think Brillat-Savarin would have been delighted with some of the odd twists of modern flavor chemistry that I describe in the next chapter.

Though osmazome has disappeared from the laboratory and the kitchen, the analysis of meat bouillon was an important stage in the development of biochemistry. And there are echoes of the work of Thouvenel and his successors in some of the great discoveries in muscle chemistry. Around 1865 the German physiologist Willy Kühne treated frog muscle with salt water and obtained a viscous extract that he associated with the generation of movement and named *myosin*. This same substance, he pointed out, could be found in the brine of traditionally pickled meats. In 1941 the Hungarian biochemists F. B. Straub and Albert Szent-Györgyi extracted Kühne's myosin with acetone—a solvent with properties similar to the alcohol used by Thouvenel—and discovered that the muscle's movement-generating mechanism has two protein components, myosin and *actin*. Szent-Györgyi, writing in 1951 about his choice of the best muscle for biochemical study, emphasized the need to minimize such extraneous materials as connective tissue, and noted that chefs and restaurateurs had already done his research for him:

> It is easy to find the muscle which contains the least amount of connective tissue, for it is the quantity of connective tissue which decides the culinary value of a muscle, to which it is inversely proportional. This culinary value is expressed numerically on the right side of any menu. If this column of numbers is studied, a significant difference is always found at the level of filet mignon, scientifically: *Musculus psoas*.

It wouldn't be surprising if cookery still had a thing or two to contribute to biochemistry.

There's something left to be said in osmazome's favor. Though it turned out to mis-name a multitude of chemical entities, osmazome did correspond to a unified sensuous experience: the rich flavor of cooked, especially roasted, meat. No wonder that even an acerbic chemist, Joseph Proust, exclaimed that "the movements of life confect and deposit" in the muscles "this animal aroma, which one can qualify without exaggeration as the quintessence of culinary art!" (In fact, exercise does seem to intensify the eventual flavor of a muscle.) In my own childhood, the flavor-charged, gelatinous, almost black drippings from oven-barbecued country ribs and chicken were the object of intense desire, so much so that my mother served them to her four children after the meal, a teaspoon at a time, in a ceremony which, but for the fleshly pleasure it gave, was reminiscent of Communion.

The passion for the flavor of the roast that inspired Brillat-Savarin's praise of osmazome was once strong enough to seduce that estimable officer of the court into a sordid act of larceny. One day, while traveling with two ladies a few miles southeast of Paris, he and his companions found themselves with enormous appetites and little hope of satisfaction because the inn they had reached had run out of provisions. A leg of lamb was roasting over the hearth, but it had been brought by three Englishmen, who were passing the time with champagne. Brillat-Savarin asked the cook whether he could scramble some eggs in the juice of the roast, and the cook agreed, saying that the juice belongs to the inn "by public right."

> When I saw that he was well occupied, I drew near to the hearth, and pulling from my pocket a traveling knife, I made in the forbidden roast a dozen or so deep cuts, from which the juice must drain to the last drop.
>
> I also watched with care the concoction of the eggs, to be sure that we were cheated of nothing, and when they were perfectly cooked I myself took them to the room which had been made ready for us.
>
> Then we feasted indeed, and laughed hysterically at the realization that we were swallowing the very essence of the roast, and leaving nothing to our English friends but the residue.

Whatever it is about a roast that inspires such devotion deserves a name, and in the absence of a better one, osmazome serves admirably.

From Raw to Cooked:
The Transformation of Flavor

Why do we like our foods cooked? In the modern world, with its stoves and barbecues, toasters and microwave ovens, that may sound like a peculiar question. But step back for a moment into the natural world, and what seems strange is that the human animal could ever enjoy morsels that have been heated just this side of pure carbon. Cocoa and coffee beans, for example, or the crust on a roast. Very strange! After all, the earth's entire animal population had eaten its foods raw for thousands of millions of years. Then a mere million years ago or so, some early humans began to apply fire to a variety of objects, including plants and animals that their ancestors had eaten raw for aeons. By and large, the new charred version prevailed. And now it's sushi and steak tartare and crisp vegetables that punctuate our meals with occasional novelty.

True, anthropologists have pointed out that cooking serves several very practical purposes: it generally makes foods easier to chew, more digestible, less likely to cause illness, slower to spoil. On these grounds alone it would have caught on as "adaptive" behavior. In fact, the purely mechanical advantages of cooking have influenced the very shape of the human face: our jaws are smaller and protrude less than the jaws of our ancestors and primate relatives. But humans had never eaten cooked foods before, and cooked flavors are not only stronger but often very different from the raw originals. So why would we have come to enjoy them?

One answer might be that as omnivores, humans are equipped to exploit a wide variety of foods. Perhaps our tastes are flexible enough that we can learn to like anything, provided there's a good reason to learn to like it. Another answer might be Brillat-Savarin's religious formulation: "The Creator, while forcing man to eat in order to live, tempts him to do so with appetite and then rewards him with pleasure." Certainly if one hungers for evidence that a benign Intelligence rules the universe, one could do worse than contemplate coffee, chocolate, and the roast.

But such answers don't offer much to chew on. Surely there's more to be said about so important a part of our life! A third approach is to look in some detail at the chemical changes caused by cooking. Perhaps a comparison of raw and cooked flavor molecules can offer a hint as to why cooked foods are so appealing. In fact, it does. The chemistry may at first seem rather esoteric and even hopelessly complicated: around six hundred different flavor compounds have been identified to date in cooked beef, for example. But the exercise is worth it. When we get down to basics, to the lowest common denominators of flavor, some very interesting patterns emerge, and with them an unexpected insight into gastronomical pleasure.

The modern-day chemistry of food flavor dates from around 1912 and the discovery of the browning reaction, also known as the Maillard reaction, which generates much of the characteristic color and aroma of foods cooked over a flame, in the oven, or in oil. It's fitting that a French scientist was at the heart of the matter, though he hadn't actually set out to build on the heritage of Thouvenel and Chaptal, Thenard and Proust, those early chemists who had explored the essence of meat flavor. The flavor of foods was far from the mind of the young doctor Louis-Camille Maillard as he pursued biochemical research at the University of Nancy. Rather, Maillard was interested in how living things string together proteins from their subunits, the amino acids. An eminent German chemist, Emil Fischer, had already succeeded in linking amino acids together in the test tube, but he did so using such unbiological means as pure alcohol, concentrated ammonia, and high temperatures. Maillard tried limiting the materials to common constituents of cells, and had some success when he heated amino acids together with glycerol, which is a part of every fat molecule.

Because glycerol has some features in common with sugars, Maillard repeated his experiment using sugars and amino acids. He observed that when these two materials were heated together, the solution in the test tube slowly turned brown. When he tried to analyze the substance responsible for the color, he found that it wasn't soluble in water, which suggested that its molecules were very large. It also contained some nitrogen, which derived from the amino acids. In this respect, as well as in the lower temperatures required to create it, the colored substance differed from the brown products of caramelized sugar, which contain no nitrogen. In his initial report of 1912, Maillard told the French Academy of Sciences that his discovery had consequences "not only in human physiology and pathology, but also in plant physiology (cyclic alkaloids, etc.), agronomy (maturation of manures, humus, diverse industries), in geology (combustible minerals, etc.)."

Louis-Camille Maillard, from a photograph taken around 1915.

Maillard's report makes no mention whatever of foods or flavor. One of these oversights is remedied in a second report of the same year, in which Maillard includes the sugar, gingerbread, and beer industries among those that should be interested in the reaction, since they use "materials of biological origin" and "are led to bring together sugars and amino acids (or the starches and proteinaceous substances capable of giving birth to them)." As one of his footnotes makes clear, Maillard was educated on this point by an English expert on brewing beer, one Arthur Robert Ling. In 1908, at a professional meeting at the Criterion Restaurant in Picadilly, London, Ling had read a paper on malting, the process of germinating barley grain for several days and then kilning it to dry it. Much of a beer's color and flavor are generated when the barley is kilned. The initial germination was thought to involve the barley's "autodigestion," or breaking down of stored starches and proteins to their fundamental building blocks, which could then be rearranged by the growing seedling. Ling imagined that these building blocks might be responsible for both the color and flavor of malted barley. So he tried the experiment of heating amino acids and sugars together, and noticed the development of a brown color and an aromatic odor.

Ling published his observations in 1908, but he never followed up on them. Maillard did devote some eight years to studying the combination under heat of amino acids and sugars, which is why the reaction was named after him, not Ling. Surprisingly, however, this countryman of Brillat-Savarin and the students of osmazome never made much of the flavorsome aspects of the browning reaction. And when Maillard died suddenly in Paris in 1936, at the age of fifty-eight, his work on browning was little remembered. For the last fifteen years of his life he had served as a professor of biological and medical chemistry at the University of Algiers, largely devoting his career to the analysis of urine and its diagnostic usefulness.

Although Maillard didn't realize how important the browning reaction is to the preparation of foods, he appears to have been quite right about a different connection that puts cooking in an interesting and unlikely perspective. As early as 1912 he pointed out the similarity between the brown compounds he could produce in the test tube and the substances that give rich organic soil its dark color. These soil substances had been studied since around 1800, when they were given the name *humic acids*: *humic* because found in humus, the Latin for "soil"; and *acid* because they could be dissolved only in alkaline solution. Nowadays, it's thought that humic acids are created by bacteria, fungi, algae, and other soil microbes that decompose the plants' structural materials, cellulose and lignin, into phenolic substances. The phenolic substances are then oxidized by enzymes that have been released into the soil from dead plants and microbes, and bond together in large, colored structures. (The same browning enzymes in plants affect the color of many of our foods; see chapter 4.) In addition, the microbial breakdown of proteins and carbohydrates generates large quantities of amino acids and sugars, which then undergo the Maillard reaction at the relatively low temperature of the soil, thanks to the presence of minerals, which may act as catalysts, and frequent changes in moisture and temperature.

To my knowledge, no one has investigated the possible contribution of the Maillard reaction to the characteristic odor of humus, which is generally attributed to a few chemicals secreted by soil bacteria. But it's an intriguing parallel: that the main chemical pathway for producing attractive colors and flavors in our foods is traveled naturally when the earth reclaims its own. Is it possible to detect a hint of fertile soil in the vapors of a roast, or a suggestion of brown-black coffee beans as one turns over the first spadefuls in the spring?

Apart from occasional studies in the brewing and sugar industries, the Maillard reaction received little attention until World War II, when American troops in the Pacific tropics complained that their powdered eggs were turning brown and developing unappetizing flavors. Laboratories assigned to analyze the problem discovered the culprit to be relatively low-temperature browning reactions made possible by the concentration of sugars and amino acids in dehydrated foods. The remedy was to remove the small quantities of glucose present in the eggs before drying them. Once browning had been identified as a cause of deterioration in processed and stored foods, the Maillard reaction became an object of great interest for both commercial and government-sponsored research. Of the many studies published in the late 1940s and the 1950s, most focused on ways to prevent browning.

A few scientists, however, bucked the trend of viewing the Maillard reaction as little more than a nuisance. One of the earliest and most notable dissents was a report issued in 1947 by H. M. Barnes and C. W. Kaufman, two chemists at General Foods Corporation. In order to piece together a basic understanding of browning in foods, they had begun by studying the reactions between individual amino acids and sugars. In doing so, they noticed that "the flavors and odors developed were apparently characteristic of the particular amino acid being used." A mixture of serine or threonine and glucose, for example, smelled like maple syrup. Such observations led Barnes and Kaufman to suggest a positive role for browning:

> The present authors now believe that, in addition to being responsible for many deteriorative changes that occur in food products, the Maillard reaction may also be the contributing factor in the development of many of our characteristic food flavors. Although no evidence is as yet available, there is reason to suspect that the distinctive flavor differences in breakfast foods, the crust of baked bread, roasted coffee, etc., may be attributed to chemical combinations brought about during the heat treatment operation.

Chocolate, maple syrup, beer, soy sauce, and roasted, broiled, and fried meats also belong on this list. And Barnes and Kaufman ended their report with a prediction that has since been fulfilled in spades: "Fundamental research on this aspect may provide a means of chemically synthesizing some flavors which will nearly approximate the natural flavors."

Within a year of this forecast, the first patent for an artificial flavor—maple—had been granted, and others were being vigorously pursued. The quality of meatiness, the erstwhile osmazome, was perhaps the most sought-after flavor of all. Before the importance of the Maillard reaction had sunk in, industrial laboratories had approximated meatiness by means of MSG (monosodium glutamate) and certain nucleotides, or compounds related to the components of DNA and RNA. These created a "brothy" flavor, and when one added vegetable protein that had been hydrolyzed (broken down into smaller chains of amino acids), a meaty aroma developed. But in 1960 a chemist at Lever Brothers patented a simpler formula based on the Maillard reaction: Heat either cysteine or cystine, two related sulfur-containing amino acids, with furan, a substance derived from sugar, and you get a meaty flavor. The amino acids arginine, glutamic acid, and proline improve the effect. Certain additional sugars produce a specifically beefy flavor. The reaction "may be carried out by adding the reagents to a food product in which a meatlike flavor is desired, e.g., deflavored codfish hydrolyzate."

The Lever Brothers patent created a sensation. According to one reviewer, it precipitated "a flood of grantings and applications" for similar patents. There were dozens of amino acids, dozens of sugars, and endless ways of combining them, each formula holding the promise of another desirable flavor. With the development in the mid-1960s of instruments that could analyze in great detail the chemical composition of natural aromas, the science of flavor chemistry reached full stride.

Today, any curious cook can explore the virtuosic nature of the Maillard reaction, thanks to those strange modern emporiums known as "health food" stores. Many of them sell capsules of individual amino acids in powdered form. The idea that they're valuable nutritional supplements is nonsense—anyone who can afford to pay five dollars for thirty half-gram capsules probably already consumes more than enough protein. But the amino acids are fun to play with on the stove. Try tapping some of the powder into a small pan of boiling water. You'll smell a faint whiff of ammonia as the molecule breaks down, and if you use cysteine, which contains sulfur, you'll detect an odor reminiscent of boiled eggs, which is mainly hydrogen sulfide. Now add some of the powder to a pan (ideally nonstick) of gently bubbling corn syrup. Almost instantly the clear liquid will begin to turn a rich brown, and you'll smell some remarkable things. With cysteine, I notice the essence of fried onions—probably more sulfur compounds—as well as ammonia, hydrogen sulfide, and a general "brothiness." With lysine the effect is much milder, something like lightly toasted bread. And with phenylalanine, an aroma strangely reminiscent of melting plastic, followed in a minute or so by essence of almonds!

Experiments like these give a vivid sense of the Maillard reaction's vast potential for creating flavor. Heat a single odorless amino acid in water, and you produce a simple aroma; heat together a single amino acid and a mixture of two sugars, the glucose and fructose in corn syrup, and you can rouse an olfactory image of an actual food, like fried onions, maple syrup, or almonds. The image may be one-dimensional rather than *trompe-le-nez*, but it's still recognizable, even uncanny. Now, even the most unadorned of raw foods—a piece of meat, a potato, a green pea, some wheat flour—contains a score of amino acids and a handful of various sugars, as well as other molecules that may contribute in other ways to the aroma. It's evident, then, that cooking must generate very complex mixtures of flavor molecules.

Just how complex the flavors of cooking are has become evident only with the development of highly sensitive analytical instruments in the last two or three decades. As of 1963 some 500 flavor compounds had been laboriously catalogued from a variety of foods. A couple of years later the gas chromatograph, which separates a mixture of volatile compounds into its pure components, was married to the mass spectrometer, which makes it possible to identify a compound even in the tiny amounts typical of food aromas. By 1984 this technology had raised the number of identified flavor compounds to 4,300. The current estimate is that perhaps 10,000 such compounds exist, with the typical cooked food containing between 300 and 800.

Here, perhaps, is our first clue to the great appeal of cooked foods. Their flavors are intricate composites of many individual aromas and are certainly much richer in taste than such uncooked originals as a handful of grain, a tuber, a share of the hunt. (This is also true of such uncooked but fermented foods as wine and cheese.) There is, however, a major exception to this rule. Ripe raw fruits also tend to have very complex flavors. The strawberry has more than three hundred component aromas, the raspberry two hundred or more. Fruits probably provided our evolutionary ancestors with refreshing sensory interludes in an otherwise bland and dull diet. Perhaps cooking with fire was valued in part because it transformed blandness into fruitlike richness. The English essayist Walter Pater once said that "All art constantly aspires to the condition of music"; perhaps the appropriate culinary paraphrase is "All cooked foods aspire to the condition of fruit."

The subtle complexity of food flavors has thwarted the chemists who have tried to produce convincing synthetic flavors. Vanillin doesn't really taste like vanilla, and imitation maple syrup seems duller than the real thing, precisely because imitations can't provide us with the fullness and depth that characterize the originals. Where a real food gives us a rich chord of sensations, the imitation product gives us only a few of the more prominent notes.

This complexity also threatens to thwart our understanding of cooked flavors. Given that modern flavor chemists have catalogued some six hundred components of beef aroma, the rest of us may wonder how such a tedious exercise could possibly illuminate the pleasure we take in a bite of roast beef. As it turns out, among all these analyses are some promising clues to the nature of that pleasure. Several important flavor components have turned up in what might otherwise seem quite unrelated biological puzzles. This common currency suggests that the puzzle of culinary pleasure is itself interlocked in a larger pattern, one that offers a new perspective on our fondness for the cooked.

The best way to get to know the flavor compounds produced by cooking is to look at their origins and family resemblances. Let's take a single simple progenitor, table sugar, and see what families arise during caramelization. Plain crystalline sucrose has no odor. Heat it to about 320°F (160°C) and it melts; to 335°F (168°C), and it begins to color and develop a rich aroma. At this point, from the initial pure population of sucrose molecules we have generated more than a hundred reaction products—probably several hundred; the cataloguing is still in progress. These products arise when the carbon, hydrogen, and oxygen atoms in sugar molecules interact with each other and with oxygen in the air at high temperatures. The heat causes the atoms in the sugar molecules to move with such force that the bonds holding them together are readily broken. The molecules fragment in a variety of ways, and these fragments then react with each other in a variety of ways: and so on throughout the cooking. The result is sucrose's myriad progeny, the substances that constitute caramelized sugar. (Fats contain the same three elements, and generate many of the same aroma molecules when heated.)

Among the reaction products, many have a low boiling point. Significant numbers of these molecules escape into the air, reach the nose, and contribute to the aroma. The volatile products of caramelization can be divided into two general groups, according to the structure of their molecules: the chains and the rings. Principal among the chain families are simple acids, alcohols, aldehydes, and esters. These each consist of a row of linked carbon atoms that is decorated with hydrogen atoms and an occasional oxygen or two. We're all familiar with representatives of each family. The acids include acetic acid, which gives vinegar its characteristic aroma. We know the alcohols from vodka, a mixture of ethyl alcohol and water, and whiskey, whose pungency comes from the presence of several longer-chain alcohols. One of the common aldehydes produces the aroma that distinguishes sherry from ordinary white wine. And the flavor of bananas is due largely to several esters.

That's already quite a heady mixture! But caramelized sugar also contains ring compounds, which are closed circles of carbon atoms, sometimes with one carbon replaced by an oxygen, again decorated with hydrogen and the odd oxygen. *Furans*, five-cornered rings that include one oxygen, can have sweet, fruity, nutty, or butterscotch flavor notes. *Pyrones* are six-cornered, with one oxygen in the ring and another attached to the opposite carbon. Maltol, a prominent pyrone, contributes a strong flavor of caramel itself. Then there are six-carbon rings, which include benzene and various derivatives, and are most familiar to us as the solvents in spot removers.

Fruits, nuts, alcohol, sherry, vinegar, spot remover, caramel—the mixture

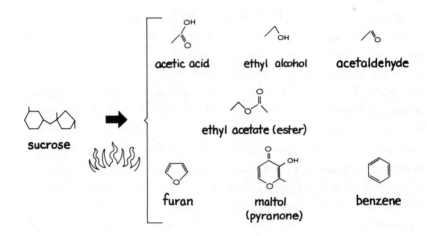

When we heat odorless table sugar—sucrose—until it browns, we generate hundreds of different chemical compounds. Among them are several families, simple representatives of which are shown here, that contribute to the rich aroma of caramel.

somehow spells caramel. Each of the hundred-plus flavor compounds is produced in a very small but characteristic quantity, and the relative proportions are essential to the overall effect they create. It's the composite impression, the chord, that we register.

It turns out that several of the flavor notes in caramel are contributed by chemical families that are common in nature, particularly in the fruits. Organic acids, alcohols, aldehydes, and esters are ubiquitous in the living world because they are all associated with the universal processes of energy production. The cook generates them by breaking up sugar molecules and scrambling the atoms with heat; fruits generate them during ripening (and microbes—yeasts, molds, and bacteria—during fermentation) by means of enzymes, which accomplish the same kinds of atomic rearrangements at lower temperatures. So at least some of the components of caramel aroma are flavors that would have been familiar to our preculinary ancestors from raw and fermented—that is, partly spoiled—fruits.

So much for browning plain sugar. Of course, nearly all our foods contain both carbohydrates and proteins, so most kitchen browning entails the Mail-

lard reaction between sugars and amino acids. When heated, these chemical ingredients will give rise to the products typical of caramelization (if the temperature is at least 335°F, or 168°C), plus products typical of heated amino acids
alone, plus the Maillard products proper. The amino acids bring two new elements into the picture: nitrogen, a constituent of all amino acids, and sulfur, a
constituent of two. Heat any amino acid in boiling water and you'll detect the
faint smell of ammonia as the nitrogen is torn away; heat a sulfur-containing
amino acid like cysteine, and you'll also detect hydrogen sulfide, that eggy note.
Both of these simple volatile compounds contribute to the aromas of cooked
eggs, meats, and dairy products, all rich in proteins and especially in sulfur-
containing amino acids.

The Maillard reaction proper begins when a nitrogen atom on an amino
acid attacks one of the carbon atoms on a sugar. A large composite molecule
forms, rearranges itself internally, and then breaks up into pieces. Each piece
continues to metamorphose until the heating stops or the molecule escapes into
the air. The participation of nitrogen seems to be a great encouragement to such
metamorphoses, because Maillard browning takes place at much lower temperatures than does caramelization.

The important families of aroma compounds produced in the Maillard reaction are all rings of carbon atoms that may also include one or two nitrogens,
sometimes an oxygen, and sometimes a sulfur. Each of these basic ring structures may be surrounded by a variety of other atoms or groups of atoms.
Sometimes two or more rings will fuse together into one large molecule. The
principal families include several five- and six-membered rings. The five-
membered rings are the *pyrroles*, with one nitrogen; the *thiophenes*, with one
sulfur; the *thiazoles*, with a nitrogen and a sulfur; and the *oxazoles*, with a nitrogen and an oxygen. The six-cornered rings are the *pyridines*, with one nitrogen, and the *pyrazines*, with two nitrogens. Currently, it's thought that the pyrazines and thiazoles are primarily responsible for the characteristic flavor of
browned foods.

These ring compounds add another dimension to the flavors produced in
sugar caramelization. Several contribute a nutty note, the sulfur rings a suggestion of browned onion and meatiness, and certain pyrazines and thiazoles a
general "roasted" impression, even hints of chocolate. But there are some surprises. Several oxazoles contribute floral odors. And many pyrazines and thiazoles, the two families that seem to be most essential to the typical browned fla-

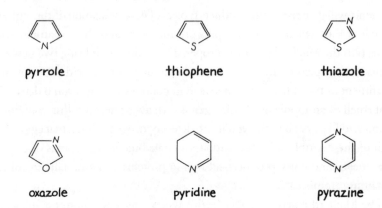

The core structures of chemical families contributing to the browned aroma of foods that contain protein.

vor, together with the pyridines, are reminiscent of green leaves and vegetables. In fact, several of the particular compounds produced by the action of heat on our foods remind us of the flavors that we encounter in plants, and that our ancestors would have encountered long before they had mastered fire.

Let's look at a few examples of characteristic roasting products whose aromas are reminiscent of plants. Two "green"-smelling pyridines, 3-methylpyridine and 2-ethylpyridine, are found in roast lamb, and 2-ethylpyridine is also found in roast beef.* Also reminiscent of green vegetables is 2-methylthiazole, formed during the cooking of beef, as is 5-ethyl-4-methylthiazole, which has nutty, green, and earthy overtones. A green note is contributed by the 2-propylpyrazine found in roast coffee and peanuts; the green, nutty 2,3-dimethylpyrazine has been noted in roast beef, cocoa, coffee, popcorn, potato chips, and a variety of nuts, as has the earthy, raw-potato aroma of 2,5-dimethylpyrazine.

This mingling of the animal and vegetable, the raw and the cooked, may seem like a remarkable coincidence. It's one thing to find shared features in

*In these chemical names, the prefix indicates by number the atom of the central ring at which a "side group" of atoms is attached, and then names the side group.

browned sugar and in fruits, which also contain sugar. But by comparison to those simple acids, esters, and so on, these nitrogen- and sulfur-containing rings, which are known as heterocyclic compounds, are rather exotic. It's harder to see how these structures would have any connection with the world of natural flavors.

In fact, many of these typical "artificial" flavor molecules have also been found in the raw natural world. They are by no means common, but they're not all that rare either. Information is scattered and preliminary at the moment, but it's also quite intriguing. Furans have been found in pineapples and strawberries, oxazoles in ryegrass and members of the aster family. There's a thiazole in passion fruit and two others in the tamarind, a tropical pod-fruit with a rich flavor reminiscent of prunes. And 2-isobutylthiazole contributes to the flavor of the tomato.

The most extensive and exciting findings have to do with the pyrazines. One regular reviewer of the field has said that "to date no other class of flavoring compounds has been shown to be as important to our foods." Members of this chemical family were first recognized in the test tube in the middle of the nineteenth century, and first found in foodstuffs—molasses and then coffee—at the beginning of the twentieth century. Around 1950, a fungus-produced antibiotic, aspergillic acid, proved to be a pyrazine derivative, and in 1962 pyrazines were extracted from fermented soy beans. In the late 1960s and early 1970s, pyrazines were identified in cocoa products, green peas, cooked beef, Gouda and Emmenthal cheeses, tamarind, wine grapes, dried red beans, soil-inhabiting bacteria, and then in a number of raw vegetables, including asparagus, green beans, beets, carrots, lettuce, and potatoes. Perhaps most renowned among flavor chemists is the potent 2-isobutyl-3-methoxypyrazine, which is found in fairly large quantities in bell peppers and is thought to be responsible for the "vegetative" or "herbaceous" character of some wines. The "bell-pepper" pyrazine can be smelled at a concentration in air of one part in a trillion, and is now a favored experimental tool for probing the mysterious means by which our olfactory cells detect aroma molecules.

So the pyrazine family is well known to microbes and plants. These organisms even synthesize some of the same pyrazines that we create when we roast meats, cocoa and coffee beans, and nuts. This is true, for example, of the earthy 2,5-dimethylpyrazine found in dried red beans and tamarind fruit. Tamarind also contains the nutty, roasted 2-methylpyrazine as well as 2,6-dimethylpyrazine, both of which are found in a wide range of browned foods. Cooking with fire may have been a great human innovation, but our ancestors and other animals have been encountering molecules characteristic of the roast for much, much longer, probably for hundreds of millions of years.

And not just in their food plants. It turns out that some animals produce their own heterocyclic aroma molecules. In 1973 a group of entomologists noticed that when ants of several species are disturbed, they secrete a chocolate-smelling substance that induces nearby ants either to retreat or to attack. That is, the substance seems to operate as an alarm pheromone. When the secretion was analyzed, it turned out to consist of several pyrazines, some of which have been found in cocoa products. Another species of ant employs a different pyrazine in its trail pheromone, which helps individual ants follow each other; that pyrazine is found in fried beef, cocoa, coffee, and roasted nuts. It's now thought that the use of pyrazines as chemical signals is widespread among the many thousands of species of ants, and perhaps among other insects as well. Recent studies have detected pyrazines in ladybugs, moths, beetles, and butterflies. Several butterflies, including the monarch, selectively extract and store pyrazines from their food plants and release them, apparently as a defensive gesture or a warning signal, when their bodies are pinched. In another sensory realm, some squids and coelenterates—including certain jellyfish, the sea pen, sea pansy, and sea cactus—incorporate the pyrazine ring in a light-emitting complex that generates visual signals. And a thiazole ring is at the core of the substance luciferin, which is responsible for the glow of the firefly.

A consistent theme emerges among these animal anecdotes: communication. Animals exploit molecules in the pyrazine and thiazole families as signals, just as they've done with alcohols, esters, aldehydes, terpenoid substances, and other volatile molecules. Odor signals are involved in a variety of important activities, from mating and egg laying to feeding, the marking of trails and territories, aggregation, and warnings and defense against predators. In the case of the insect pheromones, the efficiency of the odor-molecule signals has been well established: only small quantities of energy are required to generate them and, because the odors travel freely in the air and can be detected even when very dilute, they can be effective at distances of a few millimeters or a hundred feet.

To date, almost nothing is known about the function of pyrazines and thiazoles in plants, but it's likely to resemble their role in the animal world. These molecules are classified along with thousands of others found in plants as *secondary products*: that is, compounds that don't seem to have a direct role in the primary activities of growth, energy production and storage, and reproduction. It's thought that most of these secondary products have a defensive function. Some clearly do—for example, the poisonous alkaloids and cyanide-producing compounds—and most of the substances that we value as flavorings, the essential oils of the herb and spice plants, repel many insects and other predators. Circumstantial evidence suggests that pyrazines may have a similar function. In both insects and wild plants, the presence of pyrazines is usually associated with a defensive toxin. For example, the monarch butterfly borrows from its food plant, the milkweed, both a bitter poison and a strong-smelling trio of pyrazines. The pyrazines themselves aren't toxic. So it appears that for both plant and butterfly, the poison is the actual weapon used to deter predators, while the pyrazines are a memorable early warning signal. Once a predator has gotten sick on a bite of milkweed or monarch, the mere whiff of pyrazines is probably sufficient to cut short any subsequent attack.

The study of pyrazines in monarch butterflies was led by Miriam Rothschild, an English entomologist who has long been interested in the odorous secretions of insects. She pointed out decades ago that a number of insects emit very similar odors when handled, and many of these odors have turned out to involve pyrazines. In any event, the exploitation by insects of protective plant pyrazines, and the variety of messages carried by the pyrazine secretions of ants, are two indications that these molecules are quite versatile. They may have originated in plants as purely defensive compounds, but as life has evolved, so has their significance. Rothschild has ventured some stimulating thoughts about the versatility of the pyrazine odors:

> Certainly their evocative qualities make them ideal ingredients of a generalized warning system, but we may speculate that they probably also act as enhancers or boosters of other "interesting" signals, perhaps even heightening the attractive elements of various animal and plant secretions. Furthermore all evocative scents of this type—vanilla and chocolate are other examples—possess a certain subtle quality which stirs, if it does not actually sharpen, memory, and possibly also assists or hastens the process of learning.

Rothschild's speculations raise fascinating questions. What does it say about gastronomical pleasure that evocative odors help plants and insects survive, that the aroma of chocolate can be so important in the lives of organisms as different as ants and humans? Can biology make sense of the powerful impression that certain foods make on us?

We don't yet know enough to venture any confident answers. But it's worth noting that in the matter of smell, there's not as much difference between us and some insects as we might think. For example, in a series of remarkable experiments running from the 1920s through the 1960s, Karl von Frisch proved that the olfactory sensitivities of the bee are quite similar to those of humans. Not only do both species detect the same classes of odors, but they detect them at about the same concentrations in the air. The insects, being invertebrates, are by no means our evolutionary predecessors; the last ancestor that humans and ants had in common was nothing much like either. But that very distance indicates how important it has been for all animals to detect a wide variety of aroma molecules, and particularly molecules that are generated by plants and other animals. Maybe we're simply lucky that cooking with fire happens to create aroma molecules very similar, and sometimes identical, to those found in nature. If for some reason it hadn't turned out that way, then roasted cocoa beans might strike us as quite abominable.

Of the evocativeness of aromas, no one has written more eloquently than Marcel Proust in his *In Search of Lost Time*. "And the orange squeezed into the water seemed to yield to me, as I drank, the secret life of its ripening growth . . . countless mysteries unveiled by the fruit to my sensory perception, but not at all to my intelligence." Such moments take the narrator "deep down in that region more intimate than that in which we see and hear, in that region where we experience the quality of smells, almost in the very heart of my inmost self." It's no doubt a crime of some sort to have Proust consort on the same page with insects! But if there is something to Miriam Rothschild's musings, then our powerful response to odors may in part be a legacy of their prehistoric importance for animals, which have used them to recall and learn from their experiences. Just as an evocative odor dilates our nostrils and deepens our breath as we try to capture it and its significance, so perhaps it dilates our receptiveness and deepens our attentiveness to the circumstances of the moment as it gives that moment an indelible mark. We may come to associate a particular aroma with a particular experience, and a very familiar aroma may impart a fundamental sense of security. But initially, odors are empty of associations, and their significance can change over time. Perhaps the same element of indeterminacy that makes them so versatile also accounts for their penumbra of significant mystery.

Our quest to understand the pleasures of cooked foods has taken us quite some distance from Louis-Camille Maillard and his test tube of sugars and amino acids. But it was the census of the chemical progeny of the browning reaction that expanded our perspective to include ants and fireflies, milkweed and butterflies. These parallels remind us that the detection of useful and dangerous chemicals, the active invention of chemical signals, and their deployment for a variety of purposes have been important elements in the mutual accommodation of plant and animal life on earth. And this biochemical saga has engendered many of the table's pleasures. Spice plants have strong flavors because they are effective deterrents to many plant-eating insects; flowers have pleasant odors because long ago beetles proved to be useful agents of cross-pollination; fruits have pleasant flavors because, somewhat later, small mammals proved to be useful dispersers of seeds. It seems that browned foods taste good partly because they develop a complexity comparable to that of the fruits, and partly because the major families of aroma chemicals created by heat had already been in active use by plants and animals for millions of years.

Perhaps, then, the great triumph of cooking has not been just a matter of its mechanical and hygienic advantages. Heat transforms our foods by enriching their flavors tremendously, and by evoking, at some level, different foods and different times. In a sip of coffee or a piece of crackling there are echoes of flowers and leaves, fruit and earth, a recapitulation of moments from the long dialogue between animals and plants. The simplest morsel offers much to savor.

Appendix

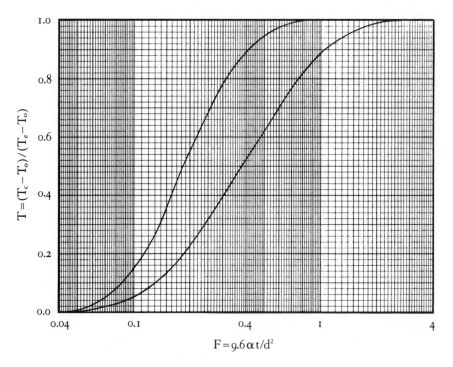

$$F = 9.6\,\alpha\,t/d^2$$

This heat conduction chart can be used to estimate cooking times in hot liquid for meat in the form of cubes (*left curve*), whose three dimensions are all the same, or "steaks" (*right curve*), whose length and width are quite large relative to their thickness.

Abbreviations: T_0 = initial temperature (all temperatures in degrees Fahrenheit); T_e = external (cooking) temperature; T_c = temperature at center of meat; t = cooking time in minutes; d = meat thickness in inches.

An average value of α for meat is 0.005. To figure the cooking time at a given temperature, use your choice of initial, cooking, and desired central temperatures to calculate T. From the chart, read off the corresponding value for F. The cooking time is then $20.8 \times F \times d^2$.

Bibliography

Introduction

Aristotle. *Meteorology*, book 4. Translated by E. W. Webster. In J. Barnes, ed., *The Complete Works of Aristotle*, vol. 1, 608–25. Princeton: Princeton University Press, 1984.

Forbes, R. J. Chemical, culinary, and cosmetic arts. In C. Singer, E. J. Holmyard, and A. R. Hall, eds., *History of Technology*, vol. 1, 238–98. Oxford: Clarendon, 1954.

Harrison, H. S. Fire-making, fuel, and lighting. In C. Singer, E. J. Holmyard, and A. R. Hall, eds., *History of Technology*, vol. 1, 216–37. Oxford: Clarendon, 1954.

Levey, M. Babylonian chemistry: A study of Arabic and second millennium B.C. perfumery. *Osiris* 12 (1956): 376–89.

McGee, H. *On Food and Cooking: The Science and Lore of the Kitchen*. New York: Scribner, 1984.

Norton, T. The ordinall of alchimy [1477]. In E. Ashmole, ed., *Theatrum Chemicum Brittanicum* [1652]. Reprint. New York: Johnson Reprint Co., 1967.

Chapter One: Searing

[Flack, I. H.] *Surgeons All*. New York: Philosophical Library, 1957.

Lawrie, R. A. *Meat Science*. 4th ed. Oxford: Pergamon, 1985.

Locker, R. H., and G. J. Daines. Effect of mode of cutting on cooking loss in beef. *Journal of the Science of Food and Agriculture* 25 (1974): 939–46.

Offer, G., D. Restall, and J. Trinick. Water-holding capacity in meat. In A. J. Bailey, ed., *Recent Advances in the Chemistry of Meat*, 71–86. London: Royal Society of Chemistry, 1984.

Pearce, J. A. *Electrosurgery*. New York: Wiley, 1986.

Chapter Two: Oil Drops

Cunnington, P., and C. Lucas. *Occupational Costume in England: From the Eleventh Century to 1914*. New York: Barnes and Noble, 1967.

Millikan, R. A. The isolation of an ion. . . . *Physical Review* 32 (1911): 349–97.

Moore, A. D., ed. *Electrostatics and Its Applications*. New York: Wiley, 1973.

Pounder, C. Charge-carrying particles from Leidenfrost boiling. *Journal of Electrostatics* 9 (1980): 159–82.

Rumford, B., Count. On the construction of kitchen fire-places and kitchen utensils [1802]. In S. C. Brown, ed., *Collected Works of Count Rumford*, vol. 3, 63–384. Cambridge, Mass.: Belknap, 1969.

Chapter Three: Simmering

Bailey, A. J., ed. *Recent Advances in the Chemistry of Meat*. London: Royal Society of Chemistry, 1984.

Bugialli, G. *The Fine Art of Italian Cooking*. New York: Times Books, 1977.

Dickerson, R. W., and R. B. Read. Calculation and measurement of heat transfer in foods. *Food Technology* 22 (1968): 1533–35, 1547–48.

Joklik, W. K., and others. *Zinsser Microbiology*, 19th ed. Norwalk, Conn.: Appleton and Lange, 1988.

Maddox, J. Heat conduction is a can of worms. *Nature* 338 (1989): 373.

Mohsenin, N. H. *Thermal Properties of Foods and Agricultural Materials*. New York: Gordon and Breach, 1980.

Schneider, P. J. *Conduction Heat Transfer*. Cambridge, Mass.: Addison-Wesley, 1955.

———. *Temperature Response Charts*. New York: Wiley, 1963.

Rumford, B., Count. On the construction of kitchen fire-places and kitchen utensils [1802]. In S. C. Brown, ed., *Collected Works of Count Rumford*, vol. 3, 63–384. Cambridge, Mass.: Belknap, 1969.

Chapter Four: Green and Brown

Beard, J. *James Beard's Theory and Practice of Good Cooking*. New York: Knopf, 1977.

Blechen, S. S., and F. J. G. Ebling. Disorders of skin colour. In A. Rook and others, eds., *Textbook of Dermatology*, 4th ed., vol. 2, 1543–55. Oxford: Blackwell, 1986.

Bugialli, G. *The Fine Art of Italian Cooking*. New York: Times Books, 1977.

Cutler, D. F., K. L. Alvin, and C. E. Price, eds., *The Plant Cuticle*. London: Academic Press, 1982.

Dampier, W. *A New Voyage Round the World*. London, 1697.

Kahn, V. Polyphenol oxidase activity and browning of three avocado varieties. *Journal of the Science of Food and Agriculture* 26 (1975): 1319–24.

Kamman, M. *The Making of a Cook*. New York: Atheneum, 1971.

Mayer, A. Polyphenol oxidases in plants— recent progress. *Phytochemistry* 26 (1987): 11–20.

Novo, S. *Cocina Mexicana: O, Historia Gastronómica de la Ciudad de México*. Mexico City: Editorial Porrúa, 1967.

Prota, G., and others. Occurrence and properties of tyrosinase in the ejected ink of cephalopods. *Comparative Biochemistry and Physiology* 68B (1981): 415–19.

Singh, R., and I. S. Sheoran. Enzymic browning of whole wheat meal flour. *Journal of the Science of Food and Agriculture* 23 (1972): 121–25.

Sodini, G., and M. Carella. Acidic butanol removal of color-forming phenols from sunflower meal. *Journal of Agricultural and Food Chemistry* 25 (1977): 822–25.

Vámos-Vigyázó, L. Polyphenol oxidase and peroxidase in fruits and vegetables. *CRC Critical Reviews in Food Science and Nutrition* 15 (1981): 49–127.

Velázquez de León, J. *Platillos Regionales de la República Mexicana*. Mexico City: A. González, 1946.

Walker, J. R. L. Studies on enzymatic browning of apple fruit. *New Zealand Journal of Science* 5 (1962): 316–24.

Young, R. E., and S. Kosiyachinda. Low-temperature storage of ripe avocado fruit. *California Avocado Society Yearbook* 60 (1976): 73–76.

Chapter Five: Jerusalem Artichoke

Brace, C. L., K. R. Rosenberg, and K. D. Hunt. Gradual change in human tooth size in the late Pleistocene and post-Pleistocene. *Evolution* 41 (1987): 705–20.

Brooke, R. *A Discourse Opening the Nature of That Episcopacie, Which Is Exercised In England*. London, 1641.

Champlain, Samuel de. *Voyages, 1613*. Translated by H. H. Langton and W. F. Ganong. In H. P. Biggar, ed., *Works of Samuel de Champlain*, vol. 1. Toronto: Champlain Society, 1929.

Coues, E., ed. *Manuscript Journals of Alexander Henry and David Thompson, 1799–1814*. New York: Harper, 1897.

David, N., and D. Muscatine. *Monday Night at Narsai's*. New York: Simon and Schuster, 1987.

Edelman, J., and T. G. Jefford. The mechanism of fructose metabolism in higher plants as exemplified in *Helianthus tuberosus*. *New Phytologist* 67 (1968): 517–31.

Gunther, R. T. *Early English Botanists and Their Gardens*. Oxford: Frederick Hall, 1922.

Hughes, J. C., and T. Swain. After-cooking blackening in potatoes. *Journal of the Science of Food and Agriculture* 13 (1962): 358–63.

Konlande, J. E., and J. R. K. Robson. The nutritional value of cooked camas as consumed by Flathead Indians. *Ecology of Food and Nutrition* 2 (1972): 193–95.

Lescarbot, M. *The History of New France*. 3d ed. [1617]. Translated by W. L. Grant. Toronto: Champlain Society, 1914.

Meier, H., and J. S. G. Reid. Reserve polysaccharides other than starch in higher plants. *Encyclopedia of Plant Physiology*, vol. 13A, 418–71. Berlin: Springer, 1982.

Nilsson, U., and others. Cereal fructans: In vitro and in vivo studies on availability in rats and humans. *Journal of Nutrition* 118 (1988): 1325–30.

Salaman, R. N. Why "Jerusalem" artichoke? *Journal of the Royal Horticultural Society* 65 (1940): 338–48, 376–83.

Schneider, E. *Uncommon Fruits and Vegetables*. New York: Harper and Row, 1986.

Thwaites, R. G., ed. *Original Journals of the Lewis and Clark Expedition, 1804–1806*. Vol. 5. New York: Dodd Mead, 1905.

Turner, N. J., and H. V. Kuhnlein. Camas and riceroot: Two liliaceous "root" foods of the northwest coast Indians. *Ecology of Food and Nutrition* 13 (1983): 199–219.

Verstraeten, L. M. J. The "autocatalytic" hydrolysis of inulin. *Zeitschrift für physikalische Chemie* 233 (1966): 91–96.

Chapter Six: Beurre Blanc

Appell, K. C., T. W. Keenan, and P. S. Low. Differential scanning calorimetry of milk fat globule membrane. *Biochimica et Biophysica Acta* 690 (1982): 243–50.

Child, J., L. Bertholle, and S. Beck. *Mastering the Art of French Cooking*. Vol. 1. New York: Knopf, 1961.

Chrysam, M. M. Table spreads and shortenings. In T. H. Applewhite, ed., *Bailey's Industrial Oil and Fat Products*, vol. 3, 41–126. New York: Wiley, 1985.

Heid, H. W., and others. Butyrophilin, an apical plasma membrane-associated glycoprotein. . . . *Biochimica et Biophysica Acta* 728 (1983): 228–38.

Kamman, M. *In Madeleine's Kitchen*. New York: Atheneum, 1984.

McDowell, F. H. *The Buttermaker's Manual*. Wellington: New Zealand University Press, 1953.

Olney, R. *Simple French Food*. New York: Atheneum, 1974.

Pépin, J. *La Méthode*. New York: Times Books, 1979.

Sokolov, R. *The Saucier's Apprentice*. New York: Knopf, 1976.

Chapter Seven: Hollandaise and Béarnaise

Baker, R. C., and others. Survival of *Salmonella typhimurium* and *Staphylococcus aureus* in eggs cooked by different methods. *Poultry Science* 62 (1983): 1211–16.

Courtine, R. J., ed. *Larousse Gastronomique*. Paris: Librairie Larousse, 1984.

David, E. *A Book of Mediterranean Food*. 2d ed. Harmondsworth, England: Penguin, 1965.

Escoffier, A. *Le Guide culinaire*. 4th ed. [1921]. Translated by H. L. Cracknell and R. J. Kaufmann. New York: Mayflower, 1982.

Gardner, R. On boiling eggs. In N. Kurti and G. Kurti, eds., *But the Crackling Is Superb: An Anthology on Food and Drink by Fellows and Foreign Members of The Royal Society*, 53–56. Bristol: Adam Hilger, 1988.

Humphrey, T. J., and others. The survival of salmonellas in shell eggs cooked under simulated domestic conditions. *Epidemiology and Infection* 103 (1989): 35–45.

Kamman, M. *In Madeleine's Kitchen*. New York: Atheneum, 1984.

Marin, F. *Dons de Comus, ou les délices de la table*. Paris, 1758.

Mennell, S. *All Manners of Food: Eating and Taste in England and France from the Middle Ages to the Present*. Oxford: Blackwell, 1985.

Olney, R. *Simple French Food*. New York: Atheneum, 1974.

St. Louis, M. E., and others. The emergence of grade A eggs as a major source of *Salmonella enteritidis* infections. *Journal of the American Medical Association* 259 (1988): 2103–7.

Salmonella enteritidis phage type 4: chicken and egg. *Lancet* 1988: ii, 720–22.

Update: *Salmonella enteritidis* infections and grade A shell eggs—United States, 1989. *Morbidity and Mortality Weekly Report* 38 (1990): 877–80.

Chapter Eight: Mayonnaise

Becher, P., ed. *Encyclopedia of Emulsion Technology*. 2 vols. New York: Dekker, 1983.

————. *Principles of Emulsion Technology*. New York: Reinhold, 1955.

Chang, C. H., W. D. Powrie, and O. Fennema. Studies on the gelation of egg yolk and plasma upon freezing and thawing. *Journal of Food Science* 42 (1977): 1658–65.

David, E. *French Provincial Cooking*. Harmondsworth, England: Penguin, 1967.

van Deenen, L. L. M., and others. Monomolecular layers of synthetic phosphatides. *Journal of Pharmacy and Pharmacology* 14 (1962): 429–44.

Giles, C. H. Franklin's teaspoon of oil. *Chemistry and Industry* (1969): 1616–24.

Gray, D. M. Chemical aspects of mayonnaise. *Oil and Fat Industries* 4 (1927): 410–25.

Guiraud, P. *Dictionnaire des étymologies obscures*. Paris: Payot, 1982.

Henisch, B. A. Photographer's cheesecake. *Petits Propos Culinaires* 17 (1984): 38–43.

Humphrey, T. J., and others. The survival of salmonellas in shell eggs cooked under simulated domestic conditions. *Epidemiology and Infection* 103 (1989): 35–45.

Koudele, J. W., and E. C. Heinsohn. The egg products industry of the United States: Historical highlights, 1900–1959. *Bulletin* 423, Kansas State University Agricultural Experiment Station (1960).

Shapiro, L. *Perfection Salad: Women and Cooking at the Turn of the Century*. New York: Farrar, Straus and Giroux, 1986.

Wakamatu, T., Y. Sato, and Y. Saito. On sodium chloride action in the gelation process of LDL from hen egg yolk. *Journal of Food Science* 48 (1983): 507–12, 516.

Weiss, T. J. *Food Oils and Their Uses*. 2d ed. Westport, Conn.: AVI, 1983.

Chapter Nine: Persimmons

Chang, K. C., ed. *Food in Chinese Culture*. New Haven: Yale University Press, 1977.

DeBakey, M., and A. Ochsner. Bezoars and concretions. *Surgery* 4 (1938): 935–63; 5 (1939): 132–60.

Gore, H. C. Experiments on the processing of persimmons to render them non-astringent. *Bulletin* 141, Bureau of Chemistry, U.S. Department of Agriculture (1911).

———. Studies on fruit respiration. *Bulletin* 142, Bureau of Chemistry, U.S. Department of Agriculture (1911).

Grigson, J., and C. Knox. *Exotic Fruits and Vegetables*. New York: Holt, 1986.

Howard, B. J. Tannin cells of persimmons. *Bulletin of the Torrey Botanical Club* 33 (1906): 567–76.

Ito, S. The persimmon. In A. C. Hulme, ed., *The Biochemistry of Fruits and Their Products*, vol. 2, 281–301. London: Academic Press, 1971.

Kaempfer, E. *Amoenitatum Exoticarum Politico-physico-medicarum Fasciculi v*. Lemgo, Westfalia, 1712.

———. *The History of Japan*. Translated by J. G. Scheuchzer [1727]. Vol. 1. Reprint. Glasgow: J. MacLehose, 1906.

Kaplan, O., and others. Persimmon bezoars as a cause of intestinal obstruction. *British Journal of Surgery* 72 (1985): 242–43.

Le Page du Pratz. *Histoire de la Louisiane*. Vol. 2. Paris, 1758.

McClure, F. A. Some preliminary notes on persimmons in Kwangtung. *Lingnaam Agricultural Review* 3 (1926): 91–95.

Matsuo, T., and S. Ito. On the mechanism of removing astringency in persimmon fruits by carbon dioxide treatment. *Plant and Cell Physiology* 18 (1977): 17–25.

Pesis, E., and R. Ben-Arie. Carbon dioxide assimilation during postharvest removal of astringency from persimmon fruit. *Physiologia Plantarum* 67 (1986): 644–48.

Pesis, E., A. Levi, and R. Ben-Arie. Deastringency of persimmon fruits by creating a modified atmosphere in polyethylene bags. *Journal of Food Science* 51 (1986): 1014–16, 1041.

Ricci, M. *China in the Sixteenth Century: The Journals of Matthew Ricci, 1583–1610.* Translated by L. J. Gallagher. New York: Random House, 1953.

Semmedo, A. *The History of That Great and Renowned Monarchy of China* [1643]. London, 1655.

Smith, F. P. *Contributions Toward the Materia Medica and Natural History of China.* London: Truebner, 1871.

Sokolov, R. *Fading Feast: A Compendium of Disappearing American Regional Foods.* New York: Dutton, 1983.

de Soto, F. *Discovery and Conquest of Terra Florida.* Translated by R. Hakluyt [1611]. Reprint. London: Hakluyt Society, 1851.

Smith, J. *A Map of Virginia* [1612]. In E. Arber, ed., *Works.* Birmingham, England, 1884.

Steingiser, S., S. P. Nemphos, and M. Salame. Barrier polymers. In *Encyclopedia of Chemical Technology*, 3d ed., vol. 3. New York: Wiley, 1978.

Strachey, W. *Historie of Travaile into Virginia Brittannia.* Edited by R. H. Major. London: Hakluyt Society, 1849.

Chapter Ten: Ices

Arbuckle, W. S. *Ice Cream.* 4th ed. Westport, Conn.: AVI, 1986.

Beard, J. *James Beard's Theory and Practice of Good Cooking.* New York: Knopf, 1977.

Courtine, R. J., ed. *Larousse Gastronomique.* Paris: Librairie Larousse, 1984.

Hazan, M. *The Classic Italian Cook Book.* New York: Knopf, 1976.

Hulme, A. C., ed. *The Biochemistry of Fruits and Their Products.* 2 vols. London: Academic Press, 1970–71.

Kamman, M. *In Madeleine's Kitchen.* New York: Atheneum, 1984.

Meade, G. P. *Spencer-Meade Cane Sugar Handbook.* 9th ed. New York: Wiley, 1963.

Middione, C. *The Food of Southern Italy.* New York: Morrow, 1987.

Schmidt, S. *Master Recipes.* New York: Ballantine, 1987.

Tarantino, J. *Sorbets!* Freedom, Calif.: Crossing Press, 1988.

Weast, R. C., ed. *CRC Handbook of Chemistry and Physics.* 69th ed. Boca Raton, Fla.: CRC Press, 1988.

Chapter Eleven: Measuring

Firth, I. Cooler? *Physics Education* 6 (1971): 32–40.

Mpemba, E. B., and D. G. Osborne. Cool? *Physics Education* 4 (1969): 172–75.

Peynaud, E. *The Taste of Wine*. Translated by M. Schuster. London: Macdonald, 1987.

Rumford, B., Count. Of the propagation of heat in fluids [1797]. In S. C. Brown, ed., *The Collected Works of Count Rumford*, vol. 1, 119–39. Cambridge, Mass.: Belknap, 1968.

Walker, J. The amateur scientist. *Scientific American* 237 (Sept. 1977): 246–52, 257.

———. *The Flying Circus of Physics With Answers*. New York: Wiley, 1977.

Chapter Twelve: Fat and the Heart

Bonanome, A., and S. M. Grundy. Effect of dietary stearic acid on plasma cholesterol and lipoprotein levels. *New England Journal of Medicine* 318 (1988): 1244–48.

Braunwald, E. On future directions for cardiology. *Circulation* 77 (1988): 13–32.

Breslow, J. L. Apolipoprotein defects. *Hospital Practice* 20 (Dec. 15, 1985): 43–49.

Brown, M. S., and J. L. Goldstein. A receptor-mediated pathway for cholesterol homeostasis. *Science* 232 (1986): 34–47.

Cantor, S. M., and M. B. Cantor. Socioeconomic factors in fat and sugar consumption. In M. R. Kare and O. Maller, eds., *The Chemical Senses and Nutrition*, 429–46. New York: Academic Press, 1977.

Dobrin, P. B. Vascular mechanics. In *Handbook of Physiology*, vol. 3, 65–102. Bethesda, Md.: American Physiological Society, 1983.

Forbes, R. J. Chemical, culinary, and cosmetic arts. In C. Singer, E. J. Holmyard, and A. R. Hall, eds., *History of Technology*, vol. 1, 238–98. Oxford: Clarendon, 1954.

Goering, H. K., and others. Effect of feeding protected safflower oil on yield, composition, flavor, and oxidative stability of milk. *Journal of Dairy Science* 59 (1976): 416–25.

Gounaris, K., and J. Barber. Monogalactosyldiacylglycerol: The most abundant polar lipid in nature. *Trends in Biochemical Sciences* 8 (1983): 378–81.

Harfoot, C. G. Lipid metabolism in the rumen. *Progress in Lipid Research* 17 (1978): 21–54.

Harrison, H. S. Fire-making, fuel, and lighting. In C. Singer, E. J. Holmyard, and A. R. Hall, eds., *History of Technology*, vol. 1, 216–37. Oxford: Clarendon, 1954.

Hilditch, T. P. *The Chemical Constitution of Natural Fats*. 4th ed. New York: Wiley, 1964.

Hunter, W. J., and others. Biohydrogenation of unsaturated fatty acids. *Journal of Biological Chemistry* 251 (1976): 2241–47.

Leaf, A., and P. C. Weber. Cardiovascular effects of n-3 fatty acids. *New England Journal of Medicine* 318 (1988): 549–57.

Leibowitz, J. O. *History of Coronary Heart Disease*. Berkeley: University of California Press, 1970.

Mann, G. V. Diet-heart: End of an era. *New England Journal of Medicine* 297 (1977): 644–50.

Meade, J. F., and others. *Lipids: Chemistry, Biochemistry and Nutrition*. New York: Plenum, 1986.

Moore, T. J. The cholesterol myth. *Atlantic*, September 1989: 37–70.

Nes, W. R., and W. D. Nes. *Lipids in Evolution*. New York: Plenum, 1980.

Ross, R. The pathogenesis of atherosclerosis. In E. Braunwald, ed., *Heart Disease*, 3d ed., vol. 2, 1135–52. Philadelphia: Saunders, 1988.

Schwartz, S. M., G. R. Campbell, and J. H. Campbell. Replication of smooth muscle cells in vascular disease. *Circulation Research* 58 (1986): 427–44.

Slattery, M. L., and D. E. Randall. Trends in coronary heart disease mortality and food consumption in the United States between 1909 and 1980. *American Journal of Clinical Nutrition* 47 (1988): 1060–67.

Small, D. M. Progression and regression of atherosclerotic lesions: Insights from lipid physical biochemistry. *Arteriosclerosis* 8 (1988): 103–29.

Spady, D. K., and J. M. Dietschy. Interaction of dietary cholesterol and triglycerides in the regulation of hepatic low-density lipoprotein transport in the hamster. *Journal of Clinical Investigation* 81 (1988): 300–309.

Stary, H. C. Macrophages, macrophage foam cells, and eccentric intimal thickening in the coronary arteries of young children. *Atherosclerosis* 64 (1987): 91–108.

Steinberg, D., and others. Beyond cholesterol: Modifications of low-density lipoprotein that increase its atherogenicity. *New England Journal of Medicine* 320 (1989): 915–24.

da Vinci, L. *Leonardo da Vinci on the Human Body*. Translated by C. D. O'Malley and J. B. de C. M. Saunders. New York: Henry Schuman, 1952.

Watkins, C., ed. *American Heritage Dictionary of Indo-European Roots*. Boston: Houghton Mifflin, 1985.

Chapter Thirteen: Food and Cancer

Alley, A. Mutagenicity of repeatedly used cooking fats. *Food and Chemical Toxicology* 26 (1988): 740–41.

Ames, B. N. Dietary carcinogens and anticarcinogens. *Science* 221 (1983): 1256–64.

Black, S. D., and M. J. Coon. P450 cytochromes: Structure and function. *Advances in Enzymology* 60 (1987): 35–87.

Cairns, J. A summary and a look ahead. In D. M. Shankel and others, eds., *Antimutagenesis and Anticarcinogenesis Mechanisms*, 531–35. New York: Plenum, 1986.

Chan, R. I. M., and others. Antimutagenic activity of browning reaction products. *Cancer Letters* 15 (1982): 27–33.

Commoner, B., and others. Formation of mutagens in beef and beef extract during cooking. *Science* 201 (1978): 913–16.

DeVita, V. T., S. Hellman, and S. A. Rosenberg, eds. *Cancer: Principles and Practice of Oncology*. 2d ed. Philadelphia: Lippincott, 1985.

Doll, R., and R. Peto. The causes of cancer: Quantitative estimates of avoidable risks of cancer in the United States today. *Journal of the National Cancer Institute* 66 (1981): 1192–1308.

Doolittle, D. J., and others. Effect of cooking methods on the mutagenicity of foods. . . . *Food and Chemical Toxicology* 27 (1989): 657–66.

Guengerich, F. P., and D. C. Liebler. Enzymatic activation of chemicals to toxic metabolites. *CRC Critical Reviews in Toxicology* 14 (1985): 259–307.

Ha, Y. L., N. K. Grimm, and M. W. Pariza. Newly recognized anticarcinogenic fatty acids. . . . *Journal of Agricultural and Food Chemistry* 37 (1989): 75–81.

Haynes, R. H. Biological context of DNA repair. In E. C. Friedberg and P. C. Hanawalt, eds., *Mechanisms and Consequences of DNA Damage Processing*, 577–84. New York: Liss, 1988.

Jakoby, W. B., ed. *Enzymatic Basis of Detoxication*. 2 vols. New York: Academic Press, 1980.

Miller, E.C., and J.A. Miller. The search for ultimate carcinogens and their reactions with cellular macromolecules. *Cancer* 47 (1981): 2327–45.

Nebert, D. W., and F. J. Gonzalez. P450 genes: Structure, evolution and regulation. *Annual Review of Biochemistry* 56 (1987): 945–93.

Searle, C. E., ed. *Chemical Carcinogens*. 2d ed. 2 vols. Washington, D.C.: American Chemical Society, 1984.

Spingarn, N. A., L. A. Slocum, and J. H. Weisberger. Formation of mutagens in cooked foods. II. Foods with high starch content. *Cancer Letters* 9 (1980): 7–12.

Stich, H. F., and others. Clastogenic activity of caramel and caramelized sugars. *Mutation Research* 91 (1981): 129–36.

Sugimura, T. Tumor initiators and promoters associated with ordinary foods. In M. S. Arnott, J. van Eys, and Y.-M. Wang, eds., *Molecular Interrelations of Nutrition and Cancer*, 3–24. New York: Raven, 1982.

Tsuda, M., and others. Inactivation of potent pyrolysate mutagens by chlorinated tap water. *Mutation Research* 119 (1983): 27–34.

———. Marked increase in the urinary level of N-nitrosothioproline after ingestion of cod with vegetables. *Cancer Research* 48 (1988): 4049–52.

Wattenberg, L. W. Chemoprevention of cancer. *Cancer Research* 45 (1985): 1–8.

———, V. L. Sparnins, and G. Barany. Inhibition of N-nitrosodiethylamine carcinogenesis in mice by naturally occurring organosulfur compounds and monoterpenes. *Cancer Research* 49 (1989): 2689–92.

Wills, E. D. *Biochemical Basis of Medicine*. Bristol, England: Wright, 1985.

Wilson, C. A. *Food and Drink in Britain: From the Stone Age to Recent Times*. Harmondsworth, England: Penguin, 1973.

Yu, Y., and others. Genotoxic activity of caramel on Salmonella and cultured mammalian cells. *Mutation Research* 139 (1984): 161–65.

Chapter Fourteen: Pots and Pans

Alfrey, A. C. Phosphorus, aluminum, and other elements in chronic renal disease. In R. W. Schrier and C. W. Gottschalk, eds., *Diseases of the Kidney*, 4th ed., vol. 3, 3371–85. Boston: Little, Brown, 1988.

Birchall, J. D., and J. S. Chappell. Aluminum, chemical physiology, and Alzheimer's disease. *Lancet* 1988: ii, 1008–10.

Candy, J. M., and others. Aluminosilicates and senile plaque formation in Alzheimer's disease. *Lancet* 1986: i, 354–57.

Christensen, O. B., and H. Möller. External and internal exposure to the antigen in the hand eczema of nickel allergy. *Contact Dermatitis* 1 (1975): 136–41.

Cooking in aluminum. *Hygeia* 26 (1948): 772–73.

Crapper, D. R., S. S. Krishnan, and A. J. Dalton. Brain aluminum distribution in Alzheimer's disease and experimental neurofibrillary degeneration. *Science* 180 (1973): 511–13.

Friberg, L., G. F. Nordberg, and V. B. Vouk, eds. *Handbook on the Toxicology of Metals.* 2d ed. 2 vols. Amsterdam: Elsevier, 1986.

Friedel, R. Silver from clay. *American Heritage of Invention and Technology* 1, no. 3 (1976): 51–57.

Gajdusek, D. C. Transmissible and nontransmissible dementias. *Mt. Sinai Journal of Medicine* 55 (1988): 3–5.

————, and A. M. Salazar. Amyotrophic lateral sclerosis and parkinsonian syndrome . . . in West New Guinea. *Neurology* 32 (1982): 107–26.

Ganrot, P. O. Metabolism and possible health effects of aluminum. *Environmental Health Perspectives* 65 (1986): 363–441.

Garruto, R. M., and Y. Yase. Neurodegenerative disorders of the western Pacific. *Trends in Neurosciences* 9 (1986): 368–74.

Godbold, D. L., E. Fritz, and A. Hüttermann. Aluminum toxicity and forest decline. *Proceedings of the National Academy of Sciences* 85 (1988): 3888–92.

Harrison, P. M., and R. J. Hoare. *Metals in Biochemistry.* London: Chapman and Hall, 1980.

Hem, S. L. Physicochemical properties of antacids. *Journal of Chemical Education* 52 (1975): 383–85.

Katzman, R. Alzheimer's disease. *New England Journal of Medicine* 314 (1986): 964–73.

Kline, M., and others. Earthenware containers as a source of fatal lead poisoning. *New England Journal of Medicine* 283 (1970): 669–72.

LaQue, F. L., and H. R. Copson, eds. *Corrosion Resistance of Metals and Alloys.* New York: Reinhold, 1963.

Lead poisoning from ceramics. *Lancet* 1988: ii, 1358.

Levick, S. E. Dementia from aluminum pots? *New England Journal of Medicine* 303 (1980): 164.

Lifshey, E. *The Housewares Story.* Chicago: National Housewares Manufacturers Association, 1973.

Lione, A. The prophylactic reduction of aluminum intake. *Food and Chemical Toxicology* 21 (1983): 103–9.

Macdonald, T. L., and R. B. Martin. Aluminum ion in biological systems. *Trends in Biochemical Sciences* 13 (1988): 15–19.

Miller, R. G. The occurrence of aluminum in drinking water. *American Water Works Association Journal* 76 (1984): 84–91.

Ministry of Agriculture, Fisheries, and Food. *Survey of Aluminum, Antimony, Chromium, Cobalt, Indium, Nickel, Thallium, and Tin in Food.* London: HMSO, 1985.

Mozar, H. N., D. G. Bal, and J. T. Howard. Perspectives on the etiology of Alzheimer's disease. *Journal of the American Medical Association* 257 (1987): 1503–7.

Phipps, D. A. *Metals and Metabolism.* Oxford: Clarendon, 1976.

Richards, J. W. *Aluminum.* 2d ed. Philadelphia, 1890.

Roberts, G. W. Immunocytochemistry of neurofibrillary tangles in dementia pugilistica and Alzheimer's disease: Evidence for common genesis. *Lancet* 1988: ii, 1456–58.

Saucepans and frying pans. *Consumer Bulletin*, April 1972: 21–29.

Selkoe, D. J. Deciphering Alzheimer's disease: The pace quickens. *Trends in Neurosciences* 10 (1987): 181–84.

Smith, E. G. *Aluminum Compounds in Food.* New York: Hoeber, 1928.

Tomlinson, H. *Aluminum Utensils and Disease: The Dangers Inherent in the Widespread Use of the Metal.* London: L. N. Fowler, 1967.

Wedeen, R. P. *Poison in the Pot: The Legacy of Lead.* Carbondale: Southern Illinois University Press, 1984.

Weiss, A. Replication and evolution in inorganic systems. *Angewandte Chemie, International Edition* 20 (1981): 850–60.

Wertime, T. A. Man's first encounter with metallurgy. *Science* 146 (1964): 1257–67.

Williams, J. W., and others. Biliary excretion of aluminum in aluminum osteodystrophy with liver disease. *Annals of Internal Medicine* 104 (1986): 782–85.

Chapter Fifteen: Brillat-Savarin

Balzac, H. de. Brillat-Savarin. In *Biographie universelle*, vol. 5, 535–38. Paris, 1854–65.

Barthes, R. In J. A. Brillat-Savarin, *Physiologie du goût, avec une lecture de Roland Barthes.* Paris: Hermann, 1975.

Brillat-Savarin, J. A. *The Physiology of Taste* [1826]. Translated by M. F. K. Fisher, 1949. Reprint. San Francisco: North Point, 1986.

Richerand, A. *Des Erreurs populaires relatives à la médecine.* Paris, 1810.

———. *Nouveaux Eléments de physiologie.* 9th ed. Paris, 1825.

Chapter Sixteen: Osmazome

Cadet de Gassicourt, C.-L. *Cours gastronomique: ou les dîners de Manant-Ville.* Paris, 1809.

———. De l'osmazome et son emploi. *Bulletin de Pharmacie* 1 (1809): 497–99.

Carême, M.-A. *L'Art de la cuisine française au XIXème siècle.* Vol. 1. Paris, 1833.

Chaptal, J. A. *Elémens de chymie.* 2d ed. Vol. 3. Paris, 1794.

Fourcroy, A. F. de. *Systèmes des connaissances chimiques.* Vol. 9. Paris, 1801.

Holmes, F. L. Analysis by fire and solvent extractions: The metamorphosis of a tradition. *Isis* 62 (1971): 129–48.

———. Elementary analysis and the origins of physiological chemistry. *Isis* 54 (1963): 50–81.

Mérat de Vaumartoise, F. J., and A. J. De Lens. *Dictionnaire universel de matière médicale*. Brussels, 1837.

de Morveau, G. *Elémens de chymie . . . pour servir aux cours publics de l'Académie de Dijon*. Dijon, 1777.

Proust, J. Extrait d'un mémoire sur les tablettes à bouillon. *Annales de Chimie et de Physique*. 2d series, 18 (1821): 170–81.

Rappaport, R. G.-F. Rouelle: 18th-century chemist and teacher. *Chymia* 6 (1960): 68–101.

Szent-Györgyi, A. *The Chemistry of Muscle Contraction*. 2d ed. New York: Academic Press, 1951.

Thenard, L. Extrait d'un rapport de M. Thenard sur l'analyse du bouillon d'os et du bouillon de viande. *Bulletin de l'Ecole de Médecine de Paris* 3 (1806): 35–36.

Chapter Seventeen: Raw and Cooked

Achard, C. Décès de M. Louis Maillard. *Comptes rendus hebdomadaires des Séances et Mémoires de la Société de Biologie* 122 (1936): 347–48.

Barnes, H. M., and C. W. Kaufman. Industrial aspects of browning reaction. *Industrial and Engineering Chemistry* 39 (1947): 1167–70.

Brain, C. K., and A. Sillen. Evidence from the Swartkrans cave for the earliest use of fire. *Nature* 336 (1988): 464–66.

Brophy, J. J., and G. W. K. Cavill. Naturally occurring pyrazines. . . . *Heterocycles* 14 (1980): 477–504.

Campbell, B. *Human Evolution*. 3d ed. New York: Aldine, 1985.

Danehy, J. P. Maillard reaction. *Advances in Food Research* 30 (1986): 77–138.

Faegri, K., and L. van der Pijl. *Principles of Pollination Ecology*. 3d ed. Oxford: Pergamon, 1979.

von Frisch, K. *The Dance Language and Orientation of Bees*. Translated by L. E. Chadwick. Cambridge, Mass.: Belknap, 1967.

Gerber, N. N. Volatile substances from actinomycetes. *CRC Critical Reviews in Microbiology* 7 (1979): 191–214.

Kawamura, S. Seventy years of the Maillard reaction. In G. R. Waller and M. S. Feather, eds., *The Maillard Reaction in Foods and Nutrition*, 3–18. Washington, D.C.: American Chemical Society, 1983.

Kremers, R. E. Imitation maple flavor. U.S. patent 2,446,478, August 3, 1948. *Chemical Abstracts* 42 (1948): 8006.

Maga, J. Pyrazines in foods: An update. *CRC Critical Reviews in Food Science and Nutrition* 16 (1982): 1–48.

Maillard, L. C. Actions des acides amines sur les sucres. *Comptes rendus hebdomadaires des Séances de l'Académie des Sciences* 154 (1912): 66–68.

———. Formation d'humus. . . . *Comptes rendus hebdomadaires des Séances de l'Académie des Sciences* 155 (1912): 1554–56.

Mihara, S., and H. Masuda. Olfactive properties of alkylpyrazines and 3-substituted 2-alkylpyrazines. *Journal of Agricultural and Food Chemistry* 36 (1988): 584–87.

———. Structure-odor relationship for disubstituted pyrazines. *Journal of Agricultural and Food Chemistry* 36 (1988): 1242–47.

Ohloff, G., and I. Flament. Role of heteroatomic substances in the aroma compounds of foodstuffs. *Progress in the Chemistry of Organic Natural Products* 36 (1979): 231–83.

Rothschild, M., and B. Moore. Pyrazines as alerting signals in toxic plants and insects. In V. Labeyrie, G. Fabres, and D. Lachaise, eds., *Insects-Plants*, 97–101. Dordrecht: Junk, 1987.

———, and W. V. Brown. Pyrazines as warning odor components in the Monarch butterfly. *Biological Journal of the Linnean Society* 23 (1984): 375–80.

Rozin, P. Human food selection: The interaction of biology, culture, and individual experience. In L. M. Barker, ed., *The Psychobiology of Human Food Selection*, 225–54. Westport, Conn.: AVI, 1982.

Stevenson, F. J. *Humus Chemistry: Genesis, Composition, Reactions*. New York: Wiley, 1982.

Swain, T. Biochemical evolution in plants. *Comprehensive Biochemistry* 29A (1974): 125–302.

Index

ABOUT THE AUTHOR

Harold McGee earned a B.S. from the California Institute of Technology and a Ph.D. in English from Yale. His first book, *On Food and Cooking*, won the 1986 André Simon Memorial Award. He lives in Palo Alto, California.